Applied Computing

Springer

London
Berlin
Heidelberg
New York
Hong Kong
Milan
Paris
Santa Clara
Singapore
Tokyo

The Springer-Verlag Series on Applied Computing is an advanced series of innovative textbooks that span the full range of topics in applied computing technology.

Books in the series provide a grounding in theoretical concepts in computer science alongside real-world examples of how those concepts can be applied in the development of effective computer systems.

The series should be essential reading for advanced undergraduate and postgraduate students in computing and information systems.

Books in this series are contributed by international specialist researchers and educators in applied computing who draw together the full range of issues in their specialist area into one concise authoritative textbook.

Arturo Trujillo

Translation Engines: Techniques for Machine Translation

 Springer

Arturo Trujillo, BSc, MPhil PhD
Department of Language Engineering, UMIST, PO Box 88, Manchester M60 1QD, UK

Series Editors
Professor Ray J. Paul, BSc MSc PhD
Department of Information Systems and Computing, Brunel University, Uxbridge, Middlesex UB8 3PH, UK

Professor Peter J. Thomas, MIEE MBCS CEng FRSA
Centre for Personal Information Management, University of the West of England, Frenchay Campus, Bristol BS16 1QY, UK

Dr Jasna Kuljis, PhD MS Dipl Ing
Department of Mathematical and Computing Sciences, Goldsmiths College, University of London, New Cross, London SE14 6NW, UK

ISBN 1-85233-057-0 Springer-Verlag Berlin Heidelberg New York

British Library Cataloguing in Publication Data
A catalogue record for this book is available from the British Library

Library of Congress Cataloging-in-Publication Data
Trujillo, Arturo, 1967-
    Translation engines : techniques for machine translation / Arturo Trujillo.
    p. cm. – (Applied computing)
    Includes examples in Spanish.
    Includes bibliographic references and index.
    ISBN 1-85233-057-0 (alk. paper)
    1. Machine translating. I. Title. II. Series.
    P308.T78 1999   99-36735
    418'.02'0285—dc21 CIP

Typeset by Ian Kingston Editorial Services, Nottingham
Printed and bound at the Athenæum Press Ltd., Gateshead, Tyne & Wear
34/3830-543210 Printed on acid-free paper SPIN 10681476

For Ana Inés, Raquel, Ron and Gonzalo

Contents

Preface

Global markets and the enormous increase in information flow across linguistic borders have forced many institutions to devote ever-increasing efforts to computer processing of natural languages, and in particular to develop tools that speed up, simplify or reduce the cost of translating texts.

The aim of this book is to present a variety of techniques spanning a wide range of topics in Machine Translation (MT) and Machine-Aided Translation (MAT), the disciplines concerned with the formulation and construction of translation tools. The book describes many approaches in sufficient detail that they can form the basis of actual implementations. A broad selection of topics is considered, ranging from character codes and input methods to disambiguation and natural language generation.

Audience

The book will be of interest to researchers and developers of Natural Language Processing (NLP), MT and MAT software, as it gives a broad overview of important theoretical and practical topics. It will also be useful to those with programming experience who wish to apply their skills to multilinguality and translation problems. Many important methods and concepts in linguistics are clearly described in the background section in order to make the book accessible to those without linguistics training. Language technologists and language engineers will find many topics on language analysis and generation, disambiguation and evaluation particularly relevant.

Postgraduate and final year undergraduate students in computer science, information retrieval, artificial intelligence (AI), computational linguists (CL) and MT will also find this book useful as it presents applications of well-known techniques to translation problems. They will benefit from the arrangement of topics in the text, and from the fact that each method and technique is given within the context of a particular goal, that of translating natural languages. This will distinguish the book from similar ones as it shows how various components and technologies fit together for a particular goal.

A third group of potential readers are translators and linguists of a technical disposition who want to have a clear understanding of MAT and MT. The structure of the book should give them an idea of important areas of research and development in these fields, thereby highlighting fundamental and practical problems that are yet to be resolved. Such knowledge may help them to assess

how and whether computers can help them in their work, and will indicate the
limitations of the technologies currently available.

Coverage and Contents

The literature on MT is now so vast that to cover all available material would
require another book. As a consequence, many theories and approaches, not to
mention systems and products, have been left out. Such omissions simply reflect
the background of the author and should not be taken as indicative of the lack of
merit of other approaches or systems. There are many ways of using computers
to translate from a source language (SL) to a target language (TL), and it is
difficult for one person to know them all intimately.

Much work in MAT and MT is reported in various books, conference proceedings, journal articles and technical reports, each with their own notation,
programming language and operating system. One of the objectives of this book
is to present, from the perspective of a single individual, some of the work produced over the last decade or so on a range of different topics.

The book can be viewed as filling a gap in the literature on MT, in which most
books either present detailed descriptions of particular MT systems, give general
overviews of the subject, collect research articles or concentrate on a specific
topic. Instead, I have tried to give a coherent yet practical description of different
systems and approaches, encompassing a variety of issues in translation.

It is also noticeable that many books have been written about MT but very
few about techniques for MAT, even though this field is having a great impact
on translation practice. Although this book is mainly about MT, it contains two
full chapters devoted to methods and algorithms for MAT.

There are four main parts to the book. Part 1, comprising the first two chapters, presents background material. Chapter 1 presents the translation context in
which MT takes place, a brief outline of its history and the main MT strategies used, namely direct, transfer and interlingua. Chapter 2 gives the linguistic
and formal background used in the rest of the book, including a brief introduction to the main levels of linguistic analysis, techniques for linguistic description
(including phrase structure grammars and finite state machines) and a brief introduction to probability and statistics.

The next two chapters comprise Part 2, where issues in text processing and
MAT are discussed. Given that the representation, rendering and editing of text
in different languages are important issues in MAT, Chapter 3 discusses character sets, fonts and input methods. Using computers to retrieve previously translated text and help in terminology compilation are the topics of Chapter 4.

Part 3 considers traditional MT. Many of the computational linguistic techniques which underlie the presentation of various approaches are presented in
Chapter 5. This mainly comprises morphological processing, parsing and generation. When the analysis stage is assumed to stop short of a language-independent representation, a transfer step is needed to convert between source and target
representations. Chapter 6 discusses three approaches to transfer MT – syntactic, semantic and lexicalist – each using different parts of the resulting analyses.

If the result of analysis is a language-independent interlingua, then no transfer step is necessary. Two interlingua MT systems are described in Chapter 7. One is linguistically oriented, while the other uses knowledge-based techniques. Four other approaches are discussed in Chapter 8. Two of these rely on corpora of bilingual materials, while the other two illustrate the application of techniques from formal semantics and constraint systems to MT.

Regardless of the approach to MT, a number of issues are important in practical applications, two of which are considered in Part 4. Chapter 9 discusses disambiguation, and in particular selecting the syntactic category of words, the syntactic analysis of a sentence, the correct sense of a word, and its correct translation. Chapter 10 considers the evaluation of MT and MAT systems. This includes a discussion of the parties interested in evaluation, techniques and measures for evaluating translations, as well as more general issues dealing with software evaluation.

At this point one should also mention certain important topics which have been omitted or which are only briefly mentioned. Perhaps the most noticeable is Human-Aided MT (HAMT) and techniques associated with human intervention in the translation process. For example, interactive MT is not considered. Neither are a variety of topics traditionally covered in MT books or topics which are clearly relevant to practical MT. These include pre- and post-editing, sublanguage and controlled language translation, organizational and management issues in translation departments, translator training and impedance, spoken language translation, translation of multimedia documents, and non-translation applications of MT technology. Space and time constraints are the main reasons for their absence.

Languages

Prolog is one of the most widely used programming languages in computational linguistics. Among the features that make it attractive are its efficient unification operation, its declarative nature and its backtracking regime. Where technical descriptions are involved in Part 3, they are given in Prolog notation. Furthermore, implementations for various techniques described in the book are available from the Web site indicated in the Appendix.

Spanish is the language I have most knowledge of, and it is no coincidence that the examples in the book are mostly for translation between English and Spanish. However, most, if not all, of the techniques presented should be applicable to at least all European languages. I see no reason either why the linguistic diversity of Asia, Africa, the Americas and Oceania could not also be enhanced through techniques similar to those presented here.

Acknowledgments

The following people have provided me with useful information, suggestions or support: Bill Black, Harold Somers, Graham Wilcock, Allan Ramsay, Fabio

Rinaldi, Jock McNaught, Mona Baker, Blaise Nkwenti-Azeh, Anouar Daghari, Lorna Smeaton, Naomi Miller, Deryck Brown, Joemon Jose, Sarah Pearce and Hayet F. Merouani. Special thanks go to Paul Bennett, Maeve Olohan, Doug Arnold, George Kiraz and Miles Osborne. Students in the MSc in Machine Translation and MSc in Natural Language Processing at UMIST and the MA in Translation and Interpreting at the University of Salford have provided useful feedback; the following should be mentioned: Pascale Stephenson, Dimitra Farmakiotou, Debora Preece, Elisabet Ricart, Kara McAlister and Simon Smith. Information supplied by Ken Church, Kai Grossjohann, Michael K. Gschwind, Roman Czyborra, Knut S. Vikor and Lance Cousins was useful at different stages of the book. Of course, all errors in the text remain my own. Thanks also to my family for their support: Ana Inés, Ron, Gonzalo, Alvaro and George.

Finally, Rebecca Mowat and Beverley Ford from Springer were very patient and encouraging through the production of the book.

Arturo Trujillo
Manchester, June 1999

Part 1
Background

1 Introduction

This chapter describes the context in which machine translation and machine-aided translation take place.

Translating between human languages has been a need in society for thousands of years. Bilingual Sumerian-Akkadian text fragments relating to the Akkadian ruler Sargon exist from the Old Babylonian period, and reference to translators and interpreters working in the ninth century BC can be found in Chinese historical records. There are also references to interpreting in the Old Testament, in Genesis 42:23 (probably mid-eighth century BC). The first recorded literary translator is reputed to be Livius Andronicus who translated the *Odyssey* from Greek into Latin in 240 BC. The Rosetta stone, which includes a translation of a hieroglyphic passage into Greek, was carved in 197 BC and provided the key to deciphering Egyptian hieroglyphics in the early 19th century. Thus, translation and translators have enabled communication and the transmission of knowledge from one culture to another for thousands of years.

Translation studies is the academic discipline concerned with research and study on translation. It draws on linguistics, anthropology, psychology, literary theory, philosophy, cultural studies and various other bodies of knowledge, as well as on its own techniques and methodologies. A number of theoretical perspectives have been proposed from which translation can be studied, including communicative and functional approaches, linguistic approaches, polysystem theory and psycho-linguistic and cognitive approaches.

Within the communicative and functional approaches one may further identify the influential *skopos* theory, which arose as a response to the growing need for non-literary translation. This theory is directed towards the contextual factors surrounding a translation, including the client who has commissioned the translation, the function which the text is to perform for a particular set of readers, and the culture of those readers. In a modern communication setting, one possible *skopos* or purpose of a translation is to convey the broad semantic content or 'gist' of a text (Sager 1994, p. 182), and it is from this perspective that MT and translation studies may have common goals.

1.1   Computers in Translation

Translation is a difficult art requiring skill in both the source and target languages, as well as the ability to choose the correct translation of an element given a variety of factors. **Literary translation** is the translation of poetry, drama and other literary works from one language to another. By contrast **technical translation** involves the translation of texts from specialist disciplines in science, commerce and industry. Technical translators must also have intimate knowledge of the vocabulary and even the subject matter of their field of specialization. It is in the area of technical translation, broadly understood to include 'gist' translation, that MAT and MT can be most fruitful.

In the present context, MAT and MT concern the application of computational techniques to aid in the translation of texts. The texts to which these techniques are applied are normally of a non-literary nature, where preservation of content is usually the most important translation criterion. Such translations are difficult for humans as well as machines. However, computer technology has been applied in technical translation in order to improve one or both of the following factors:

Speed: Translation by or with the aid of machines can be faster than manual translation.

Cost: Computer aids to translation can reduce the cost per word of a translation.

In addition, the use of MAT can result in improvements in **quality**, particularly in the use of consistent terminology within a text or for a particular kind of client. Similarly, the **availability** of MT makes it ideal for translation of Web pages and other materials on the Internet.

1.2   History of Machine Translation

The idea of using computers to translate or help translate human languages is almost as old as the computer itself. Indeed, MT is one of the oldest non-numeric applications of computers. Its history has been colourful and eventful, influenced by the politics, science and economics of different periods of modern history. It has been told many times, so only a brief summary follows.

Pre-computer: Some of the ideas that have influenced MT were already current or at least existent in the pre-computer era. Since at least the 17th century scholars and philosophers have proposed the use of language-neutral representations of meaning in order to overcome linguistic barriers. More recently, a mechanical procedure for carrying out translation was patented by the Russian Petr Smirnov-Troyanskii in 1933.

Initial efforts: Early proposals for the use of numerical techniques in MT can be traced at least to 1947, when computers had just been successfully employed in deciphering encryption methods during the Second World War. A memo from Warren Weaver proposed specific strategies for using computers to translate natural languages. This memo initiated MT research in the USA and in the rest of the world, with the first public demonstration of a Russian–English prototype MT system in 1954. This event led to similar work in the then USSR and other places around the world.

The ALPAC Report (1966): The initial over-optimism in MT came to an end in the USA when the ALPAC report, commissioned by government sponsors of MT, suggested that MT was not cost-effective. The result was divergence of funding from MT and into AI and CL, with MT research continuing mainly outside the USA, although some groups there survived.

The 1970s and operational MT: Continued effort in MT yielded operational systems in the early 1970s. Systran began Russian–English translations for the US Air Force in 1970, while Météo began translating weather reports in 1976. Also in 1976 the Commission of the European Union (then Communities) installed an English–French version of Systran.

Rebirth in the early 1980s: The late 1970s and early 1980s saw an increase in interest in MT. The Eurotra project from the European Community began in 1982, influenced by work done at Grenoble and Saarbrücken since the 1960s and 1970s. Similarly, in Japan the Mu project started in 1982, and Knowledge-Based MT started in earnest in 1983 in the USA. Some commercial systems also began to appear.

Late 1980s and early 1990s: A number of companies, especially large Japanese electronics manufacturers, began to market MT software for workstations. A number of products appeared for personal computers, and various MAT tools such as translation memory began to be commonly used. This period also saw the emergence of work on speech translation and of statistical approaches to machine translation.

Late 1990s and MAT: At the end of the decade we are seeing powerful translation engines on personal computers, translation on the Internet, widespread use of translation memory and translator's workbenches, multimedia and software localization, as well as an increased interest in Example-Based MT.

1.3 Strategies for Machine Translation

MT systems are normally classified in terms of their basic strategy for carrying out translation.

Direct: Direct systems involve extensive string pattern matching, with some rearrangement of the target string for conformance to the TL word order. Many early systems, as well as some recent MT software for personal computers employ this strategy.

Transfer systems: Transfer systems involve analysis of the source input into a transfer structure which abstracts away from many of the grammatical details of the SL. The idea is to facilitate translation by generalizing over different constructions. After analysis, the SL structure is transferred into a corresponding TL structure which is then used to generate a TL sentence. Various types of transfer system may be identified, depending on the level at which transfer takes place. In general, the more abstract the transfer representation, the easier it is to build the appropriate transfer module.

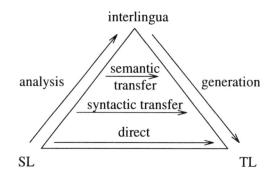

FIG. 1.1. The Vauquois triangle

Interlingua: In interlingua systems SL sentences are analysed into a language-neutral representation from which generation of TL sentences takes place, possibly after some language-independent manipulation of the interlingua representation. This strategy eliminates the need for a transfer step altogether.

These notions are illustrated using the Vauquois triangle shown in Fig. 1.1. The triangle illustrates in the vertical direction the amount of effort necessary for analysis/generation and in the horizontal dimension the amount of effort needed for transfer. At the apex, transfer effort is minimum, while analysis and generation are at a maximum.

Obviously this is a highly idealized view of MT, but it illustrates the point quite neatly. Variations on a basic strategy are possible. For example, a system may use a hybrid of interlingua and transfer elements in its representation. Similarly, a transfer system may incorporate different levels of abstraction in its representations, including syntactic, semantic and lexical information. There are also combinations of the basic direct and transfer strategies using statistical and other corpus-based techniques, as will be explained in Part 3.

1.4 Artificial Intelligence

AI is the field concerned with software and hardware systems that display intelligent behaviour, where intelligence is judged subjectively by humans observing the system. Although some work in AI involves defining what AI actually is, most work simply proceeds in a number of relatively well-defined areas. Some of the most relevant to MT and MAT include:

Computational Linguistics: CL concerns the development of computational treatments of linguistic phenomena including word formation, word ordering, meaning analysis and other aspects of communication.

Knowledge Representation (KR): This area deals with the formalisms and inference procedures needed to represent knowledge about a domain. The most common KR formalisms in use are logic, frames and semantic networks. Logic is the study of valid arguments and their associated proof procedures. Frames represent knowledge in terms of slots and values, where each slot expresses a specific piece of knowledge. Semantic networks are collections of concepts linked together through a variety of relations.

Many other areas of AI are potentially useful in MT and are briefly noted here. For example, **machine learning** involves the acquisition of new knowledge from data; techniques in this area could be used in grammar learning, terminology acquisition and learning of translation correspondences. Suitable **search** algorithms in AI can mean the difference between finding a solution to a problem and getting stuck in an infinite loop. Several of these algorithms are applicable in MT for a variety of problems.

An informal notion that is sometimes used in the AI literature is that of an **AI-complete** problem. This refers to problems whose solution would require a solution to every other major problem in AI. MT and in particular Fully Automatic High-Quality Machine Translation (FAHQMT) is sometimes seen as an AI-complete problem, since in the general case it seems to require the equivalent of human intelligence. In this book, we are not interested in FAHQMT of unrestricted text, but rather in building systems that are useful in one way or another for overcoming linguistic barriers.

1.5 Conclusion

MAT and MT can offer benefits in terms of speed, cost, quality and availability of translation. These benefits are the result of work in many areas over the last 50 years, culminating in the present range of MAT tools and translation engines available over the Web.

It is convenient to classify MT strategies according to the level of abstraction achieved during analysis, with transfer and interlingua methods employing simpler or minimal transfer components compared with direct methods. Transfer and interlingua systems in particular adopt techniques from AI and especially from CL and KR. The next chapter discusses topics in linguistics, computer science and mathematics which are directly relevant to the book's content.

1.5.1 Further Reading

A useful reference work on translation studies is Baker (1998). Sager (1994) suggests roles for MT in general translation work. A detailed description of the history of MT is given in Hutchins (1986) and Hutchins (1997). Systran is described in Whitelock and Kilby (1995); more recent is Hovy and Gerber (1997). Work on the relation between translation and computers is reported in the conference series *Translating and the Computer* published by Aslib, London. Several works on MT are available, including Hutchins (1986), Hutchins and Somers (1992), Arnold et al. (1994), Whitelock and Kilby (1995). Russell and Norvig (1998) is an excellent introduction to AI.

2 Basic Terminology and Background

Some linguistic and formal notions relevant to machine translation are introduced.

This chapter presents some introductory material in the areas of linguistics, mathematics and computer science useful for rest of the book. The presentation is brief, including just the minimum required to follow the book. Pointers to more thorough treatments are given at the end.

2.1 Linguistics

Linguistics is the study of language structure and of the way languages operate. The study of language as a serious discipline has over 2000 years of history, with work by Greek, Roman and Sanskrit philosophers and grammarians, among others. The turn of the 20th century, however, may be seen as marking the beginning of modern linguistics, with the rapid development of analysis techniques by de Saussure, Sapir, Bloomfield and others, and the application of those techniques to a number of languages. Various contrasts were articulated at this time, particularly by Saussure: *diachronic* vs. *synchronic*, *langue* vs. *parole*, *signified* vs. *signifier*, and *syntagmatic* vs. *paradigmatic*. The paradigmatic and syntagmatic contrasts seem particularly relevant here. They consider the relationships that exist between words and their contexts, and may be explained via the following diagram:

	Syntagmatic		
	She	will	run
	They	would	swim
Paradigmatic	He	can	go
	I	may	sit
	etc.	etc.	etc.

A word has a syntagmatic relationship with the words that can surround it to form a grammatical unit. For instance, *She* is in syntagmatic relation to *can go*, *will run*, *may sit* and so on. A word is in paradigmatic relation to another word if the two can be exchanged while preserving grammaticality. For example, *She* and *I* have a paradigmatic relationship; similarly for *can* and *will*, *will* and *may*, and so on. By studying such relationships it is possible to chart, codify and predict linguistic phenomena. Such studies can be extended to groups of words in order to account for the distribution of phrases and clauses. Furthermore, they can be applied to parts of words or even to sounds in a language.

2.1.1 Levels of Linguistic Description

Given the complexity of language, it is common to divide its study into different levels of linguistic description. Not only does this break down the problem into more manageable components, but it allows each level to develop its own methodology. Unfortunately, there is no standard set of levels used by all linguists, but those presented here are relatively uncontroversial.

2.1.2 Phonetics and Phonology

Phonetics is the study of the physical facts of pronunciation in terms of the way in which sounds are produced, conveyed through space and heard. The aim of this level is the description and classification of speech sounds, particularly in terms of vowels and consonants. The place and the manner of articulation of a sound are normally used to describe sound production in phonetics.

In phonology the aim is to discover how languages organize sounds to convey differences of meaning; that is, how a language selects a subset of all the possible sounds that the human speech organs can produce in order to construct utterances. Languages differ in terms of the sounds they employ. Thus English distinguishes between *r* and *l* such that *cram* and *clam* are different words. No such distinction exists in Japanese. Similar contrasts can be made for almost any pair of languages. An important notion is that of a **syllable**. A syllable, roughly speaking, is a phonological element made up of a vowel and zero or more consonants. For example, *con-sign-ment* has the three syllables indicated.

2.1.3 Morphology

Morphology is the branch of linguistics that studies the structure of words. Words are made up of **morphemes**, which are the smallest meaning-carrying units in a language. For example, the word *unhappiness* can be divided into three morphemes, *un-happi-ness*, where *un-* conveys a negative meaning, *happi* carries the meaning of *happy*, and *-ness* indicates a state or quality. **Root** morphemes are those which may appear as separate words (e.g. *happy*), while **bound** morphemes cannot appear on their own (e.g. *-ness*).

Languages may be classified in terms of the typical number of morphemes per word, and the degree of phonological alteration produced when morphemes are combined. In **analytic/isolating** languages, there is one morpheme per word and words have little or no internal structure; **synthetic** languages have a small number of morphemes per word, while **polysynthetic** languages have a large number of morphemes per word, particularly multiple roots. In terms of the degree of alteration of morphemes, a language may be **agglutinative** with simple affixation of morphemes, and **fusional** with considerable morphological and phonological alternation. Languages may represent each of these morphological types to different degrees. English, for example, can be isolating (e.g. *will ask*) or agglutinative and synthetic (e.g. *anti-dis-establish-ment-arian-ism*). Spanish verb inflections, on the other hand, are synthetic and fusional, with person, number and tense encoded in one morpheme: *ama-mos* (we loved).

Given this variety of word formation processes, the question of what counts as a word arises. In written languages this can be straightforward, as words are separated by spaces. This is the case in all European languages. Even so, there are a few problematic cases (e.g. hyphenation: *well informed* or *well-informed* – one word or two). Other written languages such as Chinese do not demarcate word boundaries in text, which makes formal word identification more difficult. In spoken language, word identification becomes even more complex.

A distinction is traditionally made between inflectional and derivational morphology. **Inflectional** morphology concerns the way words reflect grammatical information. In inflectional morphology words vary in their form but their main syntactic category remains the same. Thus, the inflections of the verb *paint*, *paints*, and *painted* are also verbs. By contrast, in **derivational** morphology new words are formed. For example, adding the suffix *-ness* turns an adjective into a noun (e.g. *happiness*, *slowness*).

English word formation employs two main types of **affixation**: **prefixation**, placing a morpheme before a word (e.g. *un-happy*), and **suffixation**, placing a morpheme after the word (e.g. *happi-ness*). Other kinds of word formation include: **conversion**, where the word changes class without changing its form (e.g. noun *bag*, verb *(to) bag*); **reduplication**, where morphemes are repeated as in Malay plurals (e.g. *rumah* (house), *rumah-rumah* (houses)); **infixation**, where an affix is inserted within the root as in Tagalog *um* (one who does) and *pīlit* (effort) to give *p-um-īlit* (one who compelled).

2.1.4 Word Classes and Grammatical Categories

Words can be grouped into word classes (also known as "parts of speech" or syntactic categories). Most grammars of English, for example, distinguish the following:

Nouns: power, apple, beauty, destruction. **Verbs:** go, run, sleep.
Adjectives: red, happy, asleep. **Adverbs:** often, happily, immediately.
Prepositions: in, under, of. **Conjunctions:** and, because, if.
Pronouns: she, it, them. **Interjections:** gosh, alas, wow.

Other categories may be identified, such as **determiners**, which includes articles (e.g. *the*, *a*) and other words (e.g. *some*, *three*), and **particles** (e.g. *up* (*give up*), *off* (*jump off*)).

Traditional definitions for these categories (e.g. "nouns name things") are less frequent now given their inadequacy (e.g. is *beauty* a thing?). Instead, structural and distributional descriptions seem more useful. For example, a noun such as *beauty* is defined as forming syntagmatic relations with articles such as *the*, and paradigmatic relations with other nouns, such as *apple*. Clearly this is not a completely satisfactory definition for word classes. It is somewhat circular (e.g. how do we decide that *apple* is a noun) and assumes that words have similar distribution, which they do not (e.g. *I ate the apple/*destruction*). Still, this technique has proved useful for much computational linguistics work. It may also be further motivated through the notion of central class or prototypical instances, where certain words are seen as clear examples of a class through some independent mechanism (e.g. semantically), and other words which resemble their distribution are then classified within the same class, possibly with varying degrees of centrality. Thus, *apple* is a typical noun (on semantic grounds). Then *destruction* is more a noun than anything else, even though it does not have exactly the same distribution pattern as other more noun-like words.

It is common to divide word categories into two classes. **Open** class words, comprising nouns, verbs, adjectives and adverbs, constitute the majority of the words in the language. New words are normally added to this class and they are generally the words that carry most **semantic content**. By contrast, **closed** class words, including determiners, pronouns, conjunctions, prepositions, particles and interjections have fewer words in them, are rarely extended, and their words frequently play a **functional** or grammatical role.

Languages often distinguish various syntactic categories in terms of contrasts such as person, number, gender and tense. The list below summarizes some of the more familiar distinctions.

Person (pronouns, verbs): Identifies speaker, addressee, third or fourth party. Typical contrasts: first, second and third person. Example: first person *I* vs. second person *you*. Some languages (e.g. Algonquian) have a fourth person for referring to an additional, distinct third party.

Number (pronouns, nouns, verbs): Indicates the number of elements referred to. Typical contrasts: singular, dual, trial, plural. Example: singular *I*, plural *we*. Various languages (e.g. some Melanesian languages) have different forms for referring to one, two, three or more than three addressees: e.g. *aijautaij* (you three).

Gender (pronouns, nouns, verbs, adjectives): Relates to whether the object referred to is male, female, sexless or living. Typical contrasts: masculine, feminine, neuter, animate, inanimate. Example: masculine *he* vs. feminine *she*. Some languages (e.g. Bantu) classify nouns, broadly speaking, according to whether they denote human beings, animals, inanimate objects and so on, and give them distinct grammatical properties accordingly.

Case (pronouns, nouns, adjectives): Indicates the role of a participant within a phrase; it distinguishes subjects, objects and various other roles. Typical contrasts: nominative, accusative, genitive, partitive. Example: nominative *they* vs. accusative *them*. Some languages (e.g. Hungarian) have around 16 cases, including the usual nominative, accusative, dative and so on, as well locative cases such as *a kocsi-ban* (the car-in = in the car). Tabasaran, a Dagestanian language of the Caucasian family, probably has the largest number with around 50 cases (Hjelmslev 1978).

Tense (verbs): Whether an action is performed in the future, present or past time. Typical contrasts: past, present, future tense. Example: present tense *she plays* vs. past tense *she played*. In some languages tense is marked in adjectives and even nouns: Japanese *shiroi* (white), *shirokatta* (was white).

Aspect (verbs): Meanings include completeness, habituality and progressiveness. Typical contrasts: perfect, imperfect. Example: habitual *she sings* vs. continuous *she is singing*.

Mood (verbs): Conveys factuality, likelihood, possibility, uncertainty. Typical contrasts: indicative, subjunctive, optative. Example: subjunctive *if he were here* vs. indicative *he is here*.

Voice (verbs): Expresses the relation of the subject or other participants of the verb to the action expressed. Typical contrasts: active, passive, middle, causative. Example: active *Mary kisses John* vs passive *John is kissed by Mary*. An example from Classical Greek illustrates middle voice: active *didàsko* (I teach) vs. middle *didàskomai* (I get myself taught).

2.1.5 Syntax

The main concern in syntax is the description of word arrangements and of the relationships of meaning that these arrangements express. Most syntactic studies focus on the **sentence**, where the most important syntactic relationships are expressed. Defining what is a sentence is not straightforward, however, although for many written languages the decision can be made by considering punctuation and other orthographic and textual cues. Thus, one simple heuristic for English and Spanish is that sentences begin with a capital letter and end with a full stop; there are many exceptions to this simple rule, of course, but it will do for our purposes. There are a variety of other ways of defining a sentence, especially for spoken language, but one working definition (although somewhat circular) might be as the largest linguistic unit to which syntactic rules apply.

Syntactic rules indicate ordering and grouping constraints on words within the language. Traditionally, a sentence was seen as consisting of two main groups, a **subject** and a **predicate**, with typical English sentences having the subject before the predicate. In the sentence *the girl likes Dublin*, the subject is *the girl* and the predicate is *likes Dublin*. **Parsing** is the process of making divisions within a sentence indicating word groupings called syntactic **constituents**. Representing these divisions through **parse trees** gives a graphical illustration of the **phrase structure** (PS) of the sentence. For the previous sentence, the parse tree would be:

Phrases themselves can be analysed into their main components. The **head** of a phrase is its central element and indicates the type of thing, activity or quality expressed by the phrase as a whole. It normally carries most syntactic and/or semantic information in the phrase. A head is surrounded by zero or more peripheral phrases that may appear before or after it. In the noun phrase *the beautiful* **songs** *on my CD* consists of the peripheral phrases *the beautiful* and *in my CD*.

In English grammars it is common to identify four types of phrase, depending on the head they have.

Verb Phrases (VP): VPs include predicates as well as phrases appearing in other contexts. Examples: **sleep** *often*, *definitely* **saw** *the sea*, **be** *in Manchester*, **think** *that Medellín is fun*. Sentences (**S**) are sometimes seen as a special kind of VP, with the predicate phrase as their head.

Noun Phrases (NP): NPs can appear as subjects, objects and in other contexts; sometimes proper names and pronouns are treated as phrases, given their distribution (syntagmatic and paradigmatic). Examples: *the* **plane**, **water**, *every* **day** *of the week*, **she**.

Adjective/Adverbial Phrases (AP): The acronym *AP* often refers to both adjective and adverbial phrases, even though the former modifies nouns while the latter modifies verbs. However, it is usually clear from the context which one is meant; if a distinction needs to be made we will use *AdjP* and *AdvP* respectively. Examples: *extremely* **angry**, *very* **easy** *to assemble*, *quite* **quickly**, **soon**.

Prepositional Phrases (PP): PPs occur in a variety of contexts and within almost all other phrase types. Examples: **in** *the park*, **under** *three minutes*, **with** *Consuelo*.

Using these phrasal structures, parse trees become more informative:

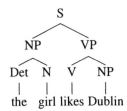

Peripheral phrases to a head can be classified in different ways, but one common distinction is that between complements and modifiers. **Complements** are obligatory phrases that need to appear in order to "complete" a headed phrase. For example, *likes* on its own is not a VP, but with its direct object complement it is: *likes Dublin*. By contrast **modifiers** are optional phrases that further qualify a phrase. There may be several modifiers in a phrase, but normally only a restricted number of complements. AdjPs, for example, can be noun modifiers: the *fast* train.

Different head words have different complement or **valency** patterns, the most studied and complex of which are those for verbs. In many modern syntactic theories (Section 5.3) valency is expressed as a **subcategorization** (or subcat for short) list or frame associated with a word. A head X, together with its complement phrases, forms an $\overline{X}$ (read "x bar") or $X1$ (read "x one") syntactic constituent. It represents a level of analysis halfway between the phrase level and the word level. For example, the phrase *desire to win* will be classified as an $N1$ constituent, as it is larger than a noun but does not seem to form an independent phrase. Modifiers are frequently analysed as applying to $X1$ constituents, even if there are no complements involved:

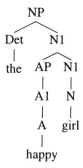

When it is irrelevant to an explanation, the extra $X1$ level is omitted. It is also common to use VP instead of $V1$, so that a PP modifies a VP:

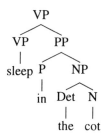

Word order patterns as described by such analyses vary widely across languages, but it is not uncommon to refer to a language as having a particular word order depending on the order of the subject, the verb and the object in simple sentences. English, for instance, is normally regarded as an SVO (Subject-Verb-Object) language, while Japanese is regarded as an SOV language, and Welsh as VSO. In fact, languages exhibiting a preference for the other possibilities, VOS, OSV and OVS, have been attested. Even within a language, different orders may coexist: German prefers SVO in main clauses, but SOV in subordinate clauses.

One important property of language is that it is **recursive**. That is, it allows phrases of one type within constituents of that same type. For example, the NP *the man with the telescope* contains within it the smaller NP *the telescope*. This property applies to sentences also. Thus, the sentence *she said that he slept* contains the sentence *he slept*. **Subordinate** clauses or sentences are those which are dependent on a main clause or sentence, as in the preceding example. **Relative** clauses are an important type of subordinate clause. They modify nouns that play simultaneous and different roles in the subordinate and in the main clause.

In *the person whom I invited left, the person* is object of *invited* but subject of *left*.

In addition to structure and word order, concord or **agreement** is another important issue in syntax. It refers to the grammatical links between words, and it arises when the form of one word requires a corresponding form of another. A typical example is subject–verb agreement, as illustrated by: *the woman walks* vs. *the women walk*. Agreement varies widely between languages. For example, Spanish nouns agree with adjectives in gender and number; Hungarian verbs agree with their objects on definiteness; in Russian there is person and number agreement between the possessor and the possessed.

2.1.6 Lexicon and Semantics

Apart from determining their boundaries, the study of language involves the identification of word equivalences. For example, are *eat, eats, eating, ate, eaten* the same or different words? From an orthographic point of view they are different, but from a semantic point of view they all belong to the same lexical item or **lexeme** "eat", from which the various word forms are derived. In many cases lexemes correspond to root morphemes, but the term is most frequent in discussions relating to meaning.

Semantics is the study of meaning in language. It is an area that has attracted special interest on the part of philosophers and logicians for many centuries. There is no standard theory of meaning at present; rather, there are a variety of approaches to the subject. This will become evident when the different semantic frameworks for MT are described, particularly those in Sections 6.2, 7.1 and 7.2. Since MT is normally applied in situations where preservation of content is the overriding factor, semantics can play a crucial role. This is even more so given that there is no simple one-to-one meaning relation between words in different languages.

Sense and **reference** are two important concepts in most semantic theories. Reference corresponds, very broadly speaking, to the relation between language and the real world. By contrast, sense is related to the way lexemes are related to other lexemes in a particular language. In a way, sense is the means by which we manipulate meaning in our minds, regardless of whether those meanings correspond to anything in the real world. We can talk of unicorns, the present king of France and other non-existent entities without having to indicate how a referential link is made to them.

Lexemes have **senses** that hold various relations to each other. **Synonyms** are lexemes that have the "same" meaning (e.g. *object/thing*). It is unlikely that words are truly synonymous for all contexts. **Antonyms** are lexemes that have some sort of opposite meaning (e.g *big/small, male/female, buy/sell*). The **hyponym** of a lexeme is included by that lexeme semantically (e.g. *rose* is a hyponym of *flower*). A **hyperonym** is its converse (*flower* is a hyperonym of *rose*). In **metonymy**, an attribute is used for the whole (*crown* instead of *king*). **Polysemy** occurs when a lexeme has different but related senses (e.g. *chip* as a piece of wood or an item of food). **Homonyms** are different lexemes that have the same form (e.g. *bank* for financial institution and side of a river); in this book we will use polysemy to include homonymy, as the distinction is somewhat arbitrary in many cases.

A **collocation** is a set of one or more lexemes that tend to occur together, either in a predictable and restricted fashion (e.g. *blond* and *hair*) or in a less predictable manner (e.g. *page* and *book*). However, in a collocation, the meaning is **compositional** in the sense that the meaning of the whole is clearly related to the meaning of its parts. Languages differ greatly in terms of their collocations: in English one *blows a whistle* while in Spanish one *toca un pito* (touches/plays a whistle). The less compositional and more fixed a collocation is, the more one thinks of it as an **idiom** (e.g. *to kick the bucket* – to die).

A **diectic** form can only be interpreted with reference to a speaker's space and time. Diectic forms include personal diexis (*I, you*), spatial diexis (*this, here*) and temporal diexis (*now, today*). **Anaphora** indicates reference to a previously introduced entity. In "*Michaela ate. She was hungry.*", *she* makes anaphoric reference to *Michaela*. **Ellipsis** occurs when part of a phrase is omitted, but it can be recovered from context: replying *I have* to the question *Have you done your homework?* involves omission of *done my homework*.

2.1.7 Pragmatics and Stylistics

Pragmatics is the branch of linguistics that deals with language in action. It relates to its use for social interaction in real world settings. Stylistics is the study of how social relationships and other extralinguistic features affect linguistic choice.

Pragmatic and stylistic choices are clearly relevant to M(A)T since translated texts must be sensitive to the TL audience. Although few MT systems employ formal theories of pragmatics and style, it is fortunate that many domains suitable for MT involve choices that can be made globally for a text and applied by the system. This is often done (if only implicitly) in a number of systems. The following are some examples of the types of choices that may be made.

Formality: Different lexical and word forms are used depending on the social relationship of the participants. For example, Spanish distinguishes between *tu* (you-informal) and *usted* (you-formal), while Japanese has an extensive system of honorifics.

Sublanguage style: Sublanguage-specific preferences exist for certain grammatical structures. For instance, Spanish instructions are normally given as infinitive forms, while English instructions are in the imperative: *Add two eggs – Añadir dos huevos* (to-add two eggs).

Lexical preferences: Certain target audiences (e.g. companies, regions, countries) prefer some lexical items over others: British English *lift* vs. American English *elevator*.

Formulaic expressions Greetings, farewells and similar standard expressions must conform to TL conventions: English *Dear Miles, –* Spanish: *Estimado Miles:* (lit: esteemed Miles:).

2.2 Formal Background

Formal and computational linguistics and M(A)T have benefited from developments in computer science and from other fields of mathematics such as set theory and statistics. This section presents some of the relevant formal background that will be useful in the rest of the book. We assume, however, that readers are familiar with basic discrete mathematics, including set theory, relations, functions, recursion and graph theory, as well as with basic calculus.

2.2.1 Formal Language Theory

Work in linguistics and computer science has resulted in a branch of mathematics known as formal language theory. This is the study of mathematical structures in which the decision about whether a given string of symbols constitutes a valid sequence is based on a set of explicitly stated rules. Two notions are fundamental in this setting: that of a string and that of a language.

A **string** is a sequence of symbols taken from some finite set of symbols Σ known as the **alphabet** for the string. Repetitions of symbols are allowed in strings, and the order of the symbols matters. An example of a string from the alphabet $\Sigma = \{a, b\}$ is $aabaabb$. The **empty string**, denoted 0 (sometimes written ϵ or λ), is a string with no symbols, and with zero length. The set of all finite strings over the alphabet Σ is denoted by Σ^* and is called the Kleene closure over the alphabet. The Kleene closure will have a countably infinite number of elements. In the example, the closure will have all possible strings that could be made from a and b, including 0:

$$\Sigma^* = \{0, a, b, aa, ab, aabb, abab, ...\}$$

In the following, we assume x and y are strings. The **concatenation** of x and y is xy; for example, if $x = aa$ and $y = bb$, their concatenation is the string $aabb$. If x is part of y, then x is a **substring** of y: if $x = ab$, $y = aabb$, then x is a substring of y; every string is a substring of itself. If z is a string of the form xy, then x is a **prefix** of z, and y is a postfix or **suffix** of z; for example, if $z = abb$, then $0, a, ab, abb$ are all prefixes of z, while $0, b, bb$ and abb are all suffixes of z.

A **(formal) language** L over an alphabet Σ is simply defined as a subset of Σ^*. For example $L = \{a, bb, aaa\}$. Thus, we say that bb is in the language L, but neither aa nor 0 is. The strings of a language are frequently expressed in terms of a phrase structure grammar, which lets us describe infinite languages through finite means.

A **phrase structure grammar** (PSG) is a 4-tuple $G = (N, T, P, S)$, where N is a finite set of non-terminal symbols, normally written in upper case; T is a finite set of terminal symbols (normally written in lower case) such that $N \cap T = \{\}$; P is a set of production rules of the form $\alpha \rightarrow \beta$, where α is a string of one or more symbols from $N \cup T$, and β is 0 or a string of one or more symbols from $N \cup T$; finally, $S \in N$ is the start symbol. Starting with the prescribed start symbol S, the derivation of a string in T^* proceeds by

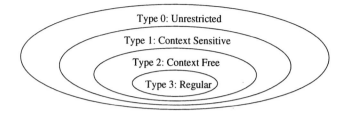

FIG. 2.1. Chomsky hierarchy of PSGs

repeatedly replacing substrings which match a left-hand side of a derivation rule by the corresponding right-hand side, as illustrated in the examples below.

This is a very general definition of PSG. By placing restrictions on the length of the left and right strings in production rules, different types of grammar can be defined. These grammars are organized in what is known as the **Chomsky hierarchy** illustrated in Fig. 2.1, and corresponds to a similar classification for formal languages (see below).

Beginning with type 3 or **regular** grammars, the restriction on these grammars is that all productions must be in either of the following forms:

1. $X \rightarrow y$ where X is a non-terminal symbol, and y is a terminal symbol.
2. $X \rightarrow yZ$ where X and Z are non-terminals, and y is a terminal.

In addition, if there is a production of the form $A \rightarrow 0$, then A does not appear as the right-hand side of any other rule. As an example, the following regular grammar generates strings consisting of ds:

$$N = \{A\} \qquad T = \{d\} \qquad S = A$$
$$P = \{A \rightarrow d, A \rightarrow dA\}$$

To generate the string ddd, we start with A and apply the second production to give dA; such a rule application would be written $A \Rightarrow dA$. Applying the same rule again extends the sequence to $A \Rightarrow dA \Rightarrow ddA$. Finally, applying the first rule gives $A \Rightarrow dA \Rightarrow ddA \Rightarrow ddd$. In general, it is easy to infer what N, T and S are from the production rules alone, so normally only rules are given as descriptions of PSGs.

Regular grammars can be efficiently implemented, and are useful for a variety of purposes including text processing, lexical analysis and even speech processing. In fact, regular languages are frequently defined using **regular expressions** (REs) which are finite representations of languages using a pre-specified set of language-defining symbols. These symbols can be combined or extended using a variety of operators. The following RE defines the language of all strings beginning with a or c, followed by zero or more bs:

$$(a \mid c)b^*$$

REs are a convenient way of describing a set of strings, and are therefore frequently used for searching and editing text in many software systems. The notation can vary from one system to another, but they mostly support similar operations. These can be described in a recursive manner as follows (in what follows x and y are REs):

Atoms: Symbols in the alphabet are REs matching themselves.

Kleene star: x^* matches sequences of zero or more strings from x. Example: a^* will match 0, a, aa, aaa, and so on.

Concatenation: xy matches all strings made by concatenating a string from the language defined by x and the language defined by y. Example: a^*b represents b, ab, aab, and so on.

One or more: x^+ matches strings comprising one or more strings from x. Example: $(ab)^+$ matches ab, $abab$, $ababab$, and so on, but not 0. Note the use of parentheses to demarcate the scope of the + operator. Also, the equivalence $x^+ = xx^*$ holds.

Either-or: $(x \mid y)$ will match strings drawn from x or from y. Example: $(ab \mid b^+)$ matches ab, b, bb, bbb, and so on, but it does not match abb nor $abbb$, for example.

These operations can be used any number of times: the RE $(a \mid b)^*a(a \mid b)^*a(a \mid b)^*$ defines the language where all strings have at least two as.

In many implementations, a variety of symbol groupings and shorthands are provided in order to simplify search operations. These include letter groupings to refer to all capital letters, all blank characters, no digits and so on; they also support wildcard characters such as . (a full stop or period) which means "match any one symbol". A variety of special "characters" such as beginning or end of word expressions are also common. The following is an example of an RE in Emacs for finding words ending in "ing": \<[a-zA-Z]+ing\> The expressions \< and \> mark the beginning and end of a word, while [a-zA-Z]+ indicates all sequences of one or more characters taken from the ranges a-z and A-Z; the sequence ing simply matches itself. This RE will match *ending*, but not *ing* on its own.

Regular grammars cannot express the type of embedded structures found in natural languages. Type 2 grammars, on the other hand, can express these structures. These grammars, known as **context-free** grammars (CFGs) are widely used for syntactic description. Also, since they are convenient for defining the syntax of programming languages, efficient techniques for processing them have been developed. In these grammars, every production is of the form $X \rightarrow y$ where X is a single non-terminal, and y is a string of zero or more terminals and non-terminals. That is, each rule can only rewrite one non-terminal at a time. The following grammar defines the language $a^n b^n$ for n a positive integer (e.g. ab, $aabb$, $aaabbb$, and so on); such a language cannot be defined using type 3 grammars.

$$S \rightarrow ab$$
$$S \rightarrow aSb$$

A simple CFG for a fragment of English is given below:

$$S \rightarrow NP\ VP \qquad Det \rightarrow the \qquad NP \rightarrow Dublin$$
$$VP \rightarrow V\ NP \qquad N \rightarrow girl$$
$$NP \rightarrow Det\ N \qquad V \rightarrow likes$$

The terminals here are *the, girl, likes, Dublin*. One rewrite sequence for this grammar would be: $S \Rightarrow NP\ VP \Rightarrow Det\ N\ VP \Rightarrow the\ N\ V\ NP \Rightarrow the\ girl\ V\ NP \Rightarrow the\ girl\ likes\ NP \Rightarrow the\ girl\ likes\ Dublin$. If in addition to rewriting each non-terminal, the complete rules used are included in the derivation, a direct correspondence with parse trees (e.g. the tree on p. 14) is established: each grammar rule corresponds to a local tree, namely a node (the mother) and all its immediate subnodes (the daughters).

This close correspondence between syntactic descriptions of natural languages and CFGs has made them a useful and popular tool in NLP. This is despite phenomena such as unbounded dependencies (Section 5.3), which are difficult if not impossible to account for using CFGs alone.

Type 1 grammars, or **context sensitive** grammars (CSGs) are less used in NLP; in these grammars, all rules are of the form $X \rightarrow y$, where X and y are sequences of terminals and non-terminals, and the number of symbols in y is greater than that for X. Thus, $AbC \rightarrow dEf$ is a CSG rule, but $AbC \rightarrow 0$ is not.

Finally, type 0 grammars, or **unrestricted** grammars have no restrictions on their production rules. As a result, they can generate recursively enumerable languages, which means that they can represent any computation that a Turing machine can represent (see below).

2.2.2 Automata Theory

Automata theory is the area of computer science that deals with formal models of computation known as automata. In particular, a hierarchy can be established which defines increasingly more powerful automata, culminating in Turing machines, the most powerful automaton in the hierarchy. This hierarchy closely resembles the Chomsky hierarchy mentioned above.

The simplest type of automaton is the **finite state machine** (FSM). Mathematically it is defined as a 5-tuple (Q, Σ, q_0, F, T) consisting of the following elements: a finite set Q of states; a finite set Σ of symbols known as the input alphabet; a start state $q_0 \in Q$; a finite set of final states $F \in Q$, and a finite set of transitions T, where each transition is a triple $(state, input, next - state)$ indicating how the machine responds to input. The machine is presented a sequence of symbols in the form of a string drawn from its input alphabet; the string is read symbol by symbol, starting from the left. Each symbol causes the machine to change state according to the transitions in T. The sequence ends when the last input letter has been read. If at this point the machine is in the final state, the machine is said to **accept** the string.

For example, define a machine as:

$$Q = \{x, y, z\} \qquad \Sigma = \{a, b\} \qquad q_0 = x \qquad F = \{z\}$$
$$T = \{(x, a, y), (x, b, z), (y, a, x), (y, b, z), (z, a, z), (z, b, z)\}$$

Start

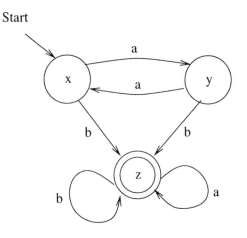

FIG. 2.2. A finite state machine.

Then the string aa is not accepted by the machine: starting in state x, the first a changes the state of the machine to y via transition (x, a, y); the next a changes the state back to x, which is not a final state and therefore the string is not accepted. A similar process would show that the string ab is accepted.

It is common to display FSMs as graphs with states represented as nodes, arcs representing transitions, and final states indicated by a double circle. This makes it easier to trace the behaviour of the machine manually. The graph for the previous machine is given in Fig. 2.2. From the graph one can see that the machine recognizes any string with at least one b in it. A **deterministic** FSM is one where there is one and only one transition from every state for every input symbol, including possibly the empty string 0; the previous example is a deterministic FSM.

By contrast, **non-deterministic** FSMs (NFSM) have the following properties: (a) more than one transition for the same input symbol from the same state is possible; (b) a state may have no transition for a particular symbol; (c) transitions with the empty string are not allowed. In procedural terms, property (a) implies that the current state and the input symbol do not determine the next state. If there is no transition for a particular input symbol, the machine blocks and backtracks to a previous decision point; if no such point exists, the input string fails to be accepted. Thus, an NFSM accepts a string if there is at least one path through the machine from the start state to one of the final states consuming all the input symbols. The NFSM in Fig. 2.3 recognizes all strings with the substrings aaa or bbb in them. Imagine tracing $baaa$ through this machine starting at state 0. First, b takes it back to state 0. Next, the a can lead to 0 or to 1. Assume 0 is chosen for this and for the two subsequent as. The machine ends in a non-final state, but with unexplored paths. Therefore it backtracks. In this case, choosing 1 as the next state after the first a leads to a final state. The string is therefore recognized by the machine.

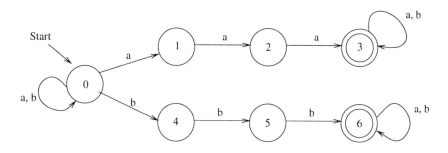

FIG. 2.3. A non-deterministic finite state machine.

It is important to note that deterministic and non-deterministic FSMs are equivalent in formal power. That is, they both accept regular languages. In fact, there are algorithms for automatically converting an NFSM into a deterministic one.

Other models of computation have a close relationship to different levels of the Chomsky hierarchy, as indicated below:

FSM: Accepts regular languages generated by type 3 grammars.

Pushdown automata: These are like FSMs but with access to memory in the form of a stack from which symbols can be access solely on a last in, first out basis. These automata accept context-free (CF) languages generated by type 2 grammars.

Linear-bounded automata: These are like FSMs but with random access to memory. The size of memory is a linear function of the size of the input. These automata accept context-sensitive languages generated by type 1 grammars.

Turing machines: These are like FSMs but with random access to unlimited amounts of memory. They accept recursively enumerable languages, generated by type 0 grammars.

2.2.3 Dynamic Programming

A very powerful and efficient technique is that of dynamic programming. It is a general approach to solving optimality problems in which parts of an optimal solution are also optimal. The problems to which this technique has been successfully applied include string comparison, bilingual alignment and Hidden Markov Model calculations.

The technique can be illustrated with the following example. Consider the problem of finding the shortest path between points A and F in Fig. 2.4. Let $F(x)$ be the minimum distance from node a to node x. Then, $F(f)$ will be whichever is the smaller of $F(d) + 8$ and $F(e) + 10$. Note that we only need to know the shortest distance from a to the immediate neighbours of f, plus the distance from them to f, to calculate the shortest distance from a to f. Similarly,

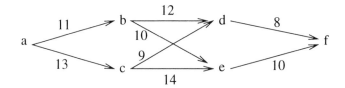

FIG. 2.4. Weighted graph representing distances between nodes.

$F(d)$ is given by: $\min(F(b) + 12, F(c) + 10)$. More generally:

$$F(x) = \min(F(y_1) + d(y_1, x), F(y_2) + d(y_1, x), ..., F(y_n) + d(y_n, x))$$

where $y_1, ..y_n$ are the immediate neighbours of x, and $d(y_i, x)$ is the distance or cost between y_i and x. If this formula is applied recursively, there will be a point when we need to compute the minimum distance to an immediate neighbour of a, say b. Defining $F(a) = 0$, the formula will reduce to $F(b) = \min(0 + d(b, a)) = 11$; similarly, $F(c) = 13$, from which $F(d) = 22$ (i.e. via c), $F(e) = 21$ (i.e. via b), and finally $F(f) = 30$ (i.e. via d). This is the shortest distance between a and f.

While the reasoning in a dynamic programming works backward through the various stages, the calculation works forward from the initial value, which is given (in this case by $F(a) = 0$) up to the desired stage. In the dynamic programming problems in this book, the result of various stages will be stored in an (at most) three-dimensional array. In the present example, however, a one-dimensional array is enough to store the values of F. An example of a dynamic programming problem involving a two-dimensional array is string edit distance calculations (Section 4.2.1), while shortest path calculations for all nodes in a graph are made using dynamic programming on a three-dimensional array (Section 9.3.2).

In addition to minimizing (or maximizing) a value, many problems require the sequence of decisions or path that led to a solution. The simplest way of obtaining this is by constructing a parallel function (array) indicating for each stage (e.g. node) the preceding stage that optimized it, and which therefore lies in the optimal path. For the preceding example, an additional function $P(x)$ would be constructed indicating the immediately preceding node x in the optimal path that led to x. Thus, $P(f) = d$, $P(d) = c$ and so on. Note that $P(a)$ would not be defined in the above example, or it would have a dummy start value.

2.2.4   Basic Probability and Statistics

Developments in NLP have led to the exploitation of language corpora to refine and develop computational models of language. Many of these models exploit basic axioms, theorems and approximations from the fields of probability theory and statistical inference. This section introduces the basic concepts assumed in the rest of the book.

The **sample space** for an experiment is the set of all possible outcomes that might be observed. An **event** is then a subset from this sample space. In statistical NLP one is frequently concerned with single element events (singleton sets). An event is said to **occur** if any one of its elements is the outcome of the experiment. For example, assume that we throw a fair die (the experiment). Then the sample space is the set of possible outcomes, namely $S = \{1, 2, 3, 4, 5, 6\}$. The event of throwing an even number $A = \{2, 4, 6\}$ occurs if any of 2, 4, or 6 is thrown.

A **probability function** is a real-valued set function defined on the class of all subsets of the sample space S: the value that is associated with a subset A is denoted by $P(A)$. The probability function P must satisfy the following three axioms:

1. $P(S) = 1$
2. $P(A) \geq 0$ for all $A \subset S$
3. $P(A \cup B) = P(A) + P(B)$ if $A \cap B = \{\}$

The first axiom states that if S includes all possible events, then an experiment will have one of those outcomes, so we are certain (probability 1) that event S will occur. The second axiom states that probabilities are non-negative (in fact they are real numbers from 0 to 1 inclusive). The last axiom states that if two events cannot occur simultaneously, then the probability that either occurs is the sum of their individual probabilities. In terms of the die example, the axioms state that $P(\{1, 2, 3, 4, 5, 6\}) = 1$ (i.e. one of the numbers will come up). $P(\{1, 2\})$ (or of any other event in S) is not negative. Finally, $P(\{1, 2\}) = P(\{1\}) + P(\{2\})$. Independently of these axioms, we can assume in this case (because the die is fair) that each single-element event is equally likely. Since there are six such events, they must all have probability 1/6. Then $P(\{1, 2\}) = 1/6 + 1/6 = 1/3$.

Technically speaking, a **random variable** is a function that associates a real value with every element in the sample space. In many cases, however, it is more convenient to treat a random variable as the uncertain outcome of the experiment. If X is a random variable, then $X = a$ indicates that the outcome of the experiment was a for some finite sample space. Under this definition, the event defined by the random variable is the singleton set $\{a\}$. So in general, we say $P(X = a)$ or simply $P(a)$ to mean the probability $P(\{a\})$ of the event $\{a\}$ given an understood sample space. For the die example, $P(3) = P(X = 3) = P(\{3\}) = 1/6$.

In many practical applications, each experiment is associated with two or more outcomes. In this case, instead of one variable, we need two or more random variables to describe the outcome of the experiment. In the case of two discrete random variables, the **joint** probability function is $P(X = x, Y = y)$, or more simply $P(x, y)$, or $P(X \cap Y)$ in terms of events, and similarly for three or more variables. The sample space in such cases is the set of all vectors of n-tuples, where each tuple is made up of the value for each variable. For example, if the experiment is to throw a die and a coin, then the sample space is $S = \{(1, H), (1, T), .., (6, H), (6, T)\}$ and a *single* experiment will result in a (set of) *pair(s)* from S. Given that each outcome is equally likely and there are $6 \times 2 = 12$ possible outcomes, each outcome has probability 1/12, for example $P(2, H) = 1/12$. In fact, for independent events (as in this case):

$$P(A, B) = P(A)P(B)$$

For instance, $P(2, H) = P(2) \times P(H) = (1/6)(1/2) = 1/12$.

Two useful relationships in probability theory are:

$$P(A \mid B) = \frac{P(A, B)}{P(B)}$$

$$P(A_1, ..., A_n) = P(A_1)P(A_2 \mid A_1)P(A_3 \mid A_1, A_2)...P(A_n \mid A_1, ..., A_{n-1})$$

The first one is known as the **conditional probability** of event A occurring given that event B has occurred. It is calculated by dividing the probability of both events occurring simultaneously by the probability of B occurring regardless of whether A occurs. For example, assume there are 100 words in a text and that the word *post* occurs five times of which four occurrences are verbs. An experiment consists of taking a word at random and checking its part of speech. If the word is *post*, the probability that it will be a verb is given by:

$$P(Verb \mid post) = \frac{P(Verb, post)}{P(post)} = \frac{(4/100)}{5/100} = 4/5$$

The second equation "breaks up" a joint probability into a product of conditional probabilities. For instance, if we are now told that, of the four *post* verbs, one occurs in a relative clause, then the probability of choosing a word at random and that this word turns out to be *post* used as a verb inside a relative clause is given by:

$$P(post, Verb, Rel) = P(post)P(Verb \mid post)P(Rel \mid post, Verb)$$
$$= (5/100)(4/5)(1/4) = 1/100$$

These two relations can be combined to derive Bayes's theorem, which gives an alternative analysis of conditional probabilities:

$$P(A \mid B) = \frac{P(A, B)}{P(B)}$$
$$= \frac{P(A)P(B \mid A)}{P(B)}$$

Returning to the *post* example, if we know that there are 50 verbs in the whole corpus, then we can get the same result as before but via a different route:

$$P(Verb \mid post) = \frac{P(Verb)P(post \mid Verb)}{P(post)} = \frac{(50/100)(4/50)}{5/100} = 4/5$$

In this simple case, $P(Verb \mid post)$ clearly could have been calculated directly from the counts or via the earlier equation. However, Bayes's theorem is useful when there is incomplete or uncertain data.

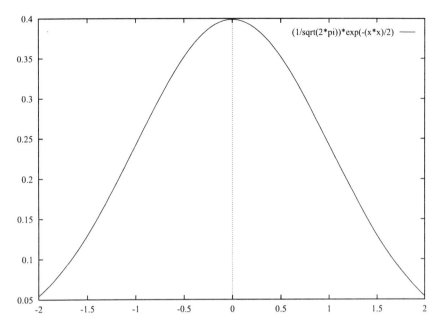

$(1/sqrt(2*pi))*exp(-(x*x)/2)$ ——

FIG. 2.5. The normal density graph.

While in simple games of chance it is quite possible to calculate precisely what probabilities to assign to different events (under certain reasonable assumptions), in more typical applications, including NLP, this is not possible. This is partly because the true probabilities of linguistic events are not easily derivable from a set of basic assumptions. Most probabilistic models of language, therefore, require a step of parameter (e.g. probabilities) estimation in which the outcome of several experiments provides a random sample for a random variable. These estimates can then be used to predict or analyse new data. One common estimation technique uses **maximum likelihood estimators** (MLEs). This technique requires us to choose the estimates which maximize the likelihood of the data given some assumed probability model of it. It can be shown that the MLE for the probability of an event from an event space is the sample proportion. For example, if there are 50 verbs taken at random from a text, and four are the word *post*, then the *estimated* probability (i.e. the MLE) that the *next* verb is *post* is given by $4/50 = 0.08$. Unfortunately, MLEs are not very reliable when there is little data. Smoothing techniques can be used to address this problem, as discussed in subsequent chapters.

The data found in many natural processes (e.g. human heights, student scores) follows a **normal distribution**, where a large number of members of the population cluster around a central value known as the **mean** (e.g. the average height), with the number of members rapidly decreasing as one moves away from the mean (e.g. there are few very short or very tall people). This distribution gives the common bell-shaped graph illustrated in Fig. 2.5. This graph shows, on the

x-axis, the value of a random variable (range $-\infty$ to $+\infty$) while on the y-axis it shows its density (range 0 to 1). In practice (e.g. with the x-axis divided into discrete intervals) the x-axis organizes the data into small intervals (e.g. of height ranges) and the y-axis indicates the frequency of data within those intervals (e.g. number of people in that height range). A normal distribution is described by the density function for a random variable X:

$$\frac{1}{\sigma\sqrt{2\pi}}e^{-\frac{(x-\mu)^2}{2\sigma^2}}$$

In this formula, e is the mathematical constant with approximate value 2.718 that is used as base for natural logarithms; μ is the mean value of X, and σ^2 is the **variance**. Variance is an indicator of how spread the population is, and it is defined, in the discrete case, as:

$$\sigma^2 = \frac{\sum_1^n (x_i - \mu)^2}{n}$$

Here $\sum$ is the summation operator (and not the alphabet set!) and σ itself (i.e. the positive square root of the variance) is called the **standard deviation**. As the name indicates, standard deviation is a measure of data variability. For example, it can be shown that regardless of the actual parameters in the formula, about 68.2% of all normally distributed data will lie within one standard deviation unit from the mean; within three standard deviations more than 99% of the data will be found. When $\mu = 0$ and $\sigma^2 = 1$, the function is simplified and we have a standard normal distribution with a standard density function (Fig. 2.5).

To estimate the mean and variance of a normally distributed population based on a relatively small sample of it, one can use the MLE method. It can be shown that $\hat{\mu}$, the MLE for μ, is the average of the data values, while for the variance it is the same as the formula for σ^2 above, with μ replaced by $\hat{\mu}$.

2.2.5 Review of Hidden Markov Models

A Hidden Markov Model (HMM) is a statistical device for modelling some probabilistic phenomenon. HMMs are sometimes explained with the "urn and ball" model (Rabiner 1989). Assume there is a room with N urns containing coloured balls, and that there are M different colours for these balls. Assume further that a genie randomly takes a ball from an urn, tells us what colour it is, and puts it back in its urn. The process is hidden because we do not see from which urn the genie gets the ball; all we know is what colour it was. We can, however, keep track of the sequence of ball colours chosen. There are two random processes in this model, the selection of urns and the selection of balls. Mathematically, an HMM is essentially a finite state machine augmented with probabilities. It is defined by a set of states (e.g. the urns), a set of output symbols (e.g. the colours), the probability of a transition from one state to another (e.g. the genie moving to the next urn), the probability of generating an output symbol m from a state n (e.g. the genie arbitrarily picking a ball in an urn), and an initial state probability

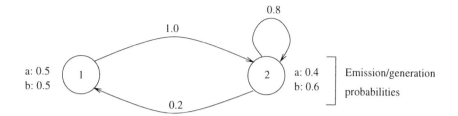

FIG. 2.6. A simple Hidden Markov Model.

for each state (e.g. the genie choosing some urn from which to start). A simple HMM is shown in Fig. 2.6.

An HMM model is normally used in one of three ways. Given a sequence of output symbols: (i) calculate its probability, (ii) calculate the most likely state sequence, and (iii) calculate the probabilities of the model which maximize the probability of that output. The following algorithms are normally used for each of these problems (Rabiner 1989). For (i) the forward algorithm can be used. This recursively computes the sum of probabilities for an output sequence emitted up to a given state; the following recursive definition can form the basis for a dynamic programming algorithm:

1. Initialization:
$$\alpha_1(i) = \pi_i g_i(1) \qquad 1 \leq i \leq S$$

   where $\alpha_t(i)$ is the probability of emitting symbols up to t, ending in state i, S is the number of states, π_i is the initial state probability for state i, and $g_i(t)$ is the probability of generating the symbol at position t from state i.

2. Induction:
$$\alpha_{t+1}(j) = g_j(t+1) \sum_{i=1}^{S} \alpha_t(i) a_{ij} \qquad 1 \leq j \leq S$$

   where a_{ij} is the transition (arc) probability of moving from state i to state j.

   The Viterbi algorithm is used for (ii). It is also a kind of dynamic programming algorithm:

1. Initialization:
$$\delta_1(i) = \pi_i g_i(1) \qquad 1 \leq i \leq S$$
$$\psi_1(i) = 0$$

   where $\delta_t(i)$ is the probability of the most likely sequence of states ending in state i and generating symbols up to t. The sequence of states is recorded in the array $\psi_t(i)$, indicating the previous state that maximizes the value of δ.

2. Recursion:

$$\delta_t(j) = g_j(t) \max_{1 \le i \le S} \{\delta_{t-1}(i)a_{ij}\} \qquad 1 \le j \le S$$

$$\psi_t(j) = \arg \max_{1 \le i \le S} \{\delta_{t-1}(i)a_{ij}\} \qquad 1 \le j \le S$$

Note that instead of a sum, it is the maximum value over the iteration that is selected this time.

Finally, the estimation–maximization (EM) algorithm (e.g. Baum–Welsh re-estimation procedure) can be used for (iii). It is a "hill-climbing" algorithm which has as input a sequence of output symbols and an HMM whose probabilities have been estimated. The algorithm then attempts to maximize the probability of the output sequence by iteratively re-estimating all the probabilities. The initial estimates for the array of transition (arc) probabilities, a, can be made, say, by making transitions leaving a state equally likely $\pm$ some small random amount to reduce the risk of getting stuck in a "ridge" during "hill-climbing". The sum of arc probabilities leaving a state must add to 1, however. The initial guesses for the array g of generation or output probabilities for each state can be made in the same way, and similarly for the vector of initial state probabilities π. The re-estimation iteration then calculates new values for all these probabilities using the estimates and the training output sequences.

The EM algorithm employs the three auxiliary functions ξ, β and γ:

$$\xi_t(i,j) = \text{probability of being in state } i \text{ when emitting the } t\text{th symbol,}$$
$$\text{and in state } j \text{ for the } (t+1)\text{th symbol}$$

$$= \frac{\alpha_t(i)a_{ij}g_j(t+1)\beta_{t+1}(j)}{\sum_{k=1}^{S} \sum_{m=1}^{S} \alpha_t(k)a_{km}g_m(t+1)\beta_{t+1}(m)}$$

where $\beta_t(i)$ is the probability of the output sequence from symbol $t+1$ onwards, given that the current state is i:

• Initialization:
$$\beta_T(i) = 1 \qquad 1 \le i \le S$$

• Induction:
$$\beta_t(i) = \sum_{j=1}^{S} a_{ij}g_j(t+1)\beta_{t+1}(j) \qquad 1 \le i \le S$$

The third auxiliary function indicates the probability of being in state i on generating the tth output symbol:

$$\gamma_t(i) = \sum_{j=1}^{S} \xi_t(i,j)$$

Given these functions, the update formulas for all three types of probabilities are:

$$\bar{\pi}_i = \gamma_1(i)$$

$$\bar{a}_{ij} = \frac{\text{expected number of transitions from state state } i \text{ to state } j}{\text{expected number of transitions from state } j}$$

$$= \frac{\sum_{t=1}^{T-1} \xi_t(i,j)}{\sum_{t=1}^{T-1} \gamma_t(i)}$$

$$\bar{g}_j(k) = \frac{\text{expected number of times in state } j \text{ and generating symbol } k}{\text{expected number of times in state } j}$$

$$= \frac{\sum \gamma_t(j) \text{ for all } 1 \le t \le T \text{ such that the } t\text{th output symbol is } k}{\sum_{t=1}^{T} \gamma_t(j)}$$

The right-hand side of each update equation is computed with the current estimates. These estimates then become the current estimates for the next iteration. Note that all the relevant values for the right-hand side are computed first, and then the updates take place. The algorithm is guaranteed to converge, although possibly to a local maximum.

The above description of HMMs could be called the standard formulation for HMMs. An alternative formulation is to have the output symbols emitted not by the states, but by the arcs (Charniak 1993). In this case, each arc is labelled by its transition probability and by the symbol that it emits. In general, the transition probability of the arc will not correspond to that for the standard formulation, as it incorporates the probability of the output symbol. Defining HMMs in this way requires a set of states and output symbols as before, the probability of moving from one state to another state while emitting an output symbol, and the initial state probability.

2.3 Review of Prolog

Much of the notation and description in Part 3 is based on Prolog, a logic programming language whose unification, backtracking and search regimes make it well suited to natural language processing. Logic programming languages contrast with more conventional languages such as C and Java in that they are declarative rather than procedural, in the sense that they can be viewed as stating what is computed, rather than how it is computed. Also, they are structured in terms of relations between entities rather than functions: in Prolog, processing is initiated by queries as to whether a particular relation holds or not. This section is simply a brief description of the terminology adopted in this book and a convenient reminder of various Prolog concepts; it is not a Prolog tutorial and it is not intended to teach those with no Prolog experience how to program in the language. For that, see the further reading section for books where such tutorials may be found.

A typical Prolog program consists of unit clauses or **facts**, and rules or **clauses**, stored in a **database** in memory. Clauses and facts are made up of **predicates** which can have zero or more **arguments** delimited by commas. The following two facts represent a parent–child relation:

```
parent_of(raquel,ana).
parent_of(ana,george).
```

The first fact, for example, indicates that the relation *parent_of* holds between the **atomic constants** *raquel* and *ana*. Such facts can be used to answer **queries** about the database. For example, the query:

```
?- parent_of(raquel,ana).
```

asks whether Raquel is a parent of Ana. It returns

```
yes
```

since the relation is true according to the database. By contrast, the query `parent_of(raquel,george).` will return no. Queries (or **goals**) in Prolog are frequently issued at the Prolog prompt (usually `?-`), which appears as soon as a Prolog session is started.

Variables in Prolog can hold different values depending on their **instantiation**. Variables always start with an upper-case letter or an underscore (_) to distinguish them from constants; an underscore on its own is the anonymous variable and indicates that its value is to be ignored. In answering a query involving variables, Prolog will search for a variable instantiation that makes the relation true:

```
?- parent_of(X,george).
X = ana
yes
```

X has been instantiated or **bound** to the constant *ana* which satisfies the relation. Predicates can have variables, atoms or **terms** as their arguments, where a term is itself a predicate.

Given the relational nature of Prolog, programs are normally non-deterministic (Section 2.2.2) in the sense that there may be multiple ways of satisfying a query at any one time. The Prolog execution mechanism automatically **backtracks** to previous choice points in order to search for alternative ways of satisfying a query. Consider the following:

```
?- parent_of(X,Y).
X = raquel, Y = ana ;
X = ana, Y = george ;
no
```

After printing the first solution *X = raquel, Y = ana*, the user types a semicolon (;) to ask for the next solution (i.e. force backtracking). The next solution is displayed, and again the user requests another solution; none exists and the result is *no*. It is important to realize that Prolog predicates are matched **in the order in which they appear in the database**; that is why the solutions are given in this particular order.

Complex clauses can be made by using a comma to separate different predicates. The comma corresponds to logical "and" indicating that both predicates must be satisfied simultaneously. The following example determines whether the grandparent–grandchild relation holds between *X* and *Y*.

```
?- parent_of(X,Z),parent_of(Z,Y).
X = raquel, Z = ana, Y = george
yes
```

Note that the instantiation of Z must be the same for both predicates.

Complex queries of this kind are normally expressed as clauses using the Prolog implication symbol : – (read "if");

```
grandparent_of(X,Y) :-
    parent_of(X,Z),
    parent_of(Z,Y).
```

Clauses consist of a single predicate to the left of the implication, called the **head** of the clause, and one or more predicates to the right called the **body**. This clause says that for X to be a grandparent of Y (the head), X must be a parent of some third entity Z, which in turn must be a parent of Y (the body). A query using this clause would look much the same as any other query:

```
?- grandparent_of(A,B).
A = raquel, B = george ;
no
```

Note that although Z must be instantiated during execution, it only forms an indirect part to the query's solution and is therefore not displayed. Execution of a body's predicates in Prolog proceeds **in the order in which they appear in the clause**.

Most Prolog programs are a collection of facts and clauses that are searched by Prolog's execution mechanism following their order in the database. Backtracking occurs when a dead end is encountered or when explicitly forced by the programmer.

A fundamental mechanism in Prolog is that of **unification**, which may be described as a mathematically well-defined technique for matching, or alternatively, as a way of combining two information structures into a more informative one. Unification occurs in Prolog automatically as clauses are searched, or it can be explicitly requested through the unification operator =. Broadly speaking, unification is a process of finding variable bindings which make two structures identical. In the simplest case, identical atoms and other constants unify:

```
?- a = a.
yes
?- a(b,c(d)) = a(b,c(d)).
yes
```

When there are variables, the unification results in a **most general unifier**, which is the variable assignment that makes least commitment to variable values. In the unification a(X) = a(Y), the same value (e.g. c) assigned to both variables would result in identity and therefore successful unification, but the result would not be the most general possible. Instead, this unification should give as its result X = Y, which simply restricts the value of the two variables to be identical (in fact, **shared**) and nothing more. Other examples of unifications include:

```
?- a(b,c(X)) = a(Y,c(d)).       ?- f(a,g(h(a,z))) = f(X,g(Y)).
X = d, Y = b ;                   X = a, Y = h(a,z)
no                               yes
?- a(b,c(d)) = a(X,c(X)).        ?- a(b,c(b)) = a(X,c(X)).
no                               X = b
                                 yes
```

Lists are an important data structure in AI in general. In Prolog they are represented using the square bracket and bar notation, and may be defined recursively as follows:

- The empty list, represented by [] is a list.
- If T is a list and H is an entity, then [H|T] is a list.

For example, [b|[]] is a list of just a single element, b, and [a|[b|[]]] is a list with two elements. This method of representing lists is cumbersome. A more convenient way of representing lists is available in Prolog using commas to separate elements. The two previous lists are written in this notation as [a] and [a,b] respectively.

Since Prolog has no repetition constructs analogous to loops in declarative programming languages, **recursion** is normally used to achieve similar effects. Typically, a recursive predicate consists of at least two clauses indicating the base case and the recursive step. For example, a program to determine whether or not an element is a member of a list is written as:

```
member(X,[X|_]).    % Base case: X is a member if it is the
                    % first element in the list

member(X,[_|T]) :- % Recursive step: X is a member if it
    member(X,T).    % is a member of the tail of the list
                    % (i.e. the elements after the first)
```

With this clause, the query member(b,[a,b]). will initially fail to unify with the base case, but it unifies with the head for the recursive step. It then tries to satisfy member(b,[b]). Since member(b,[b]) is simply a shorthand for member(b,[b|[]]) this unifies with the base case, and the original query succeeds.

In addition to its prefix notation, Prolog allows infix operators to be defined by the programmer for use by the built-in reader routine. These operators allow programs to be written in a much more natural way, greatly aiding legibility. For example, rather than use parentheses and a comma to state *parent_of* relations, an infix operator can be defined with:

```
?- op(500, xfx, parent_of).
```

This says that *parent_of* is a type of infix (xfx) operator with precedence 500, where the greater the precedence number the wider the scope of the operators (and the weaker the binding). With this operator, the previous relations in the grandparent program can be rewritten as:

```
raquel parent_of ana.
ana parent_of george.

grandparent_of(X,Y) :-
    X parent_of Z,
    Z parent_of Y.
```

Note that if a predicate is written in infix notation, all references to it must also be made in infix form. In cases where an operator can have arguments with operators of the same precedence, the associativity of the operator must be specified.

For example, xfx does not allow expressions such as raquel parent_of ana parent_of george, which would cause a syntax error. By contrast, the type xfy would allow such expressions by associating to the right; that is, by treating them as raquel parent_of (ana parent_of george). The type yfx would associate to the left.

There are Prolog features that need mentioning. Logical "or", written as a semicolon (;) is used to separate alternative ways of satisfying a clause. The cut, written as an exclamation mark (!), is used to eliminate branches of the search space. It always succeeds, but it has the effect of freezing certain choices in the search space. The following explanation is taken from (Pereira and Shieber 1987, p. 138). "If a clause

$$p :- g_1 , \ldots , g_i , ! , \ldots , g_n .$$

is being used to prove an instance of p and the cut is reached, then the choice of this clause to prove that instance of p, as well as all choices of clauses in proving g_1 through g_i, are made permanent for the duration of the overall proof of which the proof of p is a part."

An **occurs check** determines whether a variable is being unified with a term that contains it, as in:

```
X = a(X).
```

Depending on the implementation, such unifications can lead to infinite loops at different stages of processing or printing. Occurs checking, however, is computationally expensive and most Prolog implementations do not have it for their basic unification operation. However, some provide it as an additional predicate.

In many of the descriptions in later chapters, an additional notational shorthand is used which allows variables to be bound to a value within a predicate. If two or more arguments are known to be bound but (part of) their value is known, this value is only specified once in the predicate and bound to a variable. The variable can then be used at other positions in the predicate. For example, instead of writing either of

```
three(a(Y),a(Y),a(Y)).
```

```
three(X,X,X) :- X = a(Y).
```

we overload the unification operator (=) and write:

```
three(X = a(Y),X,X).
```

When a Prolog program containing linguistic data is read, each clause is preprocessed to expand out such expressions before storing them in the database. For this example, the value stored would be three(a(Y),a(Y),a(Y)). This abbreviatory extension is reasonably easy to implement in Prolog.

2.4 Conclusion

The goal of this chapter was to introduce some of the terminology and concepts that are assumed in the rest of the book. The methodological issues in linguistics regarding syntagmatic and paradigmatic contrasts are specially relevant. CFGs and their extensions will be frequently used, while the general dynamic programming algorithm will manifest itself in various ways through the book. The probability and statistics will be particularly relevant when discussing MAT and disambiguation techniques. Finally, much of the technical detail in Chapters 5–7 will use Prolog notation, and the accompanying implementations will be in Prolog.

2.4.1 Further Reading

An accessible and stimulating reference work on language is Crystal (1987). Lyons (1968) is a thorough introduction to general linguistics, although many other introductory linguistics texts exist. General issues in language typology and universals are discussed in a number of works (Comrie 1981; Mallinson and Blake 1981; Croft 1990; Shopen 1985b; Shopen 1985c; Shopen 1985a). A non-computational discussion of morphology is given by Matthews (1974); more recent is Spencer (1991). There are also many recommendable introductory books on syntax (Burton-Roberts 1997; Baker 1995); comprehensive descriptions of English are also available (Quirk et al. 1985; Huddleston 1984). Spanish is the main contrasting language used here; a clear and detailed description in English is given by Butt and Benjamin (1994). English and Spanish are contrasted at different levels of linguistic description in Whitley (1986); such contrastive grammars are available for other languages such as French (Vinay and Darbelnet 1995). For a general introduction to semantics see Kempson (1977); various topics of interest in modern formal semantics are clearly presented by Chierchia and McConnell-Ginet (1990) and in Lappin (1996). A general discussion on lexical semantics is presented in Cruse (1986). Mey (1993) is a wide-ranging and accessible introduction to pragmatics, while Kasher (1998) is encyclopaedic in its coverage. Helmreich and Farwell (1998) explain differences in translation based on assumptions about the beliefs of the translators. DiMarco and Mah (1994) discuss it with a view to MT.

Introductory texts on formal language theory and automata theory abound. Cohen (1991) is particularly accessible; Rayward-Smith (1983) and Rayward-Smith (1986) are also clear and concise. Dynamic programming is attributed to Bellman (1957). Probability theory and statistical inference are used heavily in NLP. Ross (1994) and DeGroot (1986) are introductory texts on probability and statistics and include a small amount on information theory and Markov chains, the latter being a relative of HMMs. The description of HMMs given follows Rabiner (1989). Oakes (1998) presents statistical techniques for corpus analysis.

There are several books on Prolog for natural language processing. Pereira and Shieber (1987) describe the language and its application to syntactic and semantic analysis; Gazdar and Mellish (1989) and Covington (1994) concentrate on its use for NLP. Bratko (1990) cosiders a wider range of topics in AI.

Part 2
Machine-Aided Translation

3 Text Processing

This chapter presents selected topics in text processing for MT, including formatting, character sets, fonts and input methods.

The development and widespread use of desktop publishing (DTP) has meant that translators and translation agencies now need to offer a complete service that includes not only the translation of linguistic content in a document, but also its formatting and graphic design.

Multilingual text processing includes a variety of technical issues such as formatting standards, character codes, writing direction, fonts, keyboard layout and input method, print drivers and communication protocols, as well as a number of other issues such as spell checking and online resources. A full treatment of each of these is beyond the scope of this book, and it would soon become obsolete anyway, given the speed of development in these areas. However, in this chapter we discuss three selected topics – format preservation, characters and fonts, and input methods – as illustrative of the kind of problems facing M(A)T at the moment.

3.1 Format Preservation

The structure of a document not only makes it easier to read and understand, it also portrays a view of the author or organization from which it originates. Plain text is neither appealing nor easy to read in general, so preserving the formatting of the SL is important in modern translation. The notion of formatting assumed here is very straightforward. It includes such standard fixtures as fonts, page layout, tables, lists, captions and, to a certain extent, diagrams.

The range of text formats can be very large, ranging from handwritten notes to Web pages, multimedia presentations and computer programs. In this book we are concerned with the translation of electronically represented documents. There are at least three ways in which such texts may be translated. One way is to use a WYSIWYG (What You See Is What You Get) editor to edit a copy of the SL document by overwriting it with the TL text. Another possibility is to extract the text from the document, translate it, and then reinsert it into the original formatting codes. A third possibility is to edit the internal representation of the document directly. We consider each possibility in turn.

3.1.1   WYSIWYG Editors for Translation

Perhaps the simplest way of preserving formatting information is to directly type a translation over a copy of the source document using a WYSIWYG editor such as a modern word processor, a DTP package or other document previewer system such as is found bundled with Web browsers. This method assumes that the author makes available to the translator an electronic version of the SL document in a format appropriate to the translator's editing system. Based on a copy of this document, the translator then proceeds to overwrite the SL text with its TL translation, preserving the formatting in the source document. Alternatively, the translator creates a TL version of the document from scratch, recreating or modifying the layout of the original.

It is not infrequent for WYSIWYG systems to have a macro language or some other programming language in which the functionality of the editor can be extended. Typical extensions one might be interested in include insertion or even translation of formulaic text, and complex editing operations (e.g. delete the first word of every entry in a table); additional facilities are usually provided, such as write protection of particular portions of text. Given the power of many of these macro languages, it becomes possible to create simple translation memory systems (Section 4.2) that store and retrieve previously translated translation units (usually sentences).

In order to implement a TM interface the macro language needs to include operations to select text, inspect the contents of the selection, frame it, determine the formatting properties of the text, associate actions with mouse or button events, determine the position of the cursor, record positions within the text, etc. Some of these macro languages can also be used for implementing simple sentence processing, storage and retrieval operations. In this case, the language needs to have operations for file access and window manipulation, as well as support for random access data structures such as hash tables, or at least mechanisms for fast searching of disk files. The details of such operations are very much application dependent, and are likely to change with each release of the software.

3.1.2   Text Extraction and Reinsertion

The preceding approach is normally the preferred way of maintaining formatting correspondence between source and target text, but it can be impractical in some cases. Firstly, the translator may not have access to the software and hardware to run a particular editing system, and even if access were possible, she or he may not be very proficient using it. Secondly, new formatting codes are being introduced and developed and the creation of suitable editors is not always immediate. Thirdly, certain formatting languages such as LaTeX are used via standard character-based text editors, where both formatting commands and actual text are typed in by the author of the text. Finally, if the document is to be translated by machine, the translation software might not be capable of processing the formatting codes.

Text extraction and reinsertion address these issues by dividing translation into the following phases:

1. Textual and non-textual data are extracted into different files, so that the translator is provided with a text-only version of the document to be translated (together with a fully formatted version of the document for guidance). During extraction, each linguistic unit leaves a pointer to its place of origin.
2. The textual file is translated, taking care that any pointers introduced by the extracting software are not modified.
3. The translated text is reinserted into the formatting skeleton at the appropriate locations as indicated by the pointers.

In some cases, this approach to translation is the only practical one. For example, software **localization**, the process of "translating" software into a particular language or region, is a major concern in the global market. Software **internationalization** is the process of modifying software so that it is easy to adapt to different languages and regions. During internationalization, most interface messages and other linguistic information are stored in a separate resource file and subsequently integrated into the code. This facilitates translation of the interface at minimal cost, since all material that needs translation is available in one place. One difference, however, between text extraction in documents and in software is that for a document it is impractical to extract text manually, and techniques need to be developed to automate this.

As an example, consider Hypertext Markup Language (HTML) the format used for the World Wide Web. The contents of a simple HTML file are shown in Fig. 3.1. Unless one is familiar with HTML, it can be difficult or at least tiresome and error-prone to determine which strings need to be translated. It is easy to miss portions of text, as well as inadvertently delete or otherwise modify parts of the formatting structure.

Separating text from formatting code reduces the risk of text omission or modification of format. Figure 3.2 shows the two files arising from extracting the linguistic content from the HTML code in Fig. 3.1 (pointers between the text and the format codes are delimited by < { and } >). The translation of the lower file must maintain the same index numbers as they occur in the SL so that each TL string can be reinserted into the appropriate place in the HTML skeleton file in the upper part of Fig. 3.2.

Text extraction can be achieved via two main passes through the file.

1. Identify and mark all formatting commands in a document. Depending on the formatting language, this may be possible using regular expressions or relatively simple CF extensions (Section 2.2.1) in order to match parentheses and other recursive structures. For example, an RE to match HTML tags (codes) could be (in Emacs notation): < [^>] +>. This matches any sequence of characters beginning with < followed by one or more characters in the range [^>] (this range uses the complement operator ^s which stands

```
<HTML>
<HEAD>
   <TITLE>Arcadio's Homepage</TITLE>
</HEAD>
<BODY>

<H1 ALIGN=CENTER>Welcome to Arcadio's Homepage</H1>

<P>Some links of interest:</P>

<UL>
<LI><A HREF="http://www.nowhere.co">Macondo</A></LI>

<LI><A HREF="http://www.solitude.com/">One hun-
dred years ago ...</A></LI>
</UL>

</BODY>
</HTML>
```

FIG. 3.1. A simple HTML code file.

```
<HTML>
<HEAD>
   <TITLE><{0}></TITLE>
</HEAD>
<BODY>

<H1 ALIGN=CENTER><{1}></H1>

<P><{2}></P>

<UL>
<LI><A HREF="http://www.nowhere.co"><{3}></A></LI>

<LI><A HREF="http://www.solitude.com/"><{4}></A></LI>
</UL>

</BODY>
</HTML>
```

```
<{0}>Arcadio's Homepage
<{1}>Welcome to Arcadio's Homepage
<{2}>Some links of interest:
<{3}>Macondo
<{4}>One hundred years ago ...
```

FIG. 3.2. Skeleton and text-only files for Fig. 3.1.

for all characters except those in the string *s*), followed by the character >. In other words, it matches anything between open and close angle brackets. Once matched, the strings can be marked as formatting code. For this, most text and word processors allow user-defined information to be associated with each character in a document. Note that in a few cases, strings within angle brackets *need* to be translated, as is the case with image placeholders:

```
<IMG SRC="map.gif" ALT="Map of the area">
```

Identifying these strings as translatable is slightly more complicated since they are not flanked by normal HTML tags. One simple way of detecting them is to write dedicated REs that will identify them. Other tags that could include translatable text within them include META with keywords and description, scripts and Java applets, and status bar texts.

2. The output of the first pass is an alternating sequence of marked and unmarked strings. In the second pass, this sequence is processed as follows. If the string is marked, it is appended to the skeleton HTML file. If it is unmarked, a new index is created and appended to the skeleton HTML file. In addition, the new index is also appended to the text-only file, followed by the unmarked text. The result is two files, as illustrated in Fig. 3.2. Merging the two files is then a matter of scanning the formatting file and replacing indices with their corresponding strings.

One problem with merging techniques of this kind is that the correct formatting of the TL document may not correspond to that of the SL. One example arises when textual segments change position. Consider the following one-sentence document:

```
She has a <B>red</B> car
```

The <B> and </B> are HTML tags to indicate the beginning and end of bold text. Extracting this document results in the files:

```
       Formatting File                               Text
     <{0}><B><{1}></B><{2}>                   <{0}>She has a
                                              <{1}>red
                                              <{2}>car
```

Translation of the text leads to:

```
            Target Text
        <{0}>Ella tiene un
        <{1}>rojo
        <{2}>coche
```

The problem is that merging based on the index numbers will lead to incorrect translation, since the right result should be:

```
Ella tiene un coche <B>rojo</B>
```

Different partial solutions to such problems can be formulated. One is to extract the complete sentence and let the translator rearrange the text:

```
<{0}>She has a <B>red</B> car
```

This, however, assumes that segments that can be independently translated can be identified. A variation on this idea is to extract specific formatting commands along with their textual arguments. After translation, the TL text file would contain correctly formatted TL segments, but their order would need to be determined by the translator. During merging, the order specified by the translator would override the linking established by the indices. For example, the result of extraction for the preceding example would be:

```
        Format              .          Target text file
     <{0}><{1}><{2}>                    <{0}>She has a
                                        <{1}><B>red</B>
                                        <{2}>car
```

Translation of the target text file gives:

```
<{0}>Ella tiene un
<{2}>coche
<{1}><B>rojo</B>
```

Since the relationship between index numbers in both files is lost, merging must proceed in the order of the text file, giving the correct result.

One problem with this alternative is that it assumes close correspondence between the textual fragments. When the target document needs a different set of text fragments, problems arise. For example, assume that

```
El gato <B>negro</B>
```

is extracted as:

```
        Format                          Text
     <{0}><{1}>                      <{0}>El gato
                                     <{1}><B>negro</B>
```

The goal would be to produce the TL document The `<B>black</B>` cat, but in this case there would be no simple relation between the Spanish and English textual fragments. This and similar situations can complicate format preservation significantly.

Clearly then, preserving formatting by text and code extraction is a non-trivial problem and general solutions to it need to take into consideration the full range of features of the formatting language.

3.1.3   Highlight and Protect Formatting Code

An alternative to WYSIWYG and to text and code extraction is simply to let the translator directly modify the text in the raw formatting file, but to aid her

```
<HTML>
<HEAD>
    <TITLE> Arcadio's Homepage </TITLE>
</HEAD>
<BODY>

<H1 ALIGN=CENTER> Welcome to Arcadio's Homepage </H1>

<P> Some links of interest: </P>

<UL>
<LI><A HREF="http://www.nowhere.co"> Macondo </A></LI>

<LI><A HREF="http://www.solitude.com/"> One hun-
dred years ago ... </A></LI>
</UL>

</BODY>
</HTML>
```

FIG. 3.3. An HTML document with highlighted codes.

or him by highlighting and write-protecting formatting codes. The strings that need to be translated are left unhighlighted. This approach resembles the way that some text editors colour-code syntax and keywords in programs and other types of source code to ease editing.

In order to translate a document, the unhighlighted text is replaced by its TL equivalent through direct editing of the source. Fig. 3.3 shows a file with all formatting codes highlighted and write protected; the textual part of the document could then be overwritten with its translation.

The techniques for this approach are the same as for the first pass in text and code extraction. The main difference is that marking involves write protecting and highlighting the formatting codes matched by REs. The advantage is that it lets the translator manipulate the format of the TL document directly. The disadvantage is that the translator must be proficient in the formatting language used. Also, the technique is less well suited to MT since formatting codes are not removed.

3.2   Character Sets and Typography

Of the many scripts around the world, only those for commercially or politically significant languages are widely available and supported in electronic form. For scripts of other so-called "low density languages", there are very few, if any, such resources. With the explosion in international communications, many more languages will need to be electronically manipulated, thus increasing the need for electronic formats.

The many scripts or writing systems currently in use can be divided into two types: phonological systems, which show a clear relationship between the symbols and the sounds in the language, and non-phonological systems, which do not. Starting with non-phonological systems, the following types may be identified:

Pictographic: Symbols in this system provide a recognizable picture of entities as they exist in the world. Many ancient civilizations, such as the Minoans, Easter Island and Zapotec, adopted pictographic writing systems. Nowadays they are common in road signs, some software buttons and other graphic languages.

Ideographic: This is a development of pictographic systems, in which symbols have an abstract or conventional meaning, not directly related to the shape of the symbol. Modern examples include diagonal lines across various signs to indicate prohibition and various software icons representing abstract actions.

Logographic: Symbols represent words where the relationship between the symbol and the word or meaning is effectively arbitrary. Chinese and the Chinese characters used in other languages such as Korean and Japanese are logographic systems.

Phonological systems are the most common in terms of number of languages that use them. They can divided into two main types:

Syllabic: The symbols, constituting a syllabary, correspond to spoken syllables, usually a consonant–vowel pair. The *hiragana* and *katakana* syllabaries of Japanese are typical examples of this system. In English, one sometimes sees notices such as *B4* (before) using symbols to correspond to syllables.

Alphabetic: This is the most common writing system in terms of number of languages. Each symbol or small group of symbols in the alphabet has a more or less direct correspondence to the phonemes in the language. Latin scripts (e.g. English, Spanish) as well as Arabic, Hebrew and many other languages use an alphabetic system.

The rest of this section considers two important issues in the processing of scripts: character sets and coding, and fonts.

3.2.1 Character Sets and Coding

In languages based on the Latin script, questions regarding character sets are infrequent (e.g. during spelling reform). However, for languages based on Chinese characters, where there are thousands of different symbols, it is important to identify those that are most important to learn and to be able to communicate effectively. For example, there are 1,945 Chinese characters (*kanji*) in the Japanese standard character set, compared with the 52 characters (26 upper case and 26 lower case) in what may be called the English standard character set. These sets are usually independent of whether they are used in computer applications or not; they may omit characters found in older or specialist texts (e.g. æ in English).

Electronic character sets are those made available for computer applications, and normally include more characters than non-electronic ones. For example, ASCII (American Standard for Information Interchange) contains 94 printable characters, and one of the Japanese electronic character sets contains 6,879 characters.

Since characters in a computer are stored and processed as integers, it is necessary to assign numeric codes to each character. These encoding methods are normally determined in some standard way to facilitate information interchange. Most encoding methods use one byte per character, two bytes per character, or a mixture of one and two bytes per character. There are two main ways of representing characters:

Fixed-width: In these encoding methods all characters are represented by the same number of bytes. Methods using one byte include ASCII and the ISO 8859 series (see below); Unicode is a two-byte fixed-width encoding method.

Modal and non-modal: These methods allow some characters to be encoded using one byte and others to be encoded using two bytes. They are distinguished by the way they indicate a switch between one byte and two byte codes. Modal methods indicate this through an escape sequence or through special characters; non-modal methods by contrast use the numeric value of a text stream's bytes to indicate a switch.

The main practical consequence of the various encoding methods is the amount of space taken up by a text and the difficulty with which various text-processing operations such as searching and sorting can be implemented. In general, fixed-width methods take up more space, particularly for two-byte encodings, but they simplify text-processing operations.

We now turn to specific encoding methods. In 1963 the ASCII standard was adopted for the English alphabet in the USA. This standard defines 127 codes (a 7-bit standard) which included the Latin characters used in English, together with a number of control, punctuation and symbol characters. Regardless of the languages for which it is intended, ASCII is frequently used for text-based representations of data and in source code for programs and documents. The full set of ASCII characters and their corresponding decimal codes is given in Fig. 3.4.

The intended interpretation for the control characters is: NULL (**NUL**), START OF HEADING (**SOH**), START OF TEXT (**STX**), END OF TEXT (**ETX**), END OF TRANSMISSION (**EOT**), ENQUIRY (**ENQ**), ACKNOWLEDGE (**ACK**), BELL (**BEL**), BACKSPACE (**BS**), CHARACTER TABULATION (**HT**), LINE FEED (**LF**), LINE TABULATION (**VT**), FORM FEED (**FF**), CARRIAGE RETURN (**CR**), SHIFT OUT (**SO**), SHIFT IN (**SI**), DATALINK ESCAPE (**DLE**), DEVICE CONTROL ONE (**DC1**), DEVICE CONTROL TWO (**DC2**), DEVICE CONTROL THREE (**DC3**), DEVICE CONTROL FOUR (**DC4**), NEGATIVE ACKNOWLEDGE (**NAK**), SYNCHRONOUS IDLE (**SYN**), END OF TRANSMISSION BLOCK (**ETB**), CANCEL (**CAN**), END OF MEDIUM (**EM**), SUBSTITUTE (**SUB**), ESCAPE (**ESC**), FILE SEPARATOR (**IS4**), GROUP SEPARATOR (**IS3**), RECORD SEPARATOR (**IS2**), UNIT SEPARATOR (**IS1**).

The ASCII standard is now widely used throughout the world, either fully or as a subset that includes at least all alphanumeric characters plus the space character. Unfortunately, the standard does not support the accented characters

0	NUL	1	SOH	2	STX	3	ETX	4	EOT	5	ENQ	6	ACK	7	BEL
8	BS	9	HT	10	LF	11	VT	12	FF	13	CR	14	SO	15	SI
16	DLE	17	DC1	18	DC2	19	DC3	20	DC4	21	NAK	22	SYN	23	ETB
24	CAN	25	EM	26	SUB	27	ESC	28	IS4	29	IS3	30	IS2	31	IS1
32		33	!	34	"	35	#	36	$	37	%	38	&	39	'
40	(	41	)	42	*	43	+	44	,	45	-	46	.	47	/
48	0	49	1	50	2	51	3	52	4	53	5	54	6	55	7
56	8	57	9	58	:	59	;	60	<	61	=	62	>	63	?
64	@	65	A	66	B	67	C	68	D	69	E	70	F	71	G
72	H	73	I	74	J	75	K	76	L	77	M	78	N	79	O
80	P	81	Q	82	R	83	S	84	T	85	U	86	V	87	W
88	X	89	Y	90	Z	91	[	92	\	93	]	94	^	95	_
96	`	97	a	98	b	99	c	100	d	101	e	102	f	103	g
104	h	105	i	106	j	107	k	108	l	109	m	110	n	111	o
112	p	113	q	114	r	115	s	116	t	117	u	118	v	119	w
120	x	121	y	122	z	123	{	124	|	125	}	126	~	127	DEL

FIG. 3.4. ASCII character codes.

found in most other (mainly European) languages based on the Latin alphabet. A series of subsequent 7-bit standards such as the ISO-646 series were agreed by the International Organization for Standardization (ISO) to try to redress this problem. However, these standards were not well suited to displaying several Latin alphabets at once and required each language to use a slightly different set of codes. This led to the introduction of the ISO-8859 series of 8-bit standards. Many of these standards rely on the unused 128 codes remaining when ASCII characters are encoded in bytes. At present there are 10 standards in the ISO-8859 series:

8859-1 Western Europe: Danish, Dutch, English, Faeroese, Finnish, French, German, Galician, Irish, Icelandic, Italian, Norwegian, Portuguese, Spanish and Swedish.

8859-2 Eastern Europe: Albanian, Czech, German, Hungarian, Polish, Rumanian, Croatian, Slovak and Slovene.

8859-3 Southern Europe and others: Afrikaans, Catalan, Dutch, English, Esperanto, French, Galician, German, Italian, Maltese, Spanish and Turkish.

8859-4 Northern Europe: Danish, English, Estonian, Finnish, German, Greenlandic, Lappish, Latvian, Lithuanian, Norwegian and Swedish.

8859-5 Latin/Cyrillic: Bulgarian, Byelorussian, Macedonian, Moldavian, Russian, Serbian and Ukrainian.

8859-6 Latin/Arabic: ligatures are not included (see below).

8859-7 Latin/Greek alphabet.

8859-8 Latin/Hebrew.

8859-9 Latin-5 same as 8859-1 except for Turkish instead of Icelandic.

8859-10 Latin-6 for Lappish, Nordic, Eskimo languages such as Inuit and Sami.

All these standards are supersets of ASCII and therefore allow different scripts to be used in conjunction with ASCII (e.g. Greek and English texts). Figure 3.5 gives the Latin-1 codes (note that codes 0–127 correspond to ASCII characters).

128	PAD	129	HOP	130	BPH	131	NBH	132	IND	133	NEL	134	SSA	135	ESA
136	HTS	137	HTJ	138	VTS	139	PLD	140	PLU	141	RI	142	SS2	143	SS3
144	DCS	145	PU1	146	PU2	147	STS	148	CCH	149	MW	150	SPA	151	EPA
152	SOS	153	SGCI	154	SCI	155	CSI	156	ST	157	OSC	158	PM	159	APC
160	NBS	161	¡	162	¢	163	£	164	⊗	165	¥	166	|	167	§
168	¨	169	©	170	ª	171	«	172	¬	173	-	174	®	175	‾
176	°	177	±	178	²	179	³	180	´	181	µ	182	¶	183	·
184	,	185	¹	186	º	187	»	188	¼	189	½	190	¾	191	¿
192	À	193	Á	194	Â	195	Ã	196	Ä	197	Å	198	Æ	199	Ç
200	È	201	É	202	Ê	203	Ë	204	Ì	205	Í	206	Î	207	Ï
208	Ð	209	Ñ	210	Ò	211	Ó	212	Ô	213	Õ	214	Ö	215	×
216	Ø	217	Ù	218	Ú	219	Û	220	Ü	221	Ý	222	Þ	223	ß
224	à	225	á	226	â	227	ã	228	ä	229	å	230	æ	231	ç
232	è	233	é	234	ê	235	ë	236	ì	237	í	238	î	239	ï
240	ð	241	ñ	242	ò	243	ó	244	ô	245	õ	246	ö	247	÷
248	ø	249	ù	250	ú	251	û	252	ü	253	ý	254	þ	255	ÿ

FIG. 3.5. Latin-1 character codes.

Although this is an improvement, there are disadvantages with this series. Firstly, it is difficult to mix texts from different standards; that is, Greek and Cyrillic cannot easily be mixed, nor Spanish and Arabic, for instance. Secondly, many scripts are not based on an alphabet but instead use a logographic system with thousands of different characters. It is impossible to represent each of these characters using one byte only. Finally, Japanese texts can contain up to four writing systems at once, including just under 2000 Chinese characters, two syllabic scripts, as well as Latin characters. Clearly Japanese character codes need to represent all of these systems in a unified manner.

National coding sets have been proposed in countries such as China, Korea and Japan, some differing substantially from each other in the codes they assign to essentially the same character. A process known as Hun unification, however, has led to a rationalization of these various systems; the results have been incorporated in the Unicode standard.

The Unicode character set standard is a 16-bit (2-byte) code developed by the Unicode Consortium of major software developers and other interested parties. At the time of writing the Unicode Web site lists the following scripts as supported by Unicode 2.0:

> Arabic, Armenian, Bengali, Bopomofo, Cyrillic, Devanagari, Georgian, Greek, Gujarati, Gurmukhi, Han/Chinese, Hangul, Hebrew, Kannada, Kana, Latin, Lao, Malayalam, Oriya, Tamil, Telugu, Thai, Tibetan.

Additional scripts will be included in future versions of Unicode. This standard runs in formal convergence with the ISO/IEC standard 10646-1 (the Universal Multiple-Octet Coded Character Set). As a 16-bit standard, Unicode therefore has the potential for representing 65 536 different characters, enough for all the characters of many writing systems. In addition, the standard provides an extension mechanism for about a million more characters. Popular operating systems, programming languages and markup languages have started supporting and implementing Unicode, and this ought to assure its widespread use.

The basic units in Unicode are **code elements**, which roughly correspond to characters, but also include diacritics and several other kinds of symbols and controls. For example, composite characters, those consisting of a base character and a dependent mark (e.g. ñ), can be and are defined in Unicode as a sequence of two code elements: one for *n* and one for the non-spacing mark ˜. Composite characters are also supported in pre-composed form in Unicode (i.e. as a single code element), since many existing standards already represent them with a single code (e.g. Latin-1). The standard provides (de)composition sequences to convert one representation into the other. Codes for changing script direction are also provided, to allow for situations where mixed direction text (e.g. English and Arabic) is needed.

Each code element (character) is assigned a unique number (usually written preceded by U+ and in hexadecimal notation), and a unique name. For example, U+0041 (i.e. 65 in decimal) is assigned the character name LATIN CAPITAL LETTER A and corresponds to ASCII character *A*. These Unicode names are identical to the ISO/IEC 10646 names for the same characters.

Code elements are grouped into areas throughout the range of code values. There are eight main areas as follows:

General Scripts Area: The range 0000–1FFF starts with the standard ASCII characters (0000–007F), all of whose first byte is 00; it is followed by Latin-1 and various extensions and diacritics; there follow Greek (first byte is 03), Cyrillic (04), Armenian and Hebrew (05), Arabic (06), Devanagari and Bengali (09), and so on. This area corresponds essentially to alphabetic scripts.

Symbols: Range 2000–27BF. This includes punctuation, super- and subscripts, currencies, arrows, mathematical operators, etc.

CJK Phonetics and Symbols Area: Range (3000–33FF). This includes Chinese–Japanese–Korean phonetic scripts such as Hiragana and Katakana.

CJK Ideographs Area: Range (4E00–9FFF). This includes the unified Han ideographs (e.g. *kanji*).

Hangul Syllables Area: Range (AC00–D7A3). This includes the complete set of modern Korean Hangul.

Surrogates Area: Range (D800–DFFF). Reserved for range extension mechanisms in Unicode.

Private Use Area: Users may define codes in the range E000–F8FF for their own purposes; these codes are guaranteed never to be assigned.

Compatibility Area and Specials: The end of the range (F900–FFFF) includes codes to enable mapping to earlier standards or old implementations.

Unicode representations are broadly in agreement with already established standards, particularly for alphabetic scripts; for example, Latin-1 corresponds to the 256 characters whose first byte has value 0. This means that conversion between Unicode and a number of standards is quite simple, although conversion tables are provided for a majority of national standards where necessary.

Given that many systems still work with ASCII characters, it is common to find situations where two or more ASCII characters are used to indicate a non-ASCII character. This avoids potential problems when a system cannot provide or guarantee an appropriate character set, font or input method (see below) for the script. For example, in HTML the character *á* can be represented in the source code as á similarly, in Java, the character *Á* is represented by its hexadecimal Unicode number, preceded by the escape sequence \u (i.e. \u00c1). It is possible that this will change as more scripts are supported and global code standards such as Unicode are widely adopted.

Character encoding can have important consequences for various text processing operations. For example, string comparison and sorting cannot always rely on the underlying code of a character to determine standard string ordering conventions. For example, Spanish *ñ* occurs between *n* and *o* alphabetically, but their Latin-1 codes are 241, 111 and 112 respectively. If compared using these internal codes, comparison operations could give incorrect results. Many modern programming languages such as Java have utilities that facilitate string comparison and other operations using language-specific ordering conventions, largely overcoming such problems.

3.2.2 Fonts

The character set encodings simply assign a number to each character but do not indicate the shape or typographic properties (the glyph) of the character. A font or typeface indicates the style in which a particular character or symbol is to be rendered. The following are a few examples of the many different fonts available in the Latin script:

> This is a Roman font.
> This is a Sans Serif font.
> *This is one of the italic fonts.*
> `This font is used to simulate typewriter text.`

While many of the characters in these lines are the same, their glyphs differ. In this example, the variation is only in certain qualities such as thickness of the lines (the "weight" of the font), or whether the font has serifs (the tiny cross-lines at the end of a stroke in a character). However, the manner in which fonts can vary is almost limitless. Most word and text processors, operating systems and user interfaces have several pre-installed fonts, grouped into a variety of series. Additional fonts can be added with relative ease to modern operating systems.

Fonts are available as files indicating the shape of the glyph and sometimes the code it corresponds to. The glyphs in these files are represented using one of two main types for font representation:

Bitmapped: This is one of the earliest and still widely used types of font format. In these fonts the shape of each character is defined by a bit pattern or map in which a 1 indicates a set pixel and a 0 indicates an unset pixel. Figure 3.6 shows a possible 8×8 bitmap for the letter *n*.
A common bitmapped font format is BDF (Bitmap Distribution Format), used in many Unix-based systems. It is relatively simple to use and intuitive

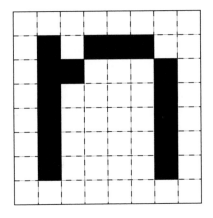

FIG. 3.6. A bitmapped character for *n*.

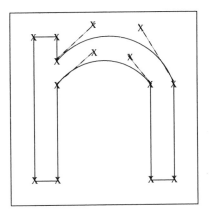

FIG. 3.7. An outline font for *n*.

to create; it is also good for very small sizes as it can be fine-tuned easily. The disadvantage of bitmapped fonts is that they are restricted to a single size, and any scaling can degrade quality substantially. Hence bitmapped fonts are usually created in a range of commonly used font sizes.

Outline: For these fonts, the outline of the character is specified mathematically using a series of straight lines and curves, where each curve is defined in terms of a set of reference points. The outline is then filled and rendered on a monitor or printer. Figure 3.7 shows a possible outline for the letter *n*. The most common outline font formats are PostScript Type 1 and TrueType, the latter normally found on PCs. The advantage of these fonts is that they are highly scalable and therefore only one set of characters is designed from which different sizes are calculated.

It is obviously possible to design a font using a font editing package or via specialized font specification languages. Thus, in principle, it should be possible to design fonts for the scripts of most languages.

In terms of complexity of interaction, the **ligature** system in languages such as Arabic is worth mentioning. For languages based on the Latin script, the position of a character has little effect on its shape, except in some special cases such as the letter sequence *fi* where the dot for the *i* is frequently joined to the *f*. However, in Arabic and some other languages these situations are the norm. Arabic characters can have up to four shapes depending on whether they appear on their own, at the beginning of a word, in the middle or at the end. The following lines show the same letter in all these positions (right to left: on its own, at the beginning, in the middle and at the end).

عَ عَد سعَة بِعَ

The difficulty in displaying the Arabic script is that after typing a character it is not known what its shape on the screen is going to be until the next character is typed. It is common to handle this by allowing characters to change as text is written or deleted, and to allow several typed keys to correspond to one shape. The net effect is to select different shapes from the current font depending on context; obviously, all the glyphs for each character to be displayed must be supported by the operating system and font in use.

There are three other aspects of the Arabic script which require special treatment. Firstly, in a similar way to Hebrew, Arabic is written from right to left. This in itself would not be a major issue except that some operating systems, display drivers and other equipment interpret newlines and other formatting codes as moving the cursor to the leftmost part of the writing area. More recent systems allow such properties to be altered, facilitating the construction of editing software for languages not written left-to-right. Secondly, Arabic writers do not normally write vowels explicitly, relying instead on context to disambiguate between words, but if vowels are used, they are represented by diacritics above and below consonants. The treatment of these diacritics may require further glyphs in their corresponding fonts. Thirdly, it is sometimes common for certain lines in Arabic characters to be extended when justifying text. By contrast the usual way of justifying text with Latin-based characters is to introduce spaces between letters and words. This means that Arabic fonts must be capable of handling such variations. These issues affect other languages as well (e.g. Japanese can be written vertically – top to bottom and right to left – in which case some characters change their shape slightly), placing special requirements on multilingual software.

3.3 Input Methods

Although speech recognition software is gradually becoming more practical for linguistic input, by far the most common input devices for M(A)T, NLP and other text-processing applications are keyboards and mice. We can group input methods via these devices into two ideal types:

Single action: These methods allow each character to be entered via a single action such as pressing a key or clicking a mouse button once.

Multiple action: In these methods, a character requires two or more actions, such as pressing the Shift key and an additional key for producing upper-case letters.

The standard QWERTY keyboard essentially provides single-action input for English characters, with some multiple-action input required for capitals and various non-alphanumeric characters. It has also proved quite adequate as a (largely) single-action input method for other languages based on the Latin script, with only some modifications. For example, keyboards for Spanish normally allow single action input of the letter ñ (to the right of *L* on the keyboard) and a few other characters, as well as multiple-action input of all accents and punctuation. Furthermore, modern operating systems and word processors have different keyboard layouts for many other alphabetic scripts such as Greek, Cyrillic, Arabic and Hebrew. These keyboards allow most of the characters in these languages to be entered using single actions. Furthermore, it is normally straightforward to extend or modify the interpretation of different keys in order to customize the keyboard.

For languages where the number of characters is in the thousands, the situation is different. Single action input devices with thousands of keys are possible, for example, for entering Chinese characters: Japanese *kanji* tablets have been used, consisting of 2160 keys (60 columns by 36 rows) with a different character on each key. However, these tablets require specialist training to operate and are not common now. More common are multiple action input methods of which there are several varieties.

Multiple action methods may themselves be grouped into four categories: pronunciation-based, shape-based, code-based and association-based. All methods, however, have mechanisms for switching to other input methods and/or to other scripts (e.g. between Chinese and English, or between the various Japanese scripts). In fact, some systems require some characters to be entered using one method, and other characters using a different method.

Pronunciation-based methods are the most productive and widely used. The user essentially types the pronunciation of one or more characters and the machine offers a range of characters with that pronunciation; the user then selects one of them using the arrow keys, the space bar or some other selection mechanism.

Pronunciations can be entered in various ways. In Japanese, for example, a keyboard with QWERTY layout can be used to enter the romanized pronunciation of the character. Normally this is then converted to a sequence of syllabic (*kana*) characters which is finally used to retrieve all the *kanji* characters with that pronunciation. An alternative mechanism is to use a keyboard with a syllabary layout so that each *kana* can be entered with at most two actions. The software then retrieves the *kanji* as before.

Entering `kan` gives, amongst others, the following characters (last one is intended one):

感 , 間 , 館 , 巻 , 管 , 関 , 観 , … , 漢

Entering `ji` gives:

時 , 次 , 自 , 事 , 辞 , 治 , 持 , … , 字

But entering `kanji` (i.e. the pronunciation for both characters) gives many less options:

幹事 , 感じ , 漢字

FIG. 3.8. A phonetic *kanji* input method.

Because several characters or character sequences may share the same pronunciation, various techniques are used to reduce or rank alternative characters. One possibility is to allow the user to type the pronunciation of a sequence of two or more characters, which can greatly reduce the number of options because of contextual constraints. For example, `kan` and `ji` on their own will retrieve tens of different characters each. However, if input together as `kanji` only a handful of character pairs will be retrieved. These ideas are illustrated in Fig. 3.8.

As their name implies, **shape-based** input methods rely on the shape of a character. The radical-based version of this method relies on the fact that most Chinese characters can be analysed into one or more radicals drawn from a set of 214. Each of these 214 radicals has a number, and most have a name. Their various combinations can produce the majority of Chinese characters. To enter a complete character, the user first specifies one or more of its radicals, upon which all characters containing those radicals are displayed, and the desired one is selected. The stroke count version of shape-based input relies on the fact that each Chinese character consists of a specific number of line strokes. Entering the number of strokes displays all the characters with that stroke count and the user selects the desired one. Both of these methods obviously rely on the user knowing what radicals or how many strokes a character has.

In a **code-based** method, the numeric code for the character is entered. This method has no selection stage as the code uniquely identifies the character. The actual code and notation used depends on the particular character set and input method used. For example, the Unicode number may be used, typed in hexadecimal notation. Code-based input is sometimes used by some operating systems for Latin characters. The user presses the ALT key and types the code for the required character. Note that the code entered may not necessarily be the internal code used by the system for processing text: Unicode may be used for input, but internal processing may be done using a corresponding one byte code.

Association-based methods operate by uniquely relating a pair of key actions with each character. The association may be mnemonic in some way, for example based on sound or meaning, or may be arbitrarily defined. In each case, the learning process for these methods can be long, but reasonable speeds can be achieved.

3.4 Conclusion

Preserving the format of the source document during translation has become almost as important as the translation of its linguistic content, particularly with the widespread use of standards such as HTML and its successors. For example, if Web pages are submitted for MT to a server, codes have to be removed and later reinserted into the appropriate place. This is a non-trivial problem which may require full interpretation of the formatting language in the general case. However, in some cases, simple techniques can work reasonably well.

For many years, text encoding has been a real barrier to international communication. Unicode and other character representation mechanisms based on the ASCII set will hopefully make this barrier all but disappear. The provision of fonts is still very uneven, with scripts like Latin-1 having far too many fonts while others have practically none, or none easily available. This is understandable given the cost of designing aesthetically pleasing fonts, but this situation may well change with cheaper font design tools. Finally, input methods seem to be relatively stable, with spoken input representing an alternative to the standard QWERTY keyboard.

3.4.1 Further Reading

A practical description of what is involved in software localization can be found in Esselink (1998) and references therein.

A description of various character code standards together with many character sets and codes for a wide variety of languages can be found in various sources (Clews 1988; Clews 1992; Parry 1992). The Unicode set is described in Unicode (1996). A thorough discussion of input, output, character codes and more for Chinese, Japanese, Korean and Vietnamese is given in Lunde (1999).

Part V in Crystal (1987) has a good overview of writing systems. Knuth (1986) and (1999) explains how to design typefaces based on mathematical descriptions of them, while other typography books such as Bringhurst (1997) explore the aesthetics of type design in more depth.

An input method for Japanese using a more ergonomic keyboard layout is described in Morita (1985). The IEEE magazine *Computer*, Vol. 18(1) of January 1985 has the theme "Chinese/Kanji Text and Data Processing".

4 Translator's Workbench and Translation Aids

A variety of techniques for MAT are presented, including those for bilingual alignment and translation memory

Martin Kay's paper (Kay 1980) on the use of computers to aid translators was at the time a departure from the place accorded to translators in an MT setting, namely that of revisors of raw MT output. Kay's conception of a translator's amanuensis or transcribing aid is of a computer system, at the command of the translator, which gradually takes over more of the translating tasks that can be reliably automated, leaving the human translator to concentrate on more interesting and challenging aspects of the art. Some of the proposals in that paper included the use of a text or word processor with features oriented to translation, as well as electronic dictionaries and retrieval software that allows translators to inspect fragments of texts similar to those being translated. These and other tools are intended to improve speed, quality or both. A development of these ideas has led to what is called a translator's workbench (TWB) or translator's workstation.

4.1 Translator's Workbench

Since Kay's paper, various TWBs have been proposed (Melby 1987; Macklovitch 1989; Kugler et al. 1992). A TWB consists of a variety of electronic translation tools integrated into a single environment, so that they can be easily accessed by the translator while keeping her or him in control. The tools that are included in any particular TWB clearly depend on the kind of translations it is intended for and the role that translation has within the overall document production cycle. The following are possible areas where tools are or could be provided.

Document processing: Word processing and text editing capabilities are the most common and widely available computer tools for translators. They can range from simple editors with basic formatting functions to complex DTP packages. The use of multiple windows is common in many research and commercial TWBs. These display the source text, the target text and a variety of resources including dictionary entries, explanations of terminology and relevant portions of source or target text. Because of the wide range of text formats currently in use (e.g. HTML, Microsoft Word, RTF) facilities for converting into and out of these formats are also desirable. Sometimes texts are supplied to translators in printed form, in which case optical character recognition (OCR) software and a scanner are needed for subsequent MAT. Being able to treat multiple languages and character sets within the same text is another feature that facilitates the production of translations within a uniform document production environment.

Monolingual resources: Spell and grammar checkers for the TL help detect typographical and other simple errors; SL checkers can be used to detect and correct OCR errors. Large translation jobs, particularly those split between two or more translators, can be facilitated by terminology preprocessing in order to ensure consistency in the use of terms and compliance with a client's preferred terminology. This can involve automatically scanning the input text and comparing it against a database (DB) of known terminology; in the case of new terminology, it involves automatically extracting phrases that are likely to be technical terms for possible cataloguing by the translator. Deciding on the translation of a particular word or phrase can be facilitated by inspecting all the occurrences of the phrase in question with all its left and right contexts as they occur in the text. Key-Word In Context (KWIC) and related tools can automatically show such information. Electronic dictionaries and encyclopaedias, technical texts and other knowledge-oriented resources are another useful source of information which translators need to access during their work. Recent advances in speech recognition mean that in the near future the classic practice of translators dictating their translations could be resumed; thus continuous speech recognition systems for the TL may also be a useful feature.

Bilingual resources: Contrastive knowledge in the form of bilingual dictionaries, multilingual terminology databanks and previously translated texts are well-established resources for translators. Recently, aligned bilingual corpora, where corresponding sentence translations are explicitly identified between the source and target texts, have also become widely used for convenient inspection of previous translations. These aligned texts, whether constructed by alignment algorithms from previously translated texts (Section 4.3), or incrementally built up by translators as they translate, can be converted into translation memories (Section 4.2) through suitable indexing. Furthermore, aligned texts can be used to assist in the compilation of bilingual terminologies (Section 4.4).

MT-oriented resources: Some TWBs allow translators to request a machine-translated version of the text. In many cases the raw translation produced is only used as a guide to terminology translation or as an inspiration for alternative ways of translating the text. Depending on the MT system used, there may also be options for pre-editing the source text, post-editing the target text or interacting with the system during translation. The effort in pre-editing the source text, for example, is usually justified when translation is into several languages. Post-editing facilities can ease the production of low-cost translations. Interaction during MT has also been suggested, for example, as a way for monolinguals to compose acceptable texts in a language they do not know.

Communications: Access to the Internet, email and the WWW are effective ways for translators to communicate with clients, other translators or domain experts, as well as being an integrated framework for accessing remote resources such as terminology databanks or specialist Web sites.

Administrative support: In large translation departments, information such as who produced a translation, when and for whom, how long it took and what quality control processes where applied to it is used for planning workflows, maintaining consistency of service, investigating queries regarding a translation, and generally maintaining a record of translation activity.

This list of features is very varied and it is unlikely that they will all be provided in a single integrated software package. Instead, generic tools such as Web browsers, document format converters and word processors can simply be added to the working environment of the translator. In fact, there is a strong argument for preferring generic tools that translators may already know and which do one thing only, but do it very well. This is clearly demonstrated by the success of MAT tools which operate as add-ons to standard word processing packages.

An important and related issue is the user-friendliness of all the tools and features in question, regardless of their orientation to translation or not. A system that involves a lengthy and complex sequence of keystrokes to look up a selected word in an electronic dictionary will hardly encourage its use.

The following sections elaborate on three important tools which seem specific to translation: translation memory, bilingual alignment and subsentential alignment.

4.2 Translation Memory

One feature of certain types of text such as technical manuals and various kinds of report is the degree to which they resemble each other. The manual for one version of a word processor will be similar to the manual for the next version. Even the manual of one software application from one company will have much in common with that for other applications from the same company. They will include phrases such as *To save a file open the File menu* or some similar instruction. Even within the same document, some portions of the text will be similar or identical to each other. For example, the instructions on how to save a file using a mouse and using the keyboard are almost identical in some manuals. One way in which such repetition can be dealt with is by copying and pasting the translation of the similar text and editing it to reflect the differences with the text being translated. This approach, however, is tedious, as it involves searching backwards through the text looking for a sufficiently similar text fragment to the one being translated. If the text searched for is in a different document, the search can become very time-consuming.

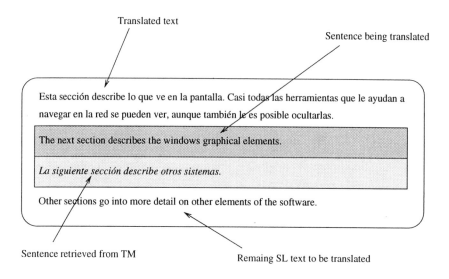

Translated text

Sentence being translated

Esta sección describe lo que ve en la pantalla. Casi todas las herramientas que le ayudan a navegar en la red se pueden ver, aunque también le es posible ocultarlas.

The next section describes the windows graphical elements.

La siguiente sección describe otros sistemas.

Other sections go into more detail on other elements of the software.

Sentence retrieved from TM

Remaing SL text to be translated

FIG. 4.1. Typical layout of a translation memory tool.

Translation memory (TM) is a translation aid which efficiently searches a DB of previously translated text fragments known as translation units (TUs) in order to locate one which closely resembles the fragment being translated. Once found, its translation is offered as a draft translation which can then be modified as necessary by the translator. The DB of TUs is sometimes also referred to as the translation memory of the system; the sense is usually clear from the context.

A minimal interaction with a TM system involves selecting a portion of text, typically a sentence, and requesting a search for a matching TU. As a result the TM system will display one or more TUs usually consisting of a sentence, its translation, and an indication of how closely the input sentence matches the source part of the TU. The translator then selects one of these translations, inserts it into the text being translated and edits it as appropriate. The newly translated fragment can then be added to the TUs DB for future retrieval. Initially the DB is empty and will be of little use, but as more texts are translated, the DB grows and the likelihood of finding a suitable TU increases. Alternatively, a DB may be provided together with the translation assignment by the client.

A common method of operation is to start with a copy of the source text and to apply TM successively to each of its sentences in turn. As sentences are translated, the SL version is deleted and replaced with the TL version. At any one time, therefore, there will be a mixture of source and target text in the same document. In addition, a portion of the screen is usually taken up by the TM system as TUs are retrieved. This area is split into two, with one half containing the selected source text and the other containing its current translation. Figure 4.1 illustrates this mode of operation for a text being translated from English into Spanish. Note how a suggested Spanish translation, from an existing TU stored in TM, is displayed in the TL input area (shown in light grey).

Some refinements of this idea are possible. For example, the system can automatically select a text fragment just by placing the cursor within it; it can paste the result immediately into the target text area; it can automatically select a text fragment, search the DB, display the results and paste the translation of the best match all by pressing a single button; and the system can even process each sentence in batch mode, replacing sentences with their best match and moving on to the next sentence. These variations involve composition of the basic steps involved in using TM, which are essentially those needed for most storage data structures, namely insertion and retrieval of TU to and from the DB. The access data structure for TM needs to allow efficient comparison of the current sentence with all previously translated sentences, returning for each a score of similarity that can assist in ranking the retrieved sentences.

4.2.1 Insertion and Retrieval

Data structures with the properties needed for sentence retrieval have been studied intensely in the field of information retrieval (IR) (van Rijsbergen 1979; Frakes and Baeza-Yates 1992). The objective of such systems is to locate complete texts or descriptions of texts from a document collection based on a query entered by the user. Examples of such systems include Internet search engines and electronic library catalogues. Some of the techniques used in IR can be applied directly to TM by viewing the query as the input sentence, and the document collection as the TUs DB.

Similarity Measure In devising a data structure for efficient TU retrieval, one needs to consider how similarity between sentences can be calculated. Ideally, the measure should give the greatest score for semantically and syntactically similar sentences. Unfortunately, quantifying or even determining semantic and syntactic similarity is very difficult for humans, let alone computer systems. For example, given the input sentence *Select one of the options*, it is difficult to decide which of the following sentences is most similar to it:

1. Choose one of the alternatives given.
2. Select none of the options.
3. Make a selection.

Each sentence is similar but not identical to the input. Semantically, sentence (2) is probably the least similar to it, even though it closely resembles it syntactically.

In IR, a variety of measures have been proposed for determining how closely a query is satisfied by a text. Although none of these measures gives perfect results, they have been found useful in practice, and may be deployed for TM. Many of these measures involve calculating the number of words in common between the input and each candidate from the DB, as illustrated by the following example (only the source text of a TU is shown):

Input: Move this data to the chart.

TU-1: You can move multiple data to the chart.
Words in common: 5

Under this scheme the TU sharing the most words with the input would be ranked at the top of the result's list. One problem with this simple proposal is that it does not take into account the length of the sentences. Using the same input as before, the score for a longer sentence would tend to be greater:

TU-2: You can always move this and other relevant data to the package and display it as a chart.   .
Words in common: 6

Clearly TU-1 resembles the input more closely than TU-2, yet TU-2 has more elements in common with it.

Normalization accounts for differences in the length of the sentences being compared. One simple normalization method is known as Dice's coefficient:

$$M = \frac{2|I \cap T|}{|I| + |T|}$$

Here I and T are the sets of words in the input and TU sentences respectively. The similarity measure M is therefore the ratio of common words and the total number of words in the two sentences, multiplied by two. This gives a number in the range 0 to 1, with 1 indicating most similar. A variety of other measures are given in van Rijsbergen (1979, Ch. 3):

$$\text{Jaccard's coefficient } M = \frac{|I \cap T|}{|I| + |T|}$$

$$\text{Cosine coefficient } M = \frac{|I \cap T|}{\sqrt{|I|} \times \sqrt{|T|}}$$

$$\text{Overlap coefficient } M = \frac{|I \cap T|}{\min(|I| + |T|)}$$

Alternatively, one may calculate a dissimilarity coefficient:

$$D = \frac{|I \triangle T|}{|I| + |T|}$$

where the symmetric difference $A \triangle B$ between two sets is the set of elements in one or the other set, but not in both. With this measure one prefers items with a low score. Whichever of these formulas is employed (they give fairly similar results), it is useful in TM retrieval to count different instances of the same word separately, so that if the input contains two occurrences of the word *file* the similarity measure should prefer matches containing exactly two occurrences.

The measure is clearly a heuristic and therefore not guaranteed to return the sentence that a human would deem closest in meaning. Two obvious shortcomings relate to word order and synonymous words. For example, the phrases *the number format* and *format the number* are considered equivalent in terms of shared words. A solution here would be to use order information in the calculation of similarities. The problem of synonymity is illustrated by the sentences *enter a digit* and *type in a number from 0–9*, which would be regarded as virtually unrelated using a words-in-common measure. The use of thesauri or statistical techniques for establishing meaning similarity between words could be employed to reduce the effect of synonymity in TM retrieval.

However, such enhancements to the basic similarity measure must be evaluated to ensure that relevant TUs are retrieved. By relevant is meant sentences that actually make the translator's task more efficient. Relevance is thus a broad notion in TM, and may refer to whether the system has suggested useful terminology or style, as well as proposing the bulk of the translation. Determining whether a retrieved TU is relevant or not is therefore a subjective matter, and potentially difficult to measure. Still, two important parameters of retrieval systems are commonly used:

Precision: This is the ratio of relevant items retrieved over all the items retrieved. For example, if a system retrieves five sentences from TM, but only one is actually useful to the translator, whatever that may be, then precision is 20%.

Recall: This is the ratio of relevant items retrieved over all relevant items in TM. If two relevant sentences are retrieved, but there are four relevant sentences in TM, then recall is 50%.

In some cases increasing one of these measures means decreasing the other. For example, adding ordering information to the search might improve precision, but it might also decrease recall. Similarly, using a thesaurus can improve recall but it may decrease precision.

Stoplists Many of the most frequent words in a language are very poor discriminators of meaning. In English, using such function words as *the*, *of*, *a*, *an*, *in* and *on* in calculating similarity measures would result in almost any sentence matching any other to some extent. What is more, for longer sentences with several of these words, the similarity measure will be dominated by them. Consider:

> Input: Delete all the files in the folder.
> TU-1: Put all the cartridges in the safe.
> TU-2: Delete folder files.

Although TU-2 is semantically the closest match, it only has three words in common with the input. By contrast, TU-1 has four elements in common because of function words. Removing such words leads to more intuitive results and better retrieval. These words are usually collected in a stoplist which simply enumerates everything that needs to be disregarded when calculating similarities.

The extent of a stoplist can depend on the particular application. Stoplists in some information retrieval applications can contain upwards of 400 words, including quite informative items such as *asked*, *give*, *today* and *room*. For sentence retrieval stoplists need not be as extensive. A possible minimal list for English and Spanish might be:

English: a, and, an, by, from, of, or, the, that, to, with.

Spanish: a, al, de, del, el, la, las, lo, los, o, que, un, una, y.

Additional prepositions, conjunctions and adverbs may be added depending on the domain, but some care must be taken, as such words contribute significantly to the syntactic and semantic structure of individual sentences, and they can help discriminate relevant TU.

String and Word Similarity Similarity measures also depend on whether words match or not, but in many languages word forms vary depending on syntactic features. Thus we have *delete* and its derived forms *deletes, deleted, deleting, deletion*. In most cases, ignoring such orthographic differences improves the usefulness of retrieved material. For example, the TU:

TU-1: Deleting a file or a folder.
Para borrar un archivo o un directorio.

can give a translator very relevant information on how to translate *It deletes all .tmp files from all folders*, even though all content words are morphologically different. Other differences, such as letter case, font and size, are irrelevant in most, although not all, cases and will therefore be ignored here.

One way to neutralize orthographic and morphological differences is to represent words in some sort of canonical or normalized form, which then becomes the single representation of different variations on the word. Thus, one may choose the singular of nouns to be their canonical form, and map plurals to this form. There are at least two ways of deriving this canonical form: morphological processing and stemming.

Morphological processing (Section 5.2) is a linguistically motivated treatment of changes in the form of words. A morphological analyser takes as input an inflected form and decomposes it into a sequence of morphemes. Morphological analysers are gaining popularity for retrieval applications, but traditionally they have not been used in typical IR tasks, since they need extensive root and affix dictionaries and comprehensive rule sets describing spelling changes. This has led to the development of stemming or affix removal as a heuristic technique for spelling normalization.

Stemming algorithms essentially relate morphologically similar words, in most cases without the need for explicit root lists. There are several types of stemmers, three of which are:

Successor variety: The successor variety of a prefix with respect to a set of words is the set of letters that can follow that prefix. For example, given the set of words:

read, readable, reading, reads, red, rope, ripe

the successor variety of prefix *r* is 3, since according to this set the prefix can be followed by *e, o, i*. The successor variety of *re* is 2 (i.e. *a, d*); for *rea* it is 1 and for *read* it is 3 (4 if one includes an end-of-word character). Successor variety decreases as the prefix gets longer, but then sharply increases at a morpheme boundary. The successor variety of a word's suffixes can be used to determine the point at which to break the word. One possibility is to break the word after the character whose successor variety is greater than that of the characters immediately before and after it. For example, *reading* is stemmed after *d* since its successor variety, 3, is greater than that of *rea* and *readi*. Determining which of the two resulting substrings is the stem or root could rely on length – the stem is the longer of the two – or frequency of occurrence – the stem is that which occurs less frequently.

Table lookup: A table of word–stem pairs is constructed. Stemming a word is then simply a matter of table lookup. For example:

Word	Canonical Form
am	be
are	be
is	be
was	be
were	be
been	be

The table can be used, for example, to determine that *are* is closer to *been* than to *art*.

Affix removal: The most common stemming algorithms remove or strip affixes from words to produce a stem. In some cases the algorithm also transforms the resulting stem to account for certain variations. A simple affix removal rule is to delete a final *s* to normalize noun plurals and the third person singular of verbs in English. There are problems with words like *flies*, which results in *flie* and which fails to match *fly*. Similar situations arise with *foxes* or in incorrect application to singulars ending in -*s*, such as *class*. Stemmers overcome these problems through elaborate sets of multiple affixes, rules, conditions and transformations to avoid overstemming and understemming, and to produce correct canonical forms. For example, alternative affixes can be used for the same phenomenon (e.g. -*s, -es* for plurals), or a rule might say that the suffix -*ing* is removed (e.g. *motor-ing*), unless the remaining stem is less than two characters long (e.g. **s-ing*).

Each type of stemming mechanism has advantages and disadvantages. Successor variety can be applied without much knowledge of the language involved, but is dependent on the words used for computing successor variety. Lookup tables are useful for highly irregular words, but compiling the tables can be expensive. Affix removal results in semantically rich stems but affixes and rules need to be developed for each language.

Stemming helps to identify words that derive from the same lexeme, but does not measure word similarity. Thus, matches involving identical words should be preferred over matches of stemmed words. For example, *relate* should be classified as more similar to itself or to *relates*, than to *relation*. Stemming schemes do not normally account for such differences. Also, they work well for languages where the root does not change much after inflection, but not for languages where the root itself changes. Techniques for string comparison, by contrast, allow for spelling variations within a word, and at the same time provide a measure of string similarity.

N-gram techniques: Orthographically related words will have similar pairs (digrams), triples (trigrams) or *n*-tuples (n-grams) of consecutive letters, and therefore, when determining whether two words are equivalent, only these tuples need to be compared. For example, using digrams to determine whether *relation* matches *relate* or *rational* better, each word is split into its unique digrams:

> relation: re el la at ti io on
> relate: re el la at te
> rational: ra at ti io on na al

A similarity measure can then be calculated, say using Dice's coefficient, to give:

> relation – relate = $2 \times \frac{4}{7+5} = 0.67$
> relation – rational = $2 \times \frac{4}{7+7} = 0.57$

Higher scores indicate greater similarity.

Edit distance: Similarity is measured by the number of insertions, deletions and substitutions to convert one string into another. To make the comparison efficient, a dynamic programming algorithm can be used. Intuitively, the algorithm tries to align two sequences of items in a way that minimizes the number of insertions, deletions and substitutions needed, giving a penalty of 1 unit for each of these operations. If the sequences are identical (e.g. ab – ab), then the alignment cost is 0; if one item needs to be substituted by another (e.g. ab – ac) the cost is 1; if an item in one sequence matches no item in the other (e.g. ab – a), the cost is also 1. Thus, the alignment cost between *man – men* is 1, since there is one substitution *a – e*; everything else matches. Similarly the cost of *boat – boats* is 1 because the *s* is inserted or deleted depending on which way the comparison is done.

The edit distance algorithm is as follows. If n and m are the lengths of the two words, then the two words are aligned on a grid $n + 1$ by $m + 1$, one letter per column and row respectively. The grid is scanned left to right, top to bottom, filling each cell with the cost of the alignment up to that cell. The cost of each cell is computed from the cost of either the cell to its left, the cell above, or the cell above and to its left, whichever is the smallest, and incrementing it by 1 if the two items at the column and row header do not match. If they do match, the cost for the cell is the minimum of adding one to the cell above or to the left, or zero to the cell above and to the left. The algorithm is initialized with cost 0 at position (0,0) which corresponds to an initial empty item. Cells above the topmost row and to the left of the leftmost column are assumed to have infinite cost and are therefore ignored. The alignment cost then is the value at the bottom right of the grid. The following two examples, comparing *man – men* and *pets – pep* illustrate the algorithm:

	–	m	a	n
–	0	1	2	3
m	1	0	1	2
e	2	2	1	2
n	3	3	2	1

	–	p	e	t	s
–	0	1	2	3	4
p	1	0	1	2	3
e	2	1	0	1	2
p	3	2	1	1	2

Once calculated, the edit distance is normalized by dividing by $\max(m, n)$. In the two cases above, the results are $1/3 = 0.33$ and $2/4 = 0.5$, giving a measure of dissimilarity. The similarity between the words can then be computed by the formula (1 – dissimilarity); for these examples it would be 0.67 and 0.5 respectively.

N-gram and edit distance measures involve little linguistic knowledge and they are therefore potentially applicable to a wide range of languages. However, they ignore relevant linguistic information about the semantic locus of a word, which in many languages is a well-defined segment of its surface form.

Both of these measures may be too expensive to calculate in a particular implementation, but they are given here because the same techniques can be applied to calculate sentence similarity by treating words as characters and sentences as strings. This is particularly useful for incorporating ordering information, as this is inherent in both algorithms. In either case, the techniques could be combined with other mechanisms which are faster at retrieving sentences from a database, as indicated in the next section. For example, affix removal could form the basis of sentence retrieval, while edit distance could then be used for a more detailed comparison of the (smaller) set of candidate matches.

Inverted Files Given that we are assuming that sentence similarity is based on the number of (orthographically) similar words, it is now time to describe how sentences (and their translations) can be retrieved efficiently from the TU DB using inverted files for indexing. A simple yet grossly inefficient way of retrieving close matches is to calculate similarity scores for each sentence in turn, and then return the n best scoring sentences. This approach would be too slow for anything but the smallest DBs.

For measures based on the number of words in common, a data structure known as an inverted file enables vastly more efficient retrieval. The rationale behind inverted file retrieval is that only those sentences in the DB that have at least one word in common with the input need to be considered. Thus, an index consisting of a list of words is maintained, with each word pointing back to all the sentences in which it is found. Such a structure is known as an inverted file.

Consider the sentences below, with their associated reference identifier (in an actual TM, each sentence also has a translation associated with it):

a. To add a bookmark, click on the Bookmarks menu.
b. Select "Add Bookmark".
c. Click on the icon.

The inverted file for this short DB, after applying a stoplist and stemming is:

add	a b
bookmark	a(2) b
click	a c
menu	a
select	b
icon	c

The number of occurrences of a word in a sentence is noted in parentheses when it is more than one. Sentence length (minus stoplist) can also be pre-computed and stored. In this case the result would be:

a: 5

b: 3

c: 2

Consider now the input sentence: *Drag the cursor to the Bookmark menu.* Before searching, the input sentence is pre-processed in the same manner as any other sentence: a stoplist is applied, words are put in a canonical form, and repeated words are totalled.

Finding a match involves four searches through the inverted file, one for each of *drag, cursor, bookmark* and *menu.* Only the last two succeed, giving an intersection of 2 items for sentence (a) and of 1 for sentence (b). Calculating Dice's coefficient gives:

For sentence (a): $2 \times \frac{2}{4+5} = 0.44$

For sentence (b): $2 \times \frac{1}{4+3} = 0.29$

Sentence (a) is therefore ranked first and given as the best match found.

The most expensive operation in this scheme is locating stems in the inverted file. A variety of improvements on linear search are possible: binary search on a sorted file, B-trees and hashing (Frakes and Baeza-Yates 1992), would all allow efficient access.

Adding a TU to TM is a process similar to retrieval. The stoplist for the SL is applied to the SL side of the TU, the remaining words are stemmed and the number of repetitions noted. A new TU id is created and the sentence length list and inverted file updated. Depending on the data structure used to store these two files, different insertion routines will apply. Figure 4.2 shows the overall structure in a TM system.

4.2.2 Further Issues

Although TM systems are useful when translating texts with a high degree of repetition, they are especially applicable when translating new versions of a document that has already been translated. A common feature of such documents (e.g. computer manuals, budgets, financial reports) is that some sentences differ from others only in elements that can be easily copied or adapted to the TL text. Thus dates can be automatically reformatted and the names of the month and day reliably translated. Numbers can be copied and reformatted as necessary

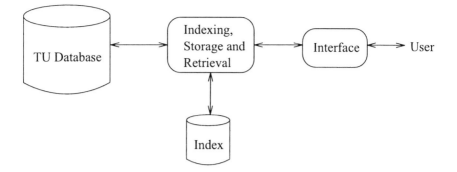

FIG. 4.2. The structure of a TM system

(e.g. 1,000 to 1.000); prices can be converted into different currencies through simple calculations, and the name and version of products can be transferred directly into some languages. Such features are being incorporated into new TM systems.

Formatting, graphics and other non-textual components pose more difficult problems. For example, if a word in the input sentence is in bold, it is non-trivial to determine which word from a previous translation should be in bold, since normally there are no word-to-word correspondences expressed in a TU DB (Section 4.4).

4.3   Bilingual Alignment

The TU database is clearly the main resource in a TM system. In the setup described above, it is built up incrementally as more and more texts are translated. However, many translators or translation organizations possess significant numbers of previously translated texts for which TU DBs have not been produced. In order to convert these bilingual texts into a TU DB, techniques have been developed to facilitate the alignment or identification of translationally equivalent text fragments.

Typical alignment is at the sentence level: the input is a text consisting of several sentences and its translation, and the output is a set of TUs where (most) TUs express one-to-one sentence correspondences. The difficulty in sentence alignment is that a sentence in the SL may correspond to none, one or more sentences in the TL, and vice versa. Furthermore, two or more sentences in the SL may correspond to two or more sentences in the TL without there being a one-to-one relation between their component sentences.

One way of aligning sentences (or other text segments) is to determine some measure of dissimilarity or distance between proposed alignments and then to align sentences such that the overall dissimilarity is minimized. Distance should be small when sentences are translations of each other, and large when they are totally unrelated. A simple yet effective way of approximating this distance without appealing to linguistic knowledge is to assume that long text fragments tend to be translated by long text fragments, and short text fragments tend to be translated by short ones. The problem is then deciding how dissimilar the lengths must be before two text fragments are deemed not to be translations of each other. The problem of alignment is constrained by the fact that the order of sentences in the target text follows very closely the order in the source text; this fact is exploited by virtually all alignment algorithms.

Starting from these observations, the alignment program of Gale and Church (1993) uses probability and statistical theory to develop a model for sentence alignment. First, the distance measure between the source and target texts to be aligned depends on their difference in length, and on the probability that a typical translation is one of various many-to-many sentence relations (i.e. 0–1, 1–0, 1–1, 2–1, 1–2, 2–2). Their distance measure is essentially a conditional probability $P(\text{match} \mid \delta)$, which indicates the probability for the type of match proposed (i.e. 1–1, 0–1, 2–2, etc.) for a particular pair of source and text fragments with difference δ.

Calculating text length can involve at least two measures: number of word tokens (Brown et al. 1991) and number of characters. Gale and Church (1993) found that measurements in characters performed better in their experiments. Furthermore, it is common for the size of a complete text to either increase or decrease in translation. Thus, before calculating the difference in lengths between source and target text fragments, the length of the target text may be scaled by the average ratio between the complete source and target text sizes. For example, if the source English text has 100 000 characters and its Spanish translation has 110 000 characters, the scaling ratio would be 1.1. To determine the difference in length between an English fragment of 50 characters and a Spanish one of 56, the English text is scaled and the result subtracted from the Spanish length: $(56 - 50 \times 1.1) = 1$. This difference tends to increase for larger portions of text, and therefore some normalization is needed. Gale and Church (1993) use the formula $\delta = (l_t - cl_s)/\sqrt{l_m s^2}$, where l_s and l_t are the lengths of the source and target text fragments respectively, l_m is the average of the two lengths (i.e. $(l_s + l_t/c)/2)$, c is the scaling factor (1.1 in the example), and s^2 is the variance for all the values of δ in a typical aligned corpus, which Gale and Church (1993) suggest is 6.8. This normalization makes δ a standard normal distribution (Section 2.2.4), with mean 0 and variance 1.

With δ as the measure for length dissimilarity, the text fragment distance, a conditional probability, can be decomposed using Bayes's theorem to give:

$$P(\text{match} \mid \delta) = \frac{P(\delta \mid \text{match})P(\text{match})}{P(\delta)}$$

Since $P(\delta)$ is a normalizing constant, the denominator can be ignored for the purposes of comparison. The probability of a match, $P(match)$, is estimated from correctly aligned corpora. Gale and Church (1993, p. 83) give one-to-one alignments a probability of 0.89, with most of the remainder probability assigned to one-to-two and two-to-one alignments.

As for $P(\delta \mid \text{match})$, Gale and Church (1993) estimate it by:

$$P(\delta \mid \text{match}) = 2(1 - P(|\delta|))$$

where $P(|\delta|)$ is the area under a standard normal density function graph from $-\infty$ to $|\delta|$. The value is defined by the standard normal distribution formula:

$$\frac{1}{\sqrt{2\pi}} \int_{-\infty}^{|\delta|} e^{-z^2/2} dz$$

The result of this calculation gives the probability that a random variable z will have magnitude less than or equal to $|\delta|$. This value ranges from 0.5 when $|\delta| = 0$, to 0.841 for $|\delta| = 1$, through to 1 for $|\delta| = \infty$. This value cannot be calculated in terms of elementary functions, but it can be approximated by the following polynomial:

Let $t = 1/(1 + 0.2316419 \times |\delta|)$. Then

$$P(|\delta|) = 1 - 0.3989423 e^{-|\delta|^2/2} t(0.319381530$$
$$+ t(-0.356563782 + t(1.781477937$$
$$+ t(-1.821255978 + 1.330274429t))))$$

The distance function then is $d(s_1, t_1, t_2, s_2) = P(\delta \mid \text{match})P(\text{match})$, where δ is a function of $s_1 + s_2 = l_s$ and $t_1 + t_2 = l_t$, as explained above. The following recurrence relation then defines $D(i, j)$, the minimum total distance for the alignment of source sentences up to i and target sentences up to j, with initial condition $D(0, 0) = 0$.

$$D(i,j) = \min \begin{cases} D(i, j-1) & + & d(0, t_j, 0, 0) & \text{Inserting} \\ D(i-1, j) & + & d(s_i, 0, 0, 0) & \text{Deleting} \\ D(i-1, j-1) & + & d(s_i, t_j, 0, 0) & \text{Substituting} \\ D(i-1, j-2) & + & d(s_i, t_j, 0, t_{j-1}) & \text{Expanding} \\ D(i-2, j-1) & + & d(s_i, t_j, s_{i-1}, 0) & \text{Contracting} \\ D(i-2, j-2) & + & d(s_i, t_j, s_{i-1}, t_{j-1}) & \text{Merging} \end{cases}$$

To solve this relation, a dynamic programming algorithm with a two-dimensional array is used. The length of source text sentences labels columns, while the length of target text sentences labels rows. Values near the top or left of the array (i.e. $i, j < 0$) are assumed to have high values and are ignored. Since it is the alignment and not the distance that is of interest, a shadow array is maintained for retrieving the best alignment.

Although aligning all the sentences in a complete text is possible, it is quite expensive computationally, and it tends to degrade performance. Fortunately, texts and their translations are normally organized around paragraphs, sections, headings, chapters etc. It is reasonable to assume that only in rare cases will a translation not adhere quite closely to this structure. Alignment may therefore consist of several stages, each working on smaller text units whose alignment provides anchor points for the next level. For example, document paragraphs are aligned within a document, then sentences can be aligned within paragraphs, and then words or phrases may be aligned within sentences. Once calculated, these alignments can be added to a translation memory after suitable indexing.

With this algorithm, Gale and Church (1993) report error rates of 4.2% on 1316 alignments. Many of the errors arise from alignments other than the 1–1 type. Furthermore, selecting the best 80% scoring alignments reduces the error rate to 0.7%. It is also relevant that the algorithm does not seem sensitive to values for c and s^2, at least for European languages. However, noisy texts (e.g. with errors due to OCR) or from very different languages can degrade performance.

4.3.1 Other Approaches

A variation on the length-based technique is that presented in Brown et al. (1991), where alignments of text fragments are seen as being generated by an HMM and the correct alignment is that which maximizes the output of the HMM.

The HMM of Brown et al. (1991) models alignment by determining probabilities for eight types of alignments or beads: s, t, st, sst, stt, $\P s$, $\P t$, $\P s \P t$, where, for example, stt indicates that one source language sentence is aligned with two target sentences, and $\P s$ indicates that a source paragraph delimiter matches nothing in the target language (i.e. it is deleted). Each bead has associated with it the probability of emitting a particular length of source and target sentences. For example, the s bead has a probability $P(l_s)$ of emitting a sentence of length l_s, which is equal to the probability of finding a sentence of that length in the source text as a whole. For an st bead, the probability of emitting sentences of length l_s and l_t depends on $P(l_s)$ as before, and $P(l_t \mid l_s)$, the probability of a target length given a source length. The latter depends on the ratio $r = \log(l_t/l_s)$ as follows:

$$P(l_t \mid l_s) = \alpha e^{-(r-\mu)^2/(2\sigma^2)}$$

where μ is the mean value or average of r and σ^2 is its variance. Constant α normalizes the result so that the sum of $P(l_t \mid l_s) = 1$. In the case of stt or sst the ratio is calculated by adding the lengths of the two target or source sentences. Furthermore, the probability of both sentences is calculated by $P(l_{t_1})P(l_{t_2})$ and $P(l_{s_1})P(l_{s_2})$ respectively. Calculation of $P(l_s)$ and $P(l_t)$ is from a corpus of 1000 sentences of length less than 81 words. The probabilities for each of the beads is computed using an EM algorithm from a large sample of text in order to estimate the parameters of the HMM. Then, given two texts, the most probable sequence of beads that maximizes the length of their respective source and target sentences is the alignment given by the model. Reported error rates for st beads in an English–French application of the algorithm are of the order of 0.9%.

Length-based alignment can be contrasted with text-based alignments. The idea is to exploit translation, similarity or identity correspondences between words and other textual components such as figures, proper names and dates. As a simple example, consider an English text and its Spanish translation, and an algorithm with access to an English–Spanish bilingual dictionary. Two sentences will then be aligned if word translation pairs from the bilingual dictionary are found with sufficient frequency between the two sentences, relative to their size and to other sentences in the corpus. Thus the measure of similarity between the sentences is based on their text rather than their length (even if their lengths are used for normalization). One disadvantage with this approach is that it requires a bilingual dictionary, something which may not be always available, particularly for low-density languages.

Kay and Röscheisen (1993) exploit the similarity of distribution between word translations in the source and target language in order to refine an estimate of sentence alignment based on relative sentence position. Once the alignment is refined, the word translations are in turn refined and used in the next iteration of the algorithm. For example, assume 10 source and 12 target sentences. Initially an estimate alignment would include, say, 3 sentences preceding and following the target sentences at the same relative position to that being aligned. Thus sentence 3 is estimated to align with sentences 1 to 6 in the target text. At the same time, a record is kept of which sentences are reliably aligned, initially only the first and last sentences of both texts.

A set of word alignments is then produced by selecting word pairs that occur in source and target sentences currently alignable. For instance, if *save* occurs in sentences 3 and 4 in the SL, and the word *grabar* occurs in sentences 2 and 5 in the TL, then they may be candidates for alignment; only if their distributions are sufficiently similar are they selected. Similarity of word alignments is based on the number of alignable sentences in which they occur and the total number of occurrences of each alignment. Assuming that $(save, grabar)$ is reliable, then sentence alignments $(2, 3)$ and $(5, 4)$ are marked as having being corroborated. If a sentence alignment is sufficiently corroborated, it is treated as reliable and becomes an anchor (i.e. first and last sentences are also anchors).

The process is then repeated by creating a new estimate alignment as before, but this time imposing the restriction that anchors may not cross; that is, a source sentence before (or after) an anchor must align with a target sentence before (or after respectively) the anchor's target sentence. Kay and Röscheisen (1993) indicate that the algorithm converges after about four or five iterations, but concede that either time or space complexity is high. When applied to the English–French Canadian Hansard corpus of parliamentary proceedings, all but seven of the first 1000 sentences were aligned correctly.

Combinations of length- and text-based approaches can offer improvements over each approach on its own. For example, Wu (1994) incorporates alignment information on days of the week, months and various titles and acronyms/abbreviations in a length-based alignment system. This results in an improvement in alignment accuracy for an English–Chinese corpus. By using cognates (e.g. *President/Presidente, respectively/respectivamente*), Simard et al. (1992) can reduce error rates by about 10% for English–French alignments in a corpus of parliamentary proceedings.

4.4   Subsentential Alignment

Accurate translation of technical terminology is difficult in human translation for a number of reasons. Firstly, while translators are language experts, they are not necessarily experts in the technical domain they are translating. Secondly, even if they are experts in the domain, they may not be familiar with the terminology and style standard for technical texts in the TL. Thirdly, the pace of technological development makes it difficult for printed and even electronic (bilingual) terminology databases to offer full coverage of all the terminology that may need to be translated. Even worse, in some fields there is no agreed terminology, and the translator must be careful to employ translations which are consistent at least with that used by the organization requiring the translation.

Apart from reference material such as (bilingual) technical dictionaries, the most useful resource to a translator is previous translations of similar texts, since these contain source and target terminology together with examples of their use in context. However, even in a sentence-aligned corpus the presentation of technical terms is less than optimal. For example, a translator looking for a translation of *debugging* might be faced with the English–Spanish sentence alignment:

A programming language must include facilities for debugging as these can increase the productivity of the programmer.	Un lenguaje de programación debe incluir medios de depuración ya que estos pueden aumentar la productividad del programador.

After reading the source and target texts, a translator will be able to determine the TL term (*depuración*) corresponding to the SL term. However, presented with a large number of such alignments, it will be quite strenuous to read through many source and target sentences, determining which of the alignments best matches the context of the sentence being translated. Furthermore, the translator might wish to see only the terms and their translations without any of their contexts. Finally, it would be useful to be able to extract bilingual terminology in order to facilitate the task of terminologists.

Each of these issues can be addressed by aligning terms in bilingual corpora, so that the portion of a target text that is the translation of an SL term is explicitly identified. Terminology alignment often (although not always) takes place after sentence alignment, and it may result in identifying zero, one or more term translations per sentence pair. In contrast to sentence alignment, where the order of sentences imposes strong constraints on possible correspondences, term alignment can take place between any two positions in the source and target sentences. In the example below, aligned terms are given in the same fonts.

En: **The optical character reader** is detected by *the operating system.*
Sp: *El sistema operativo* detecta **el lector óptico de carácteres**.

From these alignments it becomes possible to produce bilingual concordances that facilitate inspection of large sets of examples of a particular term:

.. on your SCSI port. The	optical character reader is detected by the operating system.
El sistema operativo detecta el	lector óptico de carácteres. Una ventana ..
The accuracy of an	optical character reader depends on the ..
La precisión de un	lector óptico de carácteres depende de ..

Similarly, such alignments aid in the construction of bilingual terminology and can help reduce the amount of data displayed to terminologists.

Terminology alignment is related to word alignment, where not only technical terminology but any other word or phrase in a text is linked to its translation. Algorithms for both kinds of alignment frequently exploit the fact that a word or a term and its translation have similar distributions within the two texts, and in particular they tend to occur within the same aligned sentences. The two techniques differ in that in terminology alignment, it is common to extract candidate terms from the source and target languages in separate stages, and only then is an alignment attempted. By contrast, word alignment programs construct alignments for all or most of the words and phrases in a text. Thus, word alignment algorithms may be seen as producing bilingual dictionaries made up of the aligned words.

4.4.1 Word Alignment

A simple approach to constructing a word alignment or bilingual dictionary might be to count all co-occurrences of source and target words in aligned sentences and then to postulate as word translations those words which tend to occur in the same sentence pairs but tend not to occur in other sentence pairs. For example, if *computer* appears in 30 English sentences and *computadora* appears in 29 of the corresponding Spanish sentences and nowhere else, then there is a strong chance the two are translations of each other. To make this idea into an algorithm, a measure of the co-occurrence of the two words is needed. Brown et al. (1988) suggest mutual information (MI) as a possible candidate. MI is a measure in information theory that indicates the amount of information, measured in some agreed unit, that one event carries about another. The MI between words s and t is denoted by $I(s;t)$ and it is defined as:

$$I(s;t) = \log \frac{P(s,t)}{P(s)P(t)}$$

This says that the amount of information possessed by one of the words about the occurrence of the other (in the same sentence) is related to the probability of both occurring together, divided by the probability of each occurring at all (i.e. regardless of whether the other occurs or not). For example, in an aligned corpus of 100 sentences, if *save* occurs in 30 aligned English sentences, *grabar* occurs in 20 aligned Spanish sentences, and these alignments coincide in 19 cases, then for this corpus $P(save, grabar) = 19/100, P(save) = 30/100, P(grabar) = 20/100$, and the MI is:

$$I(save; grabar) = \log(0.19/(0.3 \times 0.2)) = 1.66$$

Positive values indicate that the occurrence of one word strongly predicts that the other word will occur. A value of 0 or near zero indicates that the words occur quite independently, while negative values predict that if one word occurs the other one does not. In the Canadian Hansard, Brown et al. (1988) are able to find correct translation pairs such as *water – eau* and *yesterday – hier* using MI.

However, the MI measure is not pursued further (Brown et al. 1990) because it does not provide probabilities, making it difficult to integrate with their statistical MT system, and also because there is no motivated way of determining a threshold score below which word translations become unreliable. Oakes (1998, pp. 174–75) reports the work of Gaussier et al. (1992) who use MI for extracting bilingual word pairs: using MI between source and target words, a ranked list of candidate translations for a source word is produced using an empirically determined threshold. Candidates are then eliminated if they are found to have a greater MI score with a different source word. The best remaining candidate is then selected as a translation. Using an aligned version of the Canadian Hansard, about 65% of English words are paired with their correct French translations, 25% have no translation and 10% are given an incorrect translation.

A variation on the co-occurrence idea is the technique proposed by Dagan et al. (1993), which is in itself a variation of Model 2 in Brown et al. (1993). The input to this approach is a text and its translation, and its output is a set of word alignments which are used as computer aids in bilingual terminology compilation. The alignments produced are therefore useful even when a word is not aligned with its correct translation, but with a word near it. The technique is also intended to be robust in that it accepts noisy input, such as that produced by an OCR device. On the other hand, it relies to a certain extent on some similarities between the source and target languages, such as word order, and use of the same alphabet or the same mark-up language.

The system is in fact a combination of two programs, char_align (Church 1993) and word_align: the first one aligns text fragments delimited by cognates and other approximately equivalent character sequences; the second program uses this alignment to calculate a word alignment. Here we concentrate on the word alignment part. The basic idea in the algorithm is that a word and its translation occur in or near a text segment alignment, and that the position of a translation tends to occur at a predictable distance or offset from a naïve estimate of its position. Word alignment consists of two steps: (1) estimate word translation and offset probabilities, and (2) find the most probable alignment for the given text. The first step starts with a naïve alignment, based for example on interpolation on the aligned text fragments. For example, if a word is a quarter of the way from the beginning of a text fragment, its translation is estimated as being a quarter of the way into the target text fragment. Based around this estimate, a window of, say, 20 words either way is assumed within which the true translation of the word must lie. Translation probabilities are then estimated by counting the occurrences of word pairs within windows for the whole text. Similarly, offset probabilities are calculated by determining the frequency of a given offset for the most likely translation of a word.

For example, a simple aligned text might be:

En: Start the **operating** system. Launch the **program** via the keyboard.
Sp: Comenzar el sistema **operativo**. Empezar el **programa** mediante el teclado.

Bold words indicate the beginning and end of an aligned text segment (these are found via char_align). Assuming that the naïve alignment pairs each Spanish word with exactly one English word, ignoring function words, we might get the four naïve alignments: *comenzar – start, *sistema – start, *empezar – system, teclado – keyboard*. Although two of these are incorrect, the correct translation is close to them, and in this case, certainly within a window of 20 words. If enough text is available, the frequency of *sistema – system* will outstrip that of any other pair within the 20 word window; similarly for *empezar – launch*. Also, given enough data, it will emerge that a correct translation is likely to lie within an offset of a few words from the naive alignment.

Calculating the translation and offset probabilities involves three main equations which are then used in an EM algorithm. First, the translation probability of a target word t given a source word s is:

$$tr(s \mid t) = \frac{\text{sum of } P(con_{j,i}) \text{ where } con_{j,i} \text{ links } s \text{ to } t}{\text{sum of } P(con_{-,i}) \text{ where } con_{-,i} \text{ links any word to } t}$$

where $con_{j,i}$ is an allowed alignment (connection) in the sense that it respects the window limit, e.g. $1 \leftrightarrow 20$ but not $1 \leftrightarrow 30$. The probability of an alignment being offset k from its naïve alignment is determined by:

$$o(k) = \frac{\text{sum of } P(con_{j,i}) \text{ where } i - I(j) = k}{\text{sum of } P(con_{j,i})}$$

Here, $I(j)$ is the naïve interpolation alignment for position j in the SL. Finally, the probability of an alignment between a source word at position j and a target word at position i is defined, seemingly circularly, by:

$$P(con_{j,i}) =$$
$$\frac{tr(s_j \mid t_i).o(i - I(j))}{\text{sum of } tr(s_j \mid t_h).o(h - I(j)) \text{ where } h \text{ is within the window around } I(j)}$$

The EM iteration proceeds, say, by assigning random probabilities to $P(con_{j,i})$ and then iteratively re-evaluating them until they converge.

Finding the most probable alignment once probabilities have been established involves applying a dynamic programming algorithm that finds the set of $con_{j,i}$ that maximizes:

$$\prod tr(s_j \mid t_i).o(i - A'(j))$$

where $\prod$ is the product operator, and A' depends on the alignment of the preceding j:

$$A'(j) = A(j_{prev}) + (j - j_{prev})\frac{N_T}{N_S}$$

for N_T and N_S the length of the source and target texts, and $A(j_{prev})$ the last target position produced by A for the source word aligned before j. In this way, alignments exploit the fact that, for many European languages, words that are close together in the source language tend to translate as words that are close together in the target language.

In evaluation, this algorithm can achieve precision rates of 55%. In 84% of cases the distance to the correct alignment is at most three words, which can lead to 2–3 times faster terminology compilation by terminologists using bilingual corpora aligned in this manner.

Co-occurrence patterns are one way of estimating whether two words are translations of each other without appealing to a bilingual dictionary or any other knowledge not easily extracted from a text. An alternative is to assume that the pattern of distances, measured in number of characters, between successive occurrences of a word is similar to that of its translation (Fung and McKeown 1997). For example, if the word *keyboard* occurs 30 times in the source text at regular intervals of 100 characters, then a TL word which occurs 30 times at regular intervals of 100 characters in the target text is likely to be its translation. A recency vector recording the separation between successive occurrences of a word is determined for each word to be aligned, both in the source and target text. Their recency vectors are then compared, and those with the most similar vectors are deemed to be translations of each other. For example, if *printer* occurs at positions 100, 400 and 500 in a text, its recency vector would be $<100,300,100>$. Assume that there are two TL candidates with recency vectors (i) $<99,250,250>$ and (ii) $<20,20,300>$. Fung and McKeown (1997) use a dynamic programming algorithm to calculate the dissimilarity between the two vectors, where the distance between two vector entries is the magnitude of their difference. For these two vectors, the comparison gives:

	_	100	300	100
_	0	100	400	500
99	99	1	102	103
250	349	151	51	301
250	599	301	101	201

	_	100	300	100
_	0	100	400	500
20	20	80	360	440
20	40	100	360	440
300	340	240	200	400

The final scores in the bottom right cells are then normalized for length, say by dividing by the total number of steps in the shortest path. The final scores thus become 67.0 and 133.3, making the first pair of vectors more similar, and therefore making the word corresponding to vector (i) the translation of *printer*. Since such a comparison needs to be done for all vectors in both languages, a number of heuristics can be employed to reduce the number of dynamic programming comparisons performed. For example, if the size of the difference vectors is too great – say one is double the other – they are unlikely to be translations and are therefore not compared; similarly, if the first element in the vector is more than half the size of the text, the first occurrences of each word are too different and the vectors are not compared. When tested on English–Japanese and English–Chinese corpora, results of between 55% and 89% precision are achieved. Somers and Ward (1996) also describe work based on that of Fung and McKeown (1997), and report rates of between 76% and 95% precision by varying recall.

4.4.2 Terminology Alignment

Terminology compilation is an important and common activity in translation work, but it is also time-consuming. Automatic terminology alignment and extraction are therefore useful techniques in MAT.

Terminology alignment can be divided into two different tasks (Dagan and Church 1997; van der Eijk 1993): a monolingual terminology identification step in which candidate terms are extracted, and a bilingual step in which these terms are aligned with their translations. Terminology in this case normally means multi-word sequences describing technical concepts in a domain, with noun phrases being the most common grammatical structure used to express concepts.

Monolingual Task Terminology maintenance is a difficult task even for humans. A terminologist has to determine what constitutes a term in a domain, what its meaning is, how it relates to other terms in the domain, the degree of acceptance by domain experts, and many other issues. Many factors make it difficult to resolve these questions: use of different terms for the same concept, non-stable or evolving conceptual domains (e.g. the Internet), competing terminology within a field, and even the intended use of terms affect terminology decisions. In the monolingual task, however, we are only concerned with determining what is or may be a term in a text, rather than in a subject or domain. Computationally, this is a non-trivial problem, since even terminologists can sometimes disagree as to what counts as a term within a text (e.g. *data series* may or may not be classified as a term in a particular text).

An effective, albeit imperfect, method for automatic terminology extraction is to note that most terminology adheres to a small set of syntactic patterns that can be efficiently detected in text (Justeson and Katz 1995b). Such patterns are defined over part-of-speech (POS) sequences, and normally specify NPs consisting of a mixture of adjectives, nouns and prepositions. These patterns are conveniently expressed using REs. The following RE is adapted from that proposed by Justeson and Katz (1995b):

$$(ADJ \mid N)^+N \mid (ADJ \mid N)^*(N\ P)(ADJ \mid N)^*N$$

This will match any number of adjectives (ADJ) and nouns (N) ending in a noun, or any pair of such sequences separated by a preposition. The actual expression can be varied to cope with different texts. For example, van der Eijk (1993) uses $ADJ^*\ N^+$. Similarly, filters may be used to eliminate given categories of clearly incorrect candidates (e.g. eliminate all candidates beginning with a title such as *Mr, Dr*; eliminate terms occurring less than a given threshold frequency).

Consider the following text, where each word has been tagged with its POS (Section 9.1):

V/Choose **DET**/the **ADJ**/OK N/Button VTO/to V/close **DET**/the
N/Number N/Format N/dialog N/box.

The above regular expression will retrieve the terms:

ADJ/OK **N**/Button
N/Number **N**/Format **N**/dialog **N**/box

In this case, they are actually terms, but due to tagger errors or to structural ambiguity (e.g. PP attachment and coordinated term ambiguity) there will be extracted phrases which are not terms (precision), and there will be terms that will not be extracted (recall). Precision rates of up to 90% in a set of 237 extracted terms have been reported for such techniques (Fung et al. 1996).

An alternative mechanism for extracting multi-word constituents is described by Smadja (1993) whose XTRACT program has as input a text, and as output a list of collocations. Different types of collocations are defined:

Predicative collocations, such as *make-decision*, in which both words are repeatedly used together in a similar syntactic relation. Such collocations are flexible in the sense that they are not contiguous.

Rigid NP collocations, such as *The FSTE 100 Index*, involve uninterrupted sequences of words making up a noun phrase.

Phrasal templates, such as *The average finished the week *NUMBER* points up*, contain zero, one or several slots which need to be filled by a particular word fulfilling a specific function. In this example, the filler must be a number. Phrasal templates may contain no slots, as is the case with set phrases such as *Weather forecast till 6 a.m.*.

Collocations in this approach are considered to occur within a five-word window: for each pair of words, a vector of length 10 is computed indicating the number of times one of the words occurs at a given distance from the other. For example, given the word *market*, the frequency of *financial* and *average* at different positions before and after it in a corpus of stock market reports may be:

Position	Freq	-5	-4	-3	-2	-1	1	2	3	4	5
market financial	90	0	6	2	11	60	0	0	0	0	0
market use	14	2	1	1	2	1	1	0	1	4	1

From the vectors, the collocation of the two words is analysed and strong collocates and positions are selected. Strong collocates satisfy three conditions. First, they are sufficiently frequent. In this case, both *financial* and *use* co-occur with *market* a sufficient number of times. Second, they have one or more spikes. *Market-use* has no clear spikes and it is therefore eliminated. *Market-financial* does have a spike at position -1. Third, within a vector, strong collocations have large values (spikes); *financial* at position -1 is thus a strong collocate.

After selecting these two-word collocations a second phase builds larger collocations, both rigid and flexible, and creates phrasal templates. This is achieved by examining the frequency and position of other words around the two collocated words, using the same vector representation as for pairs of words. Larger collocations are detected by a high relative frequency of a word in the environment of the two words in question. Rigid collocations additionally have strong positional constraints with no intervening words. By using a tagged corpus, phrasal templates can also be extracted, by noting that a POS frequently appears at a given position, but with different words.

In addition to the second phase in XTRACT a robust parser is used to addition-ally filter collocations; the parser identifies the grammatical relation between the two collocated words. These relations include Subject–Verb, Noun–Noun and Verb–Object. A collocation is accepted if one of its syntactic relations occurs a sufficient number of times. For example, a collocation such as *prices-rose* would be accepted if, for instance, it appeared as a Subject–Verb relation a sufficiently large proportion of all occurrences.

Bilingual Task Once terms have been identified, the bilingual task takes place. By viewing terms as words, similar techniques to those used for word alignment can be employed, using frequency distribution, recency vectors, or cognates and other textual clues. Alternatively, word alignment can be used to induce term alignment by aligning terms containing a large proportion of aligned words. Re-sults vary depending on whether recall or precision is maximized; at one end Kupiec (1993) reports 90% precision for low recall, while Dagan and Church (1997) achieve 40% precision, but their system is robust and always includes the correct translation somewhere within its ranked list.

Yet another possibility, based on the output of XTRACT, is presented in Smadja et al. (1996). The input to the algorithm is a set of collocations as derived by XTRACT and a corpus aligned at the sentence level. To find the translation of a collocation, all single TL words which are highly correlated with the SL collo-cation are collected. Correlation is computed using Dice's coefficient. In fact, a minimum absolute frequency threshold is also used to license a possible trans-lation in order to avoid sparse data problems. From this set, the largest subset which is highly correlated with the SL term, using Dice's score, is its transla-tion. This set is found incrementally: first, all highly correlated pairs of these TL words are found. Next, highly correlated triplets are produced by adding one more word to the selected pairs. Then all sets of size four are calculated, and so on, until no larger sets are found that have a correlation value greater than an empirically determined threshold.

For example, given the SL collocation *official languages*, the following sub-sets are found (note that for each length, other subsets will have passed the threshold; only the best for each arity is shown):

officielles	0.94
officielles langues	0.95
honneur officielles langues	0.45

Once a list of such subsets is computed, the subset with the highest arity is selected as the translation. Note that it is only necessary to select from among the best for each arity. Finally, the words in each set are ordered by inspecting sample TL sentences from the bilingual corpus. Precision in terms of correct translations over total translations is about 65% for all translations produced (including those for erroneous collocations produced by XTRACT), and 73% for translations for valid collocations only.

4.5 Conclusion

TWBs, and in particular TM, have become popular tools in the translation profession. They have been particularly successful in the software localization industry, where manuals and other technical texts need to be translated and updated on a regular basis. Developments in TM technology include automatic translation of numbers, dates and other easily translatable textual units, as well as the incorporation of EBMT techniques (Section 8.1). Some vendors supply alignment software that will generate translation memories from previously translated texts. Terminology and word alignment technologies are also beginning to make an impact on bilingual lexicography and terminology management.

4.5.1 Further Reading

Kay (1980) is one of the earliest papers on the notion of a Translator's Workbench. The idea has been investigated by a number of researchers (Melby 1987; Macklovitch 1989; Kugler et al. 1992). The TWB project (Kugler et al. 1992) included a variety of options including translation memory, terminology compilation and storage, and a machine translation option, while Macklovitch (1989) describes how to build a TWB from existing software packages. A collection of articles on TWBs, alignment and other MAT topics appeared in the *Journal of Machine Translation* special issue on New Tools for Human Translators, Vol. 12(1–2), 1997. A completely different translation tool is the context-sensitive glosser described in Poznanski et al. (1998), which gives disambiguated translations of specific words in a text by taking context into account.

Melby (1995, p. 225 n. 73) refers to TM systems implemented in the 1970s and early 1980s. Keck (1991) suggests the use of HMM for TM storage and retrieval. IR algorithms and techniques can be used for both of these tasks (van Rijsbergen 1979; Frakes and Baeza-Yates 1992).

Many proposals for sentence alignment are mentioned in the text (Gale and Church 1993; Brown et al. 1991; Kay and Röscheisen 1993; Wu 1994; Simard et al. 1992). Simard and Plamondon (1998) describe work on producing robust and accurate sentence alignments, while Church (1993) employs similar character sequences for aligning text fragments. Subsentential alignment is sometimes a by-product of statistical machine translation (Brown et al. 1988; Brown et al. 1990; Brown et al. 1992; Brown et al. 1993), or of phrasal alignment (Wu 1997). Dagan and Church (1997) describe the use of word alignments for terminology compilation. The results of van der Eijk (1993) argue for the extraction of terms prior to their alignment. Smadja et al. (1996) illustrate the use of XTRACT for term alignment. Recency vectors as a technique for subsentential alignment was pioneered by Fung and McKeown (1997), and employed by Somers and Ward (1996). An algorithm for extracting discontinous phrases from text is presented in McTait and Trujillo (1999). Other work on word alignment includes Wu and Xia (1994), the evaluation presented in Macklovitch and Hannan (1998), and the flow network model of Gaussier (1998). Oakes (1998) reviews a variety of statistical techniques including some for MAT.

Part 3
Machine Translation

5 Computational Linguistics Techniques

Standard techniques for the analysis and generation of natural language sentences are presented, with an outline for their implementation.

MAT techniques are primarily designed to support humans in the translation task. However, current MAT tools fail to exploit a large body of linguistic and computational knowledge which has accumulated since the 1940s and before. This knowledge is encapsulated in a number of techniques and frameworks in the field of computational linguistics.

5.1 Introduction

In this book, CL is taken to mean the battery of algorithms and data structures that have been developed to process natural languages in a motivated and scientific manner. The CL techniques presented in this chapter are the foundations for the systems and frameworks to be elaborated in the rest of the book.

Three main areas from linguistics have received much attention in CL: morphology, syntax and semantics. In addition, natural language generation (NLG) has become a subfield in its own right, dealing with the construction of natural language sentences from meaning representations. In this chapter we consider morphological processing, syntactic processing and NLG in turn, and present some key algorithms. Different types of semantic representation and interpretation used in MT are discussed under the systems that adopt them.

5.2 Computational Morphology and the Two-level Model

Analysing and generating word forms is a crucial step in the processing of natural language. For example, in applications such as spell checkers, electronic dictionary interfaces and information retrieval systems it is important that words which are only inflectional variants of each other are identified and treated similarly. NLP and MT systems need to identify words in texts in order determine their syntactic and semantic properties. For this, lexical databases are needed.

There are two main techniques for structuring lexical databases. One is to store fully inflected forms. For example, each of the strings *play*, *played*, *playing* and *plays* could be explicitly entered in the lexicon. The other technique is to store only a citation or root form of a word, and derive inflected forms through morphological rules in combination with a small set of canonical affixes. For example, only *play* would appear in the lexicon, and the other forms would be derived by adding the suffixes *-ed*, *-ing* and *-s* respectively. Each of these approaches has advantages and disadvantages.

Storing full forms makes access to words faster, since there is no additional processing involved, and file organization techniques such as hashing (Knuth 1973; Elmasri and Navathe 1994) can be used for linear time access. Furthermore, through the use of string storage techniques such as tries (Knuth 1973, pp. 481–90), it is possible to reduce the space taken up by fully inflected representations. Finally, there is less development cost in terms of specifying appropriate morphological processes at the expense of greater lexical updating costs. The main disadvantage associated with this approach is that it fails to capture morphological regularities which can at worst make the expansion of the lexicon impossible for highly inflected or agglutinative languages. Even for relatively uninflected languages such as English, it is much simpler to enter one root form than the four inflected forms of a verb. What is more, as a system expands, changes to the content of lexical entries or of affixes are localized rather than distributed throughout many entries.

The advantages and disadvantages of only maintaining root forms in the lexicon are essentially the opposite of those just described: generalizations are captured, knowledge is localized and hence more easily maintained, and new word forms are predicted, but at the cost of longer processing times and the need for developing and maintaining morphological rules. In addition, irregular forms such as *be*, *am*, *are* and *is* still need to be entered separately.

In many cases, the modularity and linguistic motivation offered by the root and affix approach to lexical processing outweighs most of its disadvantages compared with the alternative of storing fully inflected forms. In computational terms, the best known approach to morphology is the two-level model of Koskenniemi (1983) and Kaplan and Kay (1994).

5.2.1 Two-level Morphological Processing

The two-level model of morphology takes as its starting point the observation, attributed to Johnson (1972), that the non-cyclic context-sensitive rewriting rules used by phonologists to describe pronunciation changes submit to computational treatment through finite state machines. Phonological rules of this type assume that roots and affixes are stored in a lexicon in some standard format, and apply an ordered sequence of rules to concatenations of roots and suffixes in order to produce surface realizations of words. For written language, we are interested

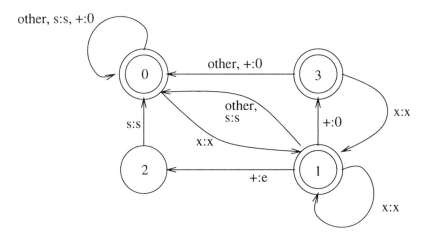

FIG. 5.1. A simple FST for inserting *e* in plurals.

in orthographic changes rather than phonological changes, which means that the rules in question deal with characters and orthography rather than phonemes. The rules are therefore more appropriately called spelling rules.

Consider a lexicon with the two roots *fox* and *cat* and the suffix +*s* (+ indicates a morpheme boundary). Spelling rules should then express the fact that a combination such as *fox+s* rewrites as *foxes* and not **foxs*, while *cat+s* should rewrite as *cats*. The following context-sensitive rules achieve these transformations:

1. + → e / x — s
2. + → 0

The first rule states that the morpheme boundary symbol + will map to the character *e* if it is preceded by character *x* and followed by character *s*. The second rule simply indicates that if the first rule does not apply, the + symbol maps to the empty string. The rules are applied in the order given, and are compulsory. They could also be applied in reverse, such that the surface form *foxes* would be analysed as the lexical form *fox+s*, whose components can then be matched against the lexicon.

Rules of this kind can be modelled using finite state transducers (FSTs), so long as the non-contextual part of a rule (e.g. + → e) cannot apply to its own output. FSTs are FSMs with a pair of symbols associated with each transition. One of these symbols acts as input and the other acts as output. The machine thus converts or "transduces" a sequence of symbols into a different sequence.

For the two rules above, the FST in Fig. 5.1 models their combined behaviour. Note that instead of using arrows to indicate symbol transductions, a colon (:) is used to separate the input and output symbols, thus emphasizing the symmetric character of the model. The label *other* is an abbreviatory convention, and stands for all identity pairs of symbols from the alphabet which are not explicitly mentioned in the rest of the machine. Thus, *other* stands for *a:a, c:c, ..., y:y,*

	x:x	s:s	+:e	+:0	other
0	1	0	–	0	0
1	1	0	2	3	0
2	–	0	–	–	–
3	1	–	–	0	0

Table 5.1. The transition table for the FST in Fig. 5.1.

z:z but not for *x:x*, *s:s*, *+:e*, *+:0*, as these pairs consist of symbols mentioned in the transducer. Note that this machine is particularly simple, and will produce incorrect plurals such as *church+s – churchs*; the machine could be extended to allow for these and other spelling changes.

The advantage of FSTs as models of morphological processes is their bidirectional character and declarative nature. FSTs can act as generators of word forms starting from lexical forms, or as analysers of word forms into canonical forms. Furthermore, they can be modelled using well-known mathematical tools such as FSMs.

The previous machine can be represented very economically as an array indicating, for each symbol pair and each state, what the next state is, as shown in Table 5.1. A dash on the table indicates that the machine blocks and then backtracks to a previous choice point, otherwise it fails.

While machines expressed as tables are efficiently interpreted by computer, they are cumbersome for linguists to write. Even the corresponding graphical representations are error-prone and unwieldy beyond simple machines. It is possible to derive FSTs manually from rules such as the one above, but this process is also tedious and error-prone. It is preferable to compile the rules automatically, leaving linguists to concentrate on the linguistic aspects of the spelling changes.

Compilation of rules normally involves two steps: compilation of individual rules into separate FSTs, and combination of these FSTs into a single transducer that models their combined behaviour. The combination step can take two forms: one is simply to keep all the machines separate and apply them all in parallel, while the other is to merge them using finite state techniques to derive a single, smaller machine in which no individual rule may be recognized.

5.2.2   Rule Format and Notation

The compilation process is intimately dependent on the particular rule formalism used. Here we adopt a formalism due to Koskenniemi. We begin by assuming two sets of largely overlapping lexical and surface alphabet symbols, with the additional symbol (+) to indicate morpheme boundaries as above and the digit zero (0) to represent the empty string. Morphological processing is seen as a transduction between a lexical tape containing canonical roots and affixes, and a surface tape representing the correct spelling of an inflected word (see Table 5.2).

Lexical tape:	f	o	x	+	s
Surface tape:	f	o	x	e	s

Table 5.2. The two-tape view of morphological processing.

Koskenniemi proposed two basic types of morphological rule (or more accurately, spelling rules), both following the general format:

```
cp op lc --- rc
```

The rules are distinguished by the operator op that they use, but they both consist of a correspondence part cp and (possibly empty) contexts, both left (lc) and right (rc).

Context restriction rules, with operator =>, state that the cp pair can only occur in the indicated context. For example, the (simplified) rule below states that the pair y:i requires r:r to its left, and the pair +:e, followed by s:s to its right.

```
y:i => r:r --- +:e s:s
```

This rule accounts for the change try+s - tries. Note that this rule allows other pairs in the context (e.g. try+s - tryes), so it needs to be restricted, as explained below.

Surface coercion rules, with operator <=, state that in the given context, the lexical symbol must map to the surface symbol indicated on the cp. For example, the (simplified) rule below forces + to be mapped into e whenever preceded by x:x and followed by s:s.

```
+:e <= x:x --- s:s
```

Mappings such as fox+s - foxes are handled by this rule. Note that the rule allows +:e in other contexts (e.g. dog+s - doges), and needs to be restricted also.

A third type of rule can be defined by merging the two rule types above into one to give **composite** rules, identified by the operator <=>. Their effect is the combination of the other two: the pair must occur in the context, and the context forces the pair (or rather, the surface symbol). Thus a more restrictive version of the y:i rule is:

```
y:i <=> r:r --- +:e s:s
```

This rule now rejects try+s - tryes but accepts try+s - tries as before; a similar modification can be made to the +:e rule.

While accurate and perspicuous, the notation so far is not very flexible. Firstly, contexts may depend on sets of pairs rather than on individual pairs: the y:i rule also applies when other consonants appear in the left context: fly+s - flies, city+s - cities, prodigy+s - prodigies. Generalized pairs represent sets of pairs, any of which may match an input pair. Thus, C:C (in capital letters) may stand for all identity pairs of consonants: b:b, c:c, d:d, ... In addition, a set of feasible pairs with a specific surface or lexical symbol may be denoted using the = notation. **Feasible pairs** are pairs of symbols that appear in a rule, or are defined as default pairs. Thus +:= stands for any pair with + on the lexical tape (e.g. +:0, +:e), but any symbol on the surface tape, as long as the resulting pair occurs in at least some rule or is a default pair.

Secondly, the left or right context can vary as to what sequences of pairs it can match: s:s h:h and c:c h:h both behave like x:x for the +:e rule, as in push+s - pushes, church+s - churches. Alternatives for a context can be expressed in the form of regular expressions over pairs of symbols. The two contexts above can be expressed as:

```
[ x:x ([s:s c:c] h:h) ]
```

Here, square brackets indicate disjunction, while parentheses group sequences. Thus, this expression represents either x:x or either of s:s or c:c followed by h:h.

Finally, pairs can occur in specific left and right contexts: in addition to the y:i context above, this pair can occur in other contexts such as n:n c:t --- +:0 a:a l:l (e.g. presidency+al - presidential). Multiple left and right contexts can be accommodated by extending the notation with the or operator. The rule below presents a fuller version of the y:i rule incorporating multiple left and right contexts:

```
y:i <=>                  [ C:C c:t ] --- ( +:= a:a =:NB )
        or [ +:= C:C (q:q u:u) ] --- ( +:= NI:= )

    where NB is {l n r t u} and
          NI is {a d e f h l m n o p s w y}
```

Note the fact that *qu* behaves as a single consonant on the left context. A pair like =:NB thus denotes any feasible pair with any symbol from the set NB on the surface tape. This rule now allows presidency+al - presidential and sun+y+er - sunnier.

It is possible to describe a substantial fragment of spelling changes for a natural language through these rules, particularly for languages not exhibiting a large degree of infixation such as English (Ritchie et al. 1992, pp. 233–36). Thus, Semitic languages and languages with morphological reduplication are not conveniently describable in the two-level model (Sproat 1992).

5.2.3 Rule Application

While sometimes referred to as morphological rules, the formalism just presented is more accurately seen as encoding spelling rules. That is, these rules state the environments that cause specific changes in the form of words. When used for analysis or generation, they will interact with each other to validate or reject particular lexical-surface mappings. In Section 5.2.6 the lexicon in a typical two-level framework is shown to constrain the strings that may appear on

	p	r	e	s	i	d	e	n	c	y	+	a	l
	p	r	e	s	i	d	e	n	t	i	0	a	l
Feasible pairs:	p:p	r:r	e:e	s:s	i:i	d:d	e:e	n:n	c:t	y:i	+:0	a:a	l:l
c-t rule								n:n	c:t	=:i	+:0	a:a	=:NB
y-i rule									c:t	y:i	+:=	a:a	=:NB

Table 5.3. Spelling rule application.

the lexical tape in order to determine a valid sequence of roots and affixes and its corresponding realization on the surface tape. For any particular lexical to surface transduction, all rules in the description of a language must be satisfied for each pair of symbols, as one would expect from the semantics of the rules.

The following two rules will suffice to exemplify rule interaction.

```
y:i <=>                    [ C:C c:t ]  ---  ( +:= a:a =:NB )
         or [ +:= C:C (q:q u:u) ]  ---  ( +:= NI:= )

c:t <=>                         n:n ---  ( =:i +:0 a:a =:NB )
```

Since the pair c:t occurs in the context of the first rule, it becomes a feasible pair, and therefore the second rule is needed to restrict the contexts in which it may appear. The rules thus allow *presidency+al – presidential* but not *face+al – *fatial*. One can think of the rules as applying to every possible subsequence of pairs in the input. If either the context or the correspondence pair matches but not the other, the transduction is invalid. Table 5.3 shows a conceptual view of this process. Note that both rules are applied several times for the complete string, but only at the indicated substrings do the context or the correspondence pair match. Feasible pairs in this case include all identity pairs made from the intersection of the lexical and surface alphabets, the pair +:0 and any pair appearing in any rule. It is up to the rule writer to ensure that non-identity pairs such as c:t and y:i are appropriately restricted to specific orthographic contexts. Indeed, one methodology for writing spelling rules is to constrain these non-identity pairs by identifying the contexts in which they may appear.

5.2.4 Rule Compilation and Interpreting

Rule compilation can take a number of routes (Ritchie et al. 1992) broadly distinguished by the amount of compilation time needed, the size of the resulting automaton, its speed and its run-time space requirements. At one extreme, one can compile each rule into standard non-deterministic FSTs, merge them into a single machine which is then determinized and finally minimized. This can be done as long as the empty string is not part of the input or output alphabet. This produces the fastest morphological analysers requiring the least run-time space, but take extra time and memory to compile, in addition to the effort of writing and maintaining the compiler. At the other extreme, one can implement rule interpreters which directly apply rules to the input lexical and surface tapes and therefore require no compilation step, but are less efficient in terms of speed and run-time memory use.

Between these two extremes, there are other possibilities, of which we consider the one due to Bear (1985), as described in Ritchie et al. (1992, pp. 148–56). Instead of compiling into standard FSTs, rules are compiled into augmented FSTs in which states can have the following labels: E(rror), T(erminal) and L(icence). There are also states with no label. The idea is that a simpler FST is built, which can nevertheless be efficiently interpreted by a modified FST interpreting procedure. The compilation produces an augmented FST for each rule and merges these into a single machine which is restarted for each symbol pair in the input. Compilation is different for each of the two types of rule, and for composite rules it is their combined result. In each case, the left and right contexts are converted into FSTs, but with different state labels depending on the side and type of rule in which they appear.

Context restriction (cp => LC --- RC) These rules are compiled into an FST which only accepts strings of the form LC cp RC. LC is compiled into a transducer with all states unmarked. The transducer for RC has its initial state marked L and the final state marked T, while other states are unmarked. An arc labelled cp is added to join the two machines.

Surface coercion (cp <= LC --- RC) The FST for these rules simply rejects strings which do not have the right surface symbol in strings of the form LC cp RC. The automata for LC and RC have no labels, except for the final state of RC which is marked E. These two transducers are joined by arcs with all feasible pairs with the lexical symbol of cp but a different surface symbol.

Composite (cp <=> LC --- RC) The FST for LC is as for the previous two rules. RC is compiled into two FSTs, one treating the rule as a context restriction rule, the other treating it as a surface coercion rule. The automaton for LC is then linked to the corresponding machine in the two ways identified above.

Each rule is compiled and all their initial states merged into one. Finally, an arc is added for each unrestricted pair, from the start state, to a state labelled both L and T. Unrestricted pairs are feasible pairs that do not appear as the cp in a context restriction or composite rule.

In order to allow for a specific transformation to occur anywhere within a string, the resulting automaton needs to be restarted each time a new symbol pair is being considered. That is, at any one time, there are several instantiations of the machine running. However, they must *all* accept the current transduction; otherwise, the string would be violating some rule.

During interpretation, all paths through the automaton are pursued by maintaining a set of configurations, one for each pair sequence being considered. Thus a configuration maintains the state of the machine in the face of ambiguity in the transductions allowed by the machine. Each configuration consists of a set of rule states, of which there are two types: simple rule states are made up of one automaton state; commit groups are sets of one or more automaton states. A rule state maintains the state of the machine in the face of non-determinism for a specific symbol pair.

The machine starts with one configuration consisting of a simple rule state: the start state. When a symbol pair is input, a new configuration is built from a previous configuration. The new configuration consists of the target states for each arc labelled with the input pair, starting at some state in the previous rule state. Different symbol pairs give rise to different configurations, and thus all possible paths through the machine are pursued in a breadth-first fashion.

New configurations must satisfy the following conditions.

1. At least one simple rule state must contain an L state.
2. No rule state can contain E states.
3. No commit group can be empty.

New configurations are then updated as follows before the next step in the recognition process.

1. Rule states with a T state are deleted.
2. All simple rule states labelled L are collected into a commit group.

The particular transduction is valid if its final configuration contains no commit groups.

5.2.5 Example

Consider again the y:i spelling rule (Ritchie et al. 1992, p. 234):

```
y:i <=>                  [ C:C c:t ] --- ( +:= a:a =:NB )
          or [ +:= C:C (q:q u:u) ] --- ( +:= NI:= )
```

First, the automata for each context are built. Each context is effectively a regular expression and therefore an automaton can be easily constructed for it. This is achieved by first creating an automaton with an initial and final state linked by an arc labelled with the whole expression. The automaton is then modified according to the following two rules:

- If an arc is labelled with [A B ...], replace the arc with separate arcs for each of A, B and so on, but preserving the original start and end states. The effect is to allow alternative paths between the two states.
- If an arc is labelled with (A B ...), replace the arc by a sequence of arcs and states, one for each of A, B and so on, between the start and final state. The effect is to move from the original two states only when the indicated sequence is present.

These rules are applied iteratively until each arc is labelled with a unique symbol pair. Figure 5.2 shows each step for the second left context in the rule. The automaton for the right contexts is constructed similarly. However, because the rule is composite, two similar automata are built. One has the initial state labelled L, and the final state labelled T. The other only has the final state labelled E. The result of compiling the second right context is shown in Fig. 5.3. These two machines are linked to that for the left context: the top one via an arc labelled

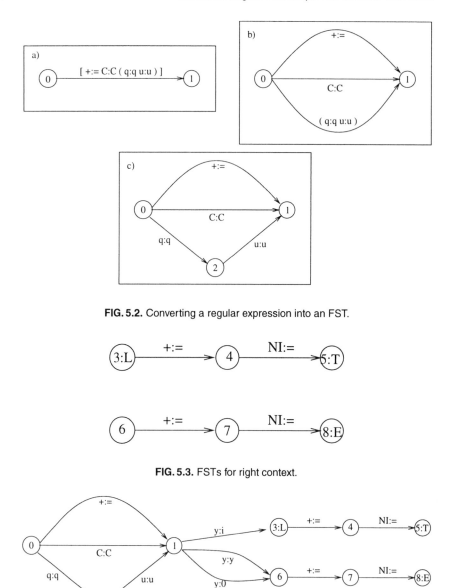

FIG. 5.2. Converting a regular expression into an FST.

FIG. 5.3. FSTs for right context.

FIG. 5.4. Automaton for a composite rule.

with the correspondence pair, the bottom one with one arc for each feasible pair containing y on the lexical tape and anything else but i on the surface tape. Figure 5.4 shows the resulting automaton. The compilation for the y : i rule also needs a machine for the top context; arcs also need to be added for

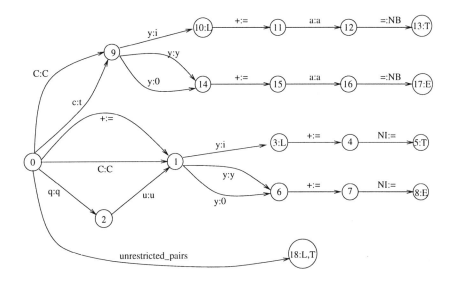

FIG. 5.5. Augmented automaton for y : i rule.

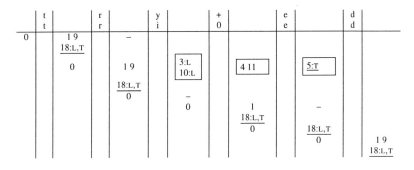

0	t / t	r / r	y / i	+ / 0	e / e	d / d
0	1 9 18:L,T	−				
	0	1 9	3:L 10:L	4 11	5:T	
		18:L,T 0				
			−	1	18:L,T	
			0	18:L,T		
				0	0	1 9
						18:L,T

Table 5.4. Accepting *try+ed - tried.*

all unrestricted pairs (note they are shown as a single arc in the diagram). The complete machine is shown in Fig. 5.5.

Table 5.4 shows a trace of the machine for a simple transduction. A single configuration is maintained in this case, with different rule states after each symbol pair is scanned. Commit groups are depicted by boxes, while deleted rule states are underlined. A dash indicates that a particular path through the machine has blocked. If different transductions are possible for a particular input (i.e. in the analysis or generation of a particular word form) two or more configurations may be maintained, each one pursuing a different analysis or synthesis of the word. The initial state is reproduced at each step in order to restart the machine. The final configuration contains no commit groups and therefore the transduction is valid.

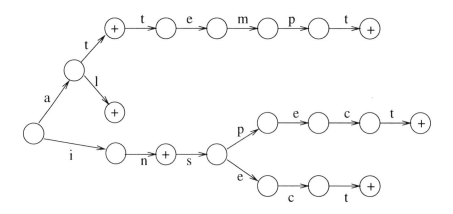

FIG. 5.6. A trie representation for a lexicon.

Implementation Details Prolog offers a relatively straightforward mechanism for interpreting rules directly, rather than compiling them as just outlined. This is achieved by maintaining a chart of activated rules whose behaviour corresponds to that of the augmented automata technique just described. Rules whose left context matches the current pair are added to the active rules list with the left context reduced by the matching pair. The next pair in the input is then matched against all the rules in the rule set and against the active rules, and, if matched, the left contexts are reduced again. Some active rules are marked as to whether they license a pair, cause an error or terminate a transduction, in a manner similar to the algorithm above.

5.2.6   Lexicon

An efficient representation for the lexicon in the two-level model is as a trie (Knuth 1973, pp. 481–90), a tree structure in which the root is the beginning of all words, arcs are labelled with symbols from the lexical alphabet, and where subtrees represent words with a common prefix. For example, the trie in Fig. 5.6 shows the subtree for the morphemes:

-al,at,attempt,in-,in,insect,inspect

Any node labelled + indicates a complete morpheme occurs at that node. Note that affixes and roots are included in the trie.

Transduction traverses the tree from the root towards the leaves, re-entering at the root when a morpheme boundary is possible. By applying feasible pairs at each step during analysis or generation, a path through the trie is transduced into a surface string, and via the spelling rules it is validated to conform to the language's spelling conventions. The tree is particularly relevant during analysis, as it reduces the amount of non-determinism on the lexical tape. Thus, given the input sing on the surface tape, the lexicon will disallow it from being analysed as s+ing as there will be no root s (see below).

5.2.7 Morphosyntactic Rules

Apart from spelling changes, morphological processes are constrained by the combinatorial properties of affixes and roots. Thus the suffix `al` only combines with nouns to give adjectives, but it is incorrect to combine the past suffix `ed` with a noun:

> [[nation]$_{Noun}$ + `al`]$_{Adj}$ (*national*)
> *[[nation]$_{Noun}$ + `ed`] (**nationed*)

There are also restrictions within the same part-of-speech. For example, "latinate" verbs such as `present` nominalize through the suffix +ation, but not "native" verbs such as `contain` which nominalize through +ment (cf. *presentation, *presentment, *containation, containment*). Different sequences of affixation are also constrained. Thus, although +able derives adjectives from verbs, inflected verbs cannot be so transformed: **readingable*. Similarly, multiple application of suffixes is not possible in general: **readinging*.

Affixes and roots can be seen as a language consisting of the allowable sequences of morphemes. As such, the language may be described through a word grammar expressed in a formal grammatical framework. The word grammar indicates how morphemes are combined to produce valid words, which may subsequently be processed by the spelling rules to produce surface words.

The vocabulary of the grammar expresses information such as a root's category (i.e. part of speech), the category that an affix expects and the category that it builds, and other language specific information (e.g. whether a verb is Latinate or not). Such information is of a highly lexical character, and it is convenient to express it in the form of complex categories reminiscent of those used in Categorial Grammar (Wood 1993), reducing grammar rules to just two:

- B → A A\B
- B → B/A A

In this scheme, affixes are assigned complex categories, indicated by the slash and backslash. Thus, a suffix like +ation might receive a category *Verb\Adj* indicating that it combines with a verb to its left to form an adjective. In a more powerful system, each of *A* and *B* will have additional features with information specific to word formation. Multiple affixes can be handled by repeated application of these rules. Thus the string un+read+able is described by the following tree:

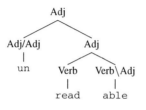

Compounding is somewhat more difficult as it involves open class words with their combinatorial properties independent of the morphology. Also, because

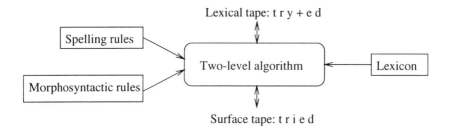

FIG. 5.7. A morphological processor.

the morphemes in compounds are effectively of unbounded length, formulating contexts spanning roots of arbitrary length becomes impossible in the present framework.

Close interaction of these "word grammars" and spelling rules can clearly enhance the efficiency of the system. For example, if a root is latinate, there is no need to explore branches of the lexicon trie corresponding to affixes that are incompatible with them.

Morphological information may be stored together with syntactic and semantic information on a word, and therefore be available to subsequent levels of processing (Evans and Gazdar 1996), or it may be stored in a separate morphological lexicon.

The overall structure of the morphological processor is shown in Fig. 5.7.

5.2.8 Implementation Details

In a possible implementation of these ideas, morpheme entries would consist of a language field, a morpheme string field, a morphological information field and a syntactic/semantic field. For example, the broad structure of the entry for the morpheme +ation could be:

```
a(en, ation, morph(latinate), cat(l,[vp] / SemV,
                                      [n,sing3] / SemN)) :-
    nominalize(SemV,SemN).
```

This says that the a(ffix) ation is a Latinate morpheme that combines to its l(eft) with a verb (as indicated by the vp category – see below), and results in a third singular noun whose semantics SemN are the result of nominalizing the semantics of the verb SemV. This last step is achieved through a predicate nominalize which is dependent on the semantic framework and representation used.

Given this structure, the morphological analyser would only handle the combination of one root with a single morpheme, but it would do so for both analysis and generation.

5.3   Syntactic Analysis

Syntactic analysis concerns the study of order and structure in a sentence and of the various relationships that words establish among themselves. Relatively speaking, syntax has received enormous attention in CL and MT, both from a linguistic perspective in terms of formalizing linguistic descriptions of sentences, and in computational terms, in devising algorithms and frameworks with which to represent and process linguistic knowledge.

Many different formal syntactic theories have been proposed, and several of these have been computationally realized; some have even been used for MT (see Further Reading section). Since this book concerns algorithms for MT, this section simply presents the skeletal linguistic structures assumed in the rest of the book, and provides pointers to more detailed linguistic analyses. The framework consists of a term unification formalism with a phrase structure backbone (Pereira and Warren 1980). This makes it flexible enough to express a variety of linguistic phenomena and to present different approaches to MT, while maintaining a bias towards computational efficiency and familiarity. Other common formalisms include those based on graph unification and typed feature structures (Shieber 1986; Carpenter 1992). However, these require additional machinery besides Prolog unification for their interpretation, and do not substantially add to the descriptions of MT approaches presented in the book.

The following section headings, dealing with aspects of syntax, are from Pollard and Sag (1994) (henceforth, HPSG-94) but do not reach their depth and breath, although some of their insights and general perspective are used. The focus here is on presenting a modicum of syntactic analysis on which to base the rest of the text.

Sign Structure   Signs are structures that relate different realms of linguistic description. Here they relate at least two kinds of knowledge, namely syntactic and semantic. Following Shieber et al. (1990), a sign will have the following general structure: Syntax / Semantics. By contrast, the signs in Pollard and Sag (1987) include phonology/orthography, while those in HPSG-94 merge syntax and semantics into a single structure, and in addition incorporate quantifier scope and phrase structure information.

The syntax/semantics division is not as strict as it appears. For example, information regarding subcategorization is stored in the syntax part, but this in turn may make reference to the semantics of a subcategorized phrase. Similarly, semantic variables in noun phrases are passed through the syntactic part and subsequently bound into the corresponding semantic predicate, as explained below.

Broad syntactic categories are used, with subcategorization constraints encoded in the subcat list. Table 5.5 shows the symbols that may be used for main syntactic categories. For example, the outline entry for the verb *put* as in *The user puts the disk in the drive* is:

```
[vp,SynVP,[ [np,SynObj]/SemObj,
            [pp,SynPP]/SemPP,
            [np,SynSubj]/SemSubj ]
   ] / GiveSem
```

s	Sentence	n	Noun	adjv	Adjective and Adverb	p	Preposition
vp	Verb and Verb Phrase	n1	N-bar Phrase	a1	A-bar Phrase	p1	P-bar Phrase
det	Determiner	np	Noun Phrase	ap	Adjective/ Adverbial Phrase	pp	Prepositional Phrase
conj	Conjunction						

Table 5.5. Symbols for syntactic categories.

Thus, *put* subcategorizes for three constituents: a direct object which is a noun phrase, a prepositional phrase oblique object, and a noun phrase subject. The information and structure in the semantic part varies depending on the MT approach taken; this may in turn influence the syntactic component of the sign (e.g. its subcat list).

An example of a phrase structure rule is:

```
[np,SynNP] / SemNP ---> [ [det,SynDet]/SemDet,
                          [n1,SynN1]/SemN1 ]
```

This rule, analogous to the CF rule $NP \rightarrow Det\ N1$, states that a noun phrase rewrites as a determiner followed by an N1 phrase. Again, as far as MT is concerned, the actual structure of the syntactic and semantic parts depends on the MT approach taken, and will vary for each one . Yet many phenomena relating to language are relevant to most of the MT systems described later; these phenomena are therefore reviewed here.

Saturation of complement signs occurs through a "popping" mechanism, illustrated through the following vp rule:

```
[vp,SynInfo,Subcat]/SemVP1 --->
            [ [vp,SynInfo,[Comp|Subcat]]/SemVP2,
              Comp ]
```

The idea is that as a phrase is analysed, the signs in the subcat list are gradually "peeled off" and unified with complement phrases, until the subcat list is empty. Note that the actual value of Comp is determined by the lexical entry for the verb. Furthermore, the subject appears at the end of the list, in order to simplify saturation by exploiting the recursive structure of lists. The subject is saturated via:

```
[s,SynInfo]/SemS --->
            [ Subj,
              [vp,SynInfo,[Subj]]/SemS ]
```

More complex situations, including control structures, are reviewed below.

Agreement Following HPSG-94, agreement here is seen as a semantic phenomenon involving nouns, verbs, determiners and, for some languages, adjectives and other syntactic categories. In most European languages, agreement involves person, number and gender; case is also an agreement feature for some languages such as German. Other linguistic phenomena such as honorific marking (HPSG-94 p. 92ff) and animacy can also be seen as instances of agreement (Croft 1990, pp. 113–14).

Agreement information is expressed through the index of an expression, where indices are referring structures constrained as to what they may refer to. The following example is of an index structure that refers to a group of two or more people and includes the speaker (i.e. the index for *we, us, our*):

```
ind(Id,ref,pl1)}
```

This structure represents a first person plural index, which must `refer` to an entity in the discourse (as opposed to being pleonastic) and has an `Identifier` field that distinguishes it from other indices in a given discourse. Indices, then, combine what are traditionally regarded as syntactic and semantic information within the same predicate. In particular, they can appear as arguments to predicates and they may be bound by quantifiers.

In addition to an index, NPs have a case slot, which in English serves to distinguish between the above pronouns, as illustrated below.

Complement Structures Apart from complement saturation, another important aspect of grammar that needs at least a cursory description is that of control. Control structures involve complement phrases lacking a particular component, but where the missing component can be inferred from the local context. The minimum to consider are equi and raising control verbs, shown in bold in the following examples:

Subject Equi Example: *They **try** to have some memory.*
   They is the subject of both *try* and *have some memory.*
Subject Raising Example: *They **seem** to have some memory.*
   They is the subject of *have some memory* only; *seem* does not have a semantic subject (cf. *It seems that they have some memory*).
Object Equi Example: *They **persuade** Kim to have some memory.*
   Kim is the object of *persuade* and the subject of *have some memory.*
Object Raising Example: *They **believe** Kim to have some memory.*
   Kim is the subject of *have some memory* only. The object of *believe* is a proposition (cf. *They believe that Kim has some memory*).

The phenomenon of equi and raising verbs has been intensely studied – (Pollard and Sag 1994, Ch. 3, 7) and references therein. For present purposes, however, these distinctions will suffice.

The treatment assumed here is that of Ch. 3 (pp. 135–36) in HPSG-94, and it contrasts in particular with the semantic approach of Ch. 7 in the same work, which derives control relations from a semantic classification of verbs and their thematic roles. In the sample entries below, controller restrictions are expressed in the lexical sign of control verbs, and more specifically, in their subcat lists.

The general syntactic structure of subject equi and raising verbs is:

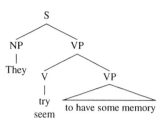

The two verbs differ in the kinds of index they allow in their subjects, and in the way they control the verb in their complement.

Try (subject equi)

```
[vp,Tense1,NumPer,[ [vp,inf,NumPer2,[ [np,Ind,CaseCont]/SemCont ]]
                    /SemVP,
                    [np,Ind = ind(Id,ref,NumPer),Case]/SemSubj ]
]/SemTry
```

The relevant aspects of this entry are that the infinitive complement vp has an unsaturated subject, and that the index of its subject is bound to the index in the subject of *try*; this index is restricted to be a referential index (i.e. not *there* or *it*) (cf. *There seems/*tries to be some memory*).

Seem (subject raising)

```
[vp,Tense1,NumPer,[ [vp,inf,NumPer2,[ NPCont ]]/SemVP,
                    NPCont = [np,ind(Id,Type,NumPer),Case]
                             /SemSubj ]
]/SemSeem
```

In this verb, the complete sign of the controlled subject is bound to the whole of the sign for the subject of *seem*, and there are no restrictions on the type of its index.

The general syntactic structure of object equi and raising verbs is:

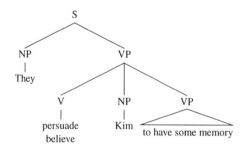

The two differ in the way in which the subjectless VP is controlled, and on index restrictions on the direct object of the main verb.

Persuade (object equi)

```
[vp,Tense1,NumPer,[ [np,IndObj = ind(IdObj,ref,NumPerObj),acc]
                    /SemObj,
                    [vp,inf,NumPer2,[ [np,IndObj,CaseCont]
                    /SemCont ]]/SemVP,
                    [np,ind(IdSubj,ref,NumPer),CaseSubj]
                    /SemSubj ]
]/SemPersuade
```

For this verb, the accusative object NP, the first in the subcat list, contains an index which is bound to the subject's index in the complement VP; this index must refer to discourse entities (cf. *The user *persuades/believes there to be a bug*).

Believe (object raising)

```
[vp,Tense1,NumPer,[ NPObj = [np,Ind,acc]/SemObj,
                    [vp,inf,NumPer2,[ NPObj ]]/SemVP,
                    [np,ind(IdSubj,ref,NumPer),CaseSubj]
                    /SemSubj ]
]/SemBelieve
```

The object of *believe* is shared with the subject of the complement VP, and there are no restrictions on the referent of its index.

It will be noticed that these two object control verbs specify case for their object, but not for their subject; nominative case is only assigned to finite verbs through a lexical rule. In this manner there is no case conflict between the accusative object of the control verb and the subject of the controlled verb.

The general approach in this analysis of control, then, is to specify constraints between structures in the subcat list of the verb and its VP complement.

Unbounded Dependency Constructions Unbounded dependency constructions (UDCs) are found in a variety of syntactic environments, including topicalization, *wh*-questions, purpose infinitives, relative clauses, and many others (HPSG-94, p. 157). Their defining characteristic is that they establish a syntactic and semantic dependency between constituents which are structurally far removed from each other. The tree below shows a dependency across three local trees:

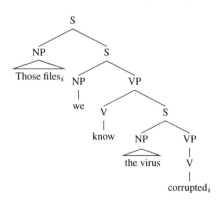

The phrase *those files*, known as the filler, is the thing *corrupted*, and hence there is a semantic relationship between the two phrases. The verb *corrupted*, being a transitive verb, contains an unsaturated object phrase, known, for historical reasons, as a gap.

Following Pereira and Shieber (1987), these dependencies can be handled by unifying filler and gap information via a list structure. This gap list is shared throughout specific branches of the tree: items are added to it wherever gaps arise, and items are elided wherever fillers arise. A variety of language-specific constraints limit the introduction and elision of items from this list (see Allen (1995, p. 138) for some English constraints). The following rules will serve to illustrate the implementation of this technique.

Three types of rule are needed to handle unbounded dependencies.

1. Bottom rules essentially introduce items to the gap list. Here they are realized as lexical rules that effectively delete a constituent from the subcat list of a lexical item and place the whole or part of that constituent in the gap list. This approach follows Sag and Wasow (1999) and differs from other treatments in that gaps do not manifest themselves as phonologically unrealized constituents. The following rule applies to verbs, and effectively moves the first constituent in the subcat list to the gap list.

   ```
   [vp,gap([NP|G]-G),Tense,NumPer,SubcatRest]/SemVP
       :-
       [vp,gap(G-G),Tense,NumPer,[ NP = [np,Ind,Case]/SemNP
                                   | SubcatRest ]
       ]/SemVP.
   ```

   In order to handle unbounded dependencies, syntactic structures have been extended to incorporate a gap list. However, because of Prolog's implementation of lists, a difference list operator – (Pereira and Shieber 1987, pp. 127–28) is used to identify the end of the list explicitly (see middle rules below). In this lexical rule, a VP now consists of a tense and number–person slot as before, and a gap difference list (identified by the predicate gap) while that for the resulting sign contains one item ([NP|G]-G). The source gap difference list is empty (e.g. G-G). This rule over- and under-generates (i.e. it allows extraction of subjects from intransitive verbs, and disallows extraction from other positions in the subcat list), but a fuller treatment is beyond the scope of this book.

2. Middle rules make the subcat list available throughout the analysis tree. They are not really separate rules, but rather additions to existing rules that effectively combine (i.e. append) gap lists and share the result with the syntactic head of a phrase. Thus, the complement saturation rules for verbs becomes:

   ```
   [vp,gap(InG-OutG),SynInfo,Subcat]/SemVP1 --->
       [ [vp,gap(InG-G),SynInfo,[Comp|Subcat]]/
         SemVP2, Comp = [X,gap(G-OutG)|SynX]/
         SemX ]
   ```

   Here, the gap list of the mother is the concatenation of the gap lists of its two daughters.

3. Top rules subtract the first item from the gap list and unify it with its filler.

```
[s,gap(InG-OutG),Tense,NumPer]/SemS --->
        [ Cat,
          [s,gap([Cat|InG]-OutG),Tense,NumPer]/SemS ]
```

The above rules essentially implement a powerful technique which allows a variety of long-distance phenomena to be expressed.

Relative Clauses Relative clauses are sentence-like phrases that modify a noun which plays a participant role within the relative clause. In this brief presentation of descriptive techniques, the following two types of relative clauses are considered:

Subject relatives Example: *The person* **who visited** *Kim left.*
  The person is the subject of both, *visited* and *left.*
Non-subject relatives Example: *The person* **who(m) Kim visited** *left.*
  The person is the object of *visited* but the subject of *left.*

Since the intended role of the NP occurs at an unbounded distance within the relative clause, the analysis of relative clauses is similar to that for other unbounded dependencies. However, their treatment requires an additional difference list through which relativized indices may be bound to the index of the modified NP, the relative pronoun, and the verb within the relative clause in which the noun is a participant. The tree below shows the analysis of a subject relative clause, with the difference list for indices indicated by the prefix r(el).

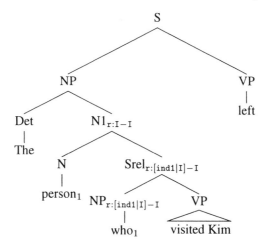

The lexical entry for *who* is:

```
[np,gap(G-G),rel([Ind|R]-R),Ind,nom]/SemWho
```

Note that the index of the pronoun is bound to the first item in the `rel` list. The rule for Srel modification of a noun is:

```
[n1,Gap,Rel,Ind,Case]/SemN1 --->
    [ [n1,Gap,Rel,Ind,Case]/SemN2,
      [s,gap([]-[]),rel([Ind]-[])|SRest]/SemSrel ]
```

In the case of non-subject relatives, the proposed analysis is given below (only relevant difference lists at each node are shown):

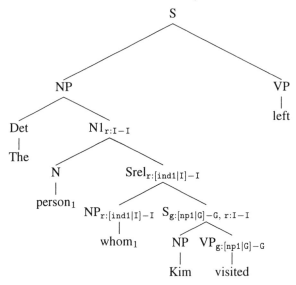

This tree assumes a lexical entry for *whom* similar to that for *who*, and the preceding grammar rule on p. 105. Top, middle and bottom rules for UDC handle the rest of the unifications, as explained above.

The analysis of relative clauses without a relative pronoun (e.g. *the person Kim visited left*) involves a rule $Srel \rightarrow S$ in which a gapped item in S is deleted and an index is introduced into the relativized indices list; a sketch of such a rule is given on p. 140.

Binding Theory Binding theory, as understood here, concerns the realization of certain pronouns in various contexts and the conditions under which reflexive and non-reflexive pronouns may occur within a sentence. The simplified theory given here is that a pronoun co-indexed with an item earlier in the subcat list of a word must be realized as a reflexive. If it is not earlier in the list, or not in the subcat list at all, it must not be realized as a reflexive (Sag and Wasow 1999). Under this formulation, earlier in the subcat list assumes that subjects are at the front of the subcat list, and hence earlier than all other items.

Reflexive pronoun Example: *Mike$_i$ likes himself$_i$/*him$_i$*.
The object pronoun refers to the subject *Mike*, and therefore must be realized as a reflexive.

Non-reflexive pronoun Example: *Ana$_i$ thought that she$_i$/*herself$_i$ had seen better films*.
The co-indexed pronoun does not appear on the subcat list of *thought* and hence may not be realized as a reflexive.

It is difficult to enforce these constraints through Prolog unification. However, they involve at least maintaining a list of index bindings as part of the lexical sign of a word. The syntactic part of the sign for *like* will be:

```
[vp,GapVP,Rel,Tense,NumPer,
    [ [np(TypeO),GapObj,RelObj,IndO,acc],   /* Subcat list */
      [np(TypeS),GapSubj,RelSubj,IndS,Case] ],
    [pron(TypeS,IndS),pron(TypeO,IndO)] ]   /* Index list (for
                                                 binding
                                                 constraints) */
```

This list is then accessed by a separate procedure to check that binding constraints are satisfied. Note that the list must include information as to the type of pronoun used, whether it is a `reflexive` pronoun or not. In this case, if `IndS` and `IndO` are bound together, then `TypeS` cannot be `refl` while `TypeO` must be so; if they are not bound, neither can be `refl`.

Aspects of Interpretation For most of the MT paradigms described here, semantic interpretation and representation are intimately connected with the paradigm in question. In consequence, semantic approaches are illustrated together with the appropriate MT system.

5.4 Parsing

Having described computationally feasible techniques for the analysis of various linguistic phenomena, this section presents a chart-parsing algorithm (Earley 1970) to derive syntactic and semantic analyses according to a grammar. The parsing algorithm presented here is an instance of a more general framework which will be used both for parsing and generation (Shieber 1988), and whose overall structure is now given.

5.4.1 General Framework

The general framework employs a memoization (i.e. storing partial/previous results) technique and a dynamic programming procedure in order to construct all possible partial solutions to a particular problem (i.e. parsing or generation). A basic implementation of the framework involves two main data structures: edges and lists of edges. An edge records a partial analysis which may form part of the final solution to a problem. In the domain of parsing and generation, edges consists of partially satisfied PS rules known as "dotted rules". In addition, edges include bookkeeping information indicating which part of the final result the edge represents. There are two types of edge:

Active edges record potential constituents during processing. They consist of a dotted rule in which at least one daughter has not been satisfied. Thus, the dotted rule *NP → Det . N1* represents an NP in which the determiner has been satisfied (i.e. it has either been analysed or generated with this rule), but not the N1 constituent.

Inactive edges record complete constituents during processing. They consist of a dotted rule in which all daughters have been satisfied. For instance, an inactive edge with dotted rule $NP \rightarrow Det\ N1$. represents an NP in which both the determiner and the N1 phrase have been analysed (generated). Note that because of local ambiguity, inactive edges may record constituents which may never form part of a final analysis tree.

The general dynamic programming algorithm keeps two lists of edges:

Chart: The chart stores edges which have been incorporated into the analysis thus far. On termination, the chart will contain the complete analyses of the input (if any), together with all their dependent subanalyses. Edges are added to the chart from the agenda one by one; for each edge that is added, the two steps below are executed to derive new edges.

Agenda: This list stores edges awaiting to be added to the chart. These edges arise from the prediction and resolution steps in the algorithm (see below). Edges are added in a last in, first out fashion, effectively treating the agenda as a stack. The result is that processing is depth first. The algorithm terminates when the agenda is empty.

The following two main steps are applied iteratively until neither can be further applied, at which point processing terminates.

Prediction: This step adds active edges to the agenda. These edges consist of rules that are potential candidates for analysing (generating from) the input:

> If an active edge $A \rightarrow \alpha.B\beta$ is about to be added to the chart, where α and β are possibly empty lists of signs, then add to the agenda all edges of the form $B' \rightarrow .\gamma$, where $B' \rightarrow \gamma$ is a rule in the grammar and B and B' unify.

This is a top-down version (de Roeck 1983) of the prediction step. It requires the agenda to be initialized with all grammar rules whose mothers unify with the start symbol.

Resolution: The resolution step combines active and inactive edges in order to satisfy rules and build a syntactic tree. This step is also known as the completion step or the fundamental rule.

> If the chart contains edges of the form $A \rightarrow \alpha.B\beta$ and $B' \rightarrow \gamma.$, where B and B' unify, then create a new edge $A' \rightarrow \alpha'B''.\beta'$, which includes the result of unifying B and B', and add it to the agenda.

The step is applied each time a new edge is added to the chart: if the new edge is active, then it is combined with appropriate inactive edges already in the chart; if it is inactive, then it is combined with active edges. Additional restrictions to the resolution step are applied depending on whether parsing or generation is being implemented.

As will be seen, the overall goal of the algorithm is to compute all possible ways of applying the grammar to the input, and to store subanalyses at each point so that they may be reused by subsequent stages.

5.4.2   Chart Parsing

Parsing is a process that has as input a string of words and as output a syntactic (and/or semantic) analysis of the input. The parser applies a grammar and a lexicon to the input, in order to determine whether the input is grammatical or not, and if so, to establish its structure.

For parsing, the main modification to the general framework is an adjacency constraint to the prediction step which causes edges to combine only when the active edge immediately precedes the inactive edge. To enforce this constraint edges must include information regarding the start and end position of the portion of the input they describe. Normally, these positions are assumed to start before the first word in the sentence and end after the last one:

$$_0 \text{ Felix } _1 \text{ ate } _2 \text{ the } _3 \text{ mouse } _4$$

Thus, the active edge $NP \rightarrow Det \,.\, N1(2,3)$ covers the string *the*. The modified version of the resolution step is therefore:

> If the chart contains edges of the form $A \rightarrow \alpha.B\beta(\mathbf{i,j})$ and $B' \rightarrow \gamma.(\mathbf{j,k})$, where B and B' unify, then create a new edge $A' \rightarrow \alpha'B''.\beta'(\mathbf{i,k})$, which includes the result of unifying B and B', and add it to the agenda.

5.4.3   Example

Assume the following grammar:

S → NP VP	NP → Felix	Det → the
VP → V	NP → Det N1	N → mouse
VP → V NP	N1 → N	V → ate

To parse the input *Felix ate the mouse*, the agenda is initialized with the edge $S \rightarrow$. $NP\ VP(0,0)$, numbered [1] in Table 5.6, and the algorithm is started. The table shows the initial and final state of the chart for this sentence. The prediction step adds edges [2] and [3] from [1] to the agenda, which is not shown in this example. The first of these, $NP \rightarrow .\ Felix(0,0)$, is then added to the chart, and causes the resolution step to be invoked (but not the prediction step), adding edge [5] to the top of the agenda; no other predictions or resolutions are possible. This edge in turn is moved to the chart. Again the prediction step is inapplicable, but the completion step is ([1] and [5]), adding edge [6] to the top of the agenda. As [6] is moved to the chart, it fires the prediction step (the resolution step is inapplicable), resulting in edges [7] and [8] being pushed onto the agenda. These edges are then moved onto the chart, and the resolution and prediction steps fired as appropriate. The procedure continues until there are no more edges on the agenda, and neither of the steps is applicable. Note that edge [3] is eventually moved to the chart after the analyses starting with *Felix* are explored. This leads to the prediction step being invoked, pushing [4] onto the agenda. When moved to the chart, neither prediction nor resolution are possible and processing would then continue with the next item in the agenda if any. The result is the triangular table in Table 5.6, with fully spanning edges given just below the top right cell.

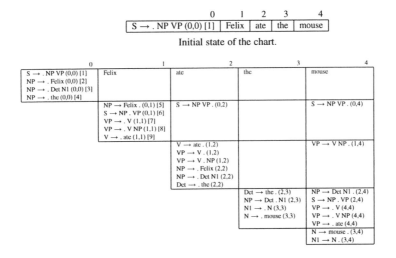

	0	1	2	3	4
S → . NP VP (0,0) [1]	Felix	ate	the	mouse

Initial state of the chart.

0	1	2	3	4
S → . NP VP (0,0) [1] NP → . Felix (0,0) [2] NP → . Det N1 (0,0) [3] NP → . the (0,0) [4]	Felix	ate	the	mouse
	NP → Felix . (0,1) [5] S → NP . VP (0,1) [6] VP → . V (1,1) [7] VP → . V NP (1,1) [8] V → . ate (1,1) [9]	S → NP VP . (0,2)		S → NP VP . (0,4)
		V → ate . (1,2) VP → V . (1,2) VP → V . NP (1,2) NP → . Felix (2,2) NP → . Det N1 (2,2) Det → . the (2,2)		VP → V NP . (1,4)
			Det → the . (2,3) NP → Det . N1 (2,3) N1 → . N (3,3) N → . mouse (3,3)	NP → Det N1 . (2,4) S → NP . VP (2,4) VP → . V (4,4) VP → . V NP (4,4) VP → . ate (4,4) N → mouse . (3,4) N1 → N . (3,4)

Final state of the chart.

Table 5.6. Chart parsing *Felix ate the mouse.*

5.4.4 Implementation Details

The parser can be divided into two main files: the chart management utilities, and the parser specific code. The former consists of the predicates for the general framework which are shared with the generators for the various MT systems. Gazdar and Mellish (1989) give actual Prolog code for an implementation. The chart management utilities essentially move edges from the top of the agenda onto the chart until the agenda is empty. Each time an edge is moved, the prediction and resolution steps are invoked on the edge, and any new edges thus created are pushed onto the agenda. When an edge is considered for addition to the chart, all edges in the chart which span the same portion of the input are tested to see if they subsume the new edge; if some such exists, the new edge is deleted. This test serves to prevent infinite left recursion loops which can arise in top-down parsers. For example, an adverbial modification dotted rule, such as *VP → . VP AP*, causes the prediction step to propose the addition of the rule *VP → . VP AP*, since the left daughter in the rule is identical to the mother. This second rule would in turn predict itself, and so on. A subsumption test eliminates the second edge and stops the rule from predicting itself infinitely many times.

The parser-specific code consists of a series of predicates which initialize the chart and the agenda, implement the prediction and resolution steps, and specify the conditions under which an edge constitutes a complete parse.

Both the chart and the agenda can be implemented as Prolog lists, with the append operation used to add items to them. For the parser, the agenda is initialized with all rules containing the start symbol as their mothers. The chart is initialized with the lexical signs for each of the words in the input, after morphological analysis has applied. This improves efficiency since top-down prediction and resolution only need to deal with lexical categories.

Finally, apart from the dotted rule and the start and end positions, each edge contains pointers to the edges and the rule from which it was derived, the input substring which it spans, and a unique identifier to facilitate reference to it.

5.5 Generation

In the most general case, Natural Language Generation (NLG) is the process of deriving linguistic expressions whose meanings correspond to some informational structure used as input. For example, the input to a natural language generator could be a set of financial statistics, with the output being an English summary of the fluctuations of various indicators (Kukich 1983). Alternatively it could be a presentation of some communicative goal and knowledge about the parts of an espresso machine, with the output being a graphical and textual explanation of how to use the machine (Wahlster et al. 1992).

5.5.1 Natural Language Generation

In Reiter and Dale (1997) the NLG generation process is decomposed into the six tasks summarized below. The description eschews many important issues, particularly in terms of the knowledge sources required for each task, and the details of the knowledge representation frameworks used. The description assumes a domain relating to students.

Content determination: This task decides on the information to be communicated and expresses it in the form of messages represented in a formal language. As an example, assume the following three messages about student George need to be communicated.

> Message(Msg1,Student(George)) *(i.e. George is a student)*
> Message(Msg2,Reside(George,London)) *(i.e. George lives in London)*
> Message(Msg3,Not(Like(George,London))) *(i.e. George does not like London)*

Discourse planning: Discourse planning orders messages into a suitable hierarchical structure, referred to as a text plan. The plan facilitates the generation of texts that have a coherent and logical structure and are therefore easier to read and understand. Messages are related to one another within a plan via discourse relations such as *explanation, justification, exemplification,* and others (Mann and Thompson 1988; Maier and Hovy 1993).

> Elaboration(Msg1,Contrast(Msg2,Msg3))

This structure indicates that message 2 contrasts with message 3, and that they are both elaborations on message 1.

Sentence aggregation: This process may be seen as taking a text plan as input and constructing a new plan in which messages have been aggregated into single sentence units consisting of one or more messages. Aggregation is not compulsory, and the above plan could easily be realized as three separate sentences. For the sake of argument, however, assume that contrasting sentences are combined into a single sentence using a conjunction:

Elaboration(Sent(Msg1),Sent(Conj,Contrast(Msg2,Msg3)))

Lexicalization: In Reiter and Dale (1997), lexicalization concerns the selection of lexical items in the language in order to represent relations or concepts, as opposed to discourse entities such as people, places, times and objects. In the current example, this phase might result in the following lexical items being selected for each predicate (note that since *George* and *London* are discourse entities, they are not lexicalized at this stage):

Student(..) → student   Reside(..) → live   Not(..) → not
Like(..) → like   Sent(Conj,Contrast(..)) → but

Different predicates can have different lexical realizations (e.g. *Reside*), in which case style, formality or other criteria may be used to select among them.

Referring expression generation: This task is similar to lexical realization, but crucially it involves the current context or discourse history in order to determine how an entity should be referred to. The options include the name of the entity, if there is one, a pronoun, and a definite phrase. Linguistic and discourse constraints lead to the following referring expressions for each entity:

First: George → George   London → London
Second: George → he   London → it
Third: George → he

Linguistic realization: This task has as input the results of the previous two tasks, and as output a syntactically and orthographically correct text. Its input can be structured as a graph of linguistic objects, and, in conjunction with a grammar, a sequence of sentences is generated.

Input: student(George)   but(live(he,London),not(like(he,it)))
Output: George is a student.   He lives in London, but he doesn't like it.

5.5.2 Semantic Head-Driven Generation

In MT, the semantic content and the broad discourse structure of a text are determined by the source text. Therefore it is usually enough for MT generation algorithms to implement only the last three tasks above: lexicalization, referring expression generation and linguistic realization. In particular, since the input to the generator is the output of a language analyser, it is convenient to build generators that effectively use a grammar in reverse, starting from a meaning representation and constructing a string of words which is grammatical, and whose meaning corresponds to the input meaning. A difficulty with this view, however, is that since the SL grammar and the TL grammars are different, there is no guarantee that the input to the generator will result in a TL sentence. This is an important problem in MT and one which has received some attention in the literature (Rosetta (pseud.) 1994; Huijsen 1998). Nevertheless, the notion of reversible grammars is an appealing one and algorithms have been developed to achieve reversibility. Semantic Head-Driven Generation (SHDG) (Shieber et al. 1990; Samuelsson 1996) is one of the better known such algorithms.

The SHDG algorithm takes as input a predicate argument structure representing the semantics to be expressed and the syntactic category of the phrase to be generated. The result is a syntactic tree with the given syntax and semantics, and whose leaves constitute the generated sentence. Three notions are needed in order to describe the algorithm.

Semantic head: The semantic head of a PS rule is the daughter whose semantics are bound to the semantics of the rule's mother. The VP is the semantic head in the following simple rule:

vp/Sem → np/SemNP vp/Sem

Chain rule: A PS rule with a semantic head. The previous rule is a chain rule.

Non-chain rule: A PS rule without a semantic head. For instance:

s/but(Sem1,Sem2) → s/Sem1 'but' s/Sem2

Processing may be seen as a virtual traversal of the final analysis tree, with those paths in the tree containing chain rules expanded first. The effect of this regime is to make available lexical information, including subcat lists, before complements are generated. The regime also enables grammars with semantic non-monotonicity to be handled. A semantically monotonic grammar is one where the semantics of each daughter is included in some portion of the semantics of the mother. The following grammar rule is not semantically monotonic:

vp/renounce(SemNP) → vp/give np/SemNP p/up

That is, the structure *renounce(SemNP)*, representing the meaning of *give up*, does not subsume *give* nor *up* (but it does include *SemNP*).

It is possible to specialize the general chart framework for SHDG. The main modifications needed are in the prediction and resolution steps:

Prediction: This step is now sensitive to chain and non-chain rules. Its effect is to expand semantic heads before other daughters.

If an active edge $A \rightarrow \alpha.B\beta$ is about to be added to the chart, where α and β are possibly empty lists of signs, then add to the agenda all edges of the form $B'' \rightarrow .\gamma$, where $B' \rightarrow \gamma$ is a **non-chain** rule in the grammar, B and B' unify **and B'' is identical to B' but with its semantics unified with those of B. Also, add to the agenda all edges of the form $B'' \rightarrow \gamma.C\delta$ where $B' \rightarrow \gamma C\delta$ is a chain rule in the grammar with semantic head C**

Resolution: When the active daughter is satisfied, it must be marked as such, and the dot moved to the leftmost unmarked (unsatisfied) daughter. Below, marked daughters are underlined.

If the chart contains edges of the form $A \rightarrow \alpha.B\beta$ and $B' \rightarrow \gamma.$, where B and B' unify, then create a new edge $\mathbf{A}' \rightarrow \delta.\mathbf{D}\zeta$ and add it to the agenda, **where $\alpha'\mathbf{B}''\beta' = \delta\mathbf{D}\zeta$, and α', B'', β' include the result of unifying B and B' (note that D is the leftmost unmarked daughter and B'' is marked).**

These conditions ensure that after satisfying the semantic head, the next daughter to be satisfied may occur before or after it. The table below gives examples of an active edge combining with an inactive edge in two different cases.

	Semantic head of Act. is leftmost	Semantic head of Act. is not leftmost
Act.:	vp/Sem → . v/Sem np/SemO	s/Sem → np/SemS . vp/Sem
Ina.:	v/eat(x,y) → 'ate' .	vp/run(x) → v/run(x) .
New:	vp/eat(x,y) → v/eat(x,y) . np/SemO	s/run(x) → . np/SemS vp/run(x)

Generation begins with a sign made up of the grammar's start category and the semantics to be generated. The agenda is then initialized as for parsing; that is, by applying the prediction step on this sign. The resulting edges are added to the agenda, and moved into the chart one by one, following the procedure outlined in Section 5.4.1.

5.5.3 Example

As an example, consider the following simple grammar, which provides much information at the lexical level, and whose semantics are not monotonic (e.g. the semantics for *calls* does not subsume that of *up*).

s/Sem → Subj vp:[Subj]/Sem
vp:Subcat/Sem → vp:[Comp | Subcat]/Sem Comp
vp:[NP/Obj, P/up, np/Subj]/ring(Subj,Obj) → 'calls'
np/ana → 'Ana'
np/raquel → 'Raquel'
p/up → 'up'

For the sign *s/ring(ana,raquel)* as input, the generation algorithm will build up the following analysis tree.

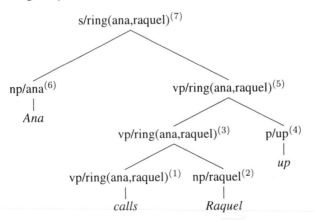

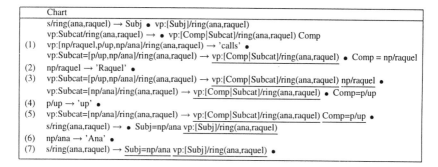

Table 5.7. A generation chart.

The superscripts indicate the order in which the nodes are built. Thus, the first lexical item to be generated is the verb, since it is the semantic head for the sentence. This in turn determines the semantic and syntactic category of the verb complements, which are then generated in turn. Table 5.7 is a detailed trace of the edges in the chart as the tree is built. Edges are added to the chart in the order given. Note that since the generator is driven top-down, the first nodes in the chart expand the tree along the branch leading to the semantic head (1). It is clear that the agenda is not shown in this trace, but it follows from the general framework that edges are first stored in the agenda prior to processing.

On comparing the charts in Tables 5.6 and 5.7 it would seem that the data structures are very different. In fact they only differ in the way the chart is organized: in the parsing chart, edges are organized by their position, so that adjacent edges may be easily selected; in the generation chart organization may be by syntactic category or by semantic representation, both of which facilitate identification of edges that are likely to combine successfully.

Two general problems that affect generation algorithms are completeness and coherence.

- Problems of **completeness** arise when the generator does not "say" everything that the semantic representation expresses. For example, if the semantics were

    $eat(john,qterm(the,X,banana(X)))$

    the grammar could potentially treat this as an instance of $eat(john,Y)$ and generate only *John ate*, rather than the correct *John ate a banana*.
- Problems of **coherence** arise when the generator "says" more than what is implied in the semantics. An example would be if the input were $eat(john,Z)$ and the generator produced *John ate the banana*.

Clearly the goal is to express all and only that which is indicated in the meaning representation. This is problematic, however, for two reasons. Technically, a unification formalism can treat semantic representations with differing information as compatible. Also, there is no guarantee that the TL grammar can express precisely what is in the meaning representation, or it may do so in an awkward way. For example, the concept of *evening* has to be approximated in Spanish by *tarde* (afternoon), which it overlaps in content but is not completely equivalent to.

One way of ensuring completeness and coherence is to build a shadow semantic representation based on the the grammar and lexical entries employed during generation (Shieber et al. 1990). After generation has terminated, the shadow structure is compared with the original input: if either contains material not in the other, then the result is not complete or coherent.

An alternative is to allow mismatches between the input semantics and the semantics of the phrase being generated. This results in several possible renderings for the same input, differing from one another in what they convey. One of these is then selected based on some measure of dissimilarity between it and the input. This measure can be the weighted sum of the over- and undergenerated material, with the weight of a meaning component correlating with its importance. This alternative approach is useful where there are clashes between the input semantics and the grammar, which occurs when metaphorical and figurative language is used (e.g. *British Gas came yesterday*).

A combination of both these alternatives is possible: a shadow representation is built, and after generation terminates, all shadow representations thus constructed are compared with the original input, and a dissimilarity measure calculated. The sentence whose meaning representation has the lowest score is chosen as the final result.

One problem with the SHDG algorithm is worth mentioning (Alshawi and Pulman 1992, p. 272): there may be situations in which the left to right generation regime for non-semantic head daughters leads to unacceptable non-determinism. Consider the following rule for auxiliary inversion in yes–no questions:

```
[s]/(E,[ynq,AuxSem]) --->
  [    [vp(aux),[ VP, Subj ]]/(E,AuxSem),
       Subj,
       VP ]
```

As a non-chain rule, daughters will be generated in left to right order. After generating the auxiliary verb, the subject phrase is processed next. However, its semantic value cannot be determined until the VP has been generated, since it is its lexical entry, and in particular its subcat value, that determines which portion of the overall semantic representation corresponds to the subject's semantics. Alshawi and Pulman (1992) therefore restrict the recursive invocation of the SHDG algorithm to daughters whose semantics are instantiated. However, this modification does not allow for partially instantiated semantics, as may be the case if a rule imposes selectional or other semantic restrictions on its daughters.

5.5.4 Implementation Details

In an implementation, the chart could be organized as a list for both parsing and generation in order to simplify the algorithm somewhat, at the expense of computational efficiency. When an edge is added, the prediction step is executed as before, but the resolution step is attempted between the new edge and all edges currently in the chart.

Edges for generation have a similar structure to parsing edges: an edge id, a mother and a list of daughter categories, a list of lexical leaves and the ids of the edges of which it is made up. In addition, the edge contains a slot with the sign for the semantic head, if any, or null if the rule is not a chain rule. When the resolution step is invoked, two cases are considered: (1) if a semantic head exists and has not been satisfied, unification is against the sign for the semantic head; (2) if the edge does not consist of a chain rule, or the semantic head has been satisfied already, unification is against the leftmost active daughter. Care must be taken to ensure that the semantic head is not satisfied twice, and that its lexical leaves are inserted into the appropriate position in the sentence being constructed. An integer can be used to record the position of the semantic head within the daughters of a rule to avoid this problem.

5.6 Conclusion

Morphological analysis, syntactic processing and NLG are important areas in CL and MT. Yet the fact that many commercial MT systems do not adopt the techniques developed in these areas indicates that such techniques are not without their problems, the most obvious being:

- Under-generation: The knowledge that these algorithms require is usually incomplete for a particular language. For example, no complete PS grammar exists for the syntax of any natural language. Clearly this affects the kinds of texts that an MT system can translate.
- Over-generation: Any non-trivial NL grammar accepts sentences which are not really acceptable by native speakers of the language. For analysis, this may not be a great problem (although see ambiguity below), but for generation, it is clearly undesirable to produce ungrammatical strings.
- Ambiguity: The morphological, lexical, syntactic and semantic structures of a sentence normally contain ambiguities that cannot be resolved easily given the knowledge bases in the system. The causes of ambiguity include over-generation and lack of contextual information.
- Brittleness: Many of the algorithms developed are sensitive to small errors in the input. If a sentence deviates slightly from its expected form, it is deemed unacceptable regardless of the severity of the deviance.
- Extendability: Extending the knowledge bases (e.g. syntactic and morphological rules) involves specialist (computational) linguistic knowledge which cannot be expected of the average user of an MT system, making it expensive for users to extend and adapt software.

Each of these issues is being actively addressed and their resolution should enable a greater degree of technology transfer between CL and MT.

5.6.1 Further Reading

Two-level morphological analysis was developed in the early 1980s (Kosken-niemi 1983; Kaplan and Kay 1994). The morphology framework adopted is based on that of Ritchie et al. (1992) and their English lexicon system. The compilation procedure is based on work by Bear (1985). Many people's first experience of two-level morphology is via the PC-KIMMO system (Antworth 1990), which is still available through the Internet. The study in Sproat (1992) presents many important multilingual issues not addressed here, while Volume 22, Number 2 (1996) is a special issue of *Computational Linguistics* devoted to Computational Phonology. The work of Kiraz (in press) extends the two-level system to multiple levels in the analysis of Semitic languages. There are algebraic algorithms for compiling rules into automata (Kaplan and Kay 1994; Mohri and Sproat 1996; Grimley-Evans et al. 1996). Two-level descriptions of languages other than English include French (Lun 1983), Finnish (Koskenniemi 1983), Rumanian (Khan 1983), Spanish and German (Dorr 1993, pp. 359–61), Japanese (Alam 1983) and Korean (Kwon and Karttunen 1996). Bennett (1993) presents translation problems from the point of view of morphology. Additional resources include the ARIES tools for Spanish processing (Coñi et al. 1997) and the Xerox finite state tools (Karttunen 1996), both accessible through the Internet.

A good starting point on contemporary formal grammar is Sag and Wasow (1999). The structure of the agreement predicate presented here is a simplified version of that in Kathol (1999). A formal treatment of English relative clauses in terms of construction types is described in Sag (1997), while Keenan (1985) surveys relative clauses cross-linguistically. Further material on the topics discussed can be found in Pollard and Sag (1994) and Borsley (1996). HPSG analyses of various Romance languages including Spanish can be found in Balari and Dini (1998). Two important areas not covered in much detail here are ellipsis (Dalrymple et al. 1991; Lappin and Shih 1996) and coordination (Grover 1996; Gazdar et al. 1985). The grammar in Alshawi (1992) also handles these and other relevant phenomena.

Many other linguistic theories have appeared. Some have even been applied to MT: Government and Binding (GB) (Dorr 1993), Lexical Functional Grammar (LFG) (Kaplan and Wedekind 1993; Emele and Dorna 1998), Head-Driven Phrase Structure Grammar (HPSG) (Copestake et al. 1995; Becker et al. 1998) and Unification Categorial Grammar (UCG) (Beaven 1992b).

Since parsing is a common process in programming language compilation as well as in NLP, it has received much attention. There are several kinds of parsing regimes and search strategies (King 1983; Aho et al. 1986; van Noord 1994). Chart parsing can be traced back to at least Earley (1970). It is described in many introductory NLP books (Allen 1995; Gazdar and Mellish 1989; Pereira and Shieber 1987). Parsers can be made more efficient by compiling grammars into LR parsing tables (Samuelsson 1994) or by using head-driven techniques (van Noord 1997); there is also work on approximating context-free grammars to finite state machines for speech recognition (Mohri and Pereira 1998). Parsing with unification grammars complicates matters somewhat, as there is a danger of non-termination (Shieber 1985; Harrison and Ellison 1992; Samuelsson 1994).

The book has omitted discussion of an important tool in contemporary computational linguistics, namely feature structures and their derivatives (Shieber

1986; Carpenter 1992), although see Section 7.2.3 for some discussion. This omission is not as grave as it may at first appear: the techniques presented here can be adapted to feature structure formalisms. Furthermore, by translating linguistic analyses found in the literature into Prolog terms, their main computational properties can be tested more easily.

A uniform framework for parsing and generation was proposed by Shieber (1988). An overview of practical aspects of NLG in general as well as a clear exposition of the main stages in NLG is given in Reiter and Dale (1997) and Reiter and Dale (2000). SHDG is based on work by Shieber et al. (1990). A relatively accessible collection of papers on generation is Adorni and Zock (1996). Wilcock and Matsumoto (1998) discuss generation in HPSG. Techniques for improving parser execution time have also been applied to generation (Samuelsson 1996). Volume 11(1–3) of the *Machine Translation* journal (1996) is a special issue on Lexical Choice, while Volume 24(4) of the *Computational Linguistics* journal (1998) is a special issue on Natural Language Generation.

It is worth noting here the doubt cast by Shieber (1993) on the completeness of generators, due to what he calls the problem of "logical-form equivalence": the problem of guaranteeing that a generator will construct a sentence from any meaning representation that is equivalent to those produced by the grammar of the language. The argument is formulated with reference to a traditional distinction between language independent strategic generation (i.e. deciding what to say) from linguistically oriented tactical generation (i.e. deciding how to say it) (Thompson 1977), and contends that either the strategic generator will need grammatical knowledge when building the semantic content of the utterance, or the tactical generator will need powerful, general-purpose reasoning to produce a sentence, possibly leading to issues of incompleteness.

Finally, the journals *Computational Linguistics*, *Language Engineering* and *Computer Speech and Language* carry CL articles.

6 Transfer Machine Translation

*The objective of this chapter is to present classic translation problems
and the way they are handled in transfer-based MT systems.*

As already outlined (Section 1.3), in transfer MT the source language is analysed into an SL-dependent representation which is then transferred into a TL-
dependent representation, from which a TL sentence is generated via some generation procedure. At a minimum, transfer systems require monolingual modules
to analyse and generate sentences, and transfer modules to relate translationally
equivalent representations of those sentences. Figure 6.1 shows the minimum
components of a multilingual transfer system for three languages.

Transfer systems are generally regarded as a practical compromise between
the efficient use of resources of interlingua systems, and the ease of implementation of direct systems. However, it is clear that for a general multilingual system
the number of transfer modules grows polynomially in the number of languages.
That is, for n languages, one needs at least $[n(n-1)]/2$ transfer modules. This
is because for each of the n languages, there are $(n-1)$ possible TL in a fully
multilingual system. If these modules are reversible, then only half of this num-

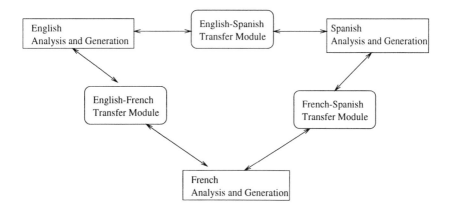

FIG. 6.1. Minimal Transfer Architecture

121

ber of transfer modules are required. This is an obvious disadvantage of transfer systems, since they become more expensive the more languages they have.

Nevertheless, there are many factors which make transfer an attractive design for MT.

1. Many systems are bilingual, or their principal use is for translation in one direction between a limited number of languages.
2. Where full multilinguality is required, it is possible to have a hub language into and out of which all translation is done.
3. Portions of transfer modules can be shared when closely related languages are involved. For example, an English–Portuguese module may share several transformations with an English–Spanish module.

One distinguishing feature of different transfer MT systems is the level to which analysis is carried out. At one end, a system may do little more than morphological processing and shallow phrase segmentation before transfer takes place. At the other end, systems have been proposed in which the only transfer that takes place is lexical transfer, with all structural differences between the two languages removed (see Fig. 1.1). What is more, some MT systems effect transfer at multiple levels of linguistic analysis, where each level supplies constraints on TL structures (Kaplan and Wedekind 1993).

This chapter describes three different types of transfer system, presented from what may be regarded as a prototypical view of the sub-strategy they instantiate. As such, they are only loosely based on actual systems, where compromises between theoretical purity and practical applicability are always necessary. For expository purposes the three types are called syntactic, semantic and lexicalist.

6.1   Syntactic Transfer MT

Syntactic transfer systems rely on mappings between the surface structure of sentences: a collection of tree-to-tree transformations is applied recursively to the analysis tree of the SL sentence in order to construct a TL analysis tree. Figure 6.2 illustrates a simple tree-to-tree transfer module to translate the English noun phrase *A delicious soup* into its Spanish translation *Una sopa deliciosa*. The transformations include translation variables, indicated by *tv*, that relate translationally equivalent portions of the source and target structures. In the case of the N1 phrase, the positions of the adjective and noun are swapped: the translation variable *tr(A)* occurs as the left daughter of $N1$ on the source tree, but as the right daughter in the target $N1'$ tree.

Given that transformations result in complete parse trees in the target language, the notion of generation as understood here is not applicable in this approach. In fact, it is possible to build syntactic transfer systems where the only generation undertaken is morphological generation. However, some syntactic transfer systems include tree-to-tree transformations during generation. These transformations deal with syntactic and semantic discrepancies not accounted

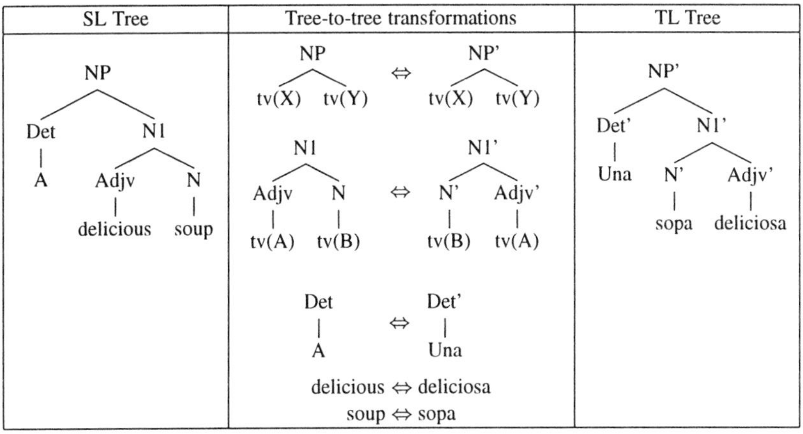
SL Tree
Tree-to-tree transformations
TL Tree
NP
Det
N1
A
Adjv
N
delicious
soup
NP ⇔ NP'
tv(X) tv(Y) tv(X) tv(Y)
N1 ⇔ N1'
Adjv N N' Adjv'
tv(A) tv(B) tv(B) tv(A)
Det ⇔ Det'
A Una
delicious ⇔ deliciosa
soup ⇔ sopa
NP'
Det'
N1'
Una
N'
Adjv'
sopa
deliciosa

FIG. 6.2. Example transfer with tree-to-tree transformations.

for during transfer. Their purpose is to simplify transfer by allowing it to produce incorrect TL trees. This aids multilinguality, since it shifts the workload from the bilingual component to the monolingual one.

The tree-to-tree transformation algorithm is a recursive, non-deterministic, top-down process in which one side of the tree-to-tree transfer rules is matched against the input structure, resulting in the structure on the right-hand side. The transformation algorithm is then called recursively on the value of the transfer variables to yield the corresponding TL structure. The following Prolog program is a standalone implementation of the NP to NP transfer example shown in Fig. 6.2.

```
:- op(500,xfx, '<==>').
:- op(450,xfx, dtrs).

[np] dtrs [ DetE, N1E ] <==> [np] dtrs [ DetS, N1S ] :-
     DetE <==> DetS,
     N1E  <==> N1S.

[n1] dtrs [ [adjv] dtrs [ AdjvE ],
            [n] dtrs [ NE ] ]     <==>
[n1] dtrs [ [n] dtrs [ NS ],
            [adjv] dtrs [ AdjvS ]]  :-
     AdjvE <==> AdjvS,
     NE    <==> NS.

[det] dtrs [a] <==> [det] dtrs [una].
delicious      <==> deliciosa.
soup           <==> sopa.
```

Given this (simple) transfer module, the following call with an English tree results in the corresponding Spanish NP.

```
[np] dtrs [ [det] dtrs [a],
```

```
        [n1]  dtrs [ [adjv] dtrs [delicious],
                     [n]    dtrs [soup]]]   <==>
    SpTree.
```

A realistic transfer module need not include fully inflected forms but only root forms. Furthermore, syntactic categories will be richer, incorporating person, number, tense and other information relevant to translation. The application of each transformation is a non-deterministic process which will normally lead to ambiguities, particularly at the lexical level. Since disambiguation is a general problem to all the approaches discussed in this book, it is discussed in Chapter 9. This section concentrates on issues pertaining particularly to syntactic transfer.

6.1.1   Translation Test Cases

Most problems common to NLP are clearly relevant to MT: disambiguation, anaphora resolution, robustness etc. However, a number of problems have been identified which relate more specifically to translation (Lindop and Tsujii 1991; Dorr 1993). These problems are regarded as peculiar to translation, since they arise from divergences and mismatches between source and target sentences, and can be potentially difficult to handle by MT systems.

A translation **divergence** normally implies that the meaning is conveyed by the translation, although syntactic structure and semantic distribution of meaning components is different in the two languages. By contrast, a translation **mismatch** implies a difference in information content between the source and target sentence. This book is mostly concerned with translation divergences, although mismatches can be approached from a KBMT perspective (Section 7.2).

The following classification of divergences is based on the works just mentioned, and includes the additional categories of collocational and multi-lexeme divergences. Some of the examples may be seen as belonging to more than one divergence class: lexicalization divergences, for instance, normally involve categorial divergences also.

The very simplest tree-to-tree transformations for each case are given in order to illustrate the problem induced by the phenomena. For the moment, only the structural aspects of the translations are discussed; issues of morphology and other markings are considered separately.

Thematic Thematic divergences relate to changes in the grammatical role played by arguments in a predicate. The classic example is that of the verb *like* and its Spanish translation *gustar*.

> En: *You* like **her**.
> Sp: **Ella** *te* gusta.
> Lit: She you-ACC pleases

The grammatical object in English appears as subject in Spanish and vice versa. A mapping between the syntactic structures of these sentences needs to access both the subject and the object within the same transformation, and place them in different positions within the target structure:

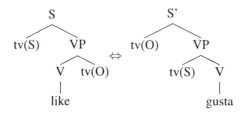

Such transformations can potentially involve a clash in the agreement properties of the verb, as well as discrepancies in the case marking and clitic structure of the target sentence. These issues will be taken up again.

Head Switching In head switching, the syntactic head of an expression in one language is not translated as a syntactic head, but as a modifier, a complement or some other constituent.

> En: The baby **just** ate.
> Sp: El bebé **acaba de** comer.
> Lit: The baby finished of to-eat

While *ate* is the syntactic head in English, its translation is not a syntactic head in Spanish; instead, it is a complement to the syntactic head.

Head switching as a translation phenomenon has received significant attention in the MT literature (Estival et al. 1990; Sadler and Thompson 1991; Whitelock 1992; Kaplan and Wedekind 1993). As a first approximation, the following transformation may be proposed:

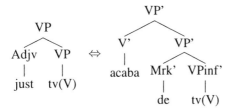

The VPinf requires the resulting verb phrase to be headed by an infinitive verb. Furthermore, transfer must ensure that the Spanish verb *acaba* receives appropriate syntactic features such as person, number and tense.

Structural The following translation exhibits structural divergence, since the English VP consists of a transitive verb and its NP complement, while the Spanish VP consists of a verb and a PP complement.

> En: Luisa **entered** the house.
> Sp: Luisa **entró a** la casa.
> Lit: Luisa entered to the house

Transfer in these cases can be achieved with:

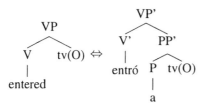

Again, we ignore morphological, tense and other non-structural phenomena for the moment.

Lexical Gap Lexical gaps are single-word concepts in one language which can only be rendered by two or more words in the other. A clear example is:

> En: Camilo **got up early**.
> Sp: Camilo **madrugó**.

The relevant transformation involves no translation variables:

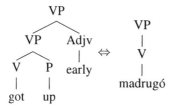

The transfer rule is just a direct mapping between the trees for the source and target phrases.

Lexicalization According to Talmy (1985), languages distribute semantic content differently within a sentence. Consider the sentences:

> En: Susan **swam across** the channel.
> Sp: Susan **cruzó** el canal **nadando**.
> Lit: Susan crossed the channel swimming

In English, manner (i.e. swimming) and motion are packaged in the verb *swam* while the notion for the path travelled is packaged in the preposition *across*. By contrast, the Spanish verb *cruzó* packages motion and path, while the manner in which the motion is carried out is encoded in the gerundive *nadando*.

A possible transformation for overcoming this particular divergence would be:

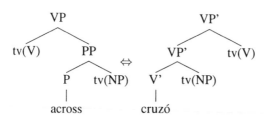

This transformation renders an English proposition as a verb in Spanish and thus could be seen as a categorial divergence. However, the fact that it involves additional structural rearrangement accords it separate mention. In addition, gerundive inflection needs to be enforced for the Spanish verb.

Categorial When otherwise semantically inter-translatable words are rendered via different syntactic categories, the translation is said to exhibit categorial divergence. In the following example, an English adjective is translated as a Spanish noun:

> En: A **little** bread.
> Sp: Un **poco de** pan.
> Lit: A bit of bread

This case is one of head switching also, and may be handled as such.

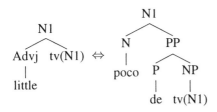

Note that not all categorial divergences involve head switching: *I am hungry – Tengo hambre (I have hunger)*.

Collocational Collocational divergences arise when the modifier, complement or head of a word is different from its default translation. Support verbs are common examples of this type of divergence (Danlos and Samvelian 1992).

> En: Jan **made** a decision.
> Sp: Jan **tomó/*hizo** una decisión.
> Lit: Jan took/*made a decision

The default Spanish translation for *make* is *hacer*, but as a support verb for *decision* it must be translated as *tomar*. In principle one could handle such divergences by listing all combinations of relevant collocations (e.g. *take a walk – dar una caminada (give a walk), be thirsty – tener sed (have thirst)*, etc.) and having specific transformations for each:

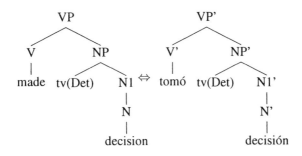

These transformations would apply before other default translations effectively overriding them. However, this makes for an inflexible solution. An alternative is to view the problem as one of disambiguation, and as such could be handled using the techniques of Chapter 9. Alternatively, lexical entries may be enriched with collocational information (Mel'čuk and Zholkovsky 1988; Danlos and Samvelian 1992), which could then be exploited by a single collocation transfer rule.

Multi-lexeme and Idiomatic Multi-lexeme and idiomatic divergences include those in which a phrase in one language corresponds to a phrase in another language, without there being a clear translation relation between their individual words. The gloss below shows that the words in the Spanish translation do not correspond to those in the English phrase:

> En: Socrates kicked the bucket.
> Sp: Socrates estiró la pata.
> Lit: Socrates stretched the leg.

The following is an example of a non-idiomatic divergence (i.e. it must be translated as a group and not word-for-word) in this category:

> En: Frank is **as** tall **as** Orlaith.
> Sp: Frank es **tan** alto **como** Orlaith.
> Lit: Frank is as tall as Orlaith.

One can do little more than establish appropriate transformations for each specific divergence in this category. The main decision to make, however, is how much structure to allow within the idiom. This in turn is determined by how variable the idiom is. For example, certain adjectives do not affect idiomatic meaning (e.g. *Socrates kicked the proverbial bucket*), but idiomatic meaning in this case is not preserved in the passive: *The bucket was kicked by Socrates*. A possible rule is:

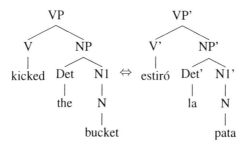

6.1.2 Generality

According to the algorithm illustrated in the Prolog code on p. 123, these transformations are structurally too specific. For example, the collocation example

(p. 127) assumes that there are no additional subtrees between *made*, the determiner and *decision*, which may not be the case (e.g. ... *made some difficult decisions* ...). Analogous situations arise with the transformations for multi-lexeme divergences, as already mentioned, but also in thematic (e.g. *You definitely like her*), head switching (*the baby obviously just ate*) (Kaplan and Wedekind 1993), lexicalisation (*Susan swam straight across the channel*) and categorial (e.g. *A little more bread*) divergences. In the general case any number of subtrees can intervene between the lexical items that trigger a transfer rule, and the point in the analysis tree at which the transfer rule needs to be applied.

At the same time, the transformations presented in the previous section are too general, since translation variables are not sensitive to the values they match. For example, the thematic divergence on p. 125 will apply to pronominal and non-pronominal subjects, which is incorrect for the latter, as they involve a redundant clitic and the translation of the non-pronominal subject (Butt and Benjamin 1994, pp. 141,153).

> En: **The students** like her.
> Sp: Ella **le** gusta a **los estudiantes**.
> Lit: She CL pleases to the students

Both these issues can be addressed through the underlying unification framework assumed in this book. Firstly, the grammar must make available, through its sign semantics, the lexical head of a phrase (Section 6.1.3). The effect is to simulate governing relations amongst lexical items, such as have been found useful in various MT systems (Durand et al. 1991; Johnson and Watanabe 1991). Secondly, the value matched by translation variables can be accessed to determine if a specific lexical item appears as the leaf of a phrasal tree. The following diagram presents the collocation example (p. 127) with these modifications:

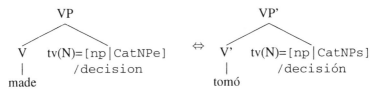

Translation variable *tv(N)* will only match noun phrases whose semantic component is *decision* and *decisión* respectively.

Other problems arise with divergences involving category changes and constituent rearrangement, deletion and insertion. For example, lexicalization divergences could be expressed as a series of transformations in order to make them more modular:

```
[vp]/_ dtrs [ Xe=[vp|RestVPe]/_, Ye=PP/Pe ]
<==>
[vp]/_ dtrs [ Ys=VPs/Vs, Xs=[vp,_,_,ing|RestVPs]/_ ] :-

                    _/Pe <==> _/Vs, % Restrict rule to licensed
                                    % p <-> vp mappings.
                    Xe <==> Xs,     % If licensed, map vp <-> vp
                    Ye <==> Ys.     %     and pp <-> vp
```

For this rule to apply, there must be a lexical transfer rule relating an English preposition and a Spanish verb:

```
[p|_]/across <==> [vp|_]/cruzar.
```

Furthermore, the complete VP and PP phrases must be transformed into one another by special rules in the transfer module. Transformations such as these need to be used with care, since they apply in very specific contexts and can lead to gross inefficiency or incorrect translations if not restricted in their application.

6.1.3 Semantics

There is little need for a theoretically motivated logic-oriented semantic representation in syntactic transfer systems. Part of the reason for this is that such theories are normally concerned with the scope of quantifiers and other operators. Instead, it is more convenient to use dependency schemes (Allegranza et al. 1991; Hudson 1984; Mel'čuk 1979) that make available relevant information to a transformation. These schemes view every phrase as consisting of a governor and optional dependents, where dependents may be optionally classified further (Somers 1987). For example, *Camilo saw the horses in the field* has the following simplified dependency analysis, with governors depicted as mothers and dependents as daughters:

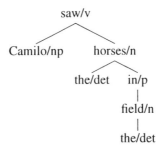

The syntactically and semantically dominating word in a phrase is selected as the governor, with modifiers and complements acting as dependents. When syntactic and semantic criteria conflict, as in the case of auxiliaries, support verbs and some specifiers, semantic criteria may override; however, this is conditioned by practical considerations in terms of the information that is needed for transfer.

Grammatical signs incorporate dependency structures in their semantic component, with PS rules determining which of the daughters is a governor. For the local trees on p. 129, the semantics of the verb and noun respectively need to be the semantics of their respective mothers, and thus the governors of the phrase:

```
[vp]/Sem --->                    [np]/Sem --->
      [ [vp]/Sem,                      [ [det]/_,
        [np]/_ ]                         [n1]/Sem ]
```

6.1.4 Compositionality

The idea of compositionality in MT was raised by Jan Landsbergen at least as early at 1980 in the context of the Rosetta project (Rosetta (pseud.) 1994). Compositionality in MT dictates that the translation of the whole is made up of the translation of the parts. As a goal, it can clearly be applied to transfer and interlingua MT.

In transfer MT it has played an important role in many experimental systems. For example, it is studied in detail in Alshawi et al. (1992, pp. 297–301) whose idea is to investigate and test the effect of complex transfer rules in different grammatical and divergence contexts. Compositionality is also considered by Sadler and Thompson (1991) and Dorr (1993, p. 277ff) among others. To illustrate some of the issues involved consider the following translation:

> En: I think Clara just swam across the pool.
> Sp: Creo que Clara acaba de cruzar la piscina nadando.
> Lit: I-think that Clara finished of to-cross the swimming-pool swimming.

These translations consist of a head switching and a lexicalization divergence embedded in a sentential complement. A possible problem that might arise is that *think* has a complement headed by *swim*, while Spanish *creo* (I think) has a complement headed by *acaba* (she finished), which additionally has a complement headed by *cruzar* (to cross). This is shown in the bracketing below, with the governor given in italics after the slash:

> [s/*think* [np/i I] [vp/*think* think [s/*swim* Clara just swam across the pool]]]
> [s/*creer* [vp/*creer* Creo [srel/*acabar* [rel/*que* que] [s/*acabar* Clara acaba de cruzar la piscina nadando]]]]

If transformations require governors of corresponding phrases to be translationally equivalent, it would be impossible to translate these sentences. However, if this requirement is relaxed, then these sentences can be transformed into each other. For example, the transformation for *think* might be expressed as:

```
[vp]/_ dtrs [ VPe, Se=[s]/_ dtrs _ ] <==>
[vp]/_ dtrs [ VPs, [srel]/_ dtrs [ [rel]/que, Ss=[s]/_ dtrs _ ]]
   :-
   VPe <==> VPs,
   Se <==> Ss.

[vp]/think <==> [vp]/creer.
```

The effect of this underspecification is that a shell TL tree is built into which lexical items are subsequently inserted by lexical transfer rules such as the *think – creer* entry given here. When the recursion enters via Se <==> Ss, different transfer rules will match. Some will fail later on, while others succeed, especially those taking into account the divergences involved. The one that succeeds then needs to be validated by the TL grammar (Section 6.1.6), since in general, the TL tree built will be underspecified. The underspecification arises because the interplay of various divergences cannot be predicted at the local level, but rather must be established once transfer rules have applied.

6.1.5 Morphological Features

Morphological features convey a variety of information crucial to sentence understanding. However, many morphological features could be said to lie at the intersection between syntax and semantics: sometimes they express actual semantic content, and sometimes they indicate purely syntactic properties, with no obvious semantic correlate. In transfer MT the following cases can arise in terms of the morphological information contained in different words:

- Information is copied when the two languages make similar use of a specific feature. English and Spanish number, for instance, tends to correspond: *dog/dogs – perro/perros, man/men – hombre/hombres*. There are exceptions, however, that can lead to difficulties. In *the trousers are dirty – el pantalón está sucio*, the Spanish sentence has a singular subject (*el pantalón*), with corresponding singular verb and adjective.
- A morphological feature leads to a divergence. For example, by and large, count and mass nouns in English and Spanish correspond, but there are situations when a count noun corresponds to a mass noun, as in *two pieces of furniture – dos muebles*. The problem is determining when a feature can be copied and when not.
- A morphological feature does not exist in one of the languages. Gender distinctions in nouns, for instance, are not made in English: *the door – la puerta*, where *puerta* has feminine gender. Such discrepancies cause problems when the distinction has semantic consequences: *a friend – un/una amigo/amiga*.
- The same feature has different translations in the TL: *the sausages* are burning – *las salchichas se* queman (the sausages burn).
- Some morphological processes do not exist or are not as productive as those in the other language. Some masculine tree names in Spanish, for instance, derive from their corresponding feminine gender fruit names: *almond – almendra, almond tree – almendro*.

Some of these problems have solutions similar to those for the divergences presented in 6.1.1. Others are instances of ambiguity or can only be solved through deeper text understanding. Yet others can be tackled by prioritizing transformations so that some are attempted first, and thus override other applicable default transformations. For example, more specific transformations may be applied before less specific ones (Estival et al. 1990), or transformations may be tried in a given order, as is done in Prolog.

However, situations in which corresponding morphological features do not have the exact same distribution raise specific issues. Consider:

En: The trousers are dirty.
Sp: El pantalón está sucio.
Lit: The trouser is dirty-SG

Given the sentence in one language, how does one determine the number marking in the other in a way that maintains as much compositionality in the transfer rules as possible. That is, in general, one should allow number to be copied across verbs:

```
[vp,_,_,_,NumPer,_,_]/be <==> [vp,_,_,_,NumPer,_,_]/estar.
```

This would enable the Spanish–English translation *Está sucio – It is dirty*. However, combining this with:

```
[n,_,_,ind(_,_,pl3),_]/trousers
<==>
[n,_,_,ind(_,_,sg3),_]/pantal\'on.
```

would result in a conflict in the inflection of the verb for the above translation. Similar situations can arise with verb forms and tenses (e.g. *swam* (fin-past) – *nadando* (ing)). It is difficult to see how to resolve these conflicts without some notion of default: certain features are copied/transferred into the TL structure but they may be overridden by other values. One alternative might include transferring certain features only for specific syntactic categories (e.g. number and person in nouns) and not transferring features whose semantic import is less well defined (e.g. infinitive markings). Such restrictions could be relaxed in specific cases such as PRO-drop sentences. Another alternative is to allow a range of feature values to be included in the TL structure and let the consolidation phase make a consistent, grammatical selection.

6.1.6 Consolidation

By consolidation we mean the process of applying TL grammar constraints (i.e. PS rules) to the TL structure in order to enforce grammaticality. This step is necessary particularly in the light of possible underspecifications remaining after transfer. Some MT systems based around syntactic transfer such as METAL (see Hutchins and Somers (1992) for an introduction) attach rules to TL structures. These rules are then invoked during the generation phase to improve the grammaticality of the TL sentence. A similar regime can be applied to the present pure syntactic transfer techniques. In this case, each side of the transfer relation specifies the applicable grammar rule at each node in the source and target structures. For example, if we assume that person and number are determined by noun phrases alone it would be necessary to percolate values to the verb phrase via grammar rule constraints. In this case, an S to S transformation rule such as in the thematic example (p. 125) would need to be augmented with the name of rules applicable at each of its nodes:

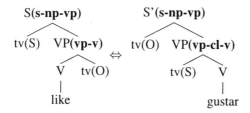

For this approach to work, each rule in the grammar must be assigned a unique identifier. After transfer is complete, the rule corresponding to the identifier is

retrieved and its constraints enforced on the node. In this example, rule identifiers are shown in bold and within parentheses. The English S node, for instance,
demands that the constraints of the rule *s-np-vp* be applied to it. If such a rule
has the general structure following, and verbs have suitable agreement bindings
between subject and verb (e.g. Try (subject equi) on p. 102), then agreement is
determined by the grammatical constraints of the TL grammar, and in particular, by constituents for which specific feature values have been transferred (e.g.
nouns).

```
rule(s_np_vp,
    [s(_)|CatS]/Sem --->
        [ NP,
          [vp,_,_,_,_,[NP]] ] )
                    .
```

6.1.7 Problems

It should be clear that syntactic transfer modules become heavily dependent on
the grammatical formalism and geometric structure assigned to sentences, and,
if consolidation is used, even on the actual grammar rules of each language. This
is highly undesirable in a multilingual system, since changes to a monolingual
component affect all transfer modules for that language.

A more technical problem with syntactic transfer relates to unbounded dependency constructions. Since such constructions are non-local, they require transformations that manipulate constituents deep within a tree. In a transfer system
like METAL (Whitelock and Kilby 1995), transformations within the analysis
phase move constituents and thus ameliorate the effects of such phenomena.
However, in the non-transformational syntactic framework assumed here, differences across languages need to be handled via transfer. The following translation
illustrates the problem:

> En: The door [s Doris came **through**] is closed.
> Sp: La puerta **por** la que [s Doris llegó] está cerrada.
> Lit: The door through it that Doris came is closed.

The translation of *through* appears outside its containing sentential phrase marker,
and so any transfer regime will have to relocate *por* to immediately after the
noun. It is difficult to ensure that the preposition is translated correctly, and that
it is inserted in the right place. It is possible that solutions based on some mechanism similar to "slash" features (Gazdar et al. 1985) could be used for this and
related phenomena in order to make information from one transfer rule available
in another transfer rule. Alternatively, transfer representations could be made
more abstract, as described in Section 6.2.

Other problems with syntactic transfer include their reliance on extensive encoding of transformation details in the lexicon (Magnúsdóttir 1993) and, in its
pure form, the diminished capabilities for complex semantic reasoning. Still,
such systems can be developed relatively quickly for one language direction or
bidirectionally for a language pair. They are robust and may be extended without
highly formal semantic analyses.

6.2   Semantic Transfer MT

One of the problems with syntactic transfer systems is that in order to account for grammatical differences between two languages, many transformations are only variations on each other. For example, PP complements in verb phrases need special treatment, since the translation of the preposition depends on the subcat frame of the TL verb, which is normally available in the TL lexical entry, and not at the point of transfer. Furthermore, long-distance dependencies are difficult to handle, as we have indicated, and semantic reasoning and additional applications for the linguistic resources developed are difficult.

Semantic transfer sees translation as a relation between language-dependent representations, which nevertheless neutralizes many language-specific idiosyncrasies. Although the representations are semantically oriented, they maintain some of the structure of their language of origin, and are therefore easier to use for analysis and generation.

Many semantic representations have been invented, and some of these have been used for semantic transfer (see Further Reading section). In this section we consider semantic transfer based on Quasi-Logical Form (QLF), which forms the basis for transfer in the BCI (Alshawi 1992). We begin by describing this semantic framework, and then explain its use in transfer-based translation.

6.2.1   Quasi-Logical Form

The description of QLF presented here is based on that in Alshawi (1992) and Allen (1995). QLF is a representation of language meaning based on predicate logic (Ramsay 1988), the classic version of which is First-Order Logic (FOL). This logic is used extensively in AI for knowledge representation, formalization of theories, reasoning, and other applications. In CL it has been used extensively for meaning representation with some extensions (Dowty et al. 1981). It is beyond the scope of this book to give a proper introduction to FOL, but a cursory overview might help the description to follow.

FOL is a formal system with a rigorous syntax and semantics. Its syntax consists of n-ary operators, constants, variables, the logical operators "and" ($\land$), "or" ($\lor$), "implies" ($\rightarrow$), "not" ($\neg$) and the two quantifiers $\exists$ and $\forall$. The semantics of FOL expressions is given through a set-theoretic model and an interpretation function. When used for representing linguistic meaning, FOL expressions indicate the truth conditions for a sentence. Thus, the following sentences have the FOL representations indicated (tense being ignored):

Sentence	FOL translation
All women are mortal	$\forall w(woman(w) \rightarrow mortal(w))$
Every man loves a woman	$\forall m(man(m) \rightarrow \exists w.woman(w)$ $\land love(m,w))$ $\exists w(woman(w) \land$ $\forall m.man(m) \rightarrow love(m,w))$
Ana saw a grey dog that Len chased	$\exists d(grey(d) \land dog(d) \land see(ana,d)$ $\land chase(len,d)$

The meaning of more complex sentences can be expressed by extending the logic, for example with intensional operators (Dowty et al. 1981), or by modelling aspects of meaning through FOL, for example by extending the ontology to include events (Parsons 1990). Thus, the FOL representation for *Omar slept* could be:

$$\exists e(event(e) \land before(e, t1) \land sleep(e, omar))$$

The variable e is an event, which occurs before time $t1$ and which is a sleeping event with role participant $omar$.

Despite such extensions, logical forms (LFs) of this type can be impractical for analysing and representing the high degree of ambiguity and underspecification present in language, which is why a QLF language has been developed. QLF expressions leave a number of ambiguities unresolved:

1. Quantifiers are unscoped. Standard predicate logic requires unambiguous expressions with respect to the scope of quantifiers (e.g. $\exists, \forall$). By contrast, quantified terms (qterms) in QLF leave the scope of a quantifier unspecified by simply representing the type of the quantifier, its bound variable and a restrictor formula within which the variable occurs. The following translation for *Every man loves a woman* encodes two qterms, and represents both FOL equivalents for this sentence:

   ```
   love(qterm(every,M,[man,M]),qterm(a,W,[woman,W]))
   ```

   Note that the quantifier corresponds to the English determiner, and hence implicitly expresses any distinctions that may exist between similar determiners.

2. There may be unresolved references. The arguments to QLF predicates may be terms to which no referent has been assigned. Compare this with FOL, where all arguments are either quantified variables or constants. Following Alshawi (1992, p. 34), these references are named anaphoric terms (aterms) here. The following QLF shows the representation for *Fabio saw her*:

   ```
   [see,fabio,aterm(pro,X,[and,[fem,X],[sing,X],[personal,X]])]
   ```

3. There may be unresolved relations. In QLF two or more entities can be related to each other, but the nature of that relation may remain unspecified. This may be compared with FOL, where predicates must be constants in all formulae. Phenomena where this is relevant include compound nouns, relational "of", ellipsis and genitives. The phrase *the laser printer* has the QLF:

   ```
   qform(the,X,aform(nn,R,[and,[printer,X],[R,laser,X]]))
   ```

   Note that the relation R applies to a type, laser, and a quantified variable, X.

By preserving underspecification in these ways, it has been argued that QLF is an appropriate level at which to carry out semantic transfer (Rayner et al.

1993). For example, resolved ellipsis can make translated sentences sound cumbersome. Definite and other references can be translated unresolved, and quantifier scope ambiguities tend to be preserved between many languages. While some relations need to be resolved for correct translation to take place, it is argued that this can be done when and if needed, depending on the language pair.

6.2.2   Analysis into QLF

At least since Montague (Montague 1974; Dowty et al. 1981) it has been possible compositionally to construct formal semantic representations for a subset of natural language sentences. These representations, in the form of LFs, are built in parallel with syntactic analysis, with each phrase type having a specific kind of semantic entity associated with it. Early work in this vein employed the lambda calculus (Church 1941) as the compositional mechanism for building LFs. However, since the introduction of computationally tractable unification formalisms it has been possible to construct semantic representations using unification. There are formal differences on the meanings that can be handled naturally by each framework. Here we employ unification to build QLFs during parsing, in parallel with syntactic analysis, ignoring for the most part any differences in expressive power.

Lexical entries handle the bulk of QLF construction, particularly as it concerns verbs and other complement structures. PS rules on the other hand, deal with unbounded dependencies, specifiers and modification. In the description below, syntactic categories omit information that is irrelevant to the description of QLF construction in order to ease the burden on the reader.

Matrix Clauses   Consider first the construction of the following QLF for *Chela reads the newspaper*:

```
[pres,[read,event(E),chela,qterm(the,N,[newspaper,N])]]
```

The predicate *pres* expresses present tense by implicitly representing a first order relation between the event variable and a contextually specified time. Event variables are assumed to be existentially quantified; from now on the event predicate will be omitted when there is no danger of confusion. This expression can be obtained with the following subcategorization list for the *read* lexical entry:

```
[vp,[ [np]/(_,SemObj),
      [np]/(_,SemSubj) ]]
/(E,[read,E,SemSubj,SemObj])
```

In conjunction with complement and subject saturation rules (p. 100), unification achieves correct binding of the semantics of the subject at the appropriate place in the verb's predicate. Each semantic expression used in compositional constructions has a distinguished semantic variable or index through which the whole expression may be identified (Kay 1996). Thus, the event variable E is the distinguished index for the VP semantics; the format is thus (Dist-Var,Formula). Note that the distinguished index of the subcat items is ignored in monolingual lexical entries.

The entry for *Chela* is:

```
[np]/(chela,chela)
```

Finally, the semantics for *the newspaper* are obtained through the following entries:

```
[det,(X,Form)]/(X,qterm(the,X,Form))
```

```
[n]/(X,[newspaper,X])
```

These, in addition to the rules for N1 and NP, build the appropriate structure:

```
[np]/SemNP ---> [ [det,Form]/SemNP,
                  [n1]/Form ]
```

```
[n1]/SemN  ---> [ [n]/SemN ]
```

Modifiers The semantics of a number of modifiers is frequently represented as a conjunction of predicates. For example, adjectives such as *red* are usually treated as predicates over the variables of the nouns they modify, with conjunction as the logical connector between the two. Thus, *a red bus* has the form $\exists x.red(x) \wedge bus(x)$. Such a representation is not too far off from the true meaning of the NP: there is something which is red and it is also a bus.

Representing modifiers of this type is done through the predicate and corresponding to logical "and". For example, the phrase *Ornella bought a purple jumper* has the QLF:

```
[past,[buy,E,ornella,qterm(a,J,[and,[purple,J],[jumper,J]])]]
```

The quantified term is derived via the entries for *purple* and *jumper* such as the two below:

```
[ap]/(X,[purple,X])                          [n]/(X,[jumper,X])
```

Such entries combine via a rule for AP modification that introduces the conjunction. A possible rule is:

```
[n1]/(X,[and,SemAP,SemN1]) ---> [ [ap]/(X,SemAP), [n1]/
                                  (X,SemN1) ]
```

A similar treatment can be given to PPs and adverbs. For example, *Claudia walked along the canal* is built with the rule:

```
[vp]/(E,[and,SemVP,SemPP]) ---> [ [vp]/(E,SemVP), [pp]/
                                  (E,SemPP) ]
```

```
[pp]/(E,[P,E,SemNP]) ---> [ [p]/(_,P), [np]/(_,SemNP) ]
```

Assuming suitable lexical entries, the result QLF would be:

```
[and,[past,[walk,E,claudia]],[along,E,qterm(the,C,[canal,C])]]
```

However, there are many adverbs, adjectives, prepositional phrases and other modifiers for which classical FOL fails to account fully for their semantic properties. One particular issue concerns expressions whose semantics cannot easily be expressed as a conjunction or disjunction of predicates. The class of non-intersective adjectives offers a good example.

Syntactically, the phrase *an alleged thief* is practically identical to *a red bus*. However, its semantics would be incorrectly represented by $*\exists x.alleged(x) \wedge thief(x)$, as this would imply that there is an alleged object and that there is also a thief, which may not be the case. Related issues arise with other expressions: *a computer message* does not imply the existence of a computer; *a fast typist* does not imply the existence of an independently fast object. The semantics of such expressions is an area of active research, but perhaps unsurprisingly, lack of suitable formalization has not meant that transfer MT systems suffer heavily because of it. Instead, one can adopt *ad hoc* analyses that enable MT to proceed without forfeiting the advantages of using formal semantic representations for transfer. In what follows, non-intersective and other modifiers that cannot easily be handled with FOL operators will be ignored, or their treatment can be assumed not to be too dissimilar from that given for intersective ones.

Control Structures The semantics of control structures follows the same pattern just presented. For instance, *Saine tries to sleep* has the QLF:

```
[pres,[try,T,saine,[sleep,E,saine]]]
```

Note in particular that the semantics of the subject of *tries* and *eat* is the same. The lexical entry for *try* is (see p. 102):

```
[vp,[ [vp,[ [np]/(X,Sem) ]]/(_,SemVP),
      [np]/(X,Sem) ]]
/(T,[try,T,Sem,SemVP])
```

By contrast, a subject raising verb has no semantic argument corresponding to its subject; *Saine seems to sleep* has QLF:

```
[pres,[seem,T,[sleep,S,saine]]]
```

The lexical entry for *seem* is then:

```
[vp,[ [vp,[ NP ]]/(_,SemVP),
      NP=[np]/(_,Sem) ]]
/(T,[seem,T,SemVP])
```

Similarly, object equi verbs (e.g. *persuade*) will have arguments corresponding to their subjects, while object raising ones (e.g. *believe*) will not.

Unbounded Dependencies The treatment of unbounded dependencies follows from the analysis given in Section 5.3. Bottom rules move a constituent from the subcat list into the gap list. Middle rules unify gap values through the analysis tree. Top rules unify the filler with the gap category, effectively instantiating the appropriate argument in the gapped constituent's QLF. Consider the sentence *the mouse, the cat chases*. A lexical rule for gap introduction generates the appropriate lexical sign for the verb:

```
[vp,gap([ [np]/(_,SemObj)|G]-G),[ [np]/(_,SemSubj) ]]
/(E,[chase,E,SemSubj,SemObj])
```

Clearly, when the gap is filled via the top rule on p. 105, the semantics of the filler will be unified into the appropriate argument slot in QLF, as identified by `SemObj`.

The situation with relative clauses is somewhat different. Consider the QLF for *The person whom Kim visited left*:

```
[past,[leave,L,qterm(the,X,[and,[person,X],
                    [past,[visit,V,kim,X]]])]]
```

In the restriction, variable X can appear at any position within the relative clause, which in this case is as the second participant in `visit`. Since it is the variable, rather than the QLF for the ñoun, that appears as the argument, the semantics of the gapped complement of *visited* must be this variable.

In Section 5.3, an index difference list was introduced to handle such constructions. This index serves the role of a variable, and hence becomes the semantics for the relative pronoun. Thus, the entry for *who* (p. 105) is:

```
[np,gap(G-G),rel([Ind|R]-R),Ind,nom]/(Ind,Ind)
```

Also, the point at which the relative clause is introduced (p. 105) needs to be modified:

```
[n1,Gap,Rel,Ind,Case]/(Ind,[and,SemN1,SemRel]) --->
   [ [n1,Gap,Rel = rel(R-R),Ind,Case]/(Ind,SemN1),
     [s(rel),Gs-Gs,rel([Ind|R]-R)|SRest]/(_,SemSrel) ]
```

The bottom and middle rules in UDC ensure that the variable is unified at the appropriate position in the QLF for the relative clause.

Sentences without a relative pronoun require a unary rule to delete an item from the gap list and introduce one into the index list.

```
[s(rel),gap(Gi-Go),rel([Ind|I]-I)]/Sem --->
   [ [s(top),gap([ [np]/(Ind,Ind) |Gi]-Go),rel(I-I)]/Sem ]
```

This quick tour of QLF construction provides sufficient background to describe the transfer rules needed for MT.

6.2.3   QLF Transfer

Transfer at the semantic level removes many language specific structures and replaces them with more standardized forms such as QLF. Still, it is possible to structure QLFs such that the similarity between QLFs varies between source and target languages. For example, one could treat prepositions as relations between event variables and qterms, as explained above, or they could have wider scope over the QLF for the VP they modify. Such decisions should ultimately be motivated by the semantic theory adopted, but in practice it is difficult to ensure that equivalent QLF representations are built for translationally equivalent sentences. Semantic transfer rules overcome discrepancies that arise in the meaning representations produced by different grammars.

QLF transfer employs the same recursive algorithm given on p. 123. The patterns, however, are given in terms of partial QLF structures rather than syntactic trees. The rules below achieve transfer between the QLFs for *the girl slept – la chica durmió*:

```
[past, FormE] <==> [past,FormS] :-
      FormE <==> FormS.
[sleep,S,ArgE] <==> [dormir,S,ArgS] :-
      ArgE <==> ArgS.
qterm(the,X,RestE) <==> qterm(def,X,RestS) :-
      RestE <==> RestS.
[girl,Y] <==> [chica,Y].
```

The quantified variables are the same for source and target structures. This maintains any binding that may be present in the source representation.

Differences between source and target QLFs can be trivial. For example, in the position and value of features or in the name of predicates, as shown above. They may also involve QLF restructuring to conform with the QLFs assumed by the TL grammar. Depending on the particular QLF analysis given to a phrase a divergence may or may not arise. For example, a phrase like *Al waited in London* could have at least three different QLFs:

```
[past,[wait,W,al,london]]
[past,[and,[wait,W,al],[in,W,london]]]
[and,[past,[wait,W,al]],[in,W,london]]
```

Depending on which analysis is adopted in different languages, more or less complex transformations will be required. Below, the divergences identified in Section 6.1.1 are used to illustrate different kinds of QLF divergences and how they may be handled.

Thematic The English and Spanish QLFs for *you like her – ella te gusta* are:

```
[pres,[like,L,aterm(pro,X,[and,[hearer,X],[personal,X]]),
          aterm(pro,Y,[and,[fem,Y],[sing,Y],
                  [personal,Y]])])]

[pres,[gustar,L,aterm(pro,Y,[and,[fem,Y],[sing,Y],
                  [personal,Y]]),
          aterm(pro,X,[and,[hearer,X],[personal,X]])])]
```

The arguments to the verb have been swapped. Transfer of such structures is unproblematic:

```
[like,E,Arg1E,Arg2E] <==> [gustar,E,Arg2S,Arg1S] :-
    Arg1E <==> Arg1S,
    Arg2E <==> Arg2S.
```

Structural Structural divergence at QLF is dependent on the analysis assigned to translationally equivalent source and target sentences. One type of divergence arises when the number of arguments to a predicate is different in each language. Assume for the sake of argument that the QLFs for *Luisa entered the house – Luisa entró a la casa* are:

```
En:  [past,[enter,E,luisa,qterm(the,X,[house,X])])]
Sp:  [past,[and,[entrar,E,luisa],
                [a_loc,E,qterm(def,X,[casa,X])])]]
```

The predicate `entrar` has one participant argument, and hence the semantics of the PP appears outside the scope of `entrar`. The transfer rule to map between these is:

```
[enter,E,Arg1E,Arg2E] <==> [and,[enter,E,Arg1S],
                                 [a_loc,E,Arg2S]]  :-
                   Arg1E <==> Arg1S,
                   Arg2E <==> Arg2S.
```

The second type of divergence concerns differences in scope. Consider the possible QLFs for *Did John sleep well? – ¿John durmió bien?*.

```
En:  [ynq,[past,[and,[sleep,S,john],[well,S]]]]
Sp:  [ynq,[and,[past,[dormir,S,john]],[bien,S]]]
```

The scope of `past` includes the adverb in English but not in Spanish. These differences might arise because of the compositional nature of QLF construction. For example, in the English sentence, the phrase *sleep well* is analysed before the tense marker from the auxiliary is applied. By contrast, the Spanish verb is inflected for tense and therefore the adverb has wide scope over it.

Such scope discrepancies can be handled for particular cases with a specific transfer rule. The following is a possibility:

```
[ynq,[past,[and,Arg1E,Arg2E]]] <==> [ynq,[and,[past,Arg1S],
                                               Arg2S]]  :-
                        Arg1E <==> Arg1S,
                        Arg2E <==> Arg2S.
```

However, if the scope operator is embedded within several layers of conjunctions, additional rules will be needed. If the depth of the nesting is unbounded, additional machinery is required to generalize the transfer rule.

Lexical Gaps A translation such as *a young bull – un novillo* is achieved through the rule:

```
[and,[young,X],[bull,X]] <==> [novillo,X].
```

This rule would apply to the restrictor part of the `qterm` derived from these NPs in order to produce a suitable TL `qterm`. The `qterm` predicate itself would need to be translated by a separate rule or via a default.

Note that this rule would not be capable of handling *young black bull – novillo negro*, since the relevant QLFs would be:

```
En:  [and,[young,X],[and,[black,X],[bull,X]]]
Sp:  [and,[negro,X],[novillo,X]]
```

The transfer rule above would fail to unify with these structures, mainly because of the extra `[black,X]` predicate.

Head Switching Problems in head switching also depend on how a sentence is analysed. Assume that *I think Carlos just fell – Creo que Carlos acaba de caer* have the following (simplified) QLFs:

```
En: [think,T,<speaker>,[and,[fall,E,carlos],[just,E]]]
Sp: [creer,T,<speaker>,[acabar,A,carlos,[caer,E,carlos]]]
```

Structurally, the two QLFs are related as follows:

```
[and,VPE,[just,E]] <==> [acabar,E,Subj,VPS] :-
                 VPE <==> VPS.
```

Note, however, that the event variables for both `acabar` and `just` are now bound, unlike the individual QLFs given above. As a result, A and E in the Spanish QLF are bound during English to Spanish transfer, and the variable for `just` is left unbound during Spanish to English transfer. This asymmetry affects translations when there is modification of only one of the verbs in Spanish, but in such cases, generation normally produces a correct sentence because of the strong structural character of QLFs, which effectively guides the generation process. Furthermore, the subject of *acabar* remains unbound. Again, generation from the Spanish QLF will force the appropriate binding as long as a suitable subject control verb entry is specified for it. Alternatively, the transfer rule can be more specific, and access the VP structure to retrieve its subject.

Lexicalization Lexicalization pattern divergences are present in the translation *Julian walked down High Peak – Julian bajó High Peak caminando*. Assume the following QLFs:

```
En: [past,[and,[walk,E,julian],[down_direction,E,high_peak]]]
Sp: [past,[and,[bajar,E,julian,high_peak],[caminar,E,julian]]]
```

This example involves head switching and categorial divergence. Transfer between the structures involved is achieved through:

```
[and,VPE,[down_direction,E,NPE]] <==> [and,[bajar,E,Subj,NPS],
                                             VPS] :-
                             VPE <==> VPS,
                             NPE <==> NPS.
```

Here, the subject of the Spanish QLF would need to be assigned a value during generation (but see Section 6.2.4 below). When the divergence appears with additional modifiers, further complications arise relating to the recursive structure of `and`.

Categorial Categorial divergences can be neutralized in QLF where a predicate can originate from different parts of speech. Categorial changes can be handled by structural divergence strategies, head switching, collocational rules, or any combination of these. Consider *a little bread – un poco de pan*:

```
En: qterm(a,X,[and,[bread,X],[little,typical_amount(bread),X]])
Sp: qterm(indef,X,aform(de,R,[and,[pan,X],[R,poco(pan),X]]))
```

The Spanish QLF says that X ranges over objects which are pan (bread), and which stand in the anaphoric relation R of type de, to an entity that is representative of a small amount of bread poco(pan). The equivalence can be established via:

```
[and,NE,[little,typical(B),X]] <==> aform(de,R,[and,NS,
                                             [R,poco(P),X]]) :-
                        NE <==> NS,
                     [B,_] <==> [P,_].
```

When modifiers are involved (e.g. *a little more bread – un poco más de pan*), this rule can be generalized, but the nature of such generalizations clearly depends on the QLFs intended to represent such phrases.

Collocational In the interest of modularity, collocational knowledge ought to reside in monolingual modules such that transfer components need not concern themselves with them. However, it is unlikely that collocational analyses will coincide for every language pair: what may be regarded as a support verb in one language may have a translation that is not a support verb construction in another language. Consider *Javier is thirsty – Javier tiene sed*. The English sentence could be assigned at least the following different QLFs:

```
E1: [pres,[thirsty,state(T),javier]]
E2: [pres,[be,state(T),[thirsty,javier]]]
```

Similarly, its Spanish translation could have any of the following QLFs (English analogues for some of these could also be proposed):

```
S1: [pres,[sed,state(T),javier]]
S2: [pres,[tener,state(T),[sed,javier]]]
S3: [pres,[tener,state(T),javier,qterm(mass,X,[sed,X])]]
S4: [pres,aform(tener,T,[T,state(T),javier,qterm(mass,X,
                                                  [sed,X])])]
```

Transfer between structures where thirsty/sed predicates over javier (i.e. E1 and S1) are straightforward. For the other cases, the default translations *be – ser/estar* and *have – tener* need to be overridden with the appropriate support verb (structural divergences are also evident in these QLFs – any of E1, E2 vs. S3, S4; their treatment has already been discussed). The issue then is determining the appropriate support verb. We take the E2, S2 pair to illustrate different solutions.

As with syntactic transfer, it would be possible to have a transfer rule for each collocation. Some simplification would be possible, say by minimally specifying collocation pairs:

```
[VE,state(T),[HeadE,Arg1E]] <==> [VS,state(T),
                                     [HeadS,Arg1S]] :-
              (VE,HeadE) <==> (VS,HeadS), % Apply only if
                                          % collocation exists.
                  Arg1E <==> Arg1S.

(be,thirsty) <==> (tener,sed).      % Valid collocations.
(be,hungry)  <==> (tener,hambre).
```

If such a transfer module did not have a *thirsty – sed* entry, there would be no question of the default translation for *be* ever applying in this case: the complete structure could only be translated into Spanish via a collocation.

A more modular alternative is to cross-linguistically identify commonalities in the semantic function of dependent collocational items, and to equate these in transfer rules. For example, following Danlos and Samvelian (1992), one can distinguish different types of collocation:

	Neutral	Inchoative
En:	be hungry/thirsty	get hungry/thirsty
Sp:	tener hambre/sed	dar hambre/sed

Transfer rules then relate the semantic head of a collocation (e.g. *hungry – hambre*) while the support verb is inferred via a monolingual collocation predicate:

```
:- op(500,xfx, '<~>').

[VE,state(T),[HeadE,Arg1E]] <==> [VS,state(T),
                                   [HeadS,Arg1S]] :-
                      Arg1E <==> Arg1S,
                      HeadE <~> HeadS,
   colloc(neutral,VE,HeadE) <==> colloc(neutral,VS,HeadS).

colloc(Type,Ve,HeadE) <==> colloc(Type,Vs,HeadS) :-
   colloc(en,Type,Ve,HeadE),
   colloc(sp,Type,Ve,HeadE).

thirsty <~> sed.
hungry  <~> hambre.
```

Since *thirsty – sed* is not a default translation (*thirst – sed* is), they are related via a separate transfer operator `<~>`. The predicate `colloc/4` is language-specific. Sample implementations for English and Spanish might be:

```
colloc(en,neutral,be,H) :- member(H,[thirsty,hungry,angry,cold,
                                      hot,lucky]).
colloc(sp,neutral,tener,H) :- member(H,[sed,hambre,rabia,frío,
                                         calor,suerte]).
```

Obviously, once these semantic roles are identified, justification for maintaining support verbs in QLF dwindles: they can now be deleted during analysis and correctly inserted during generation. However, the concomitant loss of information in eliminating the verbal predicate can diminish the robustness of the system.

Multi-lexeme and Idiomatic Like other divergences, treating multi-lexeme and idiomatic divergences in QLF transfer depends very much on the representation given to them. In general, however, transfer rules will relate complete QLF structures in the SL and TL. Consider *Amparo took a dim view of Kim – Amparo vió a Kim con malos ojos* (Amparo saw at Kim with bad eyes). Each may be given different QLFs; below are two possibilities:

```
En: [past,[take_a_dim_view,E,amparo,kim]]
Sp: [past,[ver_con_malos_ojos,E,amparo,kim]]
```

Clearly, only by relating the two predicates can transfer be achieved. Encoding the meaning of the predicate in this way ensures that transfer is non-compositional. The bulk of the processing is then undertaken by the analysis and generation grammars, which need to explicitly identify such expressions.

6.2.4 Generation and TL Filtering

Since QLF is a predicate argument structure with recursively embedded arguments, the SHDG algorithm from Section 5.5.2 is applicable to generation from it. However, for this to succeed, the transfer phase must ensure that the QLFs produced are indeed QLFs that the TL grammar can generate from. This property may be exploited for target language filtering.

Target language filtering (Alshawi et al. 1992, p. 295) is a technique for simplifying transfer in which generation is expected to weed out any incorrect structures that are produced by the transfer rules. The TL grammar effectively disambiguates the result of transfer, generating only from acceptable QLFs. As such, it serves as an alternative mechanism for handling collocations and other ambiguities, where it is difficult to select a suitable QLF representation during transfer.

6.2.5 Further Issues

QLF and similar recursive predicate argument structures still contain too much information about the source language, making it difficult to transfer structures in very different positions in QLF. For instance, the and predicate which features in several representations can create artificial embeddings that diminish the generality of transfer rules. Even if these conjunctions were "flattened" into a single list, the simple recursive model of transfer would need to be augmented with list operations that enabled rules to access different conjuncts. Furthermore, the SHDG would not be an efficient way of generating from these flat QLFs.

A related issue is that there must be agreement between grammarians as to the position of modifiers and other constituents in the source and target QLFs. Since and is not by default a commutative operator in most transfer representations, a generation grammar will expect modifiers to appear on a specific side of the head. For example, in the grammars above, all modifiers appear to the right of the constituent they modify. This need not cause problems, but it does highlight the dependence on monolingual grammars that may infiltrate semantic transfer representations, and the practical manifestation of the logical form equivalence problem (Section 5.6.1).

At the same time, one could say that a semantic representation such as QLF preserves too little SL information. For example, the informational structure in terms of topic/comment or theme/rheme is lost (e.g. topicalization is normalized). QLFs may be augmented with such details, however, to improve the correspondence in information structure between the two texts.

An issue that was overlooked was that of tense marker mappings between source and target sentences. As one would expect, tense normally coincides between source and target QLFs, but it may lead to ambiguity between tenses that are semantically related. For example present tense in Spanish corresponds to present tense or present participle in English: *I write/am writing – escribo*. In general, this ambiguity can only be resolved through contextual knowledge and/or Spanish specific grammatical constraints, and hence may be a good candidate for TL filtering. However, in a translation such as *Carlos just ate(past) – Carlos acaba(pres) de comer(inf)*, no tense in one language matches the tense in the other. This presents a problem for compositional transfer. Below are some examples of further complexities (*just* is taken to mean "very recently" as opposed to "simply" or "almost didn't"):

English	Spanish
just ate$_{past}$	acaba$_{pres}$ de comer$_{inf}$
has$_{pres}$ just eaten$_{past-part}$	acaba$_{pres}$ de comer$_{inf}$
had$_{past}$ just eaten$_{past-part}$	acababa$_{imperfect}$ de comer
having$_{pres-part}$ just eaten$_{past-part}$	acabando$_{pres-part}$ de comer

The divergences clearly stem from the effect that *just* has on the temporal semantics of the expression, and on the perfective tense that auxiliary *have* imposes. To treat them adequately, however, would require a theory of temporal meaning, aspect and aktionsart which is beyond the scope of this book. One alternative is to simply enumerate all possible combinations of tenses and *just* in transfer rules, together with their appropriate translations. This becomes more appealing when considering present and future tenses, where *just* appears to strongly favour its sense of "simply": *Carlos will just eat – Carlos simplemente comerá*.

Despite these observations, the great advantage of QLF for MT is that it is a formal, logically oriented formalism, which may be further processed to produce resolved QLFs and eventually LFs with well understood inference procedures. More importantly, much theory regarding anaphora resolution, ellipsis and coordination, not to mention theoretical semantic analyses of tense, aspect, aktionsart, motion, space and attitudes have been couched in terms of logical formalisms such as LF and QLF and thus they offer a relatively well founded strategy within which to investigate issues of primary relevance to MT.

6.3 Lexicalist MT

A major source of complication with the syntactic and semantic transfer methodologies presented above is the recursive character of their representations. In the former, analysis trees themselves consist of analysis trees. In the latter, the argument to a QLF predicate can itself be a QLF. Problems arise when the transfer structure in SL and TL are markedly different: elements of the SL structure that are geometrically distant (say because they are embedded in different branches of the structure) may need to be in close proximity in the TL. Without additional mechanisms to cope with such divergences, transfer modules fail to capture useful and interesting cross-linguistic generalizations. These mechanisms will have non-local effects on the structures being transferred, which can decrease the perspicuity of the system and add to the difficulty in transfer rule development. This and other issues relating to scope and ambiguity have given rise to non-recursive approaches to transfer, two of which are lexicalist MT (LexMT) or Shake-and-Bake MT (Whitelock 1992) and Minimal Recursion Semantics (Copestake et al. 1995). In this section we consider LexMT in some detail, leaving the latter until Section 8.3.

In LexMT, cross-linguistic relationships are established at the level of lexemes or sets of lexemes, rather than at more abstract representations. The principal advantage is that such relationships can be verified empirically by inspection of bilingual corpora, bilingual dictionaries or through validation by a bilingual. In addition, the (semi)automatic acquisition of contrastive data can be facilitated since transfer relationships are established in a format close to that found in bilingual corpora. Finally, the relations are reusable in the sense that they are to some extent independent of the syntactic and semantic theory of any particular system, and can therefore be adapted to different transfer approaches. This is unlike the previous two strategies in which one must have a significant amount of knowledge about the transfer representation and its behaviour to be able to determine whether two structures stand in a transfer relation or not, and for which painstakingly acquired contrastive knowledge cannot be easily ported to other systems.

In its simplest form, a lexicalist transfer rule consists of an SL and a TL set of lexical items that stand in translation correspondence, not too dissimilar to the way translations are given in large bilingual dictionaries. As an example, consider the following (simplified) transfer rule for a lexical gap divergence:

$$\{get, up, early\} \leftrightarrow \{madrugar\}$$

If all the items on one side of the rule match those on the SL input, then all the items on the TL side need to form part of the TL sentence. Assume also the additional rule:

$$\{Francisco\} \leftrightarrow \{Francisco\}$$

These rules enable transfer of the sentence *Francisco got up early* since its lexical items can be grouped in such a way that they match exactly the sets on the English side:

$$\{ Francisco \} \quad \{ got, up, early \}$$
$$\updownarrow \qquad\qquad \updownarrow$$
$$\{ Francisco \} \quad \{ madrugó \}$$

In LexMT the analysis phase establishes semantic relationships between the words in the SL sentence. These words, appearing at the leaves of the SL analysis tree, are then transferred into the TL with their semantic dependencies preserved. The result of transfer is a set of TL lexical items whose semantics implicitly determine a TL sentence, but whose order is underspecified. It is the task of the TL generator via the TL grammar to rearrange this set of words into an appropriate TL sentence.

Four aspects of this account need to be elaborated on: the notion of a lexical item or lexeme, semantic dependencies, and algorithms for transfer and generation.

6.3.1 Lexemes for Transfer

In its extreme form, lexicalist transfer could occur at the level of morphemes. All morphemes would be treated equivalently, and transfer would be seen as the process of turning a set of morphemes in one language into a set of morphemes in another language. The following example shows how this extreme approach would handle the lexical gap example:

> {get, up, early} ↔ {madrug}
> {-ed} ↔ {-ó}

Analysis would produce *get -ed up early*; transfer would result in *madrug -ó* and generation, including morphological synthesis, would result in *madrugó*.

Transferring morphemes in this fashion would strictly follow the philosophy of lexicalist transfer by adhering to experimentally verifiable representations, but it has some disadvantages. First it creates a large amount of non-determinism during transfer, as some morphemes need to be transferred into several alternatives in the TL. Thus, *-ed* has as its possible translations into Spanish *-ó* (third singular), *-é* (first singular), *-aste* (second singular) etc. Even if generic morphemes were used, the non-determinism created during transfer and generation makes such a representation undesirable. Secondly, and more practically, the working units of most grammars are lexical signs in which the import of various affixes forms part of the sign structure rather than being treated as separate linguistic objects.

The alternative then, and the approach illustrated here, is to use root signs for transfer, and to allow features expressing syntactic and semantic information to be copied or transferred into the TL. This means that a certain amount of abstraction in assumed, contrary to the empiricist bias underlying this approach, but the gains in compactness and generality compensate for this. The notion of root, as applied to English, say, includes the citation form of open class words, as well as all closed class words. Thus, lexicalist transfer rules will relate determiners, prepositions, conjunctions and other markers, as well as nouns, adjectives, verbs etc. Lexicalist transfer therefore takes as input a list of lexical signs. As such, the list carries all the grammatical information available in lexical categories.

Since phenomena that are lexicalized in one language may be rendered through inflections in another language, there are situations in which a word translates as a grammatical feature. Future tense between English and Spanish is a clear example of this situation:

> {will get up early} ↔ {madrugar(fut)}

To make this example more concrete, one needs to choose an actual grammatical framework in which lexical entries are expressed. Assume for the moment some version of the dependency analysis presented in Section 6.1.3.

```
[ [vp,_,_,aux|_]/will, [vp,_,_,base|_]/get, [up]/up,
  [ap]/early ]
         <==>
[ [vp,_,_,fut|_]/madrugar ]
```

The actual structure of these signs is largely irrelevant to the lexicalist transfer algorithm (Section 6.3.3), which, together with generation (Section 6.3.6), however, make one important requirement on the transfer representation, which may be loosely termed semantic dependency.

6.3.2 Semantic Dependency

Since no structure is used during transfer or generation in LexMT, semantic relationships between lexemes must be expressed in the lexemes themselves. In general these relationships are already present in many semantic representations proposed to date, in the form of bound variables or constants. With a little restructuring, these dependencies can be made available in a grammar's lexical signs. If these dependencies are not available, as in the example above, for instance, generation may produce sentences in which semantic roles are not equivalent to those of the SL. The classic example for this is *John loves Mary – John ama a Mary*.

```
[ [np]/john ] <==> [ [np]/john ].
[ [np]/mary ] <==> [ [np]/mary ].
[ [vp]/love ] <==> [ [vp]/amar, [a]/a ].
```

Applying these transfer relations, the input to the generator might be the set:

```
[ [vp]/amar, [a]/a, [np]/mary, [np]/john ]
```

Note that nothing in this list indicates who the subject and object of the loving is. Obviously this is a shortcoming of the crude semantics, but the point is laboured here in order to highlight an important issue in LexMT. Since the list represents a set, the order of its components cannot be taken as indicative in any way of the order of the TL sentence. Generation therefore involves a search for an ordering which results in a grammatical sentence. For this list there are two orderings:

```
Mary ama a John.
John ama a Mary.
```

Only the second of these is a correct translation, but without additional constraints there is no way of establishing this fact.

What is missing from the lexical items is some indication of the role played by each participant within the sentence. In most logic based representations this is indicated by a variable, an index or by a qterm appearing in the appropriate slot. Most lexical representations, however, can be easily extended with dependency markers expressing the role played by particular dependents. For the previous example, this can take the form of numerical arguments added to the lexical head of a phrase. For example, the output of transfer might be:

```
[ [vp]/(1,2,amar), [a]/(2,a), [np]/(2,mary), [np]/(1,john) ]
```

The numeric indices can be used to force *John* to be subject, and *Mary* to be object of the sentence. This would be achieved through suitable bindings in the grammar. For example:

```
[s]/Sem --->
    [   [np]/(S,_),
        [vp]/(S,_) ]
```

Alternatively, the bindings may be established at the lexical level. The entry for *amar* would then be:

```
[vp,[ [a]/(O,a), [np]/(O,_), [np]/(S,_) ]]/(S,O,amar)
```

Transfer rules bind these indices in a way that preserves the relevant relationships:

```
[ [vp]/(X,Y,love) ] <==> [ [vp]/(X,Y,amar), [a]/(Y,a) ].
[ [np]/(Z,mary) ]   <==> [ [ [np]/(Z,mary) ].
[ [np]/(W,john) ]   <==> [ [ [np]/(W,john) ].
```

These bindings, which must be enforced in both the SL and TL grammars, ensure that dependents are correctly associated with their governors.

Note, however, that after analysis, bindings are usually expressed as uninstantiated variables. This raises the issue of when these are instantiated. In simple cases, instantiation may safely be undertaken immediately after analysis. Thus, the list:

```
[ [np]/(S,john), [vp]/(S,O,love), [np]/(O,mary) ]
```

becomes:

```
[ [np]/(1,john), [vp]/(1,2,love), [np]/(2,mary) ]
```

which then serves as input to the transfer algorithm, and thence onto generation. This process is referred to as skolemization in the LexMT literature by analogy with the process of constant generation for existentially quantified variables in some FOL normal forms.

For more complex transfer rules such as head switching, the point at which skolemization takes place determines whether generation succeeds or not. Consider a possible transfer rule for *just fell – acaba de caer*:

```
[ [ap]/(E,just), [vp]/(E,S,fall) ]
   <==>
[ [vp]/(E,S,acabar), [de]/(E,E,de), [vp]/(E,S,caer) ]
```

Since Spanish *acabar* requires an index for its subject, the transfer rule equates both adverb and verb on the English side with their corresponding verb–verb translation in Spanish (see Section 6.3.4 for capturing generalizations in LexMT). Furthermore, while the Spanish translation consists of two verbs, only one event variable, E, is present. The reason for binding the corresponding two indices is that in cases of additional adverbial modification the adverb will be indexed correctly.

Consider now the result of analysing the Spanish *Nicky obviamente acaba de caer*, which may be depicted by:

```
[ [np]/(S,nicky), [ap]/(F,obviamente), [vp]/(F,S,acabar),
    [de]/(F,E,de), [vp]/(E,S,caer) ]
```

It is unlikely that the two verbs will be given the same index by the Spanish grammar, since there is no reason to believe, on monolingual grounds, that the two are one and the same event. If this set of lexical signs is now skolemized, it will not unify with the Spanish side of the transfer rule for *just fell* above, as there will be a clash between the F and E indices. Skolemizing after transfer resolves this issue, since the variables will be bound before being instantiated, thus avoiding the clash and enabling generation of the appropriate English sentence. In binding the two events however, any scope information from the Spanish is lost since any adverb indexed by F will be indistinguishable from one indexed by E. Scope is discussed again in the context of alternative semantic representations in LexMT (see Section 6.3.7).

6.3.3 Transfer Algorithm

Transfer in LexMT consists in computing the exact cover (Garey and Johnson 1979, p. 221) of a set of lexical items from the SL using the SL side of transfer rules. The result is the set union of the TL sides of all the matching transfer rules. More concretely, given an input set S of SL lexical items, lexicalist transfer consists of two main steps:

SL cover: Compute the set R of transfer rules that exactly cover S. That is, a lexical item occurs in the source side of a rule in R iff it unifies with a lexical item in S. Furthermore, each element in the source side of a rule R must unify with only one element of S and *vice versa*.

TL union: The result of transfer is the set union of all the lexical items from the target side of rules in R.

Consider the sentence *Marcela is as intelligent as Esperanza*, with transfer rules (indices given as subscripts):

$$\{\text{Marcela}_a\} \leftrightarrow \{\text{Marcela}_a\}$$
$$\{\text{be}_{e,b,c}\} \leftrightarrow \{\text{ser}_{e,b,c}\}$$
$$\{\text{as}_{d,f}, \text{as}_{f,g}\} \leftrightarrow \{\text{tan}_{d,f}, \text{como}_{f,g}\}$$
$$\{\text{intelligent}_h\} \leftrightarrow \{\text{inteligente}_h\}$$
$$\{\text{Esperanza}_i\} \leftrightarrow \{\text{Esperanza}_i\}$$

The input to transfer will be:

$$\{\text{Marcela}_o, \text{be}_{p,o,q}, \text{as}_{q,r}, \text{intelligent}_r, \text{as}_{r,s}, \text{Esperanza}_s\}$$

The transfer algorithm then maps these lexical items into the Spanish set:

$$\{\text{Marcela}_o, \text{ser}_{p,o,q}, \text{tan}_{q,r}, \text{como}_{r,s}, \text{inteligente}_r, \text{Esperanza}_s\}$$

Note in particular that transfer of *as .. as* is handled adequately resulting in the correct lexical items in Spanish; this despite unlimited lexical items possibly appearing between the two.

Each translation divergence, regardless of its structural complexity, can be translated using sets of lexical items and the transfer algorithm just outlined. It will be sufficient to present sample transfer rules in the form of Table 6.1.

Divergence	English	Spanish	Comment
Thematic	like$_{e,s,o}$	gustar$_{e,o,s}$	Indices swapped.
Head switching	just$_e$ eat$_{e,s}$	acabar$_{e,s}$ de$_{e,e}$ comer$_{e,s}$	Spanish events bound.
Structural	enter$_{e,s,o}$	entrar$_{e,s}$ a$_{e,o}$	Preposition added.
Lexical gap	get$_{e,s}$ up$_e$ early$_e$	madrugar$_{e,s}$	Phrasal translation.
Lexicalization	swim$_{e,s}$ across$_{e,o}$	cruzar$_{e,s,o}$ nadar$_{e,s}$	Spanish events bound.
Categorial	little$_b$	poco$_b$ de$_{b,b}$	Spanish indices bound.
Collocational	make$_{e,s,o}$ decision$_o$	tomar$_{e,s,o}$ decisión$_o$	Support verb added.
Multi-lexeme	kick$_{e,s,o}$ the$_o$ bucket$_o$	estirar$_{e,s,o}$ la$_o$ pata$_o$	Phrasal translation.

Table 6.1. Divergences in Lexicalist MT.

Some of these transfer relations show more or less compositionality. At one extreme multi-lexeme transfer rules are least compositional, while thematic divergences are handled purely compositionally. In particular, it would seem from this description that a large number of non-compositional transfer rules need to be written for divergences that should, intuitively, be more compositional. This issue is taken up in the next section. Note, however, that these transfer rules apply correctly regardless of how far or how many modifiers each of their components may have.

6.3.4 Bilingual Lexical Redundancy Rules

Organizing lexical resources through rules is a feature frequently used in monolingual grammatical theories (Bresnan 1982). Several linguistic processes can be described by proposing rules which derive new lexical entries from existing ones. For example, it has been suggested that the alternation depicted below should be treated by a lexical rule that adds the pronoun *it* to the subcat list of the corresponding verb (Pollard and Sag 1994, p. 150):

John *resents* that Mary left.
John *resents it* that Mary left.

The rule could be depicted schematically as:

VP[Srel,NP]
$$\Downarrow$$
VP[NP$_{it}$,Srel,NP]

Analogous to lexical rules, bilingual lexical redundancy rules (bilexical rules for short) can be formulated in the framework of LexMT in order to capture cross-linguistic regularities that would not be easily captured by the lexical transfer rules introduced earlier. A bilexical rule takes as input a transfer rule and has as output a new transfer rule. The input and output transfer rules are usually underspecified and related to each other via unification. The input rule is instantiated against a transfer rule, and the result is the (instantiated) output rule expressing a new transfer relation. Consider the following verb translations, and their corresponding imperfect tense translations:

English	Spanish	English (3sg)	Spanish
sleep	dormir	used to sleep	dormía
kiss	besar	used to kiss	besaba
give	dar	used to give	daba
think	pensar	used to think	pensaba

It is likely that on monolingual English grounds, the given tense will not be expressed as a feature value in lexical entries, but instead the verb *used* will simply be analysed as a past tense. By contrast, the Spanish lexical items on the right will be marked for imperfect tense. The bilingual relationship between the two tenses for *sleep* could be stated as:

$$\begin{array}{ccc} \text{sleep} & \leftrightarrow & \text{dormir} \\ \Downarrow & & \Downarrow \\ \text{used to sleep} & \leftrightarrow & \text{dormía} \end{array}$$

This indicates that from the translation *sleep – dormir*, a new translation *used to sleep – dormía* can be derived. Generalizing the pattern gives:

$$\begin{array}{ccc} \text{V}_{root} & \leftrightarrow & \text{V}_{root} \\ \Downarrow & & \Downarrow \\ \text{used to } \text{V}_{root} & \leftrightarrow & \text{V}_{imperfect} \end{array}$$

This rule says that root verb translations give rise to imperfect tense translations by changing the tense of the Spanish verb and adding the phrase *used to* on the English verb.

Rules of this type capture regularities between lexical and phrasal translations in a declarative manner. They also adhere to the philosophy that all bilingual correspondences must be grounded on bilingual data or can at least be verified by bilingual speakers of the languages.

Given the bilexical rule mechanism, it is now possible to give a general solution to most of the divergences dealt with via non-compositional rules in the previous section. In essence, each divergence is resolved by a bilexical rule that derives the phrasal translation from the lexical translation of its verbs or nouns.

Head switching		$\text{V}_{e,s}$ $\Downarrow$	$\leftrightarrow$		$\text{V}_{e,s}$ $\Downarrow$
	just_e	$\text{V}_{e,s}$	$\leftrightarrow$	$\text{acaba}_{e,s}\,\text{de}_{e,e}$	$\text{V}_{e,s}$
Lexicalization	$\text{V}_{e,s}$ $\Downarrow$		$\leftrightarrow$		$\text{V}_{e,s}$ $\Downarrow$
	$\text{V}_{e,s}$	$\text{across}_{e,o}$	$\leftrightarrow$	$\text{cruzar}_{e,s,o}$	$\text{V}_{e,s}$+ando
Collocational		$\text{N}_i(\text{make})$ $\Downarrow$	$\leftrightarrow$		$\text{N}_i(tomar)$ $\Downarrow$
	$\text{make}_{e,s,i}$	N_i	$\leftrightarrow$	$\text{tomar}_{e,s,i}$	N_i

The middle rule adds the preposition *across* to the English verb and the verb *cruzar* and the suffix *+ando* to the Spanish verb. The input nouns to the last rule are restricted to those having the indicated support verb (see below). Bilexical rules may be applied during a precompilation phase in which all possible transfer rules are generated prior to commencing translation. Alternatively, each rule can be applied as needed, so that only transfer rules that need to be generated are in fact generated. In this case the transfer module is expanded dynamically, depending on the input.

To avoid overgeneration, each rule needs to be constrained to specific inputs. These constraints may be motivated in a number of ways. For example, collocations for the onset of certain properties, as in *they got hungry/thirsty*, are mirrored in Spanish by *les dió hambre/sed* (self give hunger/thirst). However, for *they got lucky*, Spanish has *les llegó suerte*. It is Spanish monolingual restrictions that determine the appropriate support verb to use as translation of *get*.

Similarly, the lexicalization pattern for *across* is regular for manner and motion verbs, but with basic motion verbs such as *go*, the pattern does not apply: *she went across the street* – *cruzó la calle* (crossed-3sg the street). Note that no gerundive is involved in the Spanish translation, contrary to what is predicted by the bilexical rule. In this case, application of the rule must be restricted to manner verbs to prevent mistranslation.

These restrictions clearly form part of the lexical signs constituting the input pattern to bilexical rules. One possible location for the relevant information is the indices associated with lexical entries. For *across*, the bilexical rule could be written as:

```
:- op(520,xfx,'>>>').   % bilexical rule operator

                        [ [vp]/(E,S,Ve) ] <==> [ [vp]/(E,S,Vs) ]
                                            >>>
[[vp]/(E,S,Ve), [p]/(E,O,[across,E,O]) ] <==> [ [vp]/(E,S,O,
                                                  [cruzar,E,S,O]),
                                                  VP ]
:- E = ind(Id,manner,_,_),
   present_participle(sp,[vp]/(E,S,Vs),VP).
```

This example illustrates how bilexical rules may also exploit monolingual lexical processes, in this case the rule which derives a Spanish present participle from a verbal lexical entry. More complex examples of divergences could also be expressed within this framework by writing suitable bilexical rules:

En: Roque hammered the metal flat.
Sp: Roque martilló el metal hasta dejarlo plano.
Lit: Roque hammered the metal until leave-it flat.

An alternative to bilexical rules for treating divergences is to employ a technique analogous to the transfer variables introduced earlier. For example, under this approach, the translation of *just* could be expressed, in outline, as:

{just, tr(V)} ↔ {acabar, de, tr(V)}

Transfer variables *tr(Ve)* would then be matched against another transfer rule in order to complete transfer; for example:

{eat} ↔ {comer}

Apart from the type mismatch between the transfer variable and the transfer rule it matches – one is a lexical item, the other is a set of lexical items – transfer variables of this sort can lead to slightly unnatural translations. For example, the collocation *to be hungry – tener hambre* might involve a rule of the form:

$\{be, tr(X)\} \leftrightarrow \{tener, tr(X)\}$
$\{hungry\} \leftrightarrow \{hambre\}$

The second rule equates an English adjective with a Spanish noun. A more literal translation might be *hunger – hambre*, and indeed, this is the right translation in certain cases: *it died of hunger – murió de hambre*. Because compositionality is required by transfer variables, they can lead to unnatural transfer rules, and even to unnecessary ambiguity (i.e. *hambre* has to be translated into an English noun and into an adjective).

Another problem with using transfer variables is that monolingual resources are not fully exploited. For example, sense alternations in some English spatial prepositions can be readily described through lexical rules that have regular lexical realisations in Spanish (Trujillo 1995b):

En: The girls ran **behind** the house (*in circles*).
Sp: Las chicas corrieron **detrás de** la casa.
En: The girls ran **behind** the house (*on their way to the park*).
Sp: Las chicas corrieron **por detrás de** la casa.
En: The girls ran **behind** the house (*to hide from the boys*).
Sp: Las chicas corrieron **hasta detrás de** la casa.

The alternation between locative, path and goal sense exhibited in these examples is mirrored in Spanish by the inclusion of additional prepositions indicating the relevant spatial sense. Other prepositions such as *under, over* and *in front of* have similar alternations and translations. It is difficult to see how a transfer variable mechanism can deal with these translations without some notion of a sense extension process. A bilexical rule treatment, on the other hand, allows English sense alternation rules to be exploited in the construction of suitable transfer relations:

$$P_{loc} \quad \leftrightarrow \quad\quad P$$
$$\Downarrow\text{path} \quad\quad\quad \Downarrow$$
$$P_{path} \quad \leftrightarrow \quad por \quad P$$

This says that an extension rule that creates a path sense is applied to the English verb. Its correlate in Spanish is the introduction of the preposition *por* as modifying the input preposition.

Rule Composition As generative devices, bilexical rules can be applied to the output of other rules, making it possible to compose their effect and thus build further transfer relations. For example, derivational morphological processes sometimes have correspondences between languages:

English	Spanish	English	Spanish
accept	aceptar	believe	creer
acceptable	aceptable	believable	creíble
unacceptable	inaceptable	unbelievable	increíble

One way of capturing these regularities is through cascaded application of bilexical rules:

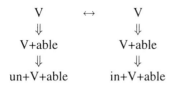

In effect, the rules in such cases establish transfer relationships between lexical processes rather than between lexical items. This may be particularly useful for closely related languages where morphological and other lexical processes have close parallels. The restrictions imposed by each language on the application of each rule in turn restricts the application of the bilexical rule (e.g. *envy/enviable/unenviable – envidiar/envidiable/poco envidiable*). The following translation illustrates a more complex case:

> En: Clara just swam across the pool.
> Sp: Clara acaba de cruzar la piscina nadando.
> Lit: Clara finished of to-cross the pool swimming.

This translation contains two head switches, one of which is also a lexicalization pattern divergence. Application of the relevant bilexical rules results in:

> {just, swam} ↔ {acaba, de, nadar}
> {swam, across} ↔ {cruzó, nadando}

The problem is that neither transfer rule will achieve the appropriate mapping given the transfer algorithm outlined in Section 6.3.3, since the lexical item *swam* appears in both transfer rules, but only one can transfer it. What is needed is:

> {just, swam, across} ↔ {acaba, de, cruzar, nadando}

The presentation so far has assumed bilexical rules to take single lexical items as input. To be able to construct this translation, the input to rules must be allowed to contain more than one item so that the following derivation is established:

> {swim}   ↔   {nadar}
> {swim, across}   ↔   {cruzar, nadando}
> {just, swim, across} ↔   {acaba, de, cruzar, nadando}

Note that *just swim across – cruzó acabando de nadar* is not built since the *across* rule requires a manner verb as input on the Spanish side, and *acabar de* is not marked as such. A simple way of including this extension is to use "rest" variables which simply match the rest of a set of lexical items. The *just* rule now looks like this:

> {V | Rest}   ↔   {V | Rest}
>   ⇓   ⇓
> {just, V | Rest}   ↔   {acaba, de, V | Rest}

This rule will now apply to entries consisting of a verb and modifiers. Note the abuse in notation: curly brackets represent sets, but the | operator applies to lists. Reconciling the two types can be done easily. For example, implementation in Prolog would exploit the recursive nature of lists and the fact that sets are usually represented as lists.

6.3.5   Contextual Restrictions in Transfer

It is well known that context plays an important part in the disambiguation of translations. While disambiguation is discussed in Chapter 9, it is a simple matter to extend the transfer algorithm presented above to allow for lexical context to restrict the possible translations of a lexical item. By context it is meant one or more lexical items in the SL sentence whose presence helps select a translation. The majority of such contexts are semantic in nature and assume a semantic classification of lexical items. Consider:

> En: Len read a book *on* photography.
> Sp: Len leyó un libro *sobre* fotografía.
> En: Len came *on* the bus.
> Sp: Len llegó *en* el bus.

In the first translation, the preposition is modifying a noun which could be classified as *information-source*, and hence the translation of *on* is *sobre*. In the second example, the complement may be classified as a *passenger-vehicle*, with the translation being *en*. The transfer rules for these alternative translations are:

> $\{on_{x,y}\}$ (N[info-source]$_x$) ↔ $\{sobre_{x,y}\}$ (N[info-source]$_x$)
> $\{on_{x,y}\}$ (N[pass-vehi]$_y$) ↔ $\{en_{x,y}\}$ (N[pass-vehi]$_y$)

Contexts are indicated by a list of lexical items within parenthesis. It is the index assigned to the noun that dictates whether the modified noun or the complement of the preposition serves as context. Intuitively, a transfer rule is applicable if after normal transfer via the non-contextual part and subsequent skolemization, all the items in the contextual part of the rule unify with elements of the SL set. The result, as before, is the union of all the items in the non-contextual part on the TL side of transfer rules. These restrictions may not be accurate in all cases, but they are given here to illustrate the way in which context can be used for disambiguation.

6.3.6   Generation Algorithm

Lexicalist generation has as input the set of lexical items resulting from the transfer phase, and as output a linear order of these lexical items as licensed by the TL grammar. Given the lack of structure in the output from transfer, lexicalist generation is prone to exponential complexity on the number of lexical items involved. In fact, it can be shown that some versions of the lexicalist generation problem are NP-complete (Brew 1992), and therefore unlikely to submit to polynomial algorithms. A simple lexicalist generation algorithm, for example, can be easily constructed by applying a parser to every permutation of the TL lexical items, until one is found that yields a grammatical sentence. Clearly, with such an algorithm a solution would be found, at worst, in time $n!$ for n the number of lexical items in the TL sentence. Still, many lexicalist generators use this as the basis for more efficient generators.

Based around the notion of a parser, a family of lexicalist generation algorithms have been proposed (see Further Reading), each relying on modifications which effectively ignore the linear order of constituents. Instead, these generators license all combinations of phrases according to the semantic contraints carried from the SL, and the syntactic constraints of the TL. Also, phrases are not allowed to have repeated lexical items. One simple way of modifying a chart parser for example, is to relax the application of the resolution step such that an active and an inactive edge may combine if their lexical leaves have no elements in common. The resulting algorithm is known as a **chart generator**.

The basic idea is to extend the representation of edges to include a lexical id set consisting of the identifiers of all the lexical leaves covered by the edge. This enables combination of edges only if they subsume different portions of the input. The modified prediction and resolution steps are therefore:

Prediction: If an active edge $A \rightarrow \alpha.B\beta(L)$ is about to be added to the chart, where α and β are possibly empty lists of signs and L is the set of lexical item identifiers covered by the edge, then add to the agenda all edges of the form $B' \rightarrow .\gamma(\{\})$, where $B' \rightarrow \gamma$ is a rule in the grammar, B and B' unify and the set of lexical item identifiers is empty.

Resolution: If the chart contains edges of the form $A \rightarrow \alpha.B\beta(L)$ and $B' \rightarrow \gamma.(M)$, where B and B' unify and $L \cap M = \{\}$, then create a new edge $A' \rightarrow \alpha'B''.\beta'(L \cup M)$, which includes the result of unifying B and B', and add it to the agenda.

Each lexical item starts as an inactive edge with its unique identifier as the only element in its set. The following example shows the resolution rule being successfully and unsuccessfully applied:

Active edge	Inactive edge	Result
NP → . Det N1 ({})	Det → the . ({1})	NP → Det . N1 ({1})
N1 → AP . N1 ({2})	N1 → AP N1 . ({2,3})	*no result*

Successful generation occurs when an inactive edge whose mother is the start category for the grammar has a lexical id set containing all the identifiers for all the lexical items in the input. Generation thus becomes a process of building all possible edges containing lexical items.

Much of the inefficiency associated with lexicalist generation in fact stems from modifiers and other optional constituents. Since the generator builds all possible edges, it will build edges that will never form part of the final solution because they do not include all the modifiers that should accompany a head. Assume the following set of lexical items is the result of transfer (lexeme id given in parentheses):

$\{the_1(1), a_2(2), fat_1(3), black_2(4), chases_{1,2}(5), dog_1(6), cat_2(7)\}$
The fat dog chases a black cat

When input to a lexicalist generator of the type just outlined, the constraints imposed on edge combination by the resolution step mean that the edge below will be built.

$NP \rightarrow Det\ N1\ .\ (\{1,6\})$ *(i.e. the dog)*

In particular, this edge omits the adjective that corresponds to *dog*. As such, this edge will never be part of the final sentence: because *fat* can only appear between *the* and *dog*, any sentence made up with this edge can never have a lexical id set consisting of all the input items. Yet, because the edge is constructed it will combine with edges throughout the generation process in the normal manner, generating yet more edges that cannot span all lexical items in the input. For this example, edges for the following strings will be built, but none of the strings in bold can form part of a complete result:

the dog
the fat dog
a cat
a black cat
chases a cat
chases a black cat
the dog chases a cat
the dog chases a black cat
the fat dog chases a black cat

Clearly the more optional constituents in the sentence, the worse the problem gets.

The solution elaborated here exploits the index structure of the grammar, relying on the observation that after an edge is constructed, only certain indices within the edges are accessible to other constituents (Kay 1996; Trujillo and Berry 1996). For example, treatments of English VPs (e.g. *chased the cat*) typically disallow adjective and other types of modification of the object NP once the VP has been constructed. Thus if *cat* received index 2, it would not be possible to bind into this index by combination with the VP *chases the cat*. Intuitively, this means that modifying the VP cannot lead to modification of the object NP, and hence any lexical items indexed by 2 (e.g. *black*) cannot be incorporated into a sentence involving that edge. Following Kay, indices not available outside a category (i.e. outside an inactive edge) are called internal indices, while those which are accessible are called external indices. When an inactive edge is constructed, none of the internal indices to the edge must appear in lexical items not spanned by the edge.

For a number of grammars it is a simple matter to calculate the internal and external indices of an edge, since these are distinguished in the semantic representation of a rule. For example, the lexical entry below makes the event index E the only external index:

```
[vp,[ [np]/(_,O), [np]/(_,S) ]]/(E,[chase,E,S,O])
```

If this lexical sign is combined with *a cat* and *the fat dog*, the resulting edge would be immediately discarded since *black* would then be indexed by an internal index.

To carry out this check efficiently, edges are augmented with the set of all their indices. When the resolution step is applied, the union of the index sets of the edges being combined makes up the index set of the resulting edge. To determine an edge's internal indices, its external indices are subtracted from this set. The external indices are established for each grammar by inspecting its mechanisms for building semantic representations. An easy way of doing this is to inspect each grammar rule and identify any indices that are made available via the mother. This implies that the effect of this particular technique on the efficiency of lexicalist generators is very much dependent on sign structure in the grammar. For example, the entry for *amar* on p. 151 has the indices for the subject and the object as external indices, making it less effective at eliminating incomplete edges than if only the index for the subject were external. It is possible to minimize the effect of different index organizations by pre-compiling all possible bindings amongst categories in the grammar (Trujillo 1997) in order to eliminate additional incomplete edges not identified by the simple internal indices check just outlined.

Taking a different approach, Poznański et al. (1995) present a greedy lexicalist generation algorithm that achieves polynomial complexity by imposing certain constraints on the grammars that it can generate from. The basis of the algorithm is a test–rewrite loop in which a partial solution is incrementally improved until a complete solution is found. The two steps in the loop are as follows:

Test step: Given a permutation of the input lexical items, the test step attempts a parse, returning all inactive edges found.

Rewrite step: The rewrite step moves an inactive edge to a new position in the emerging sentence such that the previous solution is improved. A solution improves if no inactive edge decreases in size (i.e. in the number of lexical items it spans), and at least one increases in size.

Consider for example, the input set below, corresponding to the sentence *the big brown dog barked*:

{dog,barked,the,brown,big}

Indices are omitted to illustrate the essence of the algorithm economically. Assuming that the first permutation attempted is the one given, the algorithm goes through the following steps:

Test: dog barked the brown big
Rewrite: __ barked the **dog** brown big
Test: barked (the dog) brown big
Rewrite: __ (the dog) **barked** brown big
Test: ((the dog) barked) brown big
Rewrite: the **brown** dog barked __ big
Test: ((the (brown dog)) barked) big

> **Rewrite:** the **big** (brown dog) barked __
> **Test:** ((the (big (brown dog))) barked) *(terminate)*

In this sequence double underscore (__) indicates the starting position of a moved constituent; the moved constituent itself is given in bold face; the bracketing indicates inactive edges which have been created. Each rewrite step in fact involves a search for a constituent to move and a position to move it to. In this example, only lexical items are selected for movement, but in a larger problem, longer edges could be chosen. Furthermore, this step contains the main source of nondeterminism in the algorithm: the selection of the edge to move involves a search through the current state of the algorithm, as well as intermediate test phases for each movement site considered. For example, the first rewrite step would involve moving *dog* to every possible position in turn, followed by a test step. Only when the result of the test improves the current solution does the search stop and a new constituent is selected for movement.

Originally, the algorithm was formulated for categorial grammars (i.e. binary branching) with unification, for which two restrictions were imposed in order to ensure efficiency and completeness.

Precedence monotonicity: This constraint requires that if two constituents fail to form a larger constituent, then no permutation of the elements making up either would render the combination possible. This allows the test step to be executed efficiently.

Dominance monotonicity: This requires that if a part of a constituent successfully combines with a moved constituent to form a new constituent, the rest of the original constituent will combine successfully with the new constituent. This ensures that a constituent that is successfully moved to within an existing constituent will improve the current solution.

Further efficiency is obtained by maintaining a data structure known as a Target-language Normalized Commutative Bracketing (TNCB) that records dominance information among constituents. TNCBs help determine the order in which the current solution is searched during the rewrite step.

Under these conditions, it is possible to show that the generator has order $\mathcal{O}(n^4)$ where n is the number of lexical items in the input. The complexity of the test step is $\mathcal{O}(n)$ as no more than n constituents need to be constructed via unification. The rewrite phase on the other hand is $\mathcal{O}(n^2)$ as any one of n constituents can be moved to any of $n-1$ positions. Finally, the test–rewrite loop is $\mathcal{O}(n)$, since the rewrite step needs to be executed at most $n-1$ times given that each rewrite step improves the solution by creating an edge which spans at least one more lexical item.

6.3.7   Semantics for LexMT

The previous discussion has largely glossed over issues relating to the semantic representations built by the grammar. Most of the examples simply assume that indices are somehow assigned to lexical items, but apart from basing the description on dependency constructions, no relation to formal semantic representations has been discussed. In this section we outline a way in which QLF can be used as the basis for LexMT. An alternative using Minimal Recursion Semantics is briefly discussed in Section 8.3. As indicated previously, this representation shares with the dependency constructions outlined above a lack of commitment to unambiguous quantifier scopings, choosing instead to delay resolution until it is actually needed, if at all. However, unlike the indexed lexical items, QLF can be further processed to yield scoped representations, and therefore could serve for applications other than MT, such as human–computer interfaces, validation of formal specifications etc.

If a grammar constructs QLFs as its semantic representation, one way of adapting it to LexMT is by equating lexical signs in transfer rules instead of recursively constructing a target QLF from the source QLF. Only distinguished indexes need to be bound between source and target lexical items. For example, a transfer rule for the entry *read* (p. 137) in a QLF-based LexMT might be:

```
[ [vp,[ [np]/(O,_), [np]/(S,_) ]]/(E,[read,event(E),_,_]) ]
<==>
[ [vp,[ [np]/(O,_), [np]/(S,_) ]]/(E,[leer,event(E),_,_]) ]
```

Binding the indices O and S ensures that generation constructs the TL sentence with the correct subject and object; binding E ensures that the translation of any adverbs modifying *read* modify *leer*. The minimum for lexicalist transfer is that the distinguished index of each logically dependent phrase is related to its counterpart in the TL at the lexical level. Depending on the actual structure of grammatical signs, indices may be accessed in different ways in LexMT transfer rules: they may appear as part of the subcat list (i.e. the syntactic part) of a sign, as in this example, or they may be distinguished in the semantic part of the sign, as in:

```
[vp,Subcat]/(E,S,O,[read,event(E),_,_])
```

In cases where lexical items are not actually indexed at all, they need to be assigned one or more indices based on the phrase that governs them, or, in the case of relational items, on the phrases they relate. This may involve augmenting rules and lexical entries with additional features, in order to percolate index bindings to appropriate nodes in the analysis tree. For example, in the CLE, lexical entries for auxiliaries are not indexed in the manner needed for LexMT (Alshawi 1992, p. 84):

```
sense(can,
      vp:[arglist=[(A,vp:[subjval=B,...])],
          mainv=n, subjval=B,...],
      [can1,A]).
```

This sense entry for *can* consists of a syntactic pattern which matches a node (vp:..) in the analysis tree, and a corresponding semantic part which consists of the predication [can1,A], where A is the QLF of the VP complement for this auxiliary. At least two indices are required to express the role of *can* in a sentence: one for the subject of the clause and one for the VP complement. This indexing can be superimposed on the grammar by having additional argument slots. In the codings assumed throughout this book, the entry for *can* would then be:

```
[vp,[  [vp,[  _/(C,_)  ]]/(E,A)  ]]/(F,E,C,[can1,A])
```

Indices C and E relate back to the indices for the subject and VP complement of *can* respectively, while index F is the event index for the auxiliary. To make available the right information in this manner requires grammar-wide changes in order that each constituent have a distinguished index. However, the additions can be orthogonal to the rest of the semantic machinery and need not interfere with them. A lexicalist transfer rule for *can – poder* can then be represented as:

```
[ [vp|Rest]/(F,E,C,[can1,_]) ]
<==>
[ [vp|Rest]/(F,E,C,[poder1,_]) ]
```

6.3.8 Further Issues

Efficiency remains an important issue in LexMT. In the transfer phase, a simple set-to-set type of transfer rule can lead to NP-completeness, and several restrictions can be proposed which would make the problem more efficient, including treating each side of the transfer rule as a list (and therefore forced to match the input in the order given).

Typically, the transfer phase will result in several possible translations given the SL set of lexical items. One heuristic which seems to give useful results is to choose translations employing the minimum number of transfer rules. This gives preference to large transfer relations, which, although less compositional, are more likely to be correct given that they incorporate more context.

As far as parser-based generation is concerned, there are no results as yet on whether the resulting algorithms are efficient, even when checks based on internal and external indices are used. By contrast, greedy generation still constructs a number of constituents that can never be part of a complete solution. For example, consider the step where "brown" is inserted between "the" and "dog". This action causes the complete structure for "the dog barked" to be discarded and replaced with that for "the brown dog barked", which in turn is discarded and replaced by "the big brown dog barked". It may be possible that a combination of greedy generation and restrictions on internal and external indices could lead to efficient and general generation techniques.

6.4 Conclusion

This chapter considered three important strategies in MT, and described how various typical problems are dealt with in each. Table 6.2 summarizes some of their advantages and disadvantages. This table refers to what are perceived to

Strategy	Advantages	Disadvantages
Syntactic	Simpler analysis, faster development of grammar, simpler automatic grammar induction	Complex transfer rule and interactions; expensive to maintain
Semantic	Simpler transfer rules; applications other than MT; theoretically motivated semantics	Expertise may be scarce; need for changes as semantic theory develops
Lexicalist	Transparent transfer rules; simpler acquisition of transfer modules	Difficult to include non-lexical information during transfer; danger of inefficiency

Table 6.2. Comparison of transfer strategies.

be inherent properties of the strategy, but it is likely that sufficient resources devoted to any one of them will result in a successful system, as successful MT appears to depend to a large extent on the acquisition and development of large lexical, grammatical and terminological resources. Also, human expertise in an approach and experience of its use will affect the success of the approach. What each strategy offers is a different starting point which may be more or less suitable to different MT applications.

6.4.1 Further Reading

METAL and Ariane-78 where influential systems, based mostly around the notion of syntactic transfer; discussion of these and other syntactic transfer systems can be found in Whitelock and Kilby (1995) and Hutchins and Somers (1992). Fontenelle et al. (1994) pay particular attention to the lexical component in METAL, while the short review by Lehmann (1997) discusses some of its history. METAL is now a commercial product marketed as an MT product by Lernout & Hauspie. Logic-based MT (LMT) (McCord 1989) is a Prolog based, syntactic transfer system developed at IBM. The transfer representation includes the result of some semantic choices and shows deep grammatical relations. The translation test cases are adapted from published work (Lindop and Tsujii 1991; Dorr 1993).

The semantic transfer approach outlined is based on the BCI (Alshawi 1992). A readable guide to QLF and similar semantic representations can be found in Allen (1995). The semantic analysis rules and entries used here are adapted from van Eijck and Moore (1992), where further QLF rules may be found, including a treatment of coordination and ellipsis. The Eurotra project, whose Interface Structure may be seen as implementing semantic transfer, is described in Copeland et al. (1991) and in the *Journal of Machine Translation*, in two special issues on Eurotra Volume 6, Numbers 2 and 3 (1991). Situation Semantics (Barwise and Perry 1983; Devlin 1991) is proposed by Kameyama et al. (1991) as a semantic framework for MT. LFG predicate-argument structure is used in the ELU system (Russell et al. 1991). Other MT systems have also adopted independently motivated semantic representations for transfer: Discourse Representation Structure (Kamp and Reyle 1993) is used in the system presented in Barnett et al. (1991). Montague semantics (Dowty et al. 1981) was adopted as a formalism in the Rosetta system (Rosetta (pseud.) 1994); the Verb-mobil project (Kay et al. 1994) uses Underspecified Discourse Representation Structures/F-Structures (Dorna et al. 1998; Emele and Dorna 1998). Tsujii and Fujita (1991) employ bilingual signs for transfer and also for deriving infer-ences from a knowledge base. The CRITTER system (Isabelle et al. 1988) uses predicate-argument structures for transfer based on a Prolog engine.

LexMT can be attributed to Whitelock (1992) and his Shake-and-Bake MT system. Additional references on lexicalist MT include Beaven (1992a) and Whitelock (1994). Bilingual lexical rules are discussed in Trujillo (1992), San-filippo et al. (1992) and Trujillo (1995a). A number of solutions have been pro-posed to the lexicalist generation problem. Brew (1992) suggests the compilation of ordering constraints from the grammar. Phillips (1993) modifies the control regime of the generators such that it attempts resolutions involving modifiers before any other constituents. The solution elaborated here follows Kay (1996) and Trujillo (1997).

Other transfer MT systems have been developed, as described in Hutchins and Somers (1992) and Whitelock and Kilby (1995). Of these one should mention the well known sublanguage MT system Météo, described in (Chandioux 1976) and summarised in Whitelock and Kilby (1995, Ch. 7), and SPANAM (Vascon-cellos 1987) for Spanish into English MT.

7 Interlingua Machine Translation

This chapter describes two approaches to MT that are based on a language-neutral representation of sentence meaning.

Multilingual MT systems are expensive to build, maintain and extend to new languages. Transfer systems in particular suffer from polynomial increase on the number of languages for the transfer modules required. Interlingua translation is an approach in which the work needed to construct multilingual systems is minimized by transforming sentences into a pivot or interlingua representation from which sentences in one or more TLs can be generated.

In a minimal interlingua system each language has a module that is responsible for analysing sentences into the common representation, and for generating grammatical sentences from this representation. Figure 7.1 illustrates this general architecture. Clearly the number of modules in the system grows linearly with the number of languages. For instance, if separate analysis and generation components are needed for each language, the number of modules in a system for 11 languages is 22. Compare this with a minimal transfer system where transfer modules alone, even if reversible, would total 55. Adding a 12th language would make the interlingua system grow by 1 module (2 if analysis and generation use different grammars), whereas the transfer system would grow by 11 transfer modules at least.

A distinction is sometimes made between pure interlingua systems and Knowledge-Based Machine Translation (KBMT). The former refers to systems that

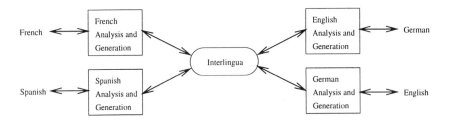

FIG. 7.1. Minimal Interlingua Architecture.

167

construct representations that are language-independent, but which nevertheless restrict themselves purely to information that is needed for linguistic realization of meanings. KBMT systems on the other hand build representations in which the content goes beyond what is linguistically implied, to contain real-world knowledge and knowledge of a particular area or domain covered by the system. From now on, the term *interlingua* will be used to refer to pure interlingua systems unless otherwise indicated.

At their respective theoretical limits, interlingua and KBMT systems are at opposite ends of a continuum, with interlingua at the language oriented end, and KBMT at the domain-oriented end. Both, however, need elements of the other to be successful in practice, particularly because the distinction of what is linguistic knowledge and what is non-linguistic world knowledge is hard to make. On the one hand, an interlingua system needs to make inferences about the world and the domain of discourse in order to resolve ambiguities or fill gaps in the literal knowledge expressed in a sentence. For this it needs non-linguistic world knowledge, just as any other type of MT system that tries to achieve high-quality translations does. On the other hand, a KBMT system needs to relate to linguistic structures to avoid excessive paraphrasing of content and, more practically, to decrease the non-determinism that would arise in generation from totally language independent representations.

The first half of this chapter describes a pure interlingua system based on that developed by Dorr (1993) and Dorr (1994). In this system, the common representation language is Lexical Conceptual Structure. The second half describes a KBMT system based on the presentation in Nirenburg et al. (1992) and Goodman and Nirenburg (1991).

7.1   Lexical Conceptual Structure MT

Interlingua systems depend crucially on the common language into and out of which all sentences accepted by the system are mapped. This language must at once be capable of representing the meaning of any sentence, and do so in a way that preserves sufficient linguistic structure such that a TL sentence is a proper translation of the original.

Cognitive linguists and other semanticists have developed formalisms for the expression of linguistic meanings in a language-oriented manner which is nevertheless independent of any specific language. Lexical Conceptual Structure (LCS) (Jackendoff 1983; Jackendoff 1990; Jackendoff 1992) is one such representation that has been employed as the basis of the English–German–Spanish system UNITRAN (Dorr 1993; Dorr 1994).

UNITRAN analyses a sentence from any of these languages and produces an LCS representation of its meaning. It then generates from this LCS into any of the other languages. The following example illustrates this process, using a simplified LCS:

English: Bill went into the house.
LCS: GO(BILL,TO(IN(HOUSE)))
Spanish: Bill entró a la casa.

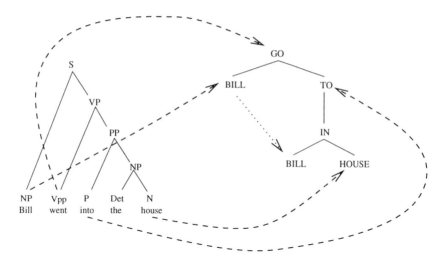

FIG. 7.2. Mapping into LCS.

As this example illustrates, LCS is a recursive framework consisting of predicates, referred to as primitives, and arguments, where arguments may themselves be LCSs. This LCS can be paraphrased as "Bill traverses a path that terminates at the interior of the house". Note that primitives may have no arguments, as in the case of BILL and HOUSE. LCS is discussed in detail in the next section.

Grammatical knowledge in UNITRAN is expressed as principles and parameters in the GB theory of Chomsky (1986). In this framework, universal and language-specific constraints operate over syntactic trees to determine their grammaticality. This makes the theory configurational in that grammaticality is specified, broadly speaking, in terms of geometric relations amongst governors and governed constituents. Principles and parameters are organized into modules, which are applied in a specific order and whose successful application deems a structure grammatical. The purpose of the grammar is to establish the syntactic structure from which LCSs are built via a linking routine. This routine uses the results of the GB analysis to build the LCS for the complete sentence. In particular, it traverses the analysis tree top-down, retrieving the LCS structure of the head daughter of a node and combining it with the recursively constructed LCS representation of the non-head daughters. This mapping is illustrated in Fig. 7.2.

The main repository of knowledge in UNITRAN is the lexicon, where uninstantiated LCS structures for each content word are stored. In fact, it will become apparent that this reliance on the lexicon makes the LCS approach to interlingua quite independent of the GB theory employed. GB is attractive from a multilingual perspective because it is intended to be easily parameterized to the specific properties of a given language, restricting the main knowledge acquisition effort to lexicon building. However, given the widespread use of non-configurational and unification-based formalisms in computational linguistics and MT, we present an LCS interlingua system based on the grammatical and computational foundations laid in previous chapters. This will follow the spirit of the LCS approach but it will make it easier to relate it and compare it with other MT paradigms.

7.1.1 Lexical Conceptual Structure

LCS may be described as a cognitive theory of grammar which in turn may be seen as a development of localist or case theories of natural language semantics of the sort some scholars have identified in work as early as that of Byzantine grammarians (Hjelmslev 1935). In these theories, descriptions of spatial expressions are used in the explanation and representation of non-spatial expressions. For example, such theories consider as semantically related the uses of *to* in *I went* **to** *Liverpool* and *I gave an apple* **to** *Alonso*.

As described by Jackendoff (Jackendoff 1990), (lexical) conceptual structure is a common representation of thought, into and out of which senses, actions and language are mapped, and through which information in different modalities is processed by the mind. Linking rules establish correspondences between inputs and LCS. Thus, grammars can be seen as linking rules for linguistic input and output, whereas other rules would be needed to link LCS and the visual, motor and auditory modalities. As well as being modality neutral, LCS is intended to be language neutral and as such fulfils the criteria for an interlingua representation.

Types, Primitives and Fields Primitives in LCS are specializations of a small set of major ontological categories referred to as types. Types determine the kinds of entities in the world that the framework can represent. The following is a complete list of all the types used in the description to follow:

Type	Description
Event	Corresponds mainly to verbs which answer "What happened?"
State	Corresponds mainly to verbs not answering "What happened?"
Position	Refers to a situation with an entity at an abstract or physical location
Path	Refers to a conceptual or physical trajectory
Thing	Corresponds mainly to nouns denoting objects
Property	A quality which is ascribed to a Thing
Location	A physical location
Time	Corresponds to temporal phrases
Manner	A quality that is ascribed to Events or States
Intensifier	Indicates a greater or lesser degree of a Property, Manner or another Intensifier
Purpose	The reason for an Event or a State

Each type acts as a "semantic parts of speech" for a number of primitives, such as GO (*Event*) and TO (*Path*). Primitives are generalizations over concepts from different domains. For example GO in the spatial domain indicates a change of location for an entity, whereas in the assignment of properties (e.g. *the apples turned yellow*) it expresses the acquisition of the property by the entity. Other examples of primitives include BE (*State*), IN (*Position*), VERY (*Intensifier*). A fuller list is given in Dorr (1993, pp. 100, 130). Some types include a large number of primitives in an almost one-to-one relationship with the open class words in the language. Thus there are a large number of *Manner* primitives such as LOVINGLY, GIFTINGLY, WRITINGLY etc., and similarly for *Thing*, *Property*, *Time* and *Location*, which need to account for a large number of different meanings.

Primitives preceded by WH- are used for questions. For example, *What did John eat?* has the LCS:

[Event EAT ([Thing JOHN], [Thing WH-THING])]

Primitives are further specialized by the addition of a field indicator stating the domain under which the primitive is to be interpreted. They are indicated by a subscript on the primitive. The table below gives the fields used here.

Field	Example sentences
Locational	Augusto is at the supermarket; they went to the shop
Possessional	I have a flat; Omar received a video
Identificational	She became a mother; Luz remained happy
Temporal	The match was at 3:30pm; dinner went from 7pm to midnight
Circumstantial	Elias kept writing books; she started composing music
Existential	Paris exists; Javier created a party
Perceptional	They saw the rain; she looked towards Platt Fields
Intentional	She signed the book for me; Debbie ate because she was hungry
Instrumental	David walked with Rose; John stabbed Mary with a knife

It is now possible to give the full LCS for *Bill went into the house*:

[Event GO_{Loc}(
   [Thing BILL],
   [Path TO_{Loc}(
      [PositionIN_{Loc}(
         [Thing BILL],
         [Thing HOUSE])])])]

Note that fields only apply to primitives that take arguments, although it is conceivable that the theory could be extended to allow different fields for *Thing* primitives also. Overall, the type organization of this LCS can be expressed as: *Event(Thing,Path(Position(Thing,Thing)))*.

A note about the Circumstantial field. This field involves primitives in which a *Thing* is "located" in an event or state, where located means that *Thing* is a participant or role player. Thus, Elias is the subject of the writing event in the first example for Circumstantial.

Dorr (1993, pp. 101–2) presents a series of constraints on type structure for argument-taking primitives. These constraints help in the interpretation of sentences by restricting the types of LCS that may appear as arguments. Basic restrictions are defined for the locational field. For example, GO takes two arguments: the first one may be a *Thing* or an *Event*, while the second must be a *Path*. When a primitive is modified by a field, these restrictions are extended. Thus, AT (*Position*) in a locational field expects two arguments, both of type *Thing*, while in the temporal field it expects a *Thing* and a *Time*.

Thus, a sentence such as *the meeting went from 2:00 to 4:00* has LCS (Dorr 1993, p. 98):

```
[Event GOTemp (
      [Thing MEETING],    .
      [Path FROMTemp (
            [Position ATTemp (
                  [Thing MEETING],
                  [Time 2:00])])],
      [Path TOTemp (
            [Position ATTemp (
                  [Thing MEETING],
                  [Time 4:00])])])]
```

The type *Exists* may be seen as a special type consisting of a single primitive with the same name. Thus, the sentence *Descartes exists* has the LCS:

```
[State BEExist (
      [Thing DESCARTES],
      [Position ATExist (
            [Thing DESCARTES],
            [Exists EXISTS])])]
```

The CAUSE and LET primitives cannot be extended to other fields (Jackendoff 1983, p. 191). The sentence *we kept the meeting at 6:00* has the LCS:

```
[Event CAUSE (
      [Thing WE],
      [Event STAYTemp (
            [Thing MEETING],
            [Position ATTemp (
                  [Thing MEETING],
                  [Time 6:00])])])]
```

Argument structure is carefully designed in UNITRAN. Each predicate can have three kinds of arguments. The first argument is always a logical subject, which normally corresponds to the subject of verbs or the complement of prepositions. After the first argument, there may be zero or more logical arguments, which normally correspond to non-subject arguments to verbs. Finally, and following the logical arguments in the structure, are zero or more logical modifiers, which, as the name implies, tend to correspond to adjectives, adverbs, prepositional phrases and other modifiers. The LCS for *John ate very happily* illustrates all three kinds of arguments:

[Event EAT (

    [Thing JOHN],

    [Thing FOOD],

    [Manner HAPPILY (

        [Intensifier VERY$_{\text{Instr}}$])])]

In addition to types, primitives and fields, the structure of LCS can be further decomposed through features that capture generalizations over several fields. For example, by positing the features *bounded* and *internal structure*, Jackendoff (1992) captures the syntactic behaviour and various aspects of semantic interpretation for plurals and events within a unified framework. For example, he identifies semantic similarities between *the light flashed until dawn* and the plural *the buses*: both consist of several instances of the same individuated entity, flashing events in the former, and buses in the latter. This commonality is captured by marking the respective events and things as *-bounded* and *+internal structure*.

What is more, a number of conceptual mapping functions are proposed which map LCSs to related LCSs, thus capturing important conceptual relationships. For example, a function *ELT* is responsible for mapping unbounded *Things* (labelled *Matter* in Jackendoff (1992)) such as water, into bounded *Things* such as drops of water. Such functions capture regularities that are manifest in different fields. Other extensions to the LCS formalism including fractional dimensionalities, polarity, direction and argument binding are described in Jackendoff (1990) and Jackendoff (1992).

Parameterization It was already mentioned that UNITRAN uses a linking routine to map the analyses produced by its GB grammars into their corresponding LCSs. As an interlingua system, these LCSs must be mapped into potentially very different analysis trees during generation into the TL. But because each language realizes the same LCS in different ways, a set of seven parameters enables the same LCS to be realized by different syntactic structures. In effect, the parameters augment LCS data structures with language specific information which is accessed by the analysis and generation modules. Most parameters essentially override a default linking routine by indicating whether part of an LCS must be realized or not, and how. The majority of these parameters are indicated in the lexical entries for each language, as these constitute the main repository of language specific information.

Star "*" The * parameter indicates that a subpart of an LCS must be realized syntactically. This parameter is used extensively as it is the way by which arguments to verbs, prepositions and other elements are realized. Consider the (simplified) LCS specified in the lexical entries for *enter* and *entrar*, which constitute an instance of structural divergence:

En: *enter* = GO(*X,TO(IN(X,*Z)))
Sp: *entrar* = GO(*X,*TO(IN(X,Z)))

Consider the English LCS first. Because the first argument to GO, namely X, is marked with *, the generation algorithm will be invoked recursively on the LCS found at this position. Contrast this with the second occurrence of X, the first argument to IN, which is not so marked and therefore need not be realized. Similarly, the second argument to IN, Z, needs to be realized syntactically. Thus, given the input LCS GO(Jack,TO(IN(Jack,House))), the sentence *Jack entered the house* will be generated, but not **Jack entered to the house/Jack entered in the house* etc.

Now consider the Spanish LCS. Again, the first argument to GO is marked * and must be realized. However, this time the complete LCS headed by TO must be recursively generated. For example, the lexical entry below would match this sub-LCS:

Sp: *a* = TO(IN(X,*Z))

Only the marked argument in this LCS needs to be generated. Given the same input as for the English example, the Spanish sentence generated would be *Jack entró a la casa*. The * operators may therefore be seen as indicating which meaning components in a lexical entry are not realized by the lexical entry and therefore need to be realized through other constituents.

:INT *and* :EXT Parameters :INT and :EXT override the default mapping for logical subjects and logical arguments making the former appear internally (i.e. within the VP as syntactic object) and the latter externally (i.e. outside the VP as grammatical subject) in the syntactic tree. To illustrate their application consider the simplified LCS for *like – gustar* exhibiting thematic divergence:

En: *like* = BE$_{\text{Ident}}$(*X,AT$_{\text{Ident}}$(X,*Y),LIKINGLY)
Sp: *gustar* = BE$_{\text{Ident}}$(*X:INT,AT$_{\text{Ident}}$(X,*Y:EXT),LIKINGLY)

Generation through the LCS for *like* leads to the LCS for logical subject X being generated as subject of the verb via default linking rules. Similarly, Y will be generated by a default rule which maps logical objects into syntactic objects.

For *gustar* both X and Y are also generated, but the :INT parameter overrides the default linking rule and results in the matching LCS being generated as direct object of the verb. In the same way, the linking rule for Y is overridden and instead the matching LCS is generated as subject to the verb.

:CAT Apart from default linking rules, UNITRAN has default syntactic realization rules that map types into syntactic categories. For example, *Event* and *State* LCSs are mapped into verbs by default, while *Thing* LCSs are mapped into nouns (Dorr 1993, p. 141).

The purpose of the :CAT parameter is to override these defaults with a different syntactic category. Consider the LCS for *Gloria is hungry – Gloria tiene hambre*:

[State BEIdent (
   [Thing GLORIA],
   [Position ATIdent (
      [Thing GLORIA],
      [Property HUNGRY])])]

The lexical entries for *be* and *tener* are:

En: *be* = [State BEIdent($*X$,[Position ATIdent(X,$*Y$)])]
Sp: *tener* = [State BEIdent($*X$,[Position ATIdent(X,$*Y$:CAT(NOUN))])]

During generation, the primitive HUNGRY will be rendered as an adjective in English by default, but in Spanish the category indicated by the argument :CAT leads to a noun being generated instead. Clearly this can only be achieved if the generator can indeed generate a noun from a property or if there is in fact a noun lexical entry with a property as its LCS.

:DEMOTE *and* :PROMOTE   In head switching divergences the default mapping of logical heads and logical modifiers is altered such that logical heads map into syntactic modifiers, and logical modifiers map into syntactic heads. The :DE-MOTE parameter causes a logical head to be generated as a syntactic modifier. That is, it is demoted in the syntactic structure. Consider the LCS for *Carlos just ate* – *Carlos acaba de comer*:

[State BECirc(
   [Thing CARLOS],
   [Position ATCirc(
      [Thing CARLOS],
      [Event EAT(
         [Thing CARLOS],
         [Thing FOOD])])],
   [Manner JUST])]

By default, the syntactic structure of the Spanish sentence will be generated since the logical head, namely that rooted at BE, corresponds to the syntactic head. To generate the English syntactic structure, the logical head must be demoted and one of its components must take its place as syntactic head. The lexical entry for *just* therefore looks like this:

[State BECirc(
   X<LOWER-SUBJECT>,
   [Position ATCirc(
      X,
      *Y:DEMOTE)]
   [Manner JUST])]

Argument *Y* will be generated, but because this argument is marked :DEMOTE, the material matching it will determine the syntactic head (it is unfortunate that the parameter name :DEMOTE indicates the sub-LCS that needs to be promoted!). The special marker <LOWER-SUBJECT> handles the control relation that exists between the logical subject of BE and the event matching Y, requiring that they be identical.

Parameter :PROMOTE is the inverse of :DEMOTE. It forces a logical modifier to become a syntactic head, thus being promoted in the syntactic structure. Consider the LCS for *Carlos usually eats – Carlos suele comer*:

[Event EAT([Thing CARLOS], [Thing FOOD], [Manner HABITUALLY])]

By default the logical modifier HABITUALLY will be generated as a syntactic modifier leading to the English sentence. In Spanish, this mapping is overridden by the :PROMOTE parameter included in the lexical entry for the verb *soler*:

[Manner HABITUALLY:PROMOTE]

During generation into Spanish, the manner modifier is matched against this lexical entry. Because of its parameter setting, the verb *soler* is generated as syntactic head, and then the rest of the input LCS is generated as its complement and subject as appropriate. Note that a :CAT parameter would not be appropriate here as this would not guarantee that the generated verb would be the syntactic head for the clause.

An important difference between :DEMOTE and :PROMOTE is that demotions involve mapping a logical head into a syntactic modifier and a logical argument into a syntactic head. By contrast, promotions map the logical head into a syntactic argument and a logical modifier into a syntactic head. In UNITRAN this means different control regimes during generation given that for demotions the parameter is visible as soon as the logical head matches a lexical entry, while for promotions the parameter can only be made available if the lexical item for the logical modifier is retrieved prior to generation of the logical head.

:CONFLATED In conflation, meaning components are included in a lexical entry such that they need not be realized syntactically. In general, this is indicated by the absence of the * parameter in UNITRAN, but it is sometimes clearer to specify this explicitly by marking the leaves of an LCS with the :CONFLATED parameter. Consider the simplified LCS for English *stab*:

CAUSE(*W,GO(KNIFE-WOUND:CONFLATED,
         TOWARDS(AT(KNIFE-WOUND,*Z))))

Generation through this lexical entry results in syntactic realizations for the LCSs matching W and Z, but not for the conflated primitive KNIFE-WOUND, blocking the incorrect * *stab knife wounds*. Note that the second, non-parameterized occurrence of this primitive is not realized either because it is not marked by *. Dorr (1993, p. 259 n. 14) justifies the conflated parameter by stating that "it specifies that the 'constant' term... [i.e. KNIFE-WOUND]... must obligatorily fill the position, and moreover, that this constant must be a legal LCS primitive of the system."

Let us summarize processing in UNITRAN in the light of these parameters. In the analysis phase parameters help construct an LCS for the input sentence based on the LCS of its individual words. The complete LCS is then stripped of these language-specific parameters, and passed onto the TL generation module. Then, during generation, portions of the input LCS are matched against the lexicon, which provides the TL specific parameters that guide syntactic realization.

7.1.2 Analysis into LCS

As we have seen, default linking, realization and other routines ensure that analysis trees give rise to appropriate LCSs and vice versa. Yet, a large amount of the knowledge needed to guide these processes is encoded in the lexicon. It is not surprising, therefore, that most of the mappings achieved by the linking routines and by the parameters just described can be modelled through suitable lexical entries and PS rules of the type introduced in Sections 5.3 and 5.4, in conjunction with Prolog's unification framework.

We begin by showing how default linking, as well as the main effects of the parameters *, :INT, :EXT, :CAT and :CONFLATED, can be achieved by establishing suitable bindings between LCS structures and the subcategorisation frames in verbs. The presentation below assumes that types, primitives and fields are indicated through predicates. Thus, the LCS:

$$[\text{Position AT}_{\text{Loc}}([\text{Thing HOUSE}], [\text{Location MALAGA}])]$$

will be represented in Prolog as:

```
[position(at(loc)),
    [thing(house)|A]++A,
    [location(malaga)|B]++B
 |C] ++ C
```

The type, primitive and optional field are the first item in a list that represents the LCS. Arguments constitute the rest of the list, each of which may itself contain arguments, as illustrated below. Furthermore, because any number of modifiers may be added as arguments to an LCS, a difference list mechanism is used to allow efficient appends of further LCSs. However, where this mechanism does not add to the explanation, the difference list will be omitted to simplify the presentation.

Consider first default linking, as illustrated by the sentence *Alvaro eats food*. Simplified lexical entries for this sentence are given below (note that tense, person, gapping and other syntactic information is also omitted for clarity):

```
[np]/[thing(alvaro)].

[n]/[thing(food)].

[vp,[ [np]/O, [np]/S ]]/
  [event(eat),S,O].
```

During parsing, the LCS for the subject and the object are unified with S and O to construct the LCS for the complete sentence. Linking is therefore achieved: the sign for *eats* explicitly indicates how the logical arguments in the LCS are mapped to the subcat items in the syntactic part of the sign.

To model parameter *, one specifies the portion of the verb's LCS that needs to be generated by a particular subcategorization sign. The following is the lexical sign for *enter*:

```
[vp,[ [np]/O, [np]/S ]]/
   [event(go(loc)),S,[path(to(loc)),[position(in(loc)),S,O]]]
```

Appropriate linking between the LCS and the subcat list is established as before. The corresponding entry for Spanish *entrar* is:

```
[vp,[ [pp]/O, [np]/S ]]/
   [event(go(loc)),S,O=[path(to(loc)),[position(in(loc)),S,Z]]]
```

Instead of an NP, the first item in the subcat list is a PP, and its LCS is bound to variable O, whose value is the LCS headed by the primitive TO. A suitable entry for *a*, the required preposition, would be:

```
[p,[ [np]/O ]]/
   [path(to(loc)),[position(in(loc)),_S,O]]
```

Parameters :INT and :EXT are modelled by changing the order of the subcat arguments. The entry for Spanish *gustar* is:

```
[vp,[ [np]/S, [np]/O ]]/
   [state(be(ident)),S,[position(at(ident)),S,O],
                       [manner(likingly)]]
```

Logical subject S is realized by the first item in the subcat list, namely the direct object of the verb.

Category switchings induced by the :CAT parameter follow directly from the category specified in the subcat list. The entry for *tener* is:

```
[vp,[ [np]/O, [np]/S ]]/
   [state(be(ident)),S,[position(at(ident)),S,O]]
```

The corresponding entry for *be* needed for *Gloria is hungry – Gloria tiene hambre* is:

```
[vp,[ [ap]/O, [np]/S ]]/
   [state(be(ident)),S,[position(at(ident)),S,O]]
```

For Spanish, the complement of the verb will be an NP, while for English the complement will be an AP.

Parameter :CONFLATED also follows naturally. English *stab* has entry:

```
[vp,[ [np]/O, [np]/S ]]/
   [event(cause),
     S,
     [event(go(poss)),
       [thing(knife-wound)],
       [path(towards(poss)),
         [position(at(poss)),
           [thing(knife-wound)],
           O]]]]
```

Primitive KNIFE-WOUND is not realized since it does not figure in the subcat list.

To account for demotions first note that, in such divergences, the LCS for the syntactic modifier (i.e. the logical head) contains the LCS of the syntactic head (i.e. a logical argument). The position of this argument is determined at the lexical level. One way of making the relevant information available in the lexical entry of the modifier is to allow modifiers to subcategorise for the modified constituents, as is done in Categorial Grammar (Wood 1993). In this approach, *just* has the entry:

```
[ap,[ [vp,[ SynNP/X ]]/LCS ]]/
    [state(be(circ)),X,[position(at(circ)),X,LCS],
    [manner(just)]]
```

This says that "just" takes a complement VP whose semantics (LCS) occur as second argument to position(at(circ)). Also, the semantics for the subject of this VP (i.e. X) occur as first argument to this primitive.

A suitable PS rule is needed to saturate this complement and to determine the LCS of the resulting constituent:

```
[vp,[Subj]]/LCS --->
 [   [ap,[ VP ]]/LCS,
     VP = [vp,[Subj]]/_ ]
```

Note that although the rule makes the VP the syntactic head, the interplay of the semantic bindings makes the AP the semantic head, and thus achieves the required demotion. The Spanish verb *acabar* is practically identical to the English adverb.

Promotion divergences can be modelled at the lexical level by requiring the promoted LCS (i.e. the logical modifier) to be treated as a syntactic head by the grammar. That is, its LCS is appended at the end of the logical modifier list of its syntactic complement's LCS. For Spanish *soler* the overall structure of its LCS is:

```
[vp,[ [vp]/LCS++[[manner(habitually)]|X], [np]/S ]]/LCS++X
```

Here the difference list mechanism enables the manner modifier to be appended to the complement's LCS, together with a new end of list variable, which then becomes the end of list variable for the semantics of *soler* as a whole. To facilitate the description, the subject of the complement VP is omitted, but its LCS should be bound to S to effect the appropriate subject raising relation. The entry for *usually* is similar to that for *just* in that it takes a VP as complement:

```
[ap,[ [vp,[ _/X ]]/LCS++[[manner(habitually)]|End ]]/
    LCS++End
```

Both the promoted and non-promoted structures are built using the same strategy: a modifier is appended to the complement's LCS and a new end of list variable is created. Promotion nevertheless occurs since the syntactic head remains the VP in both cases. The full LCS for a sentence such as *Carlos suele comer* is:

```
[event(eat),[thing(carlos)|A]++A,[thing(food)|B]++B,
  [manner(habitually)|C]++C|D]++D
```

Note the difference list for each LCS as they can all theoretically include logical arguments and modifiers. It is easy to extract an LCS in a simpler format from such a representation.

7.1.3   Generation from LCS

UNITRAN's generation mechanism employs linking routines that relate LCS components to their corresponding syntactic counterparts. The resulting deep structures are then reorganized using moving operations (i.e. Move-α) and licensed by the different GB modules to produce adequate surface forms.

However, because of the recursive, headed structure of LCSs, the SHDG algorithm can be applied to derive surface forms. In fact the algorithm can be used without many modifications. One type of extension that needs to be made, however, is related to the difference list used to represent extendible LCSs. Because these can grow as the generator searches for a parse tree, they can lead to non-termination or to cyclic Prolog structures (if no "occurs check" is incorporated). The change to the algorithm essentially involves verifying the coherence of LCS structures before they are used in the top-down generation of a (sub)tree.

7.1.4   Translation Divergences

Many of the divergences introduced in Section 6.1.1 have already been considered in the preceding discussion. In particular, it may be said that the divergences arise not so much between languages, but between a language and the interlingua representation, leaving its resolution to the monolingual grammars. Thematic, head switching, structural and categorial divergences were resolved by the parameters of UNITRAN or by specifying the required unifications and constraints in lexical entries under the framework of this book. We now briefly consider lexical gaps, lexicalizations, and collocational and idiomatic divergences.

Adhering to the interlingua philosophy, lexical gaps and idiomatic divergences require constructions in the source and target languages mapping to equivalent LCS representations. Regardless of what the specific LCS representation is, there may need to be an element of non-compositionality in one of the grammars in order to handle these divergences. To illustrate, consider again *to kick the bucket* meaning "to die". Building the necessary LCS requires a dedicated rule (a similar effect can be achieved through the subcat list of a lexical entry) that builds the required semantics:

```
[vp,[ [np]/S ]]/
  [event(go(circ)),S,[path(to(circ)),[position(at(circ)),S,
    [property(dead)]]]]]
--->
[  [vp,Subcat]/[event(kick)|_],
   [det]/the,
   [n]/[thing(bucket)] ]
```

The semantics of all the daughters are completely ignored, resulting in a non-compositional LCS at the mother node. This LCS is fed to the TL generator producing the corresponding translation. In the absence of additional information, an equivalent TL idiom (e.g. Spanish *estirar la pata*) or a non-idiomatic translation *morir* will be generated. Note that a literal interpretation of the idiom is also possible during analysis, leading to additional ambiguity. Identification of idioms could use term extraction techniques (Section 4.4) and its resolution could be based on contextual cues (Section 9.3 and Section 9.4).

For lexical gaps (e.g. *get up early* – *madrugar*), the language missing the lexical item may receive a non-compositional translation in the same manner. Alternatively, the language missing the lexical item may compositionally derive a complex LCS which is then associated with a single lexical item in the language without the gap.

In UNITRAN, lexicalizations are instances of conflational divergence (Dorr 1993, pp. 260–61). The LCS for *Susan swam across the channel* is:

```
[event(go(loc)),
  [thing(susan)],
  [path(across(loc)),
     [position(at(loc)),
        [thing(susan)],
        [location(river)]]],
  [manner(swimmingly)]]
```

In English, the verb *to swim* conflates the manner LCS, whereas Spanish *cruzar* does not, leading to SWIMMINGLY being independently generated by a gerundive. Note that if one assumes a strict ordering correspondence between logical and syntactic modifiers, the entry for *swim* in English would need to indicate a *Path* argument in its LCS regardless of whether the input contains such a PP, otherwise the LCS above would not match it.

A collocation may be viewed as a semantic concept whose lexical realization depends on other lexical or semantic elements. One way of treating collocations in LCS interlingua MT is to allow ambiguity in the realization of phrases, and to use a post-processing step to select a correct sentence. For example, the collocation divergence *be hungry* – *tener hambre*, handled as a case of categorial divergence in UNITRAN, leads to ambiguity when there is a more straightforward correspondence between the two languages, as in *Jorge is intelligent* – *Jorge es inteligente*, which can lead to the very awkward, if entirely grammatical, translation *Jorge tiene inteligencia* (Jorge has intelligence). This ambiguity arises because the LCS for Spanish *ser* (to be) and *tener* (to have) are made identical in UNITRAN in order to cope with the *hungry* divergence. The ambiguity may be resolved using a corpus or rule-based disambiguation technique as explained in Chapter 9. An alternative is to make lexical LCS expressions sensitive to complement values. For instance, the simplified entry for Spanish *tener* could be:

```
[vp,[ [np]/O=[property(nom_prop)], [np]/S ]]/[be,S,[at,S,O]]
```

Here nom_prop would need to unify only with the nominal properties THIRSTY, HUNGRY, ANGRY, COLD, HOT or LUCKY and nothing else.

7.1.5   Further Issues

Given the localist orientation of LCS, most development has been in extending spatial conceptualizations into non-spatial domains. However, this has meant that various issues of semantic description are difficult to express in LCSs. Some of these include tense and aspect (Dorr 1993), modality, quantification, informational structure, negation and scope. Even for the domains explicitly considered by workers in LCS, there are variations in the encoding of the same concept. For example, a "meeting" in Dorr (1993, p. 98) has type *Thing*, while in Jackendoff (1983, p. 191) it has type *Event*. Theoretically, this may not be a problem, but in practical terms it can lead to mismatches in the representations constructed through grammars written by different linguists.

Another issue is that of justifying LCSs for phrases which are not clearly related to locational expressions. For example, it is not clear why the *Intensifier* VERY should have instrumental field in *John ate very happily* (Dorr 1993, p. 128). Again, the issue is not whether a justification is possible or not, but a more practical issue of whether different grammarians working on different languages will actually produce corresponding LCSs for translationally equivalent sentences.

7.2   Knowledge-Based Machine Translation

The philosophy behind KBMT is that translation requires functionally complete understanding of the source text, where "functionally" means that representations of meaning should be sufficient for translation into a number of languages (Nirenburg et al. 1992, p. 27). Such a level of understanding goes beyond the propositional and literal meanings that can be derived from linguistic inputs alone to include real world knowledge. As a consequence, KBMT systems rely on an augmentor that constructs functionally complete representations based on the semantic structures produced by the analyser and other knowledge sources.

Augmentors address issues of ambiguity and coverage by adding textual as well as real-world information to a meaning representation of a text. Both human and machine augmentation are possible. Augmentation by humans takes the form of interaction with the user, while augmentation by machine involves a knowledge base or domain model and an inference mechanism operating over meaning representations. Figure 7.3 shows the conceptual organization of a multilingual KBMT system. Although the augmentor is drawn as part of the interlingua mechanism, in the case of human intervention it may need to apply during analysis. The output of the augmentor is a meaning representation of the input that is then passed onto the TL generator.

Different KR frameworks may be used to represent different kinds of meaning. For example, in an extreme case, the domain model could be expressed using FOL and the functionally complete meaning representation could be expressed using frames, while the meaning representation produced by the grammars could use f-structures from LFG. However, it is preferable, whenever possible, to adopt the same or related frameworks for all representations.

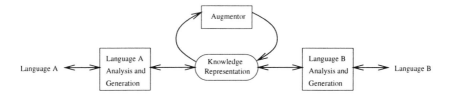

FIG. 7.3. KBMT architecture.

One should point out from the outset that the expense of constructing the knowledge bases and domain models for KBMT makes them more applicable to limited domains and sublanguages such as manuals and standard types of report. In these applications, fuller domain models can be constructed to approximate the knowledge that a human translator would have. Where appropriate, the examples in this half of the chapter will assume the domain of computer manuals. The system outlined follows the ideas presented in Nirenburg et al. (1992), Goodman and Nirenburg (1991) and the Mikrokosmos system of Onyshkevich and Nirenburg (1995).

7.2.1   Knowledge Representation and Ontology

Just as LCS formed the basis of the interlingua MT system described earlier in the chapter, so for KBMT a language is needed to represent meanings. Unlike that system however, a domain model needs to be represented also. In this section, a KR framework is presented in which the domain model is described as an ontology.

Frames   The framework we introduce is loosely based on the frames and related knowledge representation frameworks popular in AI (Minsky 1975). It consists of named slots or features and values, where values may themselves be frames. Variations on such structures have been used amply in computational linguistics, either in the form of complex feature structures (Shieber 1986) or in typed feature structure systems (Carpenter 1992).

As an example, consider the frame below which illustrates a possible meaning representation for the instruction *Save the document*:

$$
\begin{bmatrix}
\text{instance\_of:} & \text{save} \\
\text{isa:} & \text{physical\_event} \\
\text{id:} & \text{save\_43} \\
\text{agent:} & \text{user} \\
\text{patient:} & \begin{bmatrix}
\text{instance\_of:} & \text{document} \\
\text{isa:} & \text{separable\_entity} \\
\text{id:} & \text{document\_72} \\
\text{reference:} & \text{definite}
\end{bmatrix}
\end{bmatrix}
$$

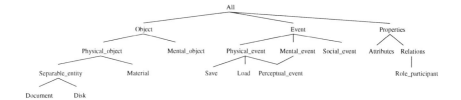

FIG. 7.4. Ontology as a hierarchy of concepts.

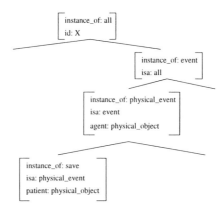

FIG. 7.5. The frame hierarchy.

Named features are shown on the left separated from their value by a colon. The main structure says that this frame is an instance of the "save" frame, which is a kind of physical event whose unique identifier is "save_43". It indicates that the user is the agent of the saving event, and the patient is itself a frame. The patient frame indicates that it is a document, which is a separable entity with an identifier "document_72", and which is referred to with a definite article. Linguistic and non-linguistic knowledge is thus combined within the same representation structure to provide a flexible and uniform framework. A number of properties of this formalism will be introduced in the sections to follow.

Ontology Hierarchy Frames can be used to represent text meaning as well as the model of the domain. As a domain model, the frames are organized as a hierarchy (technically, a lattice, but we will call it hierarchy for convenience); this hierarchy consists of the concepts and entities (the ontology) assumed in the domain. The top level for the ontology is represented in Fig. 7.4. Each node in the hierarchy is in fact a frame whose feature-value pairs are inherited by nodes below it. Fig. 7.5 illustrates a small portion of a hierarchy with some simple frames. The "isa" feature encodes the inheritance structure, and thus the geometry of the hierarchy. In this example the hierarchy states that node "save" inherits from its immediate parent node, "physical_event", which in turns inherits from "event" and from "all". The complete frame for the "save" node is:

$$
\begin{bmatrix}
\text{instance\_of:} & \text{save} \\
\text{isa:} & \text{physical\_event} \\
\text{id:} & \text{X} \\
\text{agent:} & \text{physical\_object} \\
\text{patient:} & \text{physical\_object}
\end{bmatrix}
$$

Note that neither the value for "instance_of" nor for "isa" has been inherited. Inheritance is by default, with explicitly stated values overriding inherited ones. Default inheritance allows compact descriptions of the model to be written and tailored to particular domains.

Frame definitions can also state restrictions on the type of value that may appear in a feature. For example, in this domain the feature "patient" in a "save" concept must have a frame which is an instance of a physical object frame or be compatible with it (see below). Such type constraints help ensure that correct semantic representations are built. They can also be used for disambiguation by disallowing incongruous interpretations of a text. Type constraints need not specify frames. They can restrict a feature value to be a string, a number, a predicate or any other data type made available by the system.

In addition to single parent inheritance, multiple inheritance can be useful in certain situations. For example, it may be argued that a perceptual event such as seeing and hearing is both a physical event and a mental event. Thus the description of the concept for *see* is:

$$
\begin{bmatrix}
\text{instance\_of:} & \text{perceptual\_event} \\
\text{isa:} & \text{[physical\_event, mental\_event]}
\end{bmatrix}
$$

Figure 7.4 shows the position of this event in the hierarchy. More than one parent node means that feature–value pairs are inherited from both. In the event of a clash, a left-to-right, depth-first priority ordering is assumed in this book. Thus, for "see", physical event values override those of mental events.

Properties So far features have been treated as atomic entities belonging to various frames. In some KBMT systems (Onyshkevich and Nirenburg 1995) features are in fact concepts themselves, with their own structure and place in the hierarchy. The top-level node for features is "property"; features will sometimes be referred to as properties. One may distinguish two kinds of properties: "attributes" are properties whose values are drawn from a specific set of values such as numbers, strings or atoms; "relations" have concepts as values, and as such relate one frame to another. Thus, in the "Save the document" frame on p. 183, "reference" is an attribute, while "patient" is a relation. In fact "patient" may be defined as a subtype of "role_participant" in Fig. 7.4. The kinds of features (slots) that may be defined for properties include their domain and their range. The domain indicates the type of frame in which the property may occur, while the range specifies the kinds of values that the property may have. An example frame definition for "patient" may be:

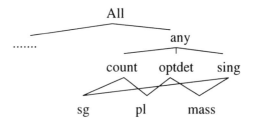

FIG. 7.6. An agreement type hierarchy.

$$
\begin{bmatrix}
\text{instance\_of:} & \text{patient} \\
\text{isa:} & \text{role\_participant} \\
\text{domain:} & \text{event} \\
\text{range:} & \text{object}
\end{bmatrix}
$$

The domain restriction prevents patients from appearing in objects such as books and screens. The range constraint is simply a broad restriction on values, which can be specialized by specific concepts that include the property. For example, an "eat" concept might further require the value of "patient" to be of type "food". Another feature that may appear in property frames are the cost of traversing that property during disambiguation (see below).

Type Hierarchy As a by-product of the ontology hierarchy a useful structure is defined, namely a type hierarchy or type lattice. A type hierarchy, as we will use the term, is a partial order with unique greatest and smallest elements (the smallest element, bottom, is usually not shown). Figure 7.4 shows a type hierarchy with "all" being the greatest element and with the smallest element omitted. Operations are defined on the elements in the hierarchy of which the most useful is that of type unification. The next few paragraphs describe type unification in more detail and present a useful technique for its implementation.

Type hierarchies organize information in a way that allows different degrees of specificity to be used while allowing compatible information to combine appropriately. Consider the type hierarchy in Fig. 7.6 (Pulman 1996). This hierarchy presents the "compatibility" of certain determiners, nouns and their corresponding NPs. The hierarchy says that determiners are optional ("optdet") for mass (e.g. *water*) and plural ("pl") count (e.g. *books*) nouns. Similarly, it states that a count noun that is ambiguous between plural and singular (e.g. *fish*) can only have optional determiners if it is plural. Succinct encoding of grammatical constraints can be achieved by using types of this sort in grammar rules and lexical entries. Thus, one would like to write rules and lexical entries along the lines of:

```
[np] ---> [ [n,optdet] ].
[np] ---> [ [det,A], [n,A] ].

the:    [det,any]          book:   [n,sg]
a:      [det,sg]           books:  [n,pl]
```

```
some:  [det,sing]          water:  [n,mass]
                           fish:   [n,count]
```

However, Prolog's unification algorithm does not allow for types organized in this manner, and a phrase such as *the water* would be rejected since the atoms any and mass do not unify. Based on work by Aït-Kaci et al. (1989) and Mellish (1988), Pulman (1996) presents a compilation algorithm that encodes types from a hierarchy as Prolog terms whose unification properties exactly mirror those indicated by the hierarchy. In this representation, "count" and "optdet" unify to give the representation for "pl", for example.

The basic idea is to calculate the reflexive, transitive closure of the super-type relation from the hierarchy and thus derive a bit string representing each node. The logical "and" operation applied to these strings will then model the required type unification. To implement logical "and" on a bit string in Prolog's term unification, an encoding attributed to Alan Colmerauer is used.

As an example, consider deriving such a representation for the previous hierarchy.

Transitive closure: First, the transitive closure is calculated by creating an $n \times n$ array of 1s and 0s where n is the number of types, and where a 1 indicates an ancestor type relation. The array is initialized with the reflexive and parent type relation:

	any	mass	count	sg	pl	sing	optdet
any	1	0	1	0	0	1	1
mass	0	1	0	0	0	0	0
count	0	0	1	1	1	0	0
sg	0	0	0	1	0	0	0
pl	0	0	0	0	1	0	0
sing	0	1	0	1	0	1	0
optdet	0	1	0	0	1	0	1

The transitive closure for the relation encoded in this array can then be calculated by recursively computing the transitive closure of the children of each type, and then calculating logical "or" for the parent and the result for each of its children. The recursion starts with the top node "any" and stops at the leaf nodes. For example, part of the calculation will involve calculating the closure for "count" (third row) which leads to the calculation of closures for "sg" and "pl". Since these two are leaf nodes, their encodings are given directly by their corresponding rows. Logical "or" with the row for "count" is then applied to both to give a new row for "count". The new row for "count" is then combined using logical "or" with the row for "any" to give: 1 0 1 1 1 1 1. This process is repeated for all possible paths through the hierarchy. The final array is:

	any	mass	count	sg	pl	sing	optdet
any	1	1	1	1	1	1	1
mass	0	1	0	0	0	0	0
count	0	0	1	1	1	0	0
sg	0	0	0	1	0	0	0
pl	0	0	0	0	1	0	0
sing	0	1	0	1	0	1	0
optdet	0	1	0	0	1	0	1

Logical "and" The logical "and" operation applied to any two rows in the array gives the row corresponding to their type unification. For instance, the logical "and" for rows "count" and "sing" is the row for "sg". The logical and of "sg" and "pl" is all 0s, which is taken to mean failure of type unification. Precisely this behaviour can be achieved by representing each row as a Prolog list of $n + 1$ 0s, 1s and bound variables. Adjacent bound variables indicate a 0 in a row, while unbound adjacent variables represent a 1. The beginning and the end of the list are instantiated to 0 and 1 respectively, to force failure of non-unifying types.

As an example, consider building the representation for "optdet". First a list of variables is created, with adjacent variables bound if the row's entry is a 0. This is shown below on the left. The first variable is then instantiated to 0, and the last to 1 to obtain the final representation, shown on the right.

```
      0 1 0 0 1 0 1
    [A,A,B,B,B,C,C,D]                              [0,0,B,B,B,C,C,1]
```

This final representation is the Prolog encoding of type "optdet". By a similar process, the encoding for "sing" can be constructed to give:

```
    [0,0,F,F,G,G,1,1]
```

Applying Prolog's term unification to these two encodings results in the bit list shown below on the left. To convert this list into its corresponding row representation, one notes a 0 for identical adjacent elements or for bound variables, and a 1 for anything else. The result is shown below on the right.

```
    [0,0,1,1,1,1,1,1]                          [0,0,1,1,1,1,1,1]
                                                  0 1 0 0 0 0 0
```

The final bit string corresponds exactly to the row for "mass" which is the correct result of type unifying "optdet" and "sing".

With type unification handled in this way, restrictions on the range of a relation can be neatly expressed: the type in the 'instance_of' feature of a concept must (type) unify with the type indicated in the restriction.

7.2.2 Interlingua Representation

While the ontology encodes mostly non-linguistic, world knowledge, the interlingua meaning representation that interfaces SL and TL must include linguistic as well as non-linguistic knowledge if translations are to be faithful. In some systems such as Mikrokosmos this interlingua takes the form of Text Meaning Representations (TMRs). In addition to propositional content, expressed as frames, TMRs are intended to capture pragmatic factors such as focus, relations among text units, speaker attitudes and intentions, stylistics, speech acts, deictic references, prior context, physical context and other information. TMRs are thus collections of propositional meanings to which these non-propositional meanings are added. Some important TMR components are briefly mentioned.

Propositional Content As already indicated, the basic semantic and literal content in terms of role participants and events is represented as instantiated frames. Propositional content includes information about "who did what to whom" and involves the identification of idioms, the treatment of metonymy and metaphor, and the resolution of reference ambiguities. For an entire text, entities in the discourse are treated by separate representations or "mentions" of the entity, even when they refer to the same thing. For example, a pronoun referring to a preceding proper name will have its own representation in TMR. This allows translation to mirror more closely the information flow in the SL by making information about an entity available in a similar order to the source text. This calls for each instance of a frame to be given a unique identifier via the "id" feature.

Attitudes and Modality These reflect the perception or disposition that a human or some other agent, particularly the speaker, has towards an object, event or situation. Attitudes need to specify at least what kind of attitude it is, who holds the attitude and about what it is held. Modalities need to specify what kind of modality they express and to what they apply. In Mikrokosmos, a value from 0 to 1 is also assigned to both attitudes and modalities, and in the case of attitudes, the time at which they hold. Some attitudes used in Mikrokosmos include: **evaluative** ranging from worst for the agent to best for the agent, and **salient** ranging from unimportant to very important. Among the modalities are: **epistimic**, ranging from agent does not believe to agent believes a proposition; **deontic**, ranging from agent believes that some entity must not X to believing that the entity must X; **volitive**, ranging from agent does not desire that X to agent desires that X; **expectative**, ranging from agent does not plan/intend X to agent plans/intends X; and **potential**, ranging from agent believes that X is not possible to believing that it is possible. The simplified TMR below shows an evaluative attitude corresponding to *a delicious mango*:

$$
\begin{bmatrix}
\text{instance\_of:} & \text{mango} \\
\text{id:} & \text{mango\_1} \\
\text{isa:} & \text{fruit} \\
\text{reference:} & \text{indefinite} \\
\text{attitude:} & \begin{bmatrix}
\text{instance\_of:} & \text{attitude} \\
\text{isa:} & \text{all} \\
\text{id:} & \text{attitude\_1} \\
\text{type:} & \text{evaluative} \\
\text{scope:} & \text{mango\_1} \\
\text{attributed\_to:} & \text{speaker} \\
\text{attitude\_value:} & 0.8 \\
\text{time:} & \text{now}
\end{bmatrix}
\end{bmatrix}
$$

The scope attribute indicates the object about which the attitude is held. In this case it is the containing frame, which must be referred to rather than being included wholesale in the attitude frame. Reference is by the frame's unique identifier. The attitude value gives some quantitative indication of how good the object is to the agent holding the attitude: anything above 0.5 is beneficial.

Stylistics Although difficult to quantify, style plays an important role in the naturalness and fluency of texts, particularly in their generation. The following stylistic indicators are suggested for the Mikrokosmos system: formality, politeness, simplicity (e.g. simple text has short sentences and simple words), colour (e.g. use personal experience to illustrate a point), force (e.g. forceful text is straightforward and uses commands), directness (e.g. use of direct personal reference) and respect (e.g. arrogant, respectful, neutral) (Hovy 1988). Each has a value between 0 and 1, and its scope may be a complete utterance or some subpart of it. For some languages such as Japanese, some of these factors become critical for appropriate rendering. The following TMR shows the effect of style settings for *delicious* on the frame above:

$$
\begin{bmatrix}
\text{proposition:} & \text{mango\_1} \\
\text{stylistics:} & \begin{bmatrix}
\text{instance\_of:} & \text{stylistics} \\
\text{isa:} & \text{all} \\
\text{id:} & \text{stylistics\_1} \\
\text{formality:} & 0.5 \\
\text{colour:} & 0.5
\end{bmatrix}
\end{bmatrix}
$$

Relations Any text contains relationships between its meaning components. TMRs in Mikrokosmos for example, include various possibilities, including textual, coreference and temporal relations. Textual relations link objects, events and textual entities to each other in terms of causality, contrast, comparison, representativeness and choice. Coreference relations combine textual references to an

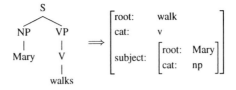

FIG. 7.7. Mapping from c-structure to f-structure.

object, an event or a state. Temporal relations establish a partial order among temporal entities.

For example, a coreference relation between a pronoun *it* (non-human-object-1) and the top frame on p. 190 might be:

$$
\begin{bmatrix}
\text{instance-of:} & \text{coreference} \\
\text{isa:} & \text{relation} \\
\text{id:} & \text{coreference-1} \\
\text{coreferring:} & \text{[non-human-object-1, mango-1]}
\end{bmatrix}
$$

Structure vs. Reference Frames such as that on p. 183 include complete frame structures as the value for some of their relations. Other frames, such as the preceding one, include only references as values. Yet other frames, such as those on p. 190 include both kinds of values. Deciding whether to use a structure or a reference to it therefore becomes an issue when building TMRs. In some cases, references must be used, for example when the value of a relation is the containing frame, as on p. 190, or for coreference. In fact, as is the case in Mikrokosmos, TMRs can be built exclusively through references. This makes for flatter structures, interlinked via a network of references. The effect is that analysis, augmentation and generation techniques make extensive use of graph processing algorithms for enforcing constraints, resolving ambiguities and performing inference operations.

7.2.3 Analysis and Augmentation

Analysis into a TMR involves syntactic-semantic processing through a parser, followed by augmentation. The Mikrokosmos system employs a variation of LFG (Kaplan and Bresnan 1982; Kaplan et al. 1989) for expressing syntactic structures, and for mapping them into the frames that make up TMRs. LFG is a formalism in which a series of mappings are specified between increasingly abstract levels of linguistic description. In Kaplan et al. (1989), for example, constituent structure (c-structure), functional structure (f-structure) and semantic structure (s-structure) are proposed. Figure 7.7 illustrates the mapping between c- and f-structure. In LFG this mapping is established through a series of equations stated in lexical items and grammar rules. A full description of such equations is beyond the scope of this book, and the reader is referred to Kaplan

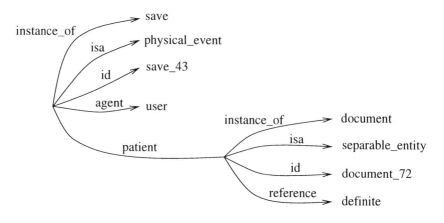

FIG. 7.8. DAG for *save* frame.

and Bresnan (1982) for further details. Similar effects, however, can be obtained through the framework developed here, as we show next.

Representing and Using Frames Just as LCS interlingua MT did not depend fundamentally on GB for SL analysis, there is no *a priori* reason either for using LFG in the construction of TMRs. In line with other chapters, therefore, we outline an approach to constructing TMRs using a unification framework.

First consider frames. These can be represented as Directed Acyclic Graphs (DAGs), commonly used to model feature structures (FS) in linguistic formalisms. In a DAG, features are encoded as directed arcs, and their target nodes correspond to values. Figure 7.8 shows the DAG corresponding to the *save* frame on p. 183.

In order to make the following discussion concrete, a Prolog notation for frames is needed. Adopting the notation of Gazdar and Mellish (1989), frames (DAGs) are expressed in terms of path equations, where a path is a sequence of features picking a particular value in a frame. The lexical entry for *walks* would be expressed as:

```
[vp,[ [np]/S ]]/Frame :-
   Frame : instance_of === *walk,
   Frame : isa === *physical_event,
   Frame : id === ref(walk,_),
   Frame : agent === S.
```

Here, `Frame` is a variable which contains the frame for the verb. This frame has four paths, each one feature long. The position at the end of each path is assigned a value for this frame: the first two are given type values, indicated by a `*`; the third simply encodes a reference identifier yet to be instantiated; the value of the `agent` feature is bound to that of the semantics for the subject of the verb. When a grammar is read, atoms with a star are replaced with their Colmerauer type encoding (Section 7.2.1). Paths can be several properties long. For example, the path equation `Frame : agent : instance_of === *an-imate_object` restricts agents of *walk* to animate objects.

It has already been noted that the value of a feature can be the complete structure of a frame, or a reference to it. In the case of paths with multiple features, the assumption is that complete structures are used as the value of features. The alternative is to use references to a frame using its id. To build frames of this kind it would be necessary to pass identifiers from one constituent to another via a similar mechanism to that used for distinguished variables in QLF (Section 6.2.2). The idea would be to have an additional argument in the semantics of a sign in which the reference id is stored. The representation for *walks* would then become:

```
[vp,[ [np]/(Ref,_) ]]/(ref(walk,Id),Frame) :-
   Frame : instance_of === *walk,
   Frame : isa === *physical_event,
   Frame : id === ref(walk,Id),
   Frame : agent === Ref.
```

Variable `Ref` is the identifier made available by the semantic structure of the subject NP, in the same way that `ref(walk,Id)` becomes the identifier for the verb's frame. Either mechanism (structure or reference) will work in practice, with the reference approach making it easier to build frame structures, while the structural approach making it easier to test semantic similarity during disambiguation.

Using DAGs means that one can use a graph unification algorithm for their combination. Unlike Prolog's term unification, graph unification is insensitive to the arity of a structure. Instead, graph unification is a special type of graph matching that is deterministic. A recursive algorithm achieves graph unification. Two structures graph-unify if the value of features (properties) with the same name graph-unify. Features that appear in one structure but not in the other are added to the result together with their values. Any other case results in unification failure. The base cases for the recursion includes uninstantiated variables, constant values and, when implemented in Prolog, predicates (Gazdar and Mellish 1989, p. 232–37). In the case of structures with no common features, unification fails by definition.

A final point about the computational framework is that rather than explicitly indicating all the features for a frame in lexical entries, these can be retrieved from the frame definition; *walks* thus becomes:

```
[vp,[ [np]/S ]]/Frame :-
   frame(walk,Frame),
   Frame : agent === S.
```

The `frame` predicate simply returns the DAG specification indicated:

```
frame(walk,Frame) :-
   Frame : instance_of === *walk,
   Frame : isa === *physical_event,
   Frame : id === ref(walk,_),
   Frame : agent : instance_of === *animate_object.
```

Constructing TMRs Various TMR construction rules can now be presented. Starting with determiners, these simply add a suitable attribute to the noun's frame. The entry for *the* and associated rule would be:

```
[det,N]/N :-
   N : reference === definite.

[np]/Frame --->
   [  [det,N]/Frame,
      [n1]/N ]
```

A verb like *save* will have entry:

```
[vp,[ [np]/O, [np]/S ]]/Frame :-
   Frame : instance_of === *save,
   Frame : isa === *physical_event,
   Frame : agent === S,
   Frame : patient === O.
```

The "attitudinal" adjective *delicious* has entry:

```
[ap,N]/N :-
   N : attitude === Attitude,
                       frame(attitude,Attitude),
   N : attitude : type === evaluative,
   N : attitude : scope === N : id,
   N : attitude : attributed_to === *speaker,
   N : attitude : attitude_value === 0.8,
   N : attitude : time === now.
```

A suitable PS rule for adjective modification would be:

```
[n1]/Frame --->
   [  [ap,N]/Frame,
      [n1]/N ]
```

A prepositional modifier such as *in* results in additional properties. In its locative sense, it adds "location" to the frame it modifies. A possible lexical entry is:

```
[p,[ [np]/Place ],N]/N :-
   N : location === Place.
```

Suitable rules would be:

```
[pp,N]/Frame --->
   [  [p,[ NP ],N]/Frame,
      NP ]

[n1]/Frame --->
   [  [n1]/N,
      [pp,N]/Frame ]
```

Note that in these examples, the semantic head in modifier constructions is the modifier rather than the syntactic head.

Grammars and lexical entries combine frames and other concepts into a TMR representation of the complete sentence. During analysis, the unification mechanism enforces type and value restrictions that are included in the lexicon or the

ontology. In Mikrokosmos, the result of this is a forest of TMRs that are then
fed to the augmentor whose role is to apply knowledge from this TMR and the
ontology, in conjunction with a series of microtheories, to achieve a variety of
goals. These include selecting between competing TMRs (disambiguate), relax-
ing constraints to account for figurative or extended usage, determining reference
(anaphora resolution), expanding ellipsis, and establishing temporal, discourse
and other relations. Microtheories are localized knowledge modules dealing with
one small aspect of linguistic theory, such as anaphora, aspect or ellipsis. To describe each of these phenomena would take complete books in themselves. Only
two are dealt with here. Firstly, disambiguation is discussed in Chapter 9. Secondly, because of the importance of anaphora resolution to the proper translation of pronouns, a simplified version of the intersentential anaphora resolution
algorithms in Goodman and Nirenburg (1991, pp. 206–11) and Allen (1995,
pp. 433–40) is outlined here.

The basic idea is to maintain a history list of possible pronoun antecedents,
with most recent first, and to search this list for one that satisfies the referring
constraints on the pronoun. The technique thus involves the following notions:

History list: The history list is in fact a list of lists, with each member list representing a local context (i.e. a sentence).

Pronoun constraints: The constraints on the pronoun arise from grammatical
constraints such as number, gender, case, participant role and binding constraints (Section 5.3), as well as semantic constraints such as selectional
restrictions (Section 9.3.1) and type constraints (see p. 193).

Search: The search starts at the most recent local context (i.e. the sentence
in which the pronoun occurs) and proceeds in reverse chronological order
through previous local contexts. Within a single local context, search is in
chronological order for an antecedent that satisfies the pronoun constraints.
Ideally some notion of discourse focus should be used, but this requires additional machinery.

To illustrate consider the following text:

Sentence	Local context
The help system will answer your question.	[help_system(sg), question(sg)]
However, *it* performs best with keyword phrases.	[keyword_phrases(pl)]
The tables show them.	[table(pl)]

To resolve the pronoun *it* in the second sentence, first its local context is searched
to try and find a referent. This fails, since the referent is plural (the fact that
it occurs after the pronoun also inhibits this choice). Next, the previous local
context is searched. The first item, "help_system" matches the constraints, and
is therefore chosen as the referent. Similarly, when resolving *them* in the third
sentence, the local context is searched. This time, binding constraints disallow
it from referring to the tables, as this would have required a reflexive pronoun.
The preceding context is searched next, resulting in "keyword_phrases" chosen

as the referent. In a TMR, bindings identified in this way would be indicated through a "coreference" relation.

7.2.4 Generation

As a domain and knowledge-oriented representation of meaning, natural language generation from TMRs can potentially involve all the stages outlined in Section 5.5. This section considers only the stages that generate one sentence given a particular portion of TMR structure. Once again SHDG forms the basis of the generator. However, the fact that graph unification is used to build meaning representations makes it necessary to change the way signs are unified: the syntactic parts still work under Prolog term unification; the semantics parts, however, use graph unification.

These changes accentuate the problems of completeness and coherence. Consider generation from the following TMR corresponding to *Click the red button*:

$$
\begin{bmatrix}
\text{instance\_of:} & \text{*click} \\
\text{isa:} & \text{*physical\_event} \\
\text{id:} & \text{click\_1} \\
\text{agent:} & \text{*hearer*} \\
\text{mood:} & \text{imperative} \\
\text{time:} & \text{now} \\
\text{patient:} & \begin{bmatrix}
\text{instance\_of:} & \text{*button} \\
\text{isa:} & \text{*screen\_object} \\
\text{id:} & \text{button\_1} \\
\text{reference:} & \text{definite} \\
\text{number:} & \text{sg} \\
\text{colour:} & \text{red}
\end{bmatrix}
\end{bmatrix}
$$

If completeness and coherence are not enforced, different sentences will be generated; some possibilities include *click the button, click the red button* and *click the red button on the screen*. Consider coherence first.

Non-termination can be an issue if incoherence is not sufficiently constrained, as any sentence compatible with the original meaning (e.g. *click the red button on the screen in front of you*) can potentially be produced. This is particularly so given that features can be consistently added to a frame via graph unification. One possible solution is to augment the DAG unification algorithm so that it ensures that all features in the grammar rules used to generate a sentence appear in the input TMR. One problem with this approach, however, is that it is too restrictive when the TL grammar must add information to a TMR. Consider: *I saw a friend yesterday. I met her at the Sandbar.* Generation into Spanish will require a gender feature with value "feminine" to be included in the TMR for *friend* since it may not be present there, even if the pronoun has been resolved (recall that anaphora resolution will relate frame references but will otherwise retain the SL TMR).

This solution can be salvaged by adopting a negotiation view of translation (Kay et al. 1994, p. 89). Broadly speaking, this view would say that the generation component may query the source TMR, and in particular its coreference relations, in order to decide whether it is correct to add such information to a nascent structure. Perhaps a more difficult problem occurs in neutral contexts, in which a default must be chosen: *Marlene talked to a doctor – Marlene habló con una doctora.* Here the Spanish object noun has been assigned feminine gender by default, even though the SL does not indicate this. Incoherence therefore can be useful to enable generation in cases of underspecification.

The issue of completeness in this context may be related to the inefficiency problem in LexMT generation: since the input is finite, a generator could attempt to produce all sentences that include less or the same semantic information as the input TMR. The effect would be a complete generation algorithm whose output would be an exponential number of sentences. The internal and external indices technique used in LexMT generation could not be used to reduce this inefficiency, however, since that technique relies on rules and lexical entries identifying specific indices that are made available at higher levels in the syntactic tree. By contrast, a grammar that constructs frames in the manner indicated above will, in the general case, make the complete frame available to higher constituents. The two rules below illustrate this:

```
[s]/Frame ---> [  NP, [vp,[ NP ]]/Frame  ] :-
   Frame : mood === declarative.

[vp,Subcat]/Frame ---> [  [vp,[Comp|Subcat]]/Frame, Comp  ]
```

From rules of this type it is difficult to determine which portions of the frame will no longer be accessible after application of the rule. One possibility is to preprocess the grammar in order to extract constraints on the kinds of constituents that must appear beneath a subtree given the input semantics (Trujillo 1997). Alternatively, if frame references are used in relations (see p. 193) it becomes easier to determine whether a constituent expresses all that it needs to express.

7.2.5 Translation Divergences

As with LCS interlingua, divergences in KBMT are resolved at the monolingual level between a language and the interlingua representation. This is achieved through a suitable encoding of lexical and grammar entries, and in particular, by building meaning representations in tandem with syntactic analysis. The main difference in this case is that the semantic representation is built through graph unification. This means that features are easier to add during analysis, but nondeterminism during generation increases, as noted above.

The techniques given in Section 7.1.2 and Section 7.1.4 for building LCS structures are also applicable here. In essence, they exploit the distinction between semantic and syntactic heads, effecting syntactic–semantic linking via subcat lists in lexical entries, and making the semantics of the modified constituent available in the modifier.

For example, the English adverb *usually* might add an attribute "frequency" to the frame for the verb it modifies:

```
[ap,[ [vp|VPrest]/Frame ]] :-
    Frame : frequency === 0.7.
```

In Spanish, by contrast, it would be the verb *soler* that would add this same feature.

7.2.6 Further Issues

KBMT assumes that high-quality translation can only be achieved if world and domain knowledge is used. Although acquiring this knowledge is very expensive, it is highly modular in that it is applicable in the analysis and generation of any language. Furthermore, it can help with disambiguation and other practical issues. However, the problems in ontology creation should not be underestimated. Deciding which concepts (nodes) to include, how to relate them to each other, and what properties to associate with each, has to be done through an interplay of theoretical insight, practical expediency and intended coverage. What is more, assigning a concept to a word or a word sense is by no means straightforward and requires considerable familiarity with the ontology and the system as a whole. Many of these issues, however, can be alleviated by providing the linguist or knowledge engineer with useful interfaces and tools to the system's domain model and linguistic resources.

Another issue in KBMT is deciding on ontology granularity. Concepts in the ontology could map one-to-one to lexical senses, or a small number of conceptual primitives (e.g. LCS) could be combined to express lexical and textual meanings. One problem with the one-to-one approach is that the ontology quickly grows as the number of languages grows. This can lead to little commonality between meaning representations from different languages. The problem with a small set of primitives is determining what the primitives should be, and whether they capture all the meaning subtleties relevant to translation. For practical systems, a position in between is probably the best choice.

While Mikrokosmos is the inspiration for the above presentation, the aim here is not to replicate it. Apart from sheer size, coverage, efficiency and user-friendliness of the resources available in Mikrokosmos, other differences need to be mentioned. Some have been pointed out: the grammatical formalism used, the linking of syntax to semantics, the use of structures rather than references for values in relations. None of the microtheories implemented or proposed in Mikrokosmos are explored here in any detail, and only one, pronoun resolution, has been briefly discussed. A system of lexical rules allows Mikrokosmos lexicons to increase their coverage; no such rules are included here. In addition to an ontology, an onomasticon also forms part of Mikrokosmos. This stores proper names such as Paris, the Battle of Gettysburg and Japan, as well as entities specific to a particular speaker or application. A well-developed graphical user interface for knowledge acquisition facilitates ontology development in Mikrokosmos. Finally, a search algorithm known as Hunter–Gatherer (Beale et al. 1996) is used to efficiently process constraints and other information in order to rank analyses, and to guide the search during generation. The expression of constraints on the value of attributes and relations is also much richer and more flexible than that described here.

7.2.7 Implementation Issues

The DAG unification algorithm (Gazdar and Mellish 1989, pp. 236–44), requires the operators === and : to be defined. DAGs are represented as open lists of features which may themselves have open lists as values. Thus, when the frame predicate on p. 193 is called, its variable returns with the following value:

```
[instance_of : *walk,
 isa : *physical_event,
 id : ref(walk,_),
 agent : [instance_of : *animate_object | _]
 | _]
```

Interpretation of the === operator results in these lists, with appropriate bindings as required.

Modifying the fail condition on the basic DAG unification algorithm gives a crude yet useful approximation to default DAG unification needed for implementing inheritance. The modification is very simple: default unification does not fail, it can only add or not add information. The predicate is essentially directed: the left DAG is default, while the right DAG inherits all the values from the left one which are compatible with it.

On loading, the ontology file would be compiled in the following way:

1. First, all inheritances are applied using the default DAG unification mechanism just described. Inheritance is depth-first, left-to-right.
2. A type hierarchy is extracted and compiled in the manner indicated in Section 7.2.1. All frames, grammar rules and lexical entries are processed replacing atoms prefixed by * with their Colmerauer encoding.
3. Domain and range constraints on properties are applied to all properties in all frames.

As already mentioned, unification of signs is now in two steps: for the syntactic part, Prolog's term unification is used; for the semantic part, DAG unification is used. Similarly, checking for subsumption involves two separate predicates, one for terms, the other for DAGs.

7.3 Conclusion

Developing MT systems for more than two languages incurs a large cost. Interlingua and KBMT are approaches which attempt to minimize these costs by constructing language-neutral representations of sentence meaning. Interlingua systems shift the burden to monolingual modules, offering modularity and compactness. The table below summarizes the two approaches:

Paradigm	Advantages	Disadvantages
Linguistic	Avoids paraphrasing; simpler knowledge acquisition.	Can lack language neutrality; does not exploit domain knowledge.
KB	Can achieve high quality; representations applicable to other tasks.	Domain dependent; complex analysis, generation or augmentation; knowledge acquisition bottleneck.

The problem for interlingua systems in general is that development of their monolingual modules is slower than that for transfer systems, and the range of texts and domains that can be dealt with is smaller. Thus, although once a domain is developed, it is relatively simple to add new languages, extending the applicability of the interlingua and monolingual grammars to completely different domains requires significant additional effort. In both cases it is also difficult to specify the interlingua representation in such a way that consistency can be achieved among all language modules.

A more fundamental problem is that of ensuring that the representation produced by the SL module can in fact be used as input to the generation module of the TL (possibly after additional processing). The problem arises when different grammars construct different representations that mean the same and should therefore give rise to translationally equivalent sentences. Depending on how meaning equivalence is defined, problems of decidability will arise. For example, if the formal power of the representation is equivalent to that of FOL, then there will be no effective procedure for determining equivalence, much less for generating from different but equivalent representations. Careful design of the interlingua can avoid this problem, but in doing so, the expressive power or flexibility of the representations could be compromised.

7.3.1   Further Reading

Wilks (1975a) describes an early interlingua system based on semantic primitives. The Rosetta system (Rosetta (pseud.) 1994) was an innovative approach to interlingua MT using isomorphic grammars as its main technique. The DLT system used Esperanto as its interlingua (Schubert 1988). Some commercial systems employing ideas from interlingua MT are described by Uchida (1989) and Harada (1986).

Several works exist on cognitive linguistics and cognitive grammar (Lakoff and Johnson 1980; Langacker 1991; Lakoff 1987). Levin and Pinker (1992) contains many interesting articles, while Ungerer and Schmid (1996) is a relatively recent introduction to the topic. The LCS system developed here is based on UNITRAN by Dorr (1993); Arnold (1996) presents a concise review of this work. The LCS framework itself is described in Jackendoff (1990); Jackendoff (1997) is a more recent expression of it. Additional articles on LCS in MT are Voss and Dorr (1995) on lexical-LCS relationships, Dorr and Olsen (1996) on generation from LCS, Dorr (1997) on dictionary construction, and Dorr et al. (1995) on GB parsing.

The 1980s saw an increase in KBMT activity in Europe, Japan and in the USA (see Hutchins (1986, Ch. 15) for a thorough survey). General discussion of KBMT is found in Nirenburg et al. (1992). The *Journal of Machine Translation* special issue on KBMT, Volume 4, numbers 1 and 2, 1989, has a collection of articles on KBMT-89, a KBMT system developed at Carnegie Mellon University. Carbonell et al. (1992) outline the approach taken in KANT, a successor of KBMT-89 that combines a variety of approaches to MT. Mitamura and Nyberg, 3rd (1995) discuss issues relating to controlled language in KANT, while lexicon acquisition is the subject of Lonsdale et al. (1995). The KBMT system outlined here is loosely based on the Mikrokosmos system; Onyshkevich and Nirenburg (1995) give an overview as well as details of its lexical organisation. Viegas et al. (1999) discuss lexical semantics issues and Raskin and Nirenburg (1998) deal with adjective meaning. For a general discussion on ontologies in NLP see, for example, Bateman (1995). A number of works give rigorous discussions of default inheritance and unification (Briscoe et al. 1993; Lascarides et al. 1996; Bouma 1992; Lascarides and Copestake 1999).

8 Other Approaches to MT

A selection of approaches to MT that illustrate a range of useful techniques is presented.

We conclude this part of the book by describing four approaches to MT that illustrate alternative solutions to various problems in translation. These techniques may be broadly divided into corpus-based MT and rule-based MT.

The corpus-based approaches presented here are Example-Based Machine Translation (EBMT) and statistical MT. These approaches rely on large amounts of bilingual corpora for carrying out translation. For the rule-based approaches we present Minimal Recursion Semantics (MRS) and a constraint-based approach. These approaches exemplify the application of developments in formal semantics and knowledge representation to the problem of machine translation.

Corpus-based systems directly address the need for MT systems to be tuned to particular sublanguages or text types by using relevant previous translations. They also attempt to simplify knowledge capture by foregoing the need to manually develop some or all the linguistic resources needed for MT.

8.1 Example-Based Machine Translation

The basic idea in EBMT is very simple: to translate a sentence, use previous translation examples of similar sentences, the assumption being that many translations are simple modifications of previous translations. This view of translation is a reasonable approximation to the saying that "a good translator is a lazy translator", by which it is meant that the production of a new translation should employ as much material from previous translations as possible. Not only does this save time, but it promotes consistency in terminology and style. It might even be necessary in legal translation. It is clear that this has a strong similarity to the use of translation memory (Section 4.2) in MAT. Indeed, TM may be seen as a special case of EBMT in which examples are retrieved but any adaptation to the current sentence must be done by a translator. By contrast, a fully fledged EBMT system may retrieve more than one example, identify fragments which match parts of the input sentence and combine these fragments into a TL expression.

EBMT can be traced at least to Nagao (1984). Since then a variety of researchers have worked within this translation paradigm (see Further Reading), possibly under various headings such as Case-Based MT (CBMT) or Memory-Based Translation (MBT), each implying certain differences that will not concern us here (e.g. CBMT seems to imply that examples come from real translations as opposed to fictitious examples supplied to the system by the user). The description in this section is based on the MBT2 system (Sato 1995), and may be introduced through the following example.

Assume that the system is asked to translate the sentence:

Julie bought a book on economics.

If this sentence has already been translated, then translation reduces to the TM case: the input is looked up in a database of translated sentences – the examples database – and its translation output. A more common case, however, is that the input only matches parts of different examples. In this case, each example will contribute towards the formulation of the TL sentence. For the sake of argument, assume the database contains the following examples:

| (a) **Julie bought** a notebook | **Julie compró** una libreta |
| (b) Ann read **a book on economics** | Ann leyó **un libro de economía** |

The bold parts in this database completely cover the input in the sense that they match each part of it without overlap. By putting together the corresponding segments from the Spanish side, a translation can be constructed:

Julie compró un libro de economía.

For a human translator, this process is very straightforward and almost trivial. However, to replicate it computationally is as difficult as MT itself. There are at least three reasons for this. Firstly, given a translation example, it is hard to determine which words and phrases correspond to each other. Algorithms for word alignment (Section 4.4.1) may be used to address this problem, but error rates are still significant. Secondly, it is not clear how matching against an example should be done, especially when words in the input and the example do not match. Finally, even if segment correspondences are identified and relevant examples have been retrieved, it is non-trivial to select the best combination of fragment correspondences whose source sides cover the input (and thus provide the segments that make up the target expression). The task of an EBMT system is to address each of these issues by providing computational (partial) solutions to them.

A typical EBMT system consists of the following main components:

1. An example database of aligned source and target sentences. Normally the dependency structure of example sentences is given (Section 6.1.3). This may be obtained through manual annotation, via a parser or through an example-based mechanism. Each example includes subsentential alignments

indicating which fragments between the source and target are in translation correspondence. Again, these alignments are made manually or through
(semi-)automated means using bilingual dictionaries or word and term alignment algorithms.
2. A matching algorithm that identifies the examples that most closely resemble all or part of the input sentence.
3. A combination algorithm which reconstructs the input sentence through a
combination of fragments from the source side of the example sentences.
4. A transfer and composition algorithm that extracts corresponding target fragments and combines them into an appropriate TL sentence.

We consider each component in turn.

8.1.1   Example Database

In Sato (1995)'s formulation of EBMT, each example in the database is made up
of three components:

- An SL word-dependency tree (SWD).
- A TL word-dependency tree (TWD).
- A correspondence list (CL) indicating translationally equivalent subtrees be-
tween source and target trees.

Figure 8.1 depicts the example database entry for (a) above. Each subtree for
source and target has a label associated with it, so that correspondences may be
expressed. Its representation might be given in a Prolog-like notation as:

```
SWD = [s1,[buy,v],                  TWD = [t1,[comprar,v],
           [s2,[julie,pron]],                  [t2,[julie,pron]],
           [s3,[notebook,n],                   [t3,[libreta,n],
              [s4,[a,det]]]]                       [t4,[una,det]]]]

CL = [ [s1,t1], [s2,t2], [s3,t3] ]
```

The correspondence list expresses basic translation alignments between subtrees. Thus, the pair [s3,t2] expresses the equivalence *the notebook – la*

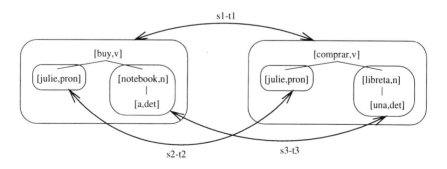

FIG. 8.1. Translation example for EBMT.

libreta. Sato extends the correspondence notation with the "−" operator to allow subtrees to be extracted. For instance s1-s3 indicates a tree consisting of s1 with s3 removed (i.e. *Julie bought _*). Using this extension, translation correspondences can be generalized to include subtrees with extracted components. Thus [s1-s3,t1-t3] is a translation correspondence representing *Julie bought _ ↔ Julie compró _*.

8.1.2 Example Composition

Matching expressions are used to encode the combination of fragments from a set of examples in order to cover the input sentence. The notation for matching expressions resembles that of word-dependency trees but it additionally includes three commands:

- [d,<ID>] Delete the subtree labelled ID.
- [r,<ID>,<ME>] Replace the subtree labelled ID with the matching expression ME.
- [a,<ID>,<ME>] Add the matching expression ME as a child of the subtree labelled ID.

In order to illustrate the use of matching expressions, assume that the database entry for (b) is:

```
SWD = [s11,[read,v],          TWD = [t11,[leer,v],
          [s12,[ann,pron]],            [t12,[ann,pron]],
          [s13,[book,n],               [t13,[libro,n],
            [s14,[a,det]],               [t14,[un,det]],
            [s15,[on,p],                 [t15,[de,p],
              [s16,[economics,n]]]]]]   [t16,[economía,n]]]]]]

CL = [ [s11,t11], [s12,t12], [s13,t13], [s16,t16] ]
```

Given this entry and that on p. 205, a matching expression that covers the original input sentence is:

```
[s1,[r,s3,[s13]]]
```

This indicates that node s3 is removed from the first example and replaced with s13 from the second, to give the word-dependency tree:

```
[[buy,v],
 [[julie,pron]],
 [[book,n],
  [[a,det]],
  [[on,p],
   [[economics,n]]]]]]
```

A matching expression is built recursively from the input sentence and a set of example SL subtrees. Sato (1995) gives a Prolog program that takes as input a database of examples, and a word depency tree, and outputs a matching expression for it based on the SL side of the database.

The algorithm effectively traverses the input word-dependency tree top-down, recursively comparing each local tree against a SL translatable subtree (i.e. appearing in the CL) from the example database. If it is possible to analyse the input by adding a child to a node from an example, then an a command is inserted. Similarly, if one of the children in the example tree can be ignored, then a d command is inserted in the nascent matching expression. Finally, if by replacing a node in an example the input tree can be analysed, then insert an r command. Thus, given the preceding word-dependency tree, the algorithm returns the ME preceding it.

Having computed an ME, transfer in MBT2 is simply the process of replacing each SL subtree id by its TL counterpart. In the current example, transfer is represented by:

```
Source = [s1,[r,s3,[s13]]]
Target = [t1,[r,t3,[t13]]]
```

During composition, a TL word-dependency tree is built according to the TL matching expression. For [t1,[r,t3,[t13]]] the result is:

```
[[comprar,v],
 [[julie,pron]],
 [[libro,n],
  [[un,det]],
  [[de,p],
   [[economía,n]]]]]]
```

Once a TWD has been built, it is possible that TL grammatical constraints are violated; Sato introduces grammatical dependency constraints in terms of the POS of parent and child nodes allowed, and which a TWD must satisfy. The following two constraints illustrate this:

- [v, [n]]: A verb can have a noun as a dependent (e.g. *John sleeps*).
- [v, [p]]: Verbs can have prepositions as dependents (e.g. *sleeps in*).

Sato's model does not include a generation component for ordering the words of the TWD into a grammatical TL sentence. However, generation from dependency constructions could be achieved through example-based generation, by reversing an analysis grammar, or by using techniques similar to those of LexMT generation.

8.1.3 Example and Translation Selection

A critical factor in the quality of translations in EBMT is the way that competing examples and translations are selected. This is clear given that the power of EBMT stems from being able to generalize from specific examples to general rules. For instance, the phrase *buy a book* ought to match *buy a newspaper* better than *buy a company*, even though the number of shared words in each case is the same. A variety of generalization mechanisms for example retrieval have been tried including matching on word strings, morphological variants, POS tags, synonyms and hyperonyms (Nirenburg et al. 1993).

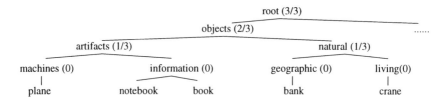

FIG. 8.2. Thesaurus hierarchy for determining semantic distance.

One common technique for matching uses a thesaurus for estimating the semantic similarity of two words in order to compute the distance between them. In one popular approach, the lowest common hyperonym of the words being compared is determined and used to define semantic distance as k/n, where n is the number of levels in the thesaurus hierarchy, and k is the level at which the lowest common hyperonym occurs. Figure 8.2 shows a semantic hierarchy with the distance between the words at the leaves given as the value at the lowest common parent node. Thus, the distance between *book* and *bank* is 0.67 (= 2/3), and between *book* and *notebook* is 0.

Such techniques however, are generally restricted to retrieval of examples from the database. In Sato (1995) a more general matching mechanism is described which scores a complete translation based on the example fragments used and their environments. Sato defines the score of a translation with respect to its source and target word dependency trees (SWD and TWD) and matching expressions (SME and TME) as follows:

$$score(SWD, SME, TME, TWD) = \min(score(SME, SWD),$$
$$score(TME, TWD))$$

The score of a matching expression (ME) with respect to the word-dependency tree (WD) that it implicitly represents is defined as:

$$score(ME, WD) = \frac{\sum_{F \in ME} score(F, WD)}{size(WD)^2}$$

where F is an example fragment in ME appearing in WD. The size of a word-dependency (sub)tree or of an example fragment F is given by the number of nodes it has. The score of a fragment F with respect to a word-dependency tree WD is defined by a composite of its size and the discrepancy between the context in its original example tree and the context in its new composed tree (i.e. WD − the tree that is the result of composing the ME):

$$score(F, WD) = size(F)(size(F) + mpoint(F, WD))$$

In this formula, the size of the fragment has a weight that depends on the matching point function *mpoint*. Using the size of F in this way gives preference to large fragments, as these are less likely to be ambiguous and hence easier to incorporate into a new sentence. The matching point function is given by:

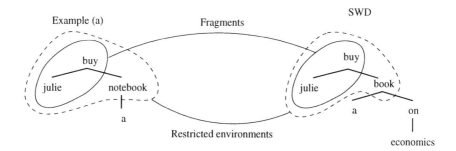

FIG. 8.3. Matching restricted environments for one example fragment.

mpoint(F,WD) = Summation of similarity values between corresponding nodes in the two restricted environments

In this definition, the restricted environments are those in which the fragment is found: the original example WD and the WD encoded by the matching expression. A restricted environment is the set of nodes one link away from nodes in the fragment, or, in the case of these links being identical, one further link away. A node in the example WD corresponds to the best matching node in the composed WD, taking into account topological restrictions on matching (e.g. the children nodes of a fragment must be matched against the children nodes in the composed tree of which they form part).

For example, consider calculating the score for the translation with the TWD given on p. 207), whose SWD is given above it, and whose matching expressions are on p. 207. First we calculate the matching point for each source fragment that appears in the SME and in the SWD. A diagram illustrating this calculation for s1 based on example entry (a) is shown in Fig. 8.3. Fragment s1-s3 (i.e. s1 with s3 removed) has size 2. The words *notebook* and *book* are one link away from the fragment and are distinct; they therefore constitute its restricted environment. Since both words are daughters of the same fragment node they may be considered for matching. Matching is as follows: for each word in the example restricted environment, find the word in the SWD restricted environment which is, according to the thesaurus, semantically closest to it. In this case there is a simple, one-to-one mapping, but in more complex cases the mapping may be *m*-to-*n* where *m* and *n* are distinct positive integers. In such cases, there may be unmatched words in either restricted environment.

Using the thesaurus hierarchy in Fig. 8.2 the semantic similarity of the two words in question is 1 (i.e. 1 − thesaurus distance). Note that now this score measures semantic similarity as opposed to distance, ranging from 0 (least similar) to 1 (most similar). Then $score(s1, SWD) = 2(2 + 1) = 6$; similarly, the size of s13 is 4 and its restricted environment includes *read* and *buy*, with (assumed) matching score 0. Therefore, $score(s13, SWD) = 4(4 + 0) = 16$.

The rest of the calculation then proceeds according to the formulas above: $score(SME, SWD) = (6+16)/6^2 = 0.61$. Similarly, $score(TME, TWD) = 0.61$ (i.e. the same as the source score). Finally, $score(SME, SWD, TWD,$

$TME) = \min(0.61, 0.61) = 0.61$. If other translations were possible, for instance, because the input could be covered in different ways by other examples in the database, the translation with the highest score would be selected.

8.1.4 Summary

The main stages in Sato's MBT2 system are summarized as follows:

1. The SL sentence is parsed into a SWD.
2. The SWD is decomposed against the example database to produce a SME.
3. The SME is translated using the correspondence links in the example database to produce the TME.
4. The TME is recomposed into a TWD, from which a TL sentence may be generated.

Each possible translation is constructed in this manner and the one that gives the best score is selected.

EBMT is an attractive approach to translation because it avoids the need for manually derived transfer rules. However, at least in the MBT2 formulation, it requires analysis and generation modules to produce the dependency trees needed for the examples database and for analysing the input sentence. Also a grammar is needed to linearize the TWD. These modules and grammars need to be constructed manually. There have been some attempts at example-based analysis and example-based generation, but in general most work has concentrated on matching mechanisms and example selection. Substantial work has been done on the translation of the Japanese particle *no* by comparing the semantic similarity of the words it connects in the input with those in the database (Sumita and Iida 1991). Another problem with EBMT is computational efficiency, especially for large databases, although parallel computation techniques can be applied to solve this problem.

8.2 Statistical Machine Translation

Statistical MT systems rely on probabilistic and statistical models of the translation process trained on large amounts of bilingual corpora. Many of the models proposed include little or no explicit linguistic knowledge, relying instead on the distributional properties of words and phrases in order to establish their most likely translation. The general idea in statistical MT is that we look for features of a bilingual corpus that are easily measured and see how these features can be used to predict translations. Features that can easily be measured include co-occurrence of two or more words in source and target texts, relative position of words within sentences, length of sentences, and many others; the idea is that these measures rely on little if any linguistic information.

One approach to statistical MT involves separate monolingual and bilingual sources of knowledge which are combined to give the probability of a translation

(Brown et al. 1990; Brown et al. 1993). In this work, there is a statistical language model that contains monolingual information and a statistical translation model that contains bilingual information. Translation then requires a method for: (a) computing the probability of a string being the translation of a SL string; (b) computing the probability of a TL string being a valid TL sentence, (c) a technique to search for the TL string which maximizes these probabilities. Mathematically, the relationship between these three processes may be expressed as:

$$\hat{\mathbf{t}} = \arg\max_{\mathbf{t}} P(\mathbf{t})P(\mathbf{s} \mid \mathbf{t})$$

The formula can be interpreted as saying that to translate source sentence $\mathbf{s}$, we search for the target word string $\mathbf{t}$ that maximizes the value of the whole formula. The idea is that given sufficiently accurate statistics, the $P(\mathbf{t})$ term biases the search towards grammatical TL word strings, while the $P(\mathbf{s} \mid \mathbf{t})$ term biases the search towards strings that are likely translations of the source sentence. This last conditional probability may appear confusing. Conditioning is on the *target* word string, as it is easier to estimate the probability of a *given* source sentence from a TL word string than the other way round. To appreciate this, we can think of the source sentence as giving us hints about the TL sentence. Then it is simpler to *estimate* from *corpora* the probability of a set of hints ($\mathbf{s}$) given a TL sentence ($\mathbf{t}$) than it is to estimate the probability of a TL sentence from the hints alone.

The monolingual language model can be based on bigram or trigram models (Brown et al. 1992), from which the likelihood of a string of words being a valid sentence can be computed. By contrast, the translation model uses the frequency of co-occurrence of source and target words, the length of the sentences in which they appear, their positions within their respective sentences, the fertility of the TL word (the number of SL words from which it arises), the actual words from which a TL word derives, and the position of these SL words in the SL string. Brown et al. (1993) propose a series of increasingly more sophisticated models that include more and more of these features.

A simple example will give a flavour of what is involved (Brown et al. 1990). The example uses word fertility to denote the number of SL words giving rise to a TL word. To determine the probability of "John does beat the dog" being a translation of *Le chien est battu par Jean* (the proper name has been translated for illustrative purposes only) given a set of fertility values involves the following computation. First, the probability from the translation model would be calculated:

$$P(\text{fertility} = 1 \mid \text{John}) \times P(\text{Jean} \mid \text{John}) \times$$
$$P(\text{fertility} = 0 \mid \text{does}) \times$$
$$P(\text{fertility} = 2 \mid \text{beat}) \times P(est \mid \text{beat})P(battu \mid \text{beat}) \times$$
$$P(\text{fertility} = 1 \mid \text{the}) \times P(Le \mid \text{the}) \times$$
$$P(\text{fertility} = 1 \mid \text{dog}) \times P(chien \mid \text{dog}) \times$$
$$P(\text{fertility} = 1 \mid \epsilon) \times P(par \mid \epsilon) \times$$

In this formula, ϵ is the empty English word onto which *par* translates. The fertility values here are just one possible (although probable) assignment for this pair of sentences. In the search process many more would be tried in order to find the one that maximized the value of the equation on p. 211. The above term would be further multiplied by the probabilities of the position of a TL word in the TL string, and by the probabilities derived from the English bigram model:

$$P(1 \mid 6,5) \times P(2 \mid 0,5) \times P(3 \mid 3,5) \times$$
$$P(3 \mid 4,5) \times P(4 \mid 1,5) \times P(5 \mid 2,5) \times$$

$$P(John \mid start) \times P(does \mid \text{John}) \times$$
$$P(beat \mid \text{does}) \times P(the \mid \text{beat}) \times P(dog \mid \text{the})$$

The first set of probabilities has the format $P(i \mid j,l)$, where i is the position of the TL word, j is the position of the SL word that gives rise to it, and l is the length of the TL string. As mentioned earlier, more complex models which include more realistic approximations to the exact position of the TL words are possible. The second set of products represents the bigram probabilities for English. The product of these and the preceding terms would be compared with those for other TL strings and their correspondences in order to select the most likely translation. Since searching for such an optimal TL string is impractically costly, a suboptimal search algorithm is used which proceeds stepwise through a number of hypotheses, pursuing at each point those whose extension is most promising.

The calculation of probabilities is done from a bilingual corpus by applying an EM algorithm iteratively until values converge to the desired level. These calculations are done on raw texts that are only aligned at the sentence level. Thus, all translation correspondences are established on the basis of textual cues.

Statistical approaches to MT have resulted in many useful technique for MT and MAT. However, they can suffer from sparse data problems, which makes them impractical in situations where large amounts of bilingual corpora are not available.

8.3 Minimal Recursion Semantics

The scope of quantifiers and semantic predicates is an important aspect of logic-based semantic descriptions, but their representation has traditionally relied on recursive structures. This recursive structure has led to complex transfer components in syntactic and semantic transfer systems. Independently of MT applications, developments in formal semantics have led to underspecified representations in which non-recursive structures (so called "flat semantics") are used to express ambiguous readings of a sentence. These representations have been motivated by the need to minimize the number of spurious and actual readings of a sentence that need to be maintained during natural language processing. One feature of these representations, however, is that fully scoped logical forms can be retrieved from them and as such represent no loss in the expressive power of the underlying logic. Minimal Recursion Semantics (Copestake et al. 1995) is a flat semantics framework that has been used in MT to account for a variety of translation problems.

At the heart of MRS are the notions of handles, lists of predicates and handle constraints. Handles are identifiers that allow one or more semantic predicates to be referred to. Lists are the actual scope-less content bearers of semantic information. The basic idea in MRS is that certain semantic elements such as quantifiers, sentential and propositional operators and other predicates that operate over formulae do not take formulae as arguments. Instead, they predicate over handles. By underspecifying and independently constraining these handles it is possible to construct underspecified, non-recursive representations that can subsequently be resolved to valid semantic formulae.

Consider the following sentence with its two FOL representations, and its corresponding single MRS representation.

En: Every brown dog chases some cat.
FOL 1: every(x,brown(x) $\wedge$ dog(x),some(y,cat(y),chase(x,y)))
FOL 2: some(y,cat(y),every(x,brown(x) $\wedge$ dog(x),chase(x,y)))
MRS: top: p
      1:every(x,2,n), 2:brown(x), 2:dog(x), 3:chase(x,y), 4:some(y,5,m), 5:cat(y)

The MRS representation consists of a top handle p, and a list of predicates, each with its own handle indicated here by separating it from the predicate by a colon. Predicates may have quantified variables or handles as arguments. For instance, *every* has a variable x as first argument, an instantiated handle, 2, as second argument, and an instantiated handle, n, as third argument. Intuitively, handle 2 indicates that the restriction on x is the formula made by *brown* and *dog*. The fact that the scope of the variable is underspecified is indicated by using a handle variable; similarly for *some*. The top handle is unused in this example, but it would be relevant in sentences containing this expression as an argument: *Sandy said that every brown dog chases some cat.*

MRS structures can express unambiguous readings. Below is the reading where *every* has wide scope:

MRS: top: 1
      1:every(x,2,4), 2:brown(x), 2:dog(x), 3:chase(x,y), 4:some(y,5,3), 5:cat(y)
Par: For each brown dog there is a cat, possibly different for each dog, that it chases.

The underspecified handles p, m, n are now instantiated to particular handles in the formula. It is therefore possible to reconstruct a fully scoped recursive logical form in a more standard notation.

In order to avoid incorrect scope assignment, restrictions may be imposed on handles. These restrictions arise from syntactic and other constraints which limit the range of possible readings of a sentence. For example, *every cat doesn't sleep and some dog barks* has the MRS:

top: 5
1:every(x,2,m), 2:cat(x), 3:not(n), 4:sleep(x), 5:and(p,q), 6:some(y,7,r), 7:dog(y), 8:bark(y)

Logical predicate *not* takes as complement a formula and therefore has a handle variable. However, it is not instantiated because in general it is not possible to determine what its handle is during parsing. Similarly, the handle for *and* is the top handle, but its arguments are handle variables since the wide scope operator in the conjuncts has not been established. Given this situation, the description of MRS so far would allow p to be bound to handle 6 to yield, among others, an expression with paraphrase *some dog barks and every cat doesn't sleep*, which does not preserve the original order of the constituents. In this case, the effect on the meaning is not great, but when *and* conveys temporal or causal sequence, the order of conjuncts must be preserved. Handle constraints in MRS thus restrict the possible readings that may be derived from an underspecified representation.

There are two types of handle constraint in MRS. The first type indicates the range of values that a handle variable might take. For the previous example, such a constraint would be expressed as $p \in \{1, 3\}$; that is, handle 6 would not be a possible instantiation for p. Similarly, $q \in \{6\}$ would disallow incorrect bindings for the second conjunct. The second type of constraint indicates that one handle must outscope another. A handle a *immediately outscopes* handle b if there is a predicate of the form a:pred(...,b,...). Handle a *outscopes* handle b if it immediately outscopes it, or if transitively outscopes it (i.e. if a handle c outscopes b and a outscopes c). Outscope constraints allow syntactically superordinate elements to have wider scope. *Maeve seldom said Gary jogged* has the MRS indicated below, with outscope constraints on the handle for *frequently* and *said*:

> top: 1
> 1:name(x,Maeve), 1:seldom(a), 2:say(x,b), 1:name(y,Gary), 3:jog(y)
> Constraints: $a > b$

The constraint states that in no resolved version of this formula must b outscope a. That is, a reading where Gary seldom jogs is not permitted, as this is not implied by the sentence. The example also illustrates the treatment of proper names. These appear as arguments to the *name* relation, with an (implicitly) quantified variable scoped at the top level. Similarly, the adverb's handle takes top scope. In this case, the only handle assignments would be $a = 2$ and $b = 3$, but for more complex sentences more than one assignment may be valid.

MRS MT has much in common with the LexMT approach and many of the techniques presented there can be adapted to MRSs (and vice versa). In particular, transfer and generation algorithms, as well as bilexical rules and contextual restrictions, seem particularly well suited to the representation. However, note that MRS MT is not restricted to lexical forms, but may include predicates that are common to a range of languages, as well as logical and other language-neutral predicates that may act as an interlingua. The approach may therefore be seen as a mixture of transfer and interlingua elements, in which language-specific predicates are transferred using a structure analogous to a bilingual lexicon, while language-neutral elements are simply copied across from the source to the target MRS representation.

8.4 Constraint Systems

While different levels of linguistic description could be included in MRS, it is semantic information that is better suited to the formalism. Constraint systems offer an alternative where translation relations are expressed as constraints between different levels of linguistic description. These approaches use syntactic and semantic information in the form of language-dependent and language-independent values to be combined within a uniform framework. They may be contrasted with other approaches in which a single level of representation is unnaturally required to hold all the information necessary for translation. Various constraint systems are described in the literature (Zajac 1989; Emele et al. 1992; Kaplan and Wedekind 1993); here we outline one such approach.

The Type Rewriting formalism for MT described by Zajac (1989) uses Typed Feature Structures (TFSs) and an associated rewriting mechanism for effecting analysis, transfer and generation (Aït-Kaci and Nasr 1986). Here only the transfer component is considered. At the heart of a Type Rewriting Transfer (TRT) system is a set of rewriting rules consisting of a type on the left-hand side and its supertype on the right-hand side. Rewriting proceeds by unifying the features of a type with those of its supertype and assigning the resulting feature structure the type of the supertype. This process is repeated recursively until no further rewritings can be made. The rewriting procedure has an additional step in which any types specified within a TFS recursively undergo type rewriting in the same manner. The result is a TFS whose type has no supertypes. The description of TRT below uses English and Spanish as example languages.

Transfer is achieved by defining a set of rules consisting of transfer types. These types have at least two features, one for the SL and one for the TL. Transfer types in general encode transfer relations, bilingual lexical entries and generalizations over them. An example of a very simple transfer type and its corresponding rule is shown below.

$$\text{speaker} = \begin{bmatrix} \text{noun} \\ \text{SPA} = & \text{s-speaker} \\ \text{ENG} = & \text{e-speaker} \end{bmatrix}$$

This type states that the speaker of a Spanish utterance translates as the speaker of an English one. In addition, it indicates that any features associated with the type **noun** are inherited by this feature structure.

Before transfer takes place, the SL input is analysed by the SL grammar in order to derive its transfer representation. This representation is assigned to the SL feature of a generic transfer type. Based on this partially instantiated type the rewriting mechanism is invoked. Its effect is to maximally expand this initial type until its TL feature is fully instantiated. At this point, the value of the TL feature effectively constitutes the result of transfer. This result can be extracted and used for generation.

A trivial example of lexical transfer using this procedure is shown below ($\sqcap$ indicates typed, graph unification):

$$
\begin{bmatrix} \textbf{prop} \\ \text{SPA} = \begin{bmatrix} \text{PRED} = & \textbf{enviar-1} \end{bmatrix} \end{bmatrix} \quad \sqcap \quad \begin{bmatrix} \textbf{send} \\ \text{SPA} = \begin{bmatrix} \text{PRED} = & \textbf{enviar-1} \end{bmatrix} \\ \text{ENG} = \begin{bmatrix} \text{PRED} = & \textbf{send-1} \end{bmatrix} \end{bmatrix} \quad =
$$

$$
\begin{bmatrix} \textbf{send} \\ \text{SPA} = \begin{bmatrix} \text{PRED} = & \textbf{enviar-1} \end{bmatrix} \\ \text{ENG} = \begin{bmatrix} \text{PRED} = & \textbf{send-1} \end{bmatrix} \end{bmatrix}
$$

The left-hand TFS is the input to transfer. Its type is **prop** which has as supertypes all the bilingual lexical entries, as indicated by the following rewriting rule:

> **prop** = **speaker** | **hearer** | **book** | **send** | ...

On rewriting, the partially instantiated **prop** TFS is unified with the transfer type **send**. This unification will cause the feature ENG in the input TFS to be instantiated to the English equivalent of Spanish *enviar*. This is the only successful rewriting that can occur, since the value of SPA:PRED, **enviar-1**, will be the only one to unify with the Spanish side.

Clearly this is an extremely simple example. To make this scheme work in general it is necessary to introduce a way of translating not only a predicate, but also any arguments that it may have. Consider again the translation of the verb "send". This verb has three arguments identified by the features AGENT, RECIPIENT and OBJECT. To translate the value of these, a recursive step must be introduced which will invoke the rewriting mechanism. This is achieved by adding the transfer features TRANS-AG, TRANS-REC, and TRANS-OBJ (agent, recipient and object transfer respectively) to the transfer type for "send". These features will act as a working area for establishing the respective transfer relationships. **Prop** is the type of these features so that any predicate that appears as argument to "send" will recursively invoke the transfer process.

The next example illustrates this mechanism. The input TFS on the left, which corresponds to the analysis of the Spanish for "you send me the book", effectively causes **enviar-1** to be transferred as "send" via the transfer relation on the right. This in turn invokes the rewriting mechanism on the value of the transfer (TRANS-) features. The initial situation is depicted below (the boxed numbers indicate reentrancy and may be thought of in the same way as bound Prolog variables):

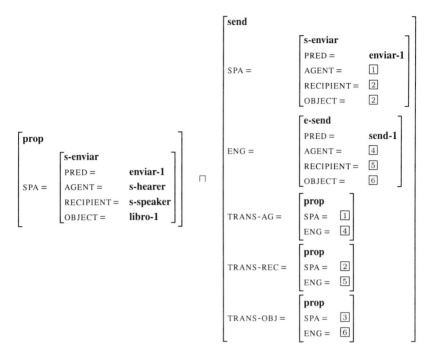

The intermediate and final values of the transfer TFS are:

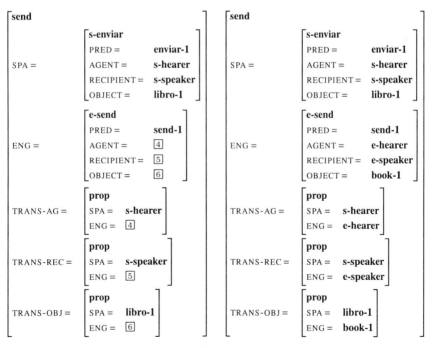

Note in particular how the TRANS- features are translated via the **prop** rewriting rule.

It is worth emphasizing that the rewriting system allows the generalization of certain transfer relations. For example, the following type specifies that there is a transfer relation between the agents of English and Spanish verbs.

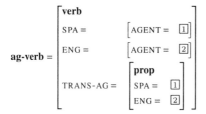

This has to be stated only once in the type hierarchy, but via the type inheritance mechanism, all verbs with **ag-verb** as one of their supertypes will inherit this transfer relation. Thus TRT allows conciseness and modularity in the description of transfer rules.

To express interlingua relationships, the value of the source and target features is bound. For example, the type definition below treats the number feature in nouns as an interlingua value:

$$
\textbf{agr-noun} = \begin{bmatrix} \textbf{noun} \\ \text{SPA} = & \begin{bmatrix} \text{S-AGR} = & \boxed{1} \end{bmatrix} \\ \text{ENG} = & \begin{bmatrix} \text{E-AGR} = & \boxed{1} \end{bmatrix} \end{bmatrix}
$$

The generality and power of type rewriting systems makes them applicable not only to transfer but also to analysis and generation. Thus it is possible to build a single system that will enforce constraints for all three processes within a unified and consistent framework. Furthermore, translation into multiple languages is possible by adding an extra feature for each extra language. Thus, a "speaker" entry for Spanish, Japanese and English might be:

$$
\text{SPEAKER} = \begin{bmatrix} \textbf{noun} \\ \text{SPA} = & \textbf{s-speaker} \\ \text{JAP} = & \textbf{j-speaker} \\ \text{ENG} = & \textbf{e-speaker} \end{bmatrix}
$$

8.5 Conclusion

New approaches to MT appear regularly in the literature. They are frequently variations on the transfer or interlingua approaches. The examples given here resemble a transfer architecture more than an interlingua one, although the last two may be used in conjunction with a suitable interlingua representation.

Corpora have always played an important role in MT, since systems frequently have to be tuned to the documents produced in a company. The development of

EBMT and statistical MT has resulted in complete paradigms based on parallel corpora. With increases in computational power and storage facilities these methodologies will be more and more feasible, either as complements to other approaches, or as MT engines in their own right.

The last two systems are rule-based and knowledge-intensive. They are useful as research models since they integrate very well with mainstream computational linguistic theory and as such provide a suitable interface between that subject and MT.

8.5.1   Further Reading

Our formulation of EBMT follows that of Sato (1995). The following is only a selection of the many articles on EBMT: Sato and Nagao (1990) gives general motivation, Watanabe (1994) presents a technique for distinguishing general from exceptional examples, Nirenburg et al. (1993) compare example matching methods, Furuse and Iida (1994) use pattern-matching to identify constituent boundaries and apply EBMT techniques for disambiguation, Collins and Cunningham (1997) use thresholding techniques to select and adapt reliable examples, Watanabe (1995) and Watanabe and Takeda (1998) describe in detail a mechanism for combining translation rules and patterns, McTait and Trujillo (1999) show how to extract non-contiguous translation patterns using string-based techniques alone.

The use of statistics was suggested early on in the history of MT. However, recent interest in the topic could be attributed to the IBM group at Yorktown Heights, NY (Brown et al. 1988; Brown et al. 1993). Apart from the articles listed in the text, Berger et al. (1996) present a maximum entropy view of statistical modelling and apply it to MT. One may also note Wu (1996) and Wang and Waibel (1998). A related approach is the use of lexical head transducers described by Alshawi et al. (1998), Alshawi et al. (1997) and Alshawi (1996). The idea is to train a statistical dependency grammar and use efficient algorithms for statistical analysis, transfer via tiling of the input and generation.

Minimal recursion semantics is a kind of underspecified semantic representation (Reyle 1993; van Deemter and Peters 1996; Pinkal 1995). Their use in MT is illustrated in Emele and Dorna (1998) and Copestake et al. (1998).

The development of LFG and its formalisation in terms of constraints led to the development of constraint-based MT systems. Kaplan et al. (1989) establish translation correspondences between different levels of linguistic analysis and, in particular, f-structures and semantic structures. However, Sadler and Thompson (1991) noted that a direct implementation of this approach led to inconsistent representations when head-switching occurred in the sentential complement of a verb. Kaplan and Wedekind (1993) rectify this by establishing the appropriate transfer relations at semantic structure rather than f-structure. Type Rewriting (Aït-Kaci and Nasr 1986) and Typed Feature Structures (Carpenter 1992) offer a more uniform formalism for expressing translation correspondences at different levels of linguistic description, as illustrated in the text. Zajac (1990) and Emele et al. (1992) give a more detailed description of this approach to constraint-based

MT. In LexMT, lexical items and their semantic relationships can be seen as constraints on possible TL structures. Thus, LexMT can also be described as a kind of constraint-based system.

Castaño et al. (1997) describe the use of recurrent neural networks and finite state models in MT for restricted domains. Work on MT for monolinguals (i.e. systems for composing documents in the TL) include the Ntran system (Wood and Chandler 1988) and others (Jones and Tsujii 1990).

Part 4
Common Issues

9 Disambiguation

Disambiguation in the analysis and transfer stages of MT is discussed here.

Disambiguation, the task of selecting the correct interpretation of a text, is one of the most important yet hardest problems in NLP and MT. For MT, it was already seen by Bar-Hillel (1960) as a major stumbling block for FAHQMT of unrestricted texts.

There are many sources of ambiguity in MT and their resolution can take place at various stages of processing. It is convenient, however, to organize disambiguation in terms of the source of the ambiguity, which in turn corresponds closely to the traditional division of MT into analysis, transfer (except for interlingua systems) and generation phases. Disambiguation during analysis involves selecting the appropriate syntactic structure and semantic interpretation of the input text. This process requires monolingual information mainly. At this stage the POS of a word, the syntactic structure of a sentence and the sense of a word are selected. In NLP this stage may also involve scope resolution, anaphora and definite reference disambiguation and ellipsis resolution, as well as a host of other problems. However, they are not considered here mainly because they would take us too far afield.

By contrast with disambiguation during analysis, transfer disambiguation is a multilingual process arising in situations where a single monolingually disambiguated SL structure induces two or more TL structures. The most common situation is that of lexical transfer ambiguity. For example, English *to know* corresponds to at least two Spanish verbs, *saber* (have knowledge of) and *conocer* (be acquainted with). It is unlikely that an English monolingual module will disambiguate between these two senses, and it is therefore a post-analysis task to select between the two. Furthermore, some MT architectures may engender additional or different disambiguation problems. For example, in syntactic transfer systems there may be alternative TL syntactic structures, one of which must be chosen. Similarly, in lexicalist transfer systems the SL bag may be covered in different ways by the bilingual lexicon, leading to transfer ambiguity.

Finally, disambiguation during generation involves selecting the most appropriate syntactic structures and discourse organization for rendering the TL sentence. This step is even more highly dependent on the actual MT paradigm or architecture used, and can include a variety of strategies and techniques. For example, in a KBMT system this might involve disambiguations at each stage in the generation process (Section 5.5). By contrast, generation in a semantic transfer system involves mainly selection of suitable grammar rules that realize the given semantic representation. Because of this dependence on the formalism used, this chapter will have little to say regarding disambiguation during generation.

All the sections include a corpus-based technique, while most also include or at least mention a non-corpus-based approach to disambiguation. Although most of the algorithms are illustrated for disambiguating English or for use in translation into or out of English, they should be adaptable to other languages. Many of the techniques employ language corpora for training the algorithms. Clearly, to apply these techniques suitable corpora in the language in question must be available electronically.

Disambiguation could easily take a whole book to do it justice. Here we simply outline various relevant techniques that are reported in the literature.

9.1   POS Tagging

Most analysis systems require the words in the input sentence to be tagged for POS before any further processing can be done. A tagger is a piece of software that assigns POS labels or tags to words in a text. Because of category ambiguity (e.g. many English nouns are also verbs), most practical taggers for unrestricted text only approximate correct tagging, since the tag of a word may depend on the full syntactic analysis and even semantic interpretation of the sentence.

Consider a large dictionary indicating, for each word, its most likely tag. A basic tagger could simply scan a text assigning the tag it found in the dictionary. Such a simple tagger would actually achieve 90% accuracy since many words in a text are in fact virtually unambiguous. Yet this still means that 1 in 10 words will be tagged incorrectly, which is unacceptable at such an early stage of processing.

A relatively simple way of improving on this is to incorporate information from the local context of the word being tagged. For example, if *can* is normally tagged as a verb but it is preceded by a determiner such as *the* then it should be tagged as a noun. Most current taggers operate by taking different amounts of context into consideration when selecting the best tag for a word.

There are at least two main components in a tagger:

Dictionary: The dictionary indicates, for each word known to the tagger, one or more POS labels. In some cases the dictionary also indicates the frequency or probability of a tag for a particular word.

Tagging algorithm: The tagging algorithm combines information from the dictionary (and from other resources depending on the tagger) in order to ratify, select or modify the POS(s) assigned to a word. The resources used may include probabilities on tag sequences, transformations on a tag sequence etc.

In addition, many taggers have a **training algorithm** by which the tagger learns to select the correct POS of a word given its context. In such cases, the tagger is trained with a representative corpus of text which may or may not be tagged.

Taggers differ along two main dimensions: supervised vs. unsupervised, and rule-based vs. stochastic. The first dimension consists of a continuum along which the degrees of automation in training and tagging vary. At the supervised end, one could have taggers which require no training in the sense that the POS disambiguation rules have to be manually entered into the system by a trained linguist. Towards the middle of this dimension, a set of tags would be determined manually for the training corpus, but the tagging algorithm would be learned automatically. Most taggers fall around this point in the spectrum. At the unsupervised end, a tagger automatically infers POS labels and disambiguation rules. The POS tags are inferred by automatically grouping words into classes resembling syntactic categories.

In rule-based tagging, the selection of a tag is done through rules which take into account the context of a word. For example a rule might say:

Mr. **goodright** NNP

which states that if a word ever appears to the right of "Mr." it should be tagged as a proper name. By contrast, stochastic tagging involves the collection and manipulation of statistics on words, their POS and sequences thereof. Based on these, the probability of a word having one or another tag can be calculated, and the most probable POS can be selected.

A problem related to tagging is that of assigning a POS to unknown words. By viewing these words as having any POS (and therefore being highly ambiguous) any technique for ambiguous words can be adapted to tag unknown words.

9.1.1 Stochastic Tagging

A stochastic tagger models context dependence through probabilities on tag sequences. Tags are assigned such that the probability of a tag sequence for a string of words is maximized. Mathematically this is defined as the tag sequence $T_1, ..., T_n$ that maximizes:

$$P(T_1, T_2, ..., T_n \mid w_1, w_2, ..., w_n)$$

where T_i is the tag of word w_i. This general form, however, would require an enormous amount of data to calculate directly. Using Bayes's theorem, it can be rewritten as:

$$P(T_1, T_2, ..., T_n \mid w_1, w_2, ..., w_n) = \frac{P(T_1, T_2, ..., T_n) P(w_1, w_2, ..., w_n \mid T_1, T_2, ..., T_n)}{P(w_1, w_2, ..., w_n)}$$

which is not much simpler to compute directly, but is simpler to approximate. First, since the word sequence is constant for the tag sequences in question, the denominator is a constant and can be ignored in the maximization process. The other factors can be approximated with:

$$P(T_1, T_2, ..., T_n) \approx \prod_{i=1}^{n} P(T_i \mid T_{i-1})$$

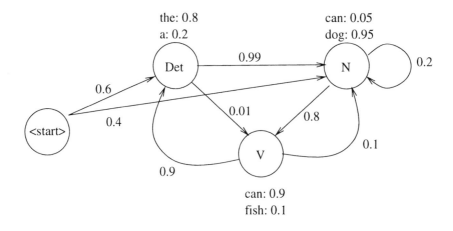

FIG. 9.1. HMM for a simple tagger.

$$P(w_1, w_2, ..., w_n \mid T_1, T_2, ..., T_n) \approx \prod_{i=1}^{n} P(w_i \mid T_i)$$

The first of these formulas implies that a bigram model is used. Trigram models, using $P(T_i \mid T_{i-2}T_{i-1})$ or other n-gram approximations are also possible. The product of these two approximations gives an estimate of the probability of a tag sequence given a word sequence. Consider tagging the phrase *the can*. Bigram probabilities could include, among others, $P(V \mid Det) = 0.01, P(N \mid Det) = 0.99, P(Det \mid < start >) = 0.6$. Lexical generation probabilities, the probability that a POS is realized as a particular word, might include $P(the \mid Det) = 0.8, P(can \mid N) = 0.05$ and $P(can \mid V) = 0.9$. The products for the two possible tag sequences are:

$$P(Det, N \mid the, can) \approx (0.6 \times 0.99) \times (0.8 \times 0.05) = 0.02376$$
$$P(Det, V \mid the, can) \approx (0.6 \times 0.01) \times (0.8 \times 0.9) = 0.00432$$

Thus, *can* is tagged as a noun in this case. Such a view of tagging can be modelled using HMMs (Section 2.2.5) in the following way: the states correspond to POS tags, with probabilities for emitting a word given by $P(w_i \mid T_i)$, while the transitions between states correspond to the bigram probabilities. For the preceding example, the HMM diagram is shown in Fig. 9.1. The tags selected correspond to the most likely state sequence that produced the observed words. To find this sequence, the Viterbi algorithm can be used.

As already mentioned, the training data is normally a manually tagged corpus, which means that transition, output and initial probabilities may be estimated directly by counting. For instance, for the bigram probabilities $P(A \mid B)$ one divides the number of times tag A follows tag B by the total number of times tag B occurs. Accuracies of around 96–97% can be achieved using stochastic taggers.

9.1.2   Rule-Based Tagging

Statistical tagging may be criticized as producing models whose parameters are difficult to interpret. Thus, transition or output probabilities are of themselves not particularly informative to humans. One of the motivations for rule-based tagging is to produce tagging models whose parameters are more easily interpreted.

The tagging technique proposed by Brill (1995) involves an initial tagging of the text by some naïve algorithm known as the initial state tagger. The naively assigned tags are then altered using an ordered list of transformations that improve the tagging accuracy of the text.

The transformations consist of a triggering environment and a rewrite rule. For example, a triggering environment might be:

The word is tagged *NN* and the preceding word is tagged *TO*.

Its corresponding rewrite rule might say:

Change the tag from *NN* to *VB*.

More concisely, this transformation could be denoted by *NN VB PREVTAG TO*. Its effect would be the following correction:

TO/to **NN**/conflict IN/with → TO/to **VB**/conflict IN/with

It is clear that the transformations must be well circumscribed for rule learning to take place. Brill (1995) proposes 14 transformation templates whose triggering environments may refer to tags and lexical items. The items inspected may be one, two or three positions before, after, or before and after the tag in question. Examples of the templates are:

- *Change tag* **a** *to tag* **b** *if:*
- The preceding (following) word is tagged *z*.
- One of the three preceding (following) words is tagged *z*.
- The preceding word is tagged *z* and the following word is tagged *w*.
- The current word is *w*, the preceding (following) word is *x* and the preceding (following) tag is *z*.

Additional transformations are included for unknown words, exploiting their morphology. One such template and an example instantiation are:

- Template: *Change the tag* **a** *of an unknown word (by default, say, a noun) to tag* **b** *if:* The first (last) (1,2,3,4) characters of the word are *x*.
- Instantiation: Change *NN* to *NNS* if the word has suffix *-s*.

The training algorithm employs transformation-based learning, taking as input a manually tagged corpus and having as output a list of transformations. The algorithm is as follows. An initial state annotator is first applied to a copy of the training corpus from which tags have been removed. The purpose of the annotator here is simply to provide an initial tagging so that learning can take place.

The annotator may simply assign the most likely tag according to the training corpus, or it may assign random tags, or it could even assign the same tag to all words.

Given this initial tagging, the transformations are then learned by comparing the tagged version of the training corpus against that produced by the initial annotator. Each possible transformation is applied independently to the text and the results of each compared with the tagged training corpus in order to determine the improvement made by each separate rule. Improvement is measured by the number of incorrect tags left by a transformation as compared with the training corpus. The transformation that produces the largest improvement becomes the first transformation in the output list. This transformation is applied to the entire text, and the process is repeated to find the second transformation. This process continues until no transformation leads to a reduction in errors.

For example, assume that there are only four transformations, T1, T2, T3 and T4, some or all of which must be learned (i.e. they must be selected and ordered) from a training corpus C. The learner starts with an untagged version of the training corpus and applies the initial state tagger to produce a tagged corpus C0. T1 is then applied to C0, and the number of different tags between C and C0 becomes the error count for T1. T2 is then applied to C0 to determine its error count; similarly for T3 and T4. Assume that T3 results in the lowest error count; T3 is then made the first learned transformation. T3 is applied to C0 to produce C1, and the process is repeated: all of T1, T2, T3 and T4 are applied and the one with the lowest error count becomes the second transformation. Eventually, applying transformations will not reduce the error rate and the algorithm stops, with the list of transformations as its result. Depending on the actual transformations, it may also be necessary to indicate whether a transformation is applied immediately or only after the entire corpus has been examined for triggering environments (Brill (1995) adopts this second approach).

Once learned, a new text is tagged as follows: the initial state tagger is applied as for learning. Then the first learned transformation is applied to the entire corpus, followed by the second one, then the third and so on until all are applied. Training on 64 000 words produced 215 transformations and an accuracy of 96.7% in evaluations of this type of tagger, while training on 600 000 words gave 97.2% accuracy for 447 transformations (Brill 1995).

9.1.3 Issues in Tagger Design

In practice the design of a tagger involves a number of decisions which may affect the utility of a tagger and its behaviour.

Tokenization Tokenization is the process of splitting a text into tokens – i.e. into the strings that need to be given a POS. In general, tokens correspond to words (e.g. "cat", "foxes", "them"), but a number of strings are difficult to classify:

> oil-eating, isms, she'd, intra- and extra-mural, cannot, shouldn't, vis-a-vis, stingray, manta ray, inasmuch as, ...

Human Assignment In many cases, humans concur on the POS of a word but again, there are a number of grey areas which lead to disagreement on label assignment. Some studies have shown that there can be up to 3.5% disagreement between linguists when tagging a text. Apart from actual mistakes and errors committed by humans, disagreements can be quite fundamental. For example, is "shopping" a verb participle or a noun? Is "average" a noun or an adjective or both (e.g. the average mark; the average for this class; he is average)? When is it which? Are "armed" and "understood" past participles or adjectives?

Tagset Design Manually designed tagsets range from a few tens of tags up to 197 tags for the London–Lund Corpus of Spoken English. By having more tags the number of grammatical distinctions that can be made increases, but so does the likelihood of a word being mistagged. For example, the Penn Treebank tagset (Marcus et al. 1993, p. 317) consists of 48 different tags, including tags for all main POS as well as punctuation and other textual elements. The tagset shows some precision with respect to number and person (e.g. *VBP* is for non-3rd person, singular present verbs), but not with respect to verb transitivity, for example.

In the case of automatically induced tagsets, the categories obtained with current techniques are so broad that they have not featured in many practical applications.

9.2 Disambiguation of Syntactic Analysis

In general, parsing a sentence with a wide coverage grammar will result in many alternative parses. For example, Briscoe and Carroll (1993) obtain 2500 analyses for a single dictionary definition. Clearly some mechanism is needed for at least selecting between these structurally ambiguous sentences, and preferably also to reduce the number of analyses calculated during parsing.

9.2.1 Psycholinguistic Preferences

One of the main causes of structural ambiguity in English is the attachment of prepositional phrases and other modifiers. Early approaches to structural ambiguity exploited various psycholinguistic preferences associated with the structure of the analysis tree. Two such preferences are reviewed in Allen (1995, pp. 159ff): minimal attachment and right association. These preferences are in fact heuristics rather than infallible predictors of structure and should therefore be used in combination with other disambiguation methods.

Minimal Attachment The principle of minimal attachment (Frazier and Fodor 1978) states that, given two possible attachment sites of a node to an incomplete constituent, the simpler attachment will be preferred. A simpler attachment is one that has fewer nodes between the new node and the nascent constituent. For example, assume that the verb *hide* is ambiguous between an NP and an NP

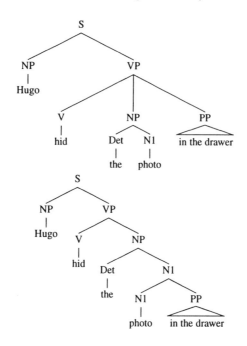

FIG. 9.2. Minimal attachment decision.

PP complement pattern. Minimal attachment prefers the top structure shown in Fig. 9.2 with 8 nodes, instead of the bottom structure with 9 nodes. This seems to accord with human preferences for this sentence, where the preferred interpretation is that of being hidden in the drawer, as opposed to the photo in the drawer being hidden somewhere else. Minimal attachment is clearly dependent on the structure assigned to a sentence by the grammar rules. In particular, it relies on rules having multiple daughters, making the principle inapplicable to binary grammars such as Categorial Grammar and grammars in Chomsky Normal Form.

   The principle was intended to account for a variety of phenomena involving attachments that had previously been accounted for using a variety of principles, including right attachment. Yet, certain preferences remained unexplained, and in the end, right association was incorporated for situations where minimal attachment could not choose among competing alternatives.

Right Association   Kimball (1973) proposed seven principles of parsing, of which right association or late closure has been used for parsing selection. This principle states that constituents are attached to the current constituent (i.e. lowest in the parse tree) in preference to other constituents higher in the parse tree. The preferred interpretation for the sentence in Fig. 9.3, where *yesterday* modifies *arrived* rather than *thought*, is predicted by the right association principle, but not by the minimal attachment principle (Garnham 1985, p. 87). Note that the

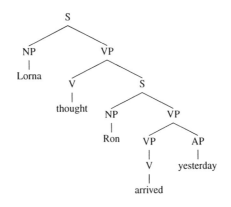

FIG. 9.3. Parse according to the right association principle.

preferred interpretation for *Hugo hid the photo in the drawer* is not predicted by right association.

9.2.2 Probabilistic Context-Free Grammars

As general and simple strategies for structural disambiguation, the above heuristics serve a useful purpose, but it is not clear how they can be improved without including further information regarding the grammar used, the lexical items found in the sentence, the way lexicon and grammar interact, and the frequency with which different phenomena occur and co-occur in real texts.

Probabilistic context-free grammars (PCFGs) have been developed as extensions of CFGs that include this information in the form of probabilities for each rule. These probabilities can be used for disambiguation, grammar learning and for dealing with ungrammatical input (Charniak 1993). Here we only consider the problem of disambiguation.

In order to see how probabilities are assigned in a PCFG, consider the task of deriving a random sentence in a top-down manner, applying each rule expansion according to its probability. Initially the start symbol would be the only symbol to be rewritten, and would therefore have a probability 1 of being used in the current derivation. Expanding this symbol will involve selecting a rule with S as its LHS and some terminal and non-terminal symbols on the RHS. Since S has been chosen it is certain that it must be expanded. Hence the probability of all rules with S on their LHS must add to one. Imagine that there is only one such rule, $S \rightarrow NP\ VP$ with probability 1. After applying this expansion, the probability that a rule with NP on the LHS will be used is 1. This means that the probability of all rules with NP on their LHSs must add up to one. Imagine there are three such rules, with probabilities as indicated below:

Rule	Probability
$NP \rightarrow Pron$	0.45
$NP \rightarrow Det\ N1$	0.35
$NP \rightarrow N1$	0.20

Randomly selecting one of these rules when expanding an NP will, for example, result in the first rule being chosen 45% of the time. Assume that the second rule is chosen. Det would then be a given and all rules with Det on their LHS must have probabilities adding to 1. One of these rules would be selected. All non-terminals can be thus expanded until there are no more non-terminals. The result would be a parse tree whose probability is given by the product of the probability of each rule applied. Consider the following tree:

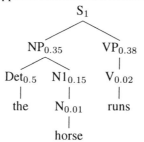

Its probability is given by $1 \times 0.35 \times 0.5 \times 0.15 \times 0.01 \times 0.38 \times 0.02 = 1.99 \times 10^{-6}$. Note that lexical generation probabilities (e.g. $P(the \mid Det) = 0.5$) are involved in such a derivation.

A PCFG consists of a set of rules where the probabilities of rules with the same LHS add up to one. These probabilities can be estimated from their frequency in a corpus of syntactically analysed sentences. For example, assume that a rule R_i of the form $C \rightarrow D_1...D_n$ is used r times in the corpus. That is, there are r subtrees in the corpus of the form:

$$
\begin{array}{c}
| \\
C \\
\overparen{\quad\quad} \\
D_1...D_n
\end{array}
$$

Then, if c rules with C as their LHS are used in the corpus, the estimate for the probability of R_i is r/c. Thus, if there are 90 occurrences of the rule $NP \rightarrow Pron$ and 200 NP rules altogether, then the probability for this rule is $90/200 = 0.45$.

Incorporating this type of probability into a chart parser leads to a straightforward mechanism for disambiguation. Each time a new inactive edge is created, its probability is calculated based on the probability of the rule being used and the probability of each edge it resolves with. The process is started by assigning lexical probabilities. Chart parsing then proceeds as expected, but with the additional calculation for the edge probabilities. Consider parsing *the can* with the grammar above plus the additional lexical generation probabilities:

$$P(can \mid N) = 0.9 \quad P(can \mid V) = 0.1$$

The chart for this NP is given below:

the	can
the/Det (0.5)	NP → Det N1 (0.5 * 0.135 * 0.35 = 0.024)
	can/N (0.9)
	can/V (0.1)
	N1 → N (0.9 * 0.15 = 0.135)
	VP → V (0.1 * 0.38 = 0.038)

The probability of the parse tree for this NP is therefore 0.047. In this simple example this is the only tree that spans the complete input. In most cases, however, many parses will be produced, in which case the one with the highest probability is selected.

In this example, lexical probabilities were calculated as lexical generation probabilities. Such probabilities are not very appropriate for use in parsing with PCFGs because they do not take context into account. One way to include context would be to use the tag assigned by a POS tagger, foregoing lexical generation probabilities altogether. Unfortunately, tagger errors are sufficiently high that the assigned tags would seriously degrade the performance of the parser. What is needed is some way of estimating more accurately the probability of a word having a POS based on the words that precede and follow the word, rather than on the preceding two or three POS tags as is done in a tagger. One way of doing this is to use forward and backward probabilities instead of lexical generation probabilities, as these have been found to give better results.

Best-First Parsing Given that our goal is to obtain the most likely parse, there is a relatively simple way of using the probabilities assigned to edges to guide the parse search. The idea is to maintain the agenda in order of probability, with the highest probability edge at the front. The effect of this change is to make the parser into a best-first parser, a parser where the first complete analysis found is also the most probable of all the possible parses for the input.

One effect of this change is that edges spanning a small number of words tend to have higher probability than edges with more words, since an edge's probability score is the product of its subconstituents. This means that smaller edges will tend to be placed at the top of the agenda, and are therefore processed first. The result is that a best-first parser can degenerate into a breadth-first parser, first producing all constituents of length one, then all of length two, and so on. To address this problem, the score of an edge can be calculated differently. For example, it can be defined as the average of the score of its subconstituents, or as the minimum between the score of the rule used to build the edge and the edge's subconstituents.

Context Dependence The fact that rule application in a PCFG is independent of context, and in particular, of the lexical items that appear within a constituent, causes major problems for PCFGs. For example, a rule such as *VP → V NP* would be equally likely whether the verb *kiss* or *sleep* was used. This makes the accuracy of PCFGs less than optimal, as it can easily lead to incorrect attachment decisions.

The problem arises for at least three reasons. First, the POS labels normally used in PCFGs are very broad. For example, the POS tag of a verb like *kill* will typically include information about inflection and tense, but rarely will it contain information about its subcategorization pattern. By contrast, if the POS label (and the grammar that used those labels) indicated that *kill* takes an NP as complement, and the rule was rewritten to indicate this (e.g. *VP → Vtra NP*), the rule would only apply when transitive verbs were present. However, using more detailed POS labels is sometimes impractical because many tagged corpora used for training contains basic tags, and because manually creating corpora with more specific tags can be error-prone, be time-consuming, be likely to include mistaggings, and aggravate sparse data problems. An alternative approach is to keep using broad tags, but to condition rules on lexical items. The effect is essentially the same: a rule that implicitly encodes the subcategorization pattern of a category is strongly associated with a lexical item having that pattern. For example, if only two *VP* rules were possible, they could be conditioned as follows:

$$P(VP \rightarrow V\ NP \mid VP, kiss) = 0.93$$
$$P(VP \rightarrow V\ NP \mid VP, sleep) = 0.07$$
$$P(VP \rightarrow V \mid VP, sleep) = 0.91$$
$$P(VP \rightarrow V \mid VP, kiss) = 0.09$$

These values indicate the probability of using the rule for a VP given that its head is the lexical item shown. Thus, *kiss* effectively prefers an NP complement while *sleep* preferably takes no complement. Conditioning is done on the head of the phrase as it is the daughter that carries most of the syntactic content for the phrase.

The second reason for the inaccuracy of PCFGs is that they do not take lexical preferences into account. Consider the following two sentences (Charniak 1993, p. 119):

> Sue bought a plant with Jane.
> Sue bought a plant with yellow leaves.

In the first sentence, the PP attaches to the verb while in the second it attaches to *plant*. In situations like this, the attachment that gives the most coherent semantic interpretation is selected. However, measuring coherence is difficult, so approximations to it need to be made based on statistical methods.

Consider the problem of determining whether a PP attaches to a verb or to a noun in this example. One simple approach would be to assume that the attachment depended principally on the two head nouns, the verb and the preposition in question (Charniak 1993, p. 120). In this approach, a function $f(p, n2, v)$ is defined that indicates the strength of the attachment to the verb v, given that p is the head of the PP and $n2$ is the head of the PP's complement NP. Similarly, a function $f(p, n2, n1)$ indicates the strength of the attachment of the PP to the noun $n1$. For the above examples, one would like $f(with, Jane, buy) >$

$f(with, Jane, plant)$ but $f(with, leaf, plant) > f(with, leaf, buy)$. Calculating the necessary strengths would involve inspecting a large amount of data in order to derive useful associations. The problem with this approach is that it is difficult to find enough data, since one potentially needs to count co-occurrences between each noun and verb, and it is unlikely that a significant number will occur even in a large corpus.

Such sparse data problems can be reduced by counting more frequent events. For example, upwards of 78% accurate PP attachments can be obtained simply by using $P(prep \mid verb)$ and $P(prep \mid noun)$ to select an attachment site, where

$$P(prep \mid verb) \approx \frac{Count(\text{prep attached to verb})}{Count(\text{verb})}$$

and similarly for nouns (Hindle and Rooth 1991).

An alternative solution to the sparse data problem is to count more general and therefore more frequent categories. For instance, by labelling verbs and nouns with their broad semantic tags, co-occurrence counts between these tags become statistically much more significant. For example, nouns like *Jane*, *Sue* and *woman* are labelled *human*, nouns such as *plant*, *leaf* and *pot* are labelled *object*, and verbs like *buy* and *grow* are labelled *physical_act*. Attachment is then determined by computing the following ($S(a)$ is the semantic tag of lexical item a)

$$P(S(n2), p, S(v) \mid p) \approx$$
$$\frac{Count(\text{verb semantic class, prep, pp noun semantic class})}{Count(\text{prep})}$$

and similarly for attachments to the noun. By choosing sufficiently representative yet broad semantic categories the probabilities estimated from a semantically tagged corpus are much more reliable and applicable. The results reported for such mechanisms are comparable with the previous technique and are in the range of 75% correct attachment decisions (Basili et al. 1992).

A third reason for inaccuracy in PCFGs is lack of information regarding case and other grammatical relations between verbs and their arguments. For example, consider the following relative clauses:

the people in the building *that we refurbished* (do not like it)
the people in the building *that refurbished our house* (want payment)

In the first example, the relative clause modifies *building*, which is the object of *refurbish*, while in the second it modifies *people* which is the subject of *refurbish*. Since in both cases the head of the relative clause is the same verb, the decision must rely on the grammatical relation between the verb and the nouns. As for prepositions, counts are extracted from a semantically annotated corpus which includes semantic tags for nouns and verbs, as well as the syntactic relation between the noun and the verb. The attachment is given by:

$$P(rel, v, S(n) \mid v) \approx \frac{Count(\text{relation,verb,noun semantic class})}{Count(\text{verb})}$$

Here, rel can be either subject or object. Note that, to give more refined probability estimates, the counts on verbs are done on the lexical items, rather than on their semantic classes. Sparse data is not as big a problem since the probabilities are conditioned on the verb itself, so as long as the verb is sufficiently frequent, reasonable estimates can be obtained.

9.3   Word Sense Disambiguation

In NLP, lexical ambiguity is normally divided into category ambiguity and word sense ambiguity. Category disambiguation, or POS tagging, has already been described. Word sense disambiguation involves selecting the most appropriate sense of a word, normally after its POS has been determined. For example, the word *crane* has two senses: a type of bird or a machine for lifting heavy objects.

Disambiguation by humans is possible in most cases because the context in which a word is used determines the most coherent or probable intended sense of the word. For example, it is clear what the preferred sense is in each of the following:

> The crane flew over the plain.
> The builder operated the crane.

In an NLP or MT system, the effect of context needs to be approximated or modelled through computational mechanisms. In this section, some common techniques for this are reviewed. These techniques are particularly useful for interlingua systems, where a language-independent and preferably unambiguous representation needs to be constructed based only on monolingual criteria.

9.3.1   Selectional Restrictions

One of the earliest and most common techniques for word sense disambiguation is that of selectional or sortal restrictions. The general idea is that lexical items indicate the broad semantic categories they can combine with, and any modifiers or complements that do not belong to these semantic categories cannot combine with them. For example, the lexical entry for the verb *fly* can specify in its lexical entry that its subject must be a bird. This constraint would immediately disallow the *machine* sense of *crane* in the above example, leaving only the correct sense. Similarly, the verb *operate* can include a restriction stating that its direct object must be a machine. This would select the correct sense from the two available in the second sentence.

There are different ways in which selectional restrictions can be implemented in NLP and MT systems. A popular approach is to use nodes from a semantic hierarchy as the restriction on constituents. Each node in the hierarchy represents a semantic type, and a restriction is violated if the semantic type of the combining constituent is not compatible with the restriction. Compatibility of semantic types can be defined in different ways, but a simple definition is as type unification (Section 7.2.1): semantic types are compatible if they share a largest common subtype. This definition has the advantage that it can be naturally incorporated into a unification framework, and can therefore be applied during parsing as part of a general analysis scheme.

For example, assume the following semantic hierarchy:

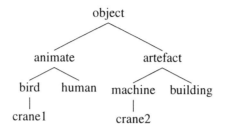

Based on it, the following schematic lexical entries can be defined:

crane(type: *crane1*)	builder(type: *human*)
crane(type: *crane2*)	operate(subj: *human*, obj: *machine*)
	fly(subj: *bird*)

Assuming that grammar rules enforce type unification between the semantic restriction on a verb's argument and its complement, any attempt at incorporating the *machine* sense of *crane* as a subject of *fly* will fail, leaving only the *bird* sense.

A related approach to disambiguation uses selectional preferences, as opposed to restrictions, so that interpretations are preferred or disfavoured rather than being completely rejected (Wilks 1975b). The idea is to use semantic preferences which encode fundamental properties of the words in question. When words combine, a process of preference satisfaction is invoked for the different possible interpretations of the sentence. The interpretation that violates the fewest preferences is the selected interpretation.

Consider the sentence:

> The policeman interrogated the crook

The word *crook* is ambiguous between the two senses: a bad person and a shepherd's staff. In determining the favoured sense for this sentence, the verb *interrogate* appears in the lexicon as preferring a human subject and object:

> interrogate(subject: *human*, object: *human*)

While processing the sentence, one interpretation, with *crook* as human, would satisfy one more preference than with the interpretation as inanimate object. The correct sense of *crook* for this context would thus be selected.

9.3.2   Frames and Semantic Distance

In Section 7.2.1 a knowledge representation framework was introduced based on simplified frames. Frames have much information that can be exploited for

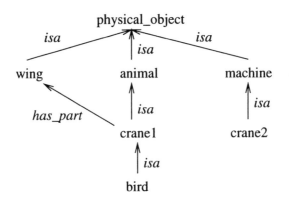

FIG. 9.4. Graph representation of a simple frame system.

disambiguation. For example, they usually include isa, has_part, made_of and other relevant details about the concept, entity or event being represented. This information can frequently be used to decide which of two or more possible senses of a word is the most appropriate in a given sentence. The general assumption is that the preferred sense of a word is that which is semantically closest to the sense of the word(s) it combines with.

Given that frames can be modelled as graphs, it is possible to apply graph-theoretic notions in order to define semantic distance. One common measure is the smallest weighted distance between the nodes corresponding to the frames in question. This distance can be calculated using standard shortest path algorithms, where the weight on an edge is treated as its distance.

Consider the following three frames for *wing*, *bird* and the two senses of *crane*.

```
[instance_of: wing,        [instance_of: crane1,
 isa: physical_object]      isa: bird]

[instance_of: bird,        [instance_of: crane2,
 isa: animal,               isa: machine]
 has_part: wing]
```

These frames can be visualized as forming a graph (Fig. 9.4). Assume that the various links have the following weights:

$$\text{isa} = 0.1 \quad \text{isa}^{-1} = 0.95 \quad \text{has\_part} = 0.3 \quad \text{has\_part}^{-1} = 0.8$$

An arc such as *has_part*$^{-1}$ indicates the inverse relation of *has_part*, namely *part_of*. Thus traversing the link in the opposite direction can have a different cost. The (semantic) distance $D(a,b)$ between nodes a and b is given by:

$$D(a, b) = \min(d(a, b), d(b, a))$$

where $d(x,y)$ is the graph distance between nodes x and y.

Consider disambiguating *crane* in *the crane's wing* assuming that the analysis step produces two representations, summarized as follows:

genitive(wing,crane1).
genitive(wing,crane2).

From Fig. 9.4 and the weights of each arc, it is easy to verify that:

d(wing,crane1) = 0.8 + 0.95 = 1.75
d(wing,crane2) = 0.1 + 0.95 + 0.95 = 2.0
d(crane1,wing) = 0.1 + 0.3 = 0.4
d(crane2,wing) = 0.1 + 0.1 + 0.95 = 1.15

This gives *D(wing,crane1) = 0.4* and *D(wing,crane2) = 1.15*; therefore, the *bird* sense of *crane* is selected, as required.

In this simple example, the shortest path was found by inspection. Efficient algorithms for computing the shortest distance between all nodes a and b in a directed weighted graph are given in books on algorithms, graph and network theory or operations research. The following dynamic programming algorithm is taken from Mitchell (1972, p. 108) and exploits the property that any subpath in a shortest path is also a shortest path (i.e. if the shortest path between Manchester and Brighton takes you through Oxford, then it will include the shortest path from Manchester to Oxford). For a graph of n nodes, we can define a series of $n \times n$ matrices denoted D^k, whose elements are:

$d_{ii}^k = 0$ (i.e. there is no distance from a node to itself).
$d_{ij}^k = $ minimum distance from i to j by a path of k or fewer links.
$d_{ij}^k = \infty$ if there is no path of k or fewer links from i to j.

The matrix D_{ij}^1 has the distances for all arcs i to j. The other elements of D^k are obtained by a succession of operations of the form:

$$d_{ij}^{2k} = \min_h(d_{ih}^k + d_{hj}^k) \qquad \text{for } h = 1 \ldots n$$

The iteration stops when $D^{2k} = D^k$ or when $2k \geq n - 1$. The elements of d_{ij}^k for the last set of values computed is the shortest distance between nodes i and j (see Section 2.2.3 for a different case of the shortest path problem). By precomputing and storing shortest distance values between all pairs of nodes, word sense disambiguation need not be unduly inefficient.

In addition to semantic distance, a frame hierarchy can also be used in constraint relaxation, a process analogous to semantic preferences, which is used when a selectional restriction (a constraint) is violated because of metaphorical or other figurative use. This is a frequent situation with verb arguments, as in the example *the company agreed the proposal*. If *agree* expects a *human* subject, and *company* is a *social_object*, the restriction will be violated. To relax the constraint, the semantic distance between the expected complement and the actual complement can be computed, and if it is below a certain threshold the proposed analysis is accepted. If a record is kept of the arcs involved in the shortest path, it is even possible to establish the type of sense extension taking place. For instance, if this path includes the feature has_part^{-1} then a "Part for Whole" sense extension might have been used.

9.3.3 Corpus-Based Techniques

Given the expense of knowledge acquisition for the preceding disambiguation strategies, corpus-based techniques have been proposed for automatically selecting word senses. The idea with these approaches is to use statistical measures of word distribution in order to model the effects of context.

Perhaps the simplest statistical technique for word sense disambiguation is to determine the most frequent sense of a word from a corpus of disambiguated words and use this sense as the default sense. This can be done with a sense-tagged corpus that might look like this:

> Pupils/STUDENT from/SOURCE a school/INSTITUTION in
> south/POSITION Manchester/CITY met/COME_TOGETHER
> with/PARTICIPANT a film/SHOW star/ENTERTAINER.

Note that several words in this sentence have other meanings: a pupil is also a part of the eye, a school is also a group of fish, a film is a piece of cellulose, and a star is also a celestial body. In a large collection of sense-tagged text, it is possible to determine the most frequent sense of a word for a particular corpus and use this as the default sense for the word. For example, assume that in a particular corpus, preferably representative of the kinds of texts to be translated, there are 1000 occurrences of *pupil/STUDENT*, but only 50 of *pupil/BODY_PART*. Then *pupil* would always be tagged as *STUDENT* under this scheme for any new, untagged text. This simple approach yields around 70% accurate tagging for general English text. Any more complex approaches incorporating context need to do significantly better than this to be acceptable.

There are at least two ways in which context can be incorporated:

Local/syntactic: Disambiguation is based on words that are local or syntactically related to the ambiguous word. Such contexts normally require a parser or a POS tagger in order to establish or estimate syntactic relations such as *verb-object* and *noun-adjective* between the ambiguous word and its local context. This type of context is useful when different senses of a word appear in similar contexts, but suffers from data sparseness problems.

Global/window Disambiguation is based on the unordered bag of words appearing within a window around the ambiguous word. Frequent window sizes in the literature range from 3 to 100 words either side of the ambiguous word. Global context contains more words and it is better at finding semantic distinctions based on the topic of the text.

The Further Reading section for this chapter includes pointers to disambiguators using local context. This section describes a simple algorithm for using global context based on the MI between the sense of a word and the words in its context. Consider first how MI would be used to select a sense tag S for a word w. The basic idea is to select the tagging w/S from all the possible taggings (senses) of w that maximizes $S(w/S, C)$, where:

$$S(w/S, C) = \sum_{w_i \in C} MI(w/S; w_i)$$

and C is the set of all words in the window around w. For example, assume the window is one content word (i.e. nouns, verbs, adjective and adverbs). Assume further that the following MI values are derived from a corpus:

MI(pupils/STUDENT;school) = 5.0
MI(school/INSTITUTION;pupils) = 6.0
MI(pupils/BODY_PART;school) = 0.6
MI(school/FISH_GROUP;pupils) = 0.7
MI(school/INSTITUTION;south) = 0.8
MI(school/FISH_GROUP;south) = 1.0

To determine the tag for *school* in *Pupils from a school in south Manchester met with a film star* we determine:

S(school/INSTITUTION,{pupils,south}) = 6.0 + 0.8 = 6.8
S(school/FISH_GROUP,{pupils,south}) = 0.7 + 1.0 = 1.7

which means that *school/INSTITUTION* is chosen as the preferred sense. Similarly, *S(pupils/STUDENT,school)* = *5.0* while *S(pupils/BODY_PART,school)* = *0.6*, and the "student" sense of *pupil* is selected (note that *pupils* has no left context in this example).

The MI values are defined by:

$$MI_n(w/S; w') = \log \frac{P(w/S, w')}{P(w/S)P(w')}$$

where $P(w/S)$ is the probability of w having tag S and being at the centre of a randomly selected window of size n. $P(w')$ is the probability of w' occurring in a randomly selected window, and $P(w/S, w')$ is the probability of both occurring in a randomly selected window. The probabilities can be estimated through frequency ratios, and so the MI value is approximated by the formula below:

$$MI(w/S; w') \approx$$
$$\log \frac{K \times (\text{Number of times w/S and w' co-occur in same window})}{(\text{Number of times w/S occurs}) \times (\text{Number of times w' occurs})}$$

where K is the number of windows, effectively the number of words or content words in the text, depending on what is being counted. For example, imagine that there are 10 000 content words in a text, *star/ENTERTAINER* occurs 20 times of which 10 have *film* as a content word within their window, and that the total number of occurrences of *film* is 15. Then,

$$MI(star/ENTERTAINER; film) \approx \log \frac{10,000 \times 10}{20 \times 15} = 5.8$$

Three main difficulties arise in disambiguation approaches of this kind. Firstly, deciding on the possible senses of a word, let alone the correct sense in a particular context, is a difficult task even for a human. This has long been realized by lexicographers, and it is immediately apparent on inspecting almost any entry in a medium sized monolingual dictionary. It is even clearer when comparing entries for the same word across dictionaries: one dictionary might have two senses, while the other might have three, with no straightforward relationship between senses across dictionaries. Solutions to this problem have included automatically inducing classes and senses from the text, or adopting external sense schemes such as may be found in a monolingual dictionary, a thesaurus, a lexical database such as WordNet or even a bilingual dictionary.

Secondly, since there are many different words, and even more senses in a language, it is simply impractical to collect co-occurrence statistics on words and their senses in the same way that they can be collected for POS. This is exacerbated by the wider variation in lexical co-occurrence patterns for different topics. The main methods for addressing this data sparseness problem are:

Class-based: Words and senses are grouped into classes and data is collected for the group as a whole. Since several words belong to the same class, there will be more windows and therefore more words in contexts of interest, thus generating more data for each class. Classes may be assigned using external resources such as thesauri, or they may be inferred from the distributional properties of words in a corpus.

Similarity-based: These methods compute similarity measures between words based on their distribution patterns; words can then be used in lieu of their resembling words when calculating co-occurrence probabilities.

Thirdly, obtaining training information is difficult because of its scarcity and because of the expense in producing it. Different methods have been tried, some directly corresponding to those for addressing data sparseness, with the following additions:

Bootstrapping: An initial set of occurrences of each sense of a word is manually tagged. This is used to derive initial training statistics which are then used to semi-automatically tag further text. This text is then re-fed into the system, thus improving its accuracy incrementally.

Bilingual corpus: Assuming that different senses of a word translate differently, the co-occurrence of a word with one or another word in the TL is a reflection of its sense in the given context, and therefore acts as a semantic tag on the word. Clearly if the ambiguity is preserved in the TL, no tagging can take place.

A technique that addresses some of the above issues might operate as follows (Yarowsky 1992). First, each sense of a word is assigned a unique top level category from the 1042 in *Roget's International Thesaurus* (Chapman 1988). The thesaurus effectively acts as a sense inventory for the words in the text. In the training phase, a 100-word window for each thesaurus category is extracted from a corpus and co-occurrences between the words in these windows and the category are computed. Then in the test phase, to disambiguate a new word, its 100-word window is extracted and the co-occurrence of each of its senses (i.e. *Roget's* categories) with the words in the window is calculated. The category with the strongest affinity to the words in the window is taken as the sense of the word.

For example, assume that training has been carried out, and the word *star* needs to be disambiguated. Then, the sense selected is simply that which gives the larger of:

$$\sum_{w_i \in C} \log \left(\frac{P(w_i \mid ENTERTAINER)P(ENTERTAINER)}{P(w_i)} \right)$$

$$\sum_{w_i \in C} \log \left(\frac{P(w_i \mid UNIVERSE)P(UNIVERSE)}{P(w_i)} \right)$$

where C is the set of words in the window centered on *star*. This formula may be simplified by omitting the denominator $P(w_i)$, the probability of w_i occurring in the entire corpus, since it is the same for all possible senses of the word. Similarly, assuming that $P(Cat)$, the probability of a thesaurus category occurring in the corpus is constant for all categories, this factor (e.g. *P(ENTERTAINER)*) can also be ignored. This means that in the training phase, only $P(w_i \mid Cat)$, the probability of word w_i appearing within the context of Cat, needs to be computed.

Ideally, $P(w_i \mid Cat)$ should be estimated by collecting all the words appearing within 50 words of Cat, counting the number of times w_i occurred in this set of words, and dividing by the size of the set. Unfortunately, for this to be possible, all words with Cat as one of their senses would have to be disambiguated, which is unfeasible for a large training corpus. Instead, Yarowsky (1992) found that simply by collecting the contexts around all words with Cat as one of their senses it was possible to collect useful statistics. For example, to collect contexts for the category TOOLS/MACHINERY, the contexts around words such as *adze, shovel, generators, drills* and *crane* are used. This counting procedure clearly includes incorrect contexts in cases where a word is used in another of its senses. For example, this procedure collects words around *crane* and *drill* even when used in their animal or other senses. However, such levels of noise are tolerated in the algorithm, especially when compared with the cost of disambiguating the entire corpus. In addition, rather than simply count words in the contexts, Yarowsky (1992) normalized the counts in order not to give too much weight to words occurring around frequently mentioned tools: if a word such as *drill* occurred k times in the corpus, all words in the context of *drill* contribute $1/k$ to the frequency sums.

From the frequency sums, $P(w_i \mid Cat)$ is estimated. However, a simple estimate based on the frequency count of w_i divided by the count for all the context words collected would be unreliable for words with low frequency counts. An interpolation mechanism, described in Section 9.4.2, is adopted which uses the global probabilities $P(w_i)$ to estimate local probabilities when the frequency counts are low in order to reduce the effects of sparse data. After training on the 10 million word *Grolier's Encyclopedia*, the system successfully disambiguated 92% of the occurrences of 12 ambiguous words.

9.4   Transfer Disambiguation

Often an unambiguous word with respect to the SL will result in two or more translations into the TL. Such situations are particularly common in transfer systems where it is expected that the transfer module will carry out language-pair specific disambiguations. This section discusses three techniques for disambiguation in these cases.

9.4.1   Knowledge-Based Methods

Sometimes it is sufficient to use information already present in the source or target grammars in order to select a correct translation. Thus, although the analysis stage will not distinguish different senses of a word, different transfer rules may depend on the context of a word. The typical example for this situation is illustrated by the English verb *eat* and its German translations *essen* for human subjects and *fressen* for animal subjects. Making the reasonable assumption that nouns are semantically marked as to whether they are human or animal, lexical transfer rules with appropriate selectional restrictions may be specified as outlined below:

eat(subject: *human*) $\leftrightarrow$ essen
eat(subject: *animal*) $\leftrightarrow$ fressen

Note that *eat* still has one sense, with the language pair-specific distinction being made only in these two transfer rules. Given these rules, the correct translation would be selected for each sentence below:

The girl ate.
The cat ate.

It could be argued that an even more modular solution is possible by using TL filtering (Section 6.2.4). With the same example, the transfer rules could be simplified to:

eat $\leftrightarrow$ essen
eat $\leftrightarrow$ fressen

These rules would give rise to at least two different TL transfer structures. Crucially, each of these structures would contain the translation of the verb's subject. TL filtering would work on the assumption that the TL lexicon indicated (a) the semantic class of the subject's noun, and (b) the selectional restriction imposed by the verb on its subject. During generation, the disambiguation mechanism would use this information to eliminate (or disfavour if semantic preferences are used) a translation where the restriction is not satisfied.

These methods for disambiguation may be seen as knowledge-based techniques whose main disadvantage is the knowledge acquisition bottleneck. To address this problem, a number of corpus-based approaches for transfer disambiguation have been suggested. The following two sections illustrate two of them.

9.4.2 Using Statistics from the Source Language

Consider first the technique presented in Gale et al. (1992) and Gale et al. (1993). The basic idea is to use an aligned bilingual corpus containing instances of the ambiguous source word, together with its TL translations. In the training phase, instances of each sense of the word in question and its translation are collected, and statistics calculated on them. In the testing phase, a new instance of the source word is disambiguated by comparing its SL context with the contexts of already disambiguated instances of the word.

To train such a system, a sentence-aligned bilingual corpus as well as word alignments of the word being studied are needed. For experimental work, the word can be aligned semi-automatically. In a fuller system that attempts to disambiguate a large number of words, a word alignment algorithm would need to be used (Section 4.4.1).

Consider the testing phase first, and take as an example the disambiguation of English *duty* between French *droit* (tax) and *devoir* (obligation). First we calculate:

$$\prod_{w_i \in C} \frac{P(w_i \mid droit)}{P(w_i \mid devoir)}$$

$$\prod_{w_i \in C} \frac{P(w_i \mid devoir)}{P(w_i \mid droit)}$$

where C is the set of 100 words in a window centred around the instance of *duty* being disambiguated. The TL word appearing as numerator that gives the largest value of the two products is selected as the translation of *duty*. For instance, if the first calculation gives a greater value than the second, *droit* is chosen as the translation.

The probabilities in the above formula are estimated as follows. $P(w' \mid t)$ is estimated, in principle, by collecting all the windows around the SL word s when it is translated as t, counting the number of times w' appears in these windows, and dividing by the total number of words in the windows. Unfortunately, these conditional estimates suffer heavily because of sparse data. A smoothing technique is employed (Gale et al. 1993, p. 426), which interpolates between $P(w')$, the probability of w' occurring in the text, and $P(w' \mid t)$. The idea is that if w' occurs very few times in the context, then its true conditional probability is better estimated via its global probability. Conversely, if it occurs frequently in the context, its true conditional probability is close to that computed using local counts. The interpolation uses the following parameters: the size of the conditional corpus n (i.e. the total number of words in all the windows around s), the total number of words in the remainder of the corpus (the residual corpus) N, the number of occurrences of w' in the conditional corpus a, and the number of occurrences of w' in the residual corpus A. The result is the expected value of p, denoted $E(p \mid a)$, which is the interpolated estimate of $P(w' \mid t)$ given a particular a. This value is given by:

$$E(p \mid a) = \frac{r\frac{B(A+a+1.5,N-A+n-a+0.5)}{B(A+0.5,N-A+0.5)} + (1-r)\frac{B(a+1.5,n-a+0.5)}{B(0.5,0.5)}}{r\frac{B(A+a+0.5,N-A+n-a+0.5)}{B(A+0.5,N-A+0.5)} + (1-r)\frac{B(a+0.5,n-a+0.5)}{B(0.5,0.5)}}$$

where

$$B(x,y) = \frac{\Gamma(x)\Gamma(y)}{\Gamma(x+y)}$$
$$\Gamma(n) = (n-1)\Gamma(n-1), \text{ for } n > 1$$
$$\Gamma(1) = 1$$
$$\Gamma(0.5) = \sqrt{\pi}$$

Finally, r is an empirically determined and application specific constant, which Gale et al. (1993) give as 0.8.

Assume there are 100 words in the corpus and 10 words in the window around *duty* when translated as *droit*. Then $n = 10$ and $N = 90$. The effect of smoothing can be seen in the small table below:

n	N	a	A	$E(p \mid a)$
10	90	2	2	.111
10	90	0	5	.054
10	90	5	0	.500

For example, if *against* does not occur in the windows around *duty* when this word is translated as *droit*, but it does occur five times in the rest of the corpus (third row), then $P(against \mid droit) = 0.054$ rather than 0. This is a better indicator of the true likelihood of *against* occurring in the given window, which takes into account its frequency in the rest of the corpus. Using techniques of this kind it is possible to achieve disambiguation accuracies of around 92% on a small set of ambiguous nouns.

9.4.3   Using Statistics from the Target Language

The technique in the previous section uses probabilities calculated from the SL. One disadvantage of this is that it is better suited to ambiguities which are apparent from SL contexts. In particular, it does not take into account TL collocational preferences and other TL specific co-occurrences. The technique described by Dagan and Itai (1994) by contrast employs TL statistics to select the most appropriate translation. In the training phase, co-occurrence statistics between TL words in various syntactic relations are computed from a target monolingual corpus. In the testing phase, a set of possible candidate translations are produced via a bilingual dictionary. Those which form frequent collocations in the TL are then chosen as the disambiguated translations. The resources needed for this technique are:

1. Parsers for both the SL and the TL capable of locating relevant syntactic relations such as subj-verb, verb-obj and noun-adj.

2. A bilingual lexicon that lists alternative translations.
3. A TL corpus for calculating the frequency of TL syntactic relations between words.

Once again, we start the description with the testing phase, using the following Spanish–English example:

Sp: *El sistema graba todos los archivos antes de ejecutar un programa del disco.*
Lit: the system saves all the files before of running a program from the disk.

The translation of this sentence is given below:

The system $\left\{ \begin{array}{c} \text{saves} \\ \text{engraves} \end{array} \right\}$ every file before running a $\left\{ \begin{array}{c} \text{program} \\ \text{syllabus} \end{array} \right\}$ from the $\left\{ \begin{array}{c} \text{disk} \\ \text{record} \end{array} \right\}$.

The multiple translations of ambiguous words are given in curly brackets, with the correct translation given first.

The disambiguation procedure starts by identifying syntactic relations in the SL involving ambiguous words. These relations are expressed in terms of syntactic tuples of the words involved. In this example, the SL relations are given on the left column of Table 9.1. From these tuples, a bilingual dictionary is used to

Source tuples	Target tuples	Counts
(a) (subj-verb: *sistema graba*)	(subj-verb: *system saves*)	0
	(subj-verb: *system engraves*)	0
(b) (verb-obj: *graba archivo*)	(verb-obj: *saves file*)	25
	(verb-obj: *engraves file*)	0
(c) (verb-obj: *ejecutar programa*)	(verb-obj: *running program*)	26
	(verb-obj: *running syllabus*)	3
(d) (noun-pp: *programa de disco*)	(noun-pp: *program from disk*)	8
	(noun-pp: *program from record*)	0
	(noun-pp: *syllabus from disk*)	2
	(noun-pp: *syllabus from record*)	2

Table 9.1. SL syntactic tuples and their alternative translations.

generate all possible translations of the tuple, shown on the second column. For instance, since *programa* and *disco* each have two possible translations in this simplified example, there are four possible English tuples. The last column indicates the frequency of each tuple in the TL corpus. Thus (noun-pp: *syllabus from disk*) would have occurred twice in the corpus. This is determined in the training phase and it requires a TL parser that can identify the appropriate relations.

Disambiguation proceeds using a constraint propagation algorithm. In a simplistic model this would just involve choosing the most frequent tuple in the

TL as the translation of the SL tuple. The effect of this choice would then be propagated to other tuples. For example, once (verb-obj: *running program*) is chosen under (c), only the two alternatives that include *program* under (d) are left. Selection and constraint propagation are iteratively applied until no ambiguity remains or no further selections can be made.

The problem with this simplistic model is that it takes no account of the level of confidence on each choice of TL tuple. For example, if the tuples arising from Spanish *asignar* (allocate, assign) are:

(verb-obj: *allocates resources*) 10
(verb-obj: *assigns resources*) 5

There is a strong chance that a mistake will be made if the first translation is selected, given that its alternative is so frequent. Dagan and Itai (1994) use confidence intervals to guard against this: if their algorithm cannot decide which is the most likely translation with a given threshold of confidence, it refrains from doing so. To develop their decision technique they start with estimates for the probability p_i that tuple T has translation T_i:

$$\hat{p}_i = \frac{n_i}{\sum_{j=1}^{k} n_j}$$

where n_i is the number of times T is translated by T_i. If n_i is 0, a smoothing value of 0.5 is added to all the counts. For instance, the most frequent TL tuple for (c), (verb-obj: *running program*), has $\hat{p}_1 = 26/29 = 0.9$, while (verb-obj: *running syllabus*) has $\hat{p}_2 = 3/29 = 0.1$ (rank indicated by the subscript). In order to select a translation, the ratio p_1/p_2 for the two most frequent TL tuples must be greater than a specified threshold, which Dagan and Itai (1994) choose as 1.22. In fact, for convergence reasons it is the log of the ratio that is used for testing against the threshold, which is now set to $\theta = \log(1.22) = 0.2$. However, because this ratio can only be *estimated* from the data via $\log(\hat{p}_1/\hat{p}_2) = \log(n_1/n_2)$, a minimum confidence on this estimate must be set. The value used in their experiments is 90% (i.e. only select a translation when we are 90% confident that $\log(p_1/p_2) \geq 0.2$, based on the value of $\log(n_1/n_2)$). The formula they suggest is:

$$\log\left(\frac{n_1}{n_2}\right) - Z_{1-\alpha}\sqrt{\frac{1}{n_1} + \frac{1}{n_2}} \geq \theta$$

The value $Z_{1-\alpha}$ is a statistical constant and can be determined from statistical tables for a given α. Since we require 90% confidence, $\alpha = 0.1$, and $Z_{1-\alpha} = 1.282$. This inequality tells us that the estimate for $\log(p_1/p_2)$ must be greater than θ plus an amount dependent on the size of the samples. In what follows, $B_\alpha(n_1, n_2)$ is defined as the left-hand side in this inequality.

Consider for example the tuple (c) with $n_1 = 26$, $n_2 = 3$:

$$B_\alpha(26, 3) = \log(26/3) - 1.282\sqrt{1/26 + 1/3} = 1.378$$

which is clearly greater than 0.2 and therefore *program* is chosen. However, if $n_1 = 10$ and $n_2 = 5$, then $B_\alpha(10, 5) = -0.009$ and a selection cannot be made reliably.

Constraints are still propagated as before. The translation with the largest value for B_α that is above the threshold is selected first. In Table 9.1 this occurs for (b), with $B_\alpha(25.5, 0.5) = 2.1$, thus disambiguating tuples (b), and via constraint propagation, (a). Next (c) is disambiguated since $B_\alpha(26, 3) > 0.2$, resulting in only two consistent possibilities for (d). $B_\alpha(8.5, 0.5) = 0.967$ is then computed for (d) and the final choice is made. Disambiguation is therefore complete. This technique is reported to achieve from about 78% to 92% correct disambiguation rates when it actually applies; the technique applies (i.e. $B_\alpha \geq \theta$) for about 50% to 68% of all ambiguous words in a Hebrew–English translation task.

9.5 Conclusion

Disambiguation is an important issue in NLP and MT, but it is also thought to be an AI-complete problem. Different types of ambiguity exist. This chapter considered categorial (POS), structural, lexical and transfer ambiguity, ignoring ambiguity in morphological analysis, quantifier scope ambiguity and various kinds of ambiguity during generation.

Improvements in ambiguity resolution will have a major impact on translation quality. At the moment the most promising approaches are those based on large corpora, and in particular those using probabilistic and statistical techniques. One problem with these techniques is that of sparse data, and various mechanisms are adopted to overcome them. The need for large amounts of electronic text makes the techniques less suitable for low-density languages, although work aimed at reducing the minimum size of the training corpus is under way. Another problem is that of overfitting. During training, an algorithm may become too good at analysing the training data and fail to deal adequately with novel input.

For restricted domains, frames and selectional restrictions are an appealing and flexible disambiguation mechanism. However, specifying these for a large vocabulary and grammar is costly. Defining adequate frames is also difficult and subjective, potentially leading to inconsistent coding by different knowledge engineers. Several disambiguation techniques using frames and other hierarchies are sensitive to their topology also. Because this topology depends on subjective decisions, weights and other costs associated with arcs and nodes have to be tuned to a particular system and application.

9.5.1 Further Reading

Many of the techniques described in this chapter rely on statistical approaches to language processing. Early work in this area, including tagging and parsing, is presented in Garside et al. (1987) and references therein. The *International Journal of Corpus Linguistics* is dedicated to corpus analysis. The *Journal of Computational Linguistics*, special issues on Using Large Corpora I (Volume 19(1)) and II (Volume 19(2)), 1993, and on Word Sense Disambiguation (Volume 24(1)), 1998, include historical overview and a bibliography on statistical methods for NLP. Here we identify a few other papers which seem relevant to disambiguation, particularly those not appearing in these collections or published after these special issues were published. Introductions to some of the techniques presented here are given in a number of texts (Manning and Schütze 1999; Allen 1995; Charniak 1993; Oakes 1998).

Stochastic taggers have been investigated by several researchers, including Church (1988) and Weischedel et al. (1993). The rule-based tagger presented is that of Brill (1995). Roche and Schabes (1995) describe techniques for improving the time efficiency of rule-based taggers, while Dermatas and Kokkinakis (1995) compare the effect of tagset choice on several languages for an stochastic tagger. Guessing the POS of unknown words is the topic of Mikheev (1997).

Hobbs and Bear (1990) discuss parsing principles and include further pointer to the literature. PCFGs are described by Charniak (1993) but may be traced to Baker (1982). Hindle and Rooth (1991) present a mechanism for statistical PP attachment. Stolcke (1995) presents algorithms for computing probabilities in PCFG for parses, substrings and other values. Johnson (1998) considers the effect of tree shape on PCFGs, concluding that they can have a significant effect on parser performance. Caraballo and Charniak (1998) assess different ranking mechanisms in best-first PCFG chart parsing. Fisher and Riloff (1992) discuss relative clause attachment disambiguation. Bod (1999) is a recent book on statistical language analysis.

Wilks (1975b) introduces the idea of semantic preferences, while the semantic closeness technique is used in Mikrokosmos (Beale et al. 1995). Yarowsky (1992) presents the statistical word sense disambiguation technique described in the chapter. Justeson and Katz (1995a) present a linguistically motivated technique for the disambiguation of adjectives. The evaluation of sense disambiguation programs is the subject of Kilgarriff (1998)

Some of the material covered in Chapter 6 is essentially concerned with disambiguation during transfer, particularly those techniques used for selecting collocations and idiomatic expressions. Using statistics from the source language for transfer disambiguation was suggested in Gale et al. (1992), while the use of statistics from the TL is explored by Dagan and Itai (1994).

10 Evaluation

Strategies for assessing the translation quality of a system as well as its cost-effectiveness are given.

The evaluation of MT and MAT systems is an important issue which has received considerable attention. There are many reasons for evaluating MT software. For example, one might want to decide whether the quality of the output is sufficiently high for a particular purpose, or one might wish to determine the savings (or costs) arising from using a particular system.

Unfortunately, given the wide range of potential applications and settings where MT and MAT software is found, it is not surprising that there is no simple or unique way of evaluating M(A)T software. This chapter presents a variety of important concepts in evaluation and a number of strategies that have been proposed to assess the merits of translation software. We begin by reviewing the different social groups that may be interested in evaluation, followed by a variety of common evaluation issues.

10.1 Evaluation Participants

Evaluation is of interest to all the different groups involved in the creation, deployment, use and maintenance of M(A)T software. Given that each group has different goals and constraints, they will have different, although hopefully related and compatible, evaluation needs. It is therefore not surprising that each group will be interested in specific and possibly non-overlapping aspects of the system and its environment.

The following groups are adapted from those suggested in King (1991) and Hutchins and Somers (1992). These groups are both producers and audiences of evaluation in the different areas of M(A)T.

10.1.1 Researchers

Researchers develop and explore new theories or adapt theories from related fields, and apply them in an M(A)T context. Evaluation in this context consists of building and debugging a prototype that embodies the theoretical framework to be explored. Several issues need to be addressed by this group, but ideally the emphasis ought to be on the abstract properties of the translation engine, independent as far as possible of any application or intended languages.

Researchers can, where applicable, situate their approach by reference to other frameworks, indicating how the new theory or technique resembles or differs from existing ones. For example, the new framework may be compared to the classical transfer vs. interlingua paradigm, either indicating that one or the other best describes the new system, or, for other types of systems, indicating why neither paradigm is an adequate characterization of it. This makes it easier for other researchers to relate to the work and possibly identify its strengths and weaknesses.

In terms of the algorithms and formalisms developed, it is useful to identify their limits and illustrate the way in which they handle (or fail to handle) a range of typical or standard problems in M(A)T. For example, evaluation at this stage should indicate whether the system can treat unbounded dependencies in a general and motivated manner and, if so, illustrate how this would be done for specific examples. At this point it might also be useful to indicate how the new approach improves on previous work.

New ways of viewing well-known problems in the field, or general treatments to these problems can also be presented in evaluations by and for researchers. Such alternative or unifying views tend to throw light on research issues and it is worth stating them explicitly.

The typical vehicles for evaluation by researchers are peer review, academic and other research journals, research conferences and academic books. This body of literature is also a source of test phenomena, benchmarks and other theoretical work against which to compare a research system.

10.1.2 Research Sponsors

Research sponsors or agencies, particularly governmental ones, invest in research at the precompetitive stage. Their aim is to determine whether a particular research project should continue to be funded, or to choose which project to fund from among a group of projects.

A sponsor needs to consider the organization and management of the research project, the current state of development in relation to the stated goals, the resources requested and whether they are adequate or excessive to achieve stated goals. Other issues that need to be assessed include the relevance of the project to other areas funded by the agency or indeed by other policies pursued by the parent organization, the standing of the researchers involved and their previous track record if available, and any other issues relating to the technological, economic and political situation in which the project will be undertaken.

In addition to these strategic and organizational issues, funding agencies will also assess the technical foundations of the project, its generality, its novelty and technical feasibility, results to date, quality of output and other evaluation issues common to other areas, as discussed below.

Evaluation by funding agencies can have considerable impact on the climate in which M(A)T research takes place, and indeed, whether it takes place at all. The ALPAC report is said to be responsible for causing a lull in MT research in the USA in the late 1960s and early 1970s, while the Eurotra project is claimed to have spurred NLP work in European languages for which few computational resources were available.

10.1.3 Developers

There are two aspects to evaluation by developers: first, deciding on the acquisition of a prototype or other system to be developed, and secondly, developing that system. In both cases there is close interaction between the developers and the researchers who produced the prototype.

In deciding on which prototype to develop, close attention is paid to the potential for development and the additional work that would be needed to make it comply with general software quality standards. If the system does not handle a particular construction, it should be possible to determine with relative ease why the construction is not handled. This implies that the internals of the system should be visible to the developer. Developers also need to consider the ease with which knowledge can be expressed and expanded. For example, is the grammatical formalism powerful enough for the intended text types? How difficult would it be to hire personnel with the required computational and linguistic expertise? Is the system modular and without unpredictable interactions between modules?

Having committed themselves to a particular type of M(A)T system, system developers need to assess their progress towards the economic viability of the system. This includes determining the coverage of their linguistic resources, the efficiency of the computational devices, the features that will enhance the attractiveness of the final product and its added value over and above other systems.

At this stage, the practical, as opposed to theoretical, limitations of the system are identified and documented. The basic system is enhanced and further debugged to the point that it can be sold as a product under explicitly stated functionality. Developers will translate substantial amounts of text of the intended type, and identify and implement the necessary changes to dictionaries, grammars and interfaces.

This second phase of evaluation for and by developers concerns successive stages of the same system, and it includes a cycle of translation, error identification, correction and retranslation until no more changes can be made cost-effectively and without diminishing the quality of other areas of the system. Sometimes development continues by specifying a ratio threshold of improvement over degradation that must be crossed. For example, a ratio of 10:1 would mean that a change is accepted only if it results in 10 or more improvements in the output for each new error that it introduces.

10.1.4 Purchasers

Purchasers of M(A)T systems range from individual translators to large translation departments or companies. They are distinguished from developers in that they do not sell M(A)T software; rather they buy and use M(A)T tools for their main activities. Evaluation by and for purchasers shares some criteria with developers' evaluation, including translation quality, efficiency and extendability. However, purchaser evaluations tend not to involve reference to the internal workings of the system, nor are they concerned with extending the basic software environment. These evaluations are sometimes called user evaluations, but a more specific term is used here to distinguish these evaluations from translator evaluations, described below.

The main concerns in purchaser evaluation are deciding whether a particular system meets the user needs. These may include text types handled, volume and quality of the output, and economic feasibility of the system. It is important in the methodology for purchaser evaluations to consider the software within the overall document production and management environment, rather than as an isolated translation module. This means that several criteria need to be considered:

Translational needs: M(A)T is particularly suited to large volumes of repetitive texts; consequently, the actual translation needs of the individual or organization must justify the purchase of the technology.

Linguistic capabilities: Representative sample texts are submitted to the system for translation and the quality of the output measured (Section 10.3). The kinds of errors produced are identified and the difficulty in fixing them should be established. Interaction with developers may be necessary to estimate the relevant level of difficulty.

Technical assessment: The software and hardware requirements for system installation and operation are established. Operating system, networking needs, word processing and desktop publishing requirements, character encodings, OCR facilities, processor speed, memory requirements and related issues are identified.

Extendability: Since every MT system must be extendable at least with new terminology, the degree to which this and other expansions are facilitated, or even possible, is determined. Can the grammar be extended, and, if so, how easy would this be for a non-expert user? Are there user-defined semantic checks? How many specialist dictionaries can be used at any one time? How easily can the system be extended to other subject domains or to other languages?

Organizational changes: The changes involved in the working practices of the organization need to be assessed, since this can affect the environment of translators and other people involved in document production. Training may be needed for translators and system administrators, maintenance contracts might be required, terminologists could be needed. Furthermore, hostility towards the system can prevent the successful introduction of M(A)T into the organization; such hostility can be particularly acute if the system is not user-friendly or has a dehumanizing effect on the user.

Costs and benefits: In addition to the basic cost of the software, the cost of installation, use and maintenance of an M(A)T system needs to be considered. The main sources of expenditure include staff training, data input, terminology and grammar updating, pre- and post-editing and system maintenance and upgrading. Any purchaser evaluation must include an estimate of the proposed costs and benefits that the system will bring. Costs may well diminish with time as dictionaries are compiled, users become more proficient at using the system, and resources are gradually tailored to the particular subject field and house style. Among the possible benefits, one can include: more consistent terminology and possibly style, faster translations, easier translation into multiple languages and faster translation of large volumes of text. As mentioned earlier, cost–benefit evaluations must be done for the complete system, taking into account the linguistic capabilities, technical environment and organizational changes that the system installation implies. In some evaluations a period of at least six months is allowed for, in order to accurately estimate the long term benefits of the installation.

Stability of vendor: The corporate situation of the M(A)T developer and supplier is also an important factor in these evaluations. The main criteria to consider are the size of the company, the relation of M(A)T to the rest of the product range, market share, the company's financial situation, the degree of product support in terms of training and help lines, its customer base, and its corporate relations within the computing and language industries.

10.1.5 Translators

Until the advent of MT over the Internet via portal services (e.g. search engines) and chat forums, a significant proportion of all M(A)T software was used by translators. Evaluation for and by translators emphasizes the operational and user interface aspects of the system. User-friendliness is paramount, as are facilities for pre- and post-editing. The types of linguistic errors can affect translator satisfaction enormously. For example, a system may translate a table of terms from English into Spanish, but if the system fails to insert articles, it will take almost as much time (and it will be very annoying) to go through each entry adding the appropriate article. The ease with which terminology is updated, exported and imported plays an important role, as does the intuitive look and feel of the user interface. It is preferable if the system is simply a plug-in to standard document editors. It should follow the conventions of the host package, and it should be able to read different file formats adequately. User support and efficient help lines can increase translator satisfaction. Contact with other users of the software through bulletin boards or the developer's Web site and Frequently Asked Questions (FAQs) can quickly increase expertise in the product with only a little effort on the part of the developer.

10.1.6 Recipients

The recipients of translations are normally monolinguals in the TL and their main concerns are with the cost, speed and linguistic quality of the translation. At least four types of recipients may be identified depending on the use they will make of the translation (Jordan et al. 1993):

Scanning: Users need to determine whether the text is relevant, so that it can be classified or a higher quality translation requested. In these cases, the cost and speed of translation are the most important criteria, as well as the technical environment in which the translation takes place: can the translation be done over the Internet? Are Web pages acceptable?

Content: Users may be experts in the field and need to know the contents of the text, but will allow for various errors in grammar and style. The semantic content of the translation must be as faithful to the original as possible, and the terminology bank must have wide coverage and be up to date. Cost and speed are also important, with different weighting depending on the subject domain and urgency of the translation.

Conversation: Users communicate verbally, either synchronously (e.g. chat forums or speech-to-speech translation) or asynchronously (e.g. email or bulletin boards). Speed is more important in the former, while quality has perhaps more impact on the latter.

Publication: Translations for publication require human involvement, in which case all three criteria, quality, cost and speed are important.

10.2   Evaluation Strategies

Regardless of the evaluation participant, there are different strategies for assessing an M(A)T system: the evaluation may adopt a "black box" or a "glass box" model, and it may use a test suite or a test corpus.

10.2.1   Black vs. Glass Box

In black box evaluation, the M(A)T system is seen as a black box whose operation is treated purely in terms of its input–output behaviour, without regard for its internal operation. Black box evaluations are particularly suited to evaluation by users and translators. They should not be conducted by the author of the software, and may or may not include the intended users of the system. Without user involvement, black box tests assess functionality, volume of data handled, recovery situations, etc. Black box testing with user involvement may take the form of laboratory tests or of field tests where users are observed using the system at their normal workplace.

By contrast, in glass box evaluation the various components that make up the system are inspected and their effect on the overall workings of the system is assessed. Glass box evaluation is particularly relevant to researchers and developers, who need to identify modules whose operation is deficient in some way. It is normally divided into static and dynamic analysis. Static glass box analysis involves checking the system without actually running it. This might include automatic syntax and type checking by a compiler, manual inspection of the system, symbolic execution, data flow analysis, etc. By contrast, dynamic glass box analysis requires running the program. It generally includes trying the program on as many logical paths as possible, and ensuring that every logical branch is executed at least once. The use of source code and visual debugging tools as well as debugging routines and libraries is common in dynamic analysis.

A recursive use of these concepts can also be adopted, where a glass box evaluation treats individual components in the system as black boxes. After being selected for further inspection, these system components can then be treated as glass boxes with their subcomponents treated as black boxes and so on.

10.2.2 Test Suite vs. Test Corpus

Test suite evaluations involve a carefully constructed set of examples, each testing a particular linguistic or translation problem. For example, Arnold et al. (1993) automatically construct test suites that systematically test various linguistic phenomena. Similarly, Gambäck et al. (1991) test the degree of compositionality of their MT system by constructing sentences in which different known transfer problems are included in different linguistic contexts. For instance, translation of "like" into the Swedish phrasal verb *tycka om* (lit. "think about") is tested in contexts such as negation, wh-questions and others. Test suite evaluations are useful for assessing generality of M(A)T systems.

However, one problem with test suite evaluations is that they assume the behaviour of a system can be projected from carefully constructed examples to real texts. In other words, test suite evaluations only indirectly evaluate the behaviour of the system on naturally occurring sentences. Also, test suite evaluations are difficult to compare. For example, given two systems, if one is better at handling coordination while the other is better at handling relative clauses, which one is better? Test suites are also difficult or virtually impossible to construct comprehensively since they potentially need to test bilingual phenomena for each pair of languages.

By contrast, in corpus evaluations a possibly specialized corpus of text is used as input to the M(A)T system. Such evaluations have been performed for both commercial and experimental systems. For example, Bennett and Slocum (1988, p. 128) report the then ongoing evaluations of the METAL system with approximately 1000 pages of actual texts over a period of five years. Rates of between 45% and 85% translations requiring no post-editing were achieved. The spoken language translation system described by Rayner et al. (1993) has been evaluated using a set of 633 sentences selected from the ATIS corpus. Rates of 41.8% acceptable translations, based on the scores of bilingual judges, are reported.

Corpus evaluation is not without its shortcomings. One problem is that it does not systematically test all possible sources of incorrect translations. Instead, it considers the most commonly occurring constructions, since these are likely to abound in any randomly selected text. It is therefore difficult to estimate the behaviour of the system for other types of text. Ideally, one should apply a mixture of text suite and test corpus evaluation in order to gain insight from both. For example, King and Falkedal (1990) propose two sets of test data: one based on the type of text the system is expected to translate, and the other based on more general examples such as may be constructed without any particular text type in mind. Such tests would evaluate both suitability to actual texts and extendability of the system, but of course they are lengthier and more expensive to conduct.

10.2.3 Cost of Evaluation

It should be quite clear that the cost of evaluation should in general be small in relation to the cost of the system and the budget allocated to it. Furthermore, evaluation is time-consuming and therefore cannot be done at frequent intervals. About 12 person-months for a large-scale operational evaluation (i.e. on site and with the system performing its intended operations) is sometimes suggested, which can give an indication of the personnel costs involved.

10.3 Quality Measures

Measuring the quality of a translation is not only a difficult problem in M(A)T but for translation in general. Part of the problem is that for any given text there is a possibly infinite number of correct translations. Even within the narrower domain of technical translation, there is enough variability that no simple measure exists for determining quality. As a result, different strategies for assessing translation quality have been developed.

The most common approach is to ask a translator or subject expert to rank the output texts for quality, defined in terms of the monolingual intelligibility of the target text, and the bilingual accuracy of content preservation. This clearly makes measures of quality in MT subjective, but it is difficult to see how they could be otherwise. One of the first evaluations of this type was undertaken as part of the ALPAC report (ALPAC 1966). It was a highly controlled assessment which has influenced subsequent evaluation methodologies. Intelligibility and accuracy are discussed in the next two sections.

10.3.1 Intelligibility

Intelligibility or clarity measures the fluency and grammaticality of the TL text, without concern for whether it faithfully conveys the meaning of the SL. Intelligibility can be measured by speakers fluent in the TL without reference to the source text. A typical intelligibility test consists of a group of readers who are given a piece of machine-translated text and a scale along which to rank the readability of the text's sentences. Arnold et al. (1994) suggest a minimum of a four-point scale ranging from "hopelessly unintelligible" to "perfectly intelligible", while for the ALPAC report a ten-point scale was used. A frequently used scale is that suggested by Nagao et al. (1988) consisting of five categories, presented below in a slightly adapted form:

1. The meaning of the sentence is clear, and there are no questions. Grammar, word usage, and/or style are all appropriate, and no rewriting is needed.
2. The meaning of the sentence is clear, but there are some problems in grammar, word usage, and/or style, making the overall quality less than 1.

3. The basic thrust of the sentence is clear, but you are not sure of some detailed parts because of grammar and word usage problems. You would need to look at the original SL sentence to clarify the meaning.
4. The sentence contains many grammatical and word usage problems, and you can only guess at the meaning after careful study, if at all.
5. The sentence cannot be understood at all.

It is clear that objectivity is not achieved through this scale: what someone classifies as a 1 may be classified as a 2 by someone else. To reduce subjectivity, the scores of several evaluators can be combined and statistical means used to approximate a more objective assessment of intelligibility.

The scale can be tested before it is used in order to achieve greater consistency in its wording, interpretation and application. Scale testing should be repeated until the scales are being applied uniformly by evaluators.

Perhaps less subjective alternatives are suggested by the use of Cloze tests, where words in the translated text are masked and evaluators are asked to guess the masked word. The correlation between the masked word and the guessed word, say in terms of part of speech, semantic category or other semantic criterion, is an indication of how intelligible the text is. Another possibility is the use of comprehension tests, where after reading the machine-translated text evaluators are tested on their understanding of it using standard reading comprehension techniques such as are used for educational purposes.

10.3.2 Accuracy

Once intelligibility has been assessed, the accuracy of the translation can be measured. Accuracy is an indication of how the translated text preserves the content of the source text. To a certain extent, this is dependent on the intelligibility score since a text scoring, say 4 or 5 on the Nagao intelligibility scale is unlikely to convey any content, let alone the content of the source text. It has even been claimed that accuracy evaluation can be omitted in certain cases because this relation is so strong. However, a highly intelligible sentence may not convey the meaning of the source text at all because of incorrect disambiguation. Thus a thorough evaluation would include accuracy testing.

A typical methodology consists of a group of bilinguals presented with a set of SL sentences and their translations, along with a scale with which to rank the translation for accuracy. Nagao et al. (1988) give the following seven-point scale for accuracy, presented here in a slightly adapted form:

1. The content of the SL sentence is faithfully conveyed to the TL sentence. The translated sentence is clear to a native speaker of the TL and no rewriting is needed.
2. The content of the SL sentence is faithfully conveyed to the TL sentence, and can be clearly understood by a native speaker, but some rewriting is needed.
3. The content of the SL sentence is faithfully conveyed in the TL sentence, but some changes are needed in word order.

4. While the content of the SL sentence is generally conveyed faithfully in the TL sentence, there are some problems with things like relationships between phrases and expressions, and with tense, plurals, and the position of adverbs. There is some duplication of nouns in the sentence.

5. The content of the SL sentence is not adequately conveyed in the TL sentence. Some expressions are missing, and there are problems with the relationships between clauses, between phrases and clauses, or between sentence elements.

6. The content of the SL sentence is not conveyed in the TL sentence.

7. The content of the SL sentence is not conveyed at all. The output is not a proper sentence; subjects and predicates are missing.

Once again, the scale cannot be applied objectively, since evaluators may be more or less stringent.

An alternative measure of accuracy is that of practical performance evaluation in the translation of instruction manuals. An accurate translation of a set of instructions is one whose content can be followed by a target text reader in the same way that they would be followed by a source text reader. Perhaps a more tenuous approach is to back-translate the target text into the SL and compare it with the original text. Apart from requiring a bidirectional system, this approach can lead to an overestimate of errors, given that errors might be increased or magnified by translating a less than perfect text. Back-translation, however, can be used in interlingua MT where paraphrases of the pivot representation help identify errors prior to generation into the TL.

Intelligibility and accuracy scores are useful indicators of quality, but they may not always be useful or adequate. For example, if we wish to select between two systems, and one produces most sentences around the middle of the scales (i.e. of medium quality), while another produces sentences in roughly equal numbers around the high and low end of the scales (i.e. either high quality or low quality but few of medium quality), how could one choose between the two systems? Furthermore, it has been claimed that quality is not kept constant when an M(A)T system is introduced, as translators will tend to produce merely correct rather than good post-edited translation.

10.3.3 Error Analysis

Given the subjective character of quality measures in MT, one useful and popular way of assessing intelligibility and accuracy is to count the errors in the text in order to assess translation quality. One version of this approach is to count the number of words inserted, modified, deleted and moved by a post-editor revising the machine-translated text in order to convert it into an acceptable form. Different kinds of error are given different weightings, and the overall quality of a translation is determined by the weighted sum of errors in the text, normalized by the size of the text.

Error weighting can depend on the severity of the error in terms of its effect on intelligibility or accuracy, the difficulty in updating the system to correct it, the time taken by the post-editor to correct it, or a combination of all three. For example, deletion of a word may be given a weight of 2, deletion of a clause a weight of 4, while correction of a conjunction may be given a weighting of 12 (Minnis 1993).

There are at least three problems with error analysis. Firstly, deciding what is an acceptable translation is a subjective question: one post-editor's acceptable translation is another's deluge of errors. Secondly, determining the weight of particular error classes can involve conflicting reasoning: correcting the tense of a verb is relatively straightforward to do by a post-editor, but can completely mislead a reader and can involve considerable changes to the system's grammars. It is also questionable whether one single weight per error class accurately represents the effect of an error in a given sentence. Finally, classifying errors into these classes is problematic: a missing auxiliary verb could be classified as a missing word error, or as an incorrect verb form error. Furthermore, errors are interlinked, making counting difficult. For example, incorrect gender marking on a Spanish noun will cause its article and adjective to be incorrect. Should this be counted as one or three errors? In pathological cases where a translation is practically useless, error counting is of little help since it is unclear even what corrections to make.

10.4   Software Evaluation

Given that an M(A)T system is in essence a piece of software, it is profitable to see any of the stages in its creation, installation and maintenance as those of a software system. This perspective on M(A)T has been emphasized recently by the Evaluation of Natural Language Processing Systems group in the EAGLES project (EAGLES 1996), when it adopted the ISO standard 9126 on software quality. This standard sets out six quality characteristics to be considered in the evaluation of software products: functionality, reliability, usability, efficiency, maintainability and portability. Each characteristic is further subdivided into a number of more specific subcharacteristics. These six characteristics are intended to apply to all software products, and therefore can apply to translation software. The characteristics are independent of the type of evaluation participant and can therefore play an important role at any stage in translation software production and use. However, they are clearly more directly applicable to researchers, developers, purchasers and translators. In this section, the term user will be taken to include these four groups. It should also be clear that while researchers and evaluators will be concerned with including these characteristics in the software they produce, purchasers and translators will be concerned with finding them in the software they use.

10.4.1   Functionality

The functionality of a software system determines the degree to which it fulfils the stated or implied needs of a user. It consists of the following subcharacteristics:

Suitability: The presence and appropriateness of functions for a task, e.g. translation of individual sentences.

Accuracy: The provision of right or agreed results, e.g. the quality of the translated sentences.

Interoperability: Ability to interact with specified systems, e.g. MT system works with popular word processors.

Compliance: Software adheres to application related standards or regulations. There are no widely accepted M(A)T standards, but the EAGLES project is an attempt to provide these for NLP.

Security: Ability of the software to prevent unauthorized access, whether accidental or deliberate, to data and programs, e.g. translation memory updating is protected by a password.

10.4.2 Reliability

Reliable software is that which maintains its level of performance under specified conditions and for a specified period of time. It consists of:

Maturity: Frequency of failure by faults in the software. Mature software is less likely to crash or otherwise fail, as more bugs and errors will have been identified and corrected.

Fault tolerance: Software maintains a specified level of performance in cases of software faults or of infringement of its specified interface, e.g. clicking inappropriate buttons on the interface does not crash the system.

Recoverability: Capability to re-establish the system's level of performance and to recover the data directly affected in case of failure; also the time and effort needed to achieve these. For example, if a TM system is accidentally switched off, any TUs produced up to or just before failure can be recovered.

10.4.3 Usability

The usability of a software system indicates the effort needed to use the software by a stated or implied set of users. Usability also includes individual assessments by users on the ease of operation of the software. Its subcharacteristics are:

Understandability: Effort by the user in recognizing the logical concept embodied by the software and its applicability, e.g. it should be easy to see what a TM system is intended to do and/or what it can do.

Learnability: Effort in learning to use the software, e.g. an MT system is learnable if it can be used after little training.

Operability: Effort in using and controlling the system, e.g. an MT system in which deeply nested menus need to be accessed to enable Web page translation is not highly operable.

10.4.4   Efficiency

Efficiency bears on the relationship between the level of performance of the software and the amount of resources used to achieve that level of performance under specified conditions. Subcharacteristics:

Time behaviour: Response and processing times and throughput rates of the software in performing its function, e.g. the words per hour/minute translated by the system.

Resource Behaviour: Amount of resources used by the software and the duration of such use in performing its function, e.g. the amount of memory and disk space needed by the system.

10.4.5   Maintainability

Maintainability relates to the effort needed to make specified modifications to the software. It consists of:

Analysability: Effort needed for diagnosis of deficiencies or causes of failures, or for identification of parts to be modified, e.g. the system indicates in advance of translation what terminology is missing from its dictionaries.

Changeability: Effort needed for modification, fault removal or environmental change, e.g. the possibility and ease of adding terminology and other linguistic resources to the system.

Stability: The risk of unexpected effects after modifications, e.g. adding terminology should improve translation quality in a predictable manner.

Testability: Effort needed to validate the modified software, e.g. once changes are made to the terminology database, it should be possible immediately to test whether the database has been updated properly.

10.4.6   Portability

Portability indicates the ability of the software to be transferred from one environment to another. Subcharacteristics:

Adaptability: Opportunity for the software's adaptation to different specified environments without applying other actions or means other than those provided for this purpose, e.g. a plug-in is available that allows the system to translate between additional languages.

Installability: Effort needed to install the software in a specified environment, e.g. the installation software should infer as many properties about the operating system and hardware environment as possible; other installation parameters should be elicited through clear simple questions.

Conformance: Adherence of the software to standards or conventions relating to portability, e.g. a TM system should be able to import and export translation memories in standard formats.

Replaceability: Opportunity and effort of using the software in the place of other specified software, e.g. the ease with which a terminology management tool can replace an existing tool in a TWB.

In addition to software characteristics, the ISO 9126 has been extended by EAGLES, together with the TEMAA LRE project (TEMAA 1997), to include the formulation of user needs, which are outlined below.

10.5 Software User Needs

In order to assess any of the above characteristics for a particular group of evaluation participants, the needs that the software product must fulfill need to be identified in a systematic fashion, as can be inferred from the definition of some of the preceding characteristics. However, identifying the explicit or implicit needs in M(A)T is far from simple, with the fields of requirements analysis and engineering dedicated to the study and development of appropriate techniques.

10.5.1 Requirements Analysis

Requirements analysis is one of the principal stages in the software cycle. Traditionally, it takes place early on, prior to software design and implementation. However, requirements analysis is frequently an iterative process during development, or it can take place after the implementation of a prototype, or even when no development is in prospect, for example when evaluating an existing product.

When used for evaluating NLP and M(A)T systems, the following sequence of steps may be proposed:

Top-level tasks: A set of tasks describing the top-level functionality of the system. For example, a spell checker can be defined as taking a unproofed text as input and producing a proofed text as output, by analogy with a human proofreader.

Setup: Here the situation and environment variables affecting the task are identified. For example, if the input to the spell checker is the result of optical character recognition, this needs to be identified at this stage.

Quality requirements: These are task-independent descriptions of the features the output of the system must have. For example, this could refer to the quality of error detection of the software.

Transformation to reportable attributes: At this stage, the top-level tasks, setup and quality requirements are re-expressed in terms of measurable attributes. Here a bottom-up approach is applicable, where system performance and behaviour is matched against higher level domain requirements. Error rates are an example of a reportable attribute corresponding to a quality requirement.

Describing how these requirements would be elicited and formalized from users would require a complete volume, and the reader is referred to Macaulay (1996) for a practical introduction.

10.5.2   Consumer Report Paradigm

When presenting the results of an evaluation, it is convenient to adopt the consumer report paradigm. Such reports are often produced by consumer associations or specialist magazines on a wide range of products, including computers, printers, cars and universities. Results are displayed in such a way that measures for all reportable attributes are presented, possibly in tabular form, so that users can consider only those features that they deem most relevant to their requirements. Sometimes such tests additionally assume a typical or standard user and make a recommendation based on a particular weighting of features, but this weighting can be modified to suit different requirements.

Consumer reports consist of a series of product tests from which comparisons can be made. There are a number of desirable properties of product tests. Firstly, they must be reliable in the sense that repeatedly applying the test to the same product or to identical products produces the same results. For example, translating the same text with different copies of the same software on different machines should produce the same results. Secondly, tests must be valid in that the results obtained must reflect functionality as perceived by the user. For example, precision and recall scores for a TM system should correlate with perceived usefulness of retrieved sentences. Thirdly, tests must be relevant in that they consider features that are important to the user. Thus, for a standalone user of an MT system, tests on the networking features of the system will be irrelevant. Finally, the tests must be feasible in terms of the resources available to the evaluator.

Consumer reports can be produced using the following six steps:

1. Product classes and products are selected for evaluation.
2. Selection and definition of attributes to be compared. These should relate directly to the primary function of the product, its use and maintenance, cost etc.
3. Development of measuring methods. Here different kinds of values may be obtained: nominal (presence/absence of a product characteristic), ordinal (ordering of values – high, middle, low), interval (absolute numbers) etc.
4. Measurement.
5. Analysis of results, where values are compared with each other, plotted etc.
6. Interpretation of the data, where the results are simplified to give an overall picture for each product, and possibly give a best buy.

The consumer report paradigm clearly has advantages for M(A)T evaluation in terms of familiarity and accessibility, although it is by no means perfect. For example, such tests fail to test all variants of a product, they can become obsolete quickly, alternative products are not evaluated (e.g. an MT product test would not test TM systems), and they give little indication about actual product use.

10.6   Conclusion

There is no standard approach to evaluation, and each application of MAT or MT may require its own distinct evaluation methodology and measures. Deciding on the evaluation participants and determining the user needs are the first steps in an evaluation. From this, various aspects of the software can be identified for evaluation. Some of these, particularly those related to translation quality, are difficult to assess and a variety of evaluation strategies and quality measures are possible.

However, the cost of a thorough and/or realistic evaluation is high, and usually involves installation specific parameters, making it difficult to compare different systems.

10.6.1   Further Reading

Since the early days of MT, particular attention has been paid to evaluation (ALPAC 1966). Many books on MT include at least a chapter on evaluation (Lehrberger and Bourbeau 1988; Hutchins and Somers 1992; Arnold et al. 1994). King (1991) is an interesting panel discussion on evaluation. The intelligibility and accuracy measures are taken from Nagao et al. (1988). The Journal of Machine Translation, Special Issue on Evaluation, Volume 8, 1993, includes several useful articles. General topics in NLP evaluation are discussed by Sparck Jones and Galliers (1995), King (1996) and as part of the EAGLES project (EAGLES 1996). Chinchor et al. (1993) describe the evaluation methodology for the Third Message Understanding Conference.

11 Conclusion

Concluding remarks regarding the book and the future of MT and MAT.

Demand for MT has grown and will continue to grow steadily. The advent of the Internet and electronic commerce in particular have increased the demand for automatic translation of sufficient quality for determining the content of a Web page. A variety of authoring tools and document production techniques have also made linguistic information available in a variety of formats. This information will need to be translated if it is to have the widest possible distribution.

The techniques presented in this book vary substantially in their purpose and orientation. In selecting the most suitable technique for a particular application one has to consider a variety of criteria. Perhaps the most important questions are the quality of translation and the degree of automation needed. Broadly speaking, MAT techniques achieve higher quality but require more user involvement, while MT techniques have a greater degree of automation but generally have lower quality on unrestricted input. Transfer systems tend to be less costly to build for a pair of languages, but in multilingual environments the costs quickly mount as several transfer modules need to be updated and refined. Interlingua systems would be particularly useful for translation into multiple languages for restricted domains since unrestricted domains are too difficult to treat with this approach. These are but broad rules of thumb for deploying translation engines in particular applications. In fact, one can combine different strategies within a single system. For example, it is common to see TM systems that revert to an MT system when the best match from the TUs database does not exceed the specified threshold. Similarly, one can conceive of multi-engine systems where transfer, interlingua and EBMT engines compete to produce the best translation of a sentence.

11.1 Trends

The success of TM systems is one of the most noticeable trends in translation in general, and MAT in particular. Many companies expect translators to know and to be able to use TM tools. This success has led to an increase in research in TM and EBMT with the goal of producing ever more useful translation tools.

Web page translation is particularly suitable for MT. Browsers with built-in or added MT capabilities may become commonplace. The advantage of these systems is that they can translate quickly and at any time, enabling access to information in a variety of languages.

However, even if MT is available on a browser or over the Internet, finding a page to translate can be difficult if the person doing the search does not know the language in which the page is written. Imagine wishing to find all Web pages about art galleries in France. Assuming that all these pages are in French, a query in English will probably fail to retrieve many relevant pages. Cross-language information retrieval is the study of techniques for formulating queries in one language but retrieving documents written in a different language. At present it is a growing area of research and development and it is likely to have an impact on multilingual communication (Grefenstette 1998).

The explosion in electronic communication and the use of computers has meant that endangered languages can take advantage of technology to record, disseminate, and maybe even preserve, the language, and to exploit approaches and techniques that are already tried and tested on more common languages. M(A)T could help the preservation and revival of these languages.

Speech recognition rates are continually improving, and it is possible that spoken translation will some day come out of the research labs and into the market-place. Indulging in speculation even further, is is conceivable that automatic captioning and subtitling of films and videos into a different language may be attempted. Indeed, machine translation of text subtitles has shown the usefulness of such applications (Popowich et al. 1997).

The use of grammar learning and other machine-learning techniques is improving and will continue to improve the coverage of monolingual, bilingual and multilingual resources. This should simplify the creation of MT systems for new domains and/or languages. Further integration of interlingua and transfer approaches should lead to a reduction of their disadvantages and a fruitful interplay of their advantages.

11.2 Further Reading

Research in MAT and MT is reported in the journal *Machine Translation* published by Kluwer and in the proceedings of the International Conference on Theoretical and Methodological Issues in Machine Translation (TMI), MT Summit and the conferences by Association for Machine Translation in the Americas (AMTA). The conference series *Translating and the Computer*, published by Aslib in the UK also has relevant articles. The *Computational Linguistics* journal, published by the MIT Press for the Association for Computational Linguistics, also contains many useful articles. The proceedings of other conferences, including those of the Association for Computational Linguistics (ACL) and the International Conference on Computational Linguistics (COLING), contain relevant papers.

Appendix: Useful Resources

The following is a list of resources on the Internet that are relevant to readers of this book. Web sites are constantly changing and one cannot guarantee that they will exist when readers try to access them. At the time of writing (May 1999) they were still available. URLs may be assumed to have the `http://` prefix unless an alternative is explicitly given.

Introduction and Background

The implementations for most of the algorithms presented in Chapters 5–7 are available via:

```
www.ccl.umist.ac.uk/resources/ccl/
  langeng_resources.html
```

The code has been tested using Jan Wielemaker's SWI-Prolog:

```
www.swi.psy.uva.nl/usr/jan/SWI-Prolog/
```

For information on Prolog see:

```
www.comlab.ox.ac.uk/archive/logic-prog.html
```

The LINGUIST List homepage has many links on linguistics:

```
www.linguistlist.org
```

A good starting point for AI is the American Association for Artificial Intelligence site:

```
www.aaai.org
```

John Carew's introduction to probability and statistics is at:

```
www.cms.wisc.edu/~carew/statistics/index.html
```

For HMMs see Section 11.2 below.

Text Processing

XEmacs is a widely used multilingual text editor:

```
www.xemacs.org
```

Internationalization and Localization

Internationalization links from the WWW Consortium are at:

`www.w3.org/International/`

The Localization Industry Standards Association (LISA)'s web site is at:

`www.lisa.org`

Other links, particularly on character sets are available via:

`anubis.dkuug.dk/maits/`
`www.vlsivie.tuwien.ac.at/mike/i18n.html`

The second of these includes font links for Unix and X11. Web Internationalization and Multilingualism links provided by M. T. Carrasco Benitez are at:

`www.dragoman.org`

Character Sets

Some internationalization links include information on character sets (see above). The Unicode Web site is:

`www.unicode.org`

An explanation of Chinese–Japanese–Korean information processing is provided by Ken Lunde:

`ftp://ftp.ora.com/pub/examples/nutshell/ujip/`
  `doc/cjk.inf`

Microsoft's character sets are explained in:

`www.microsoft.com/typography/unicode/cs.htm`

Fonts

The fonts FAQ is available at:

`www.nwalsh.com/comp.fonts/FAQ/index.html`

The Yamada Language Center home page has links to font archives mainly for Macs and PCs:

`babel.uoregon.edu/yamada/guides.html`

For X11 fonts for Unix see under internationalization. Discussion of various font editors and of TrueType fonts is at:

`www.truetype.demon.co.uk`

Information on PostScript Type 1 fonts can be found at:

`www.adobe.com/type/`

There are also a few shareware font editors. For example, `xfedor` is a bitmap editor for producing `.bdf` fonts:

`avahi.inria.fr/pub/xfedor/`

The Metafont system is a macro package that allows the mathematical definition of scalable fonts. It is particularly suited for use with TEX and LATEX. Instructions for obtaining it are at:

`www.tex.ac.uk/tex-archive/systems/web2c/unixtex.ftp`

Multilingual support for LATEX can be obtained from:

`www.tex.ac.uk/tex-archive/languages/`

or any of its mirror sites.

Input Methods

An early version of the ISO-10646 input method standard proposal is at:

`www-rocq.inria.fr/~deschamp/www/divers/ALB-WD.html`

Ordering information on the ISO/IEC 14755:1997 standard for input methods is at:

`www.iso.ch/cate/d25491.html#0`

Radical and stroke based input for Chinese characters is explained in:

`student-www.uchicago.edu/users/jcwicent/wubihua.html`

An introduction to T-Code is given in Japanese at:

`www.cc.rim.or.jp/~tarokawa/tcode/intro.html`

Machine-Aided Translation

Descriptions and links on MAT may be found at:

`www.languagepartners.com`
`www.who.int/pll/cat/cat_resources.html`

OpenTag is a standard for representing text extracted from different formats in order to facilitate manipulation (e.g. translation) and subsequent merging into an original skeleton format file:

`www.opentag.org`

The TMX file format for translation memory exchange is described in:

`www.lisa.unige.ch/tmx/tmx.htm`

The source code (in C) to accompany Frakes and Baeza-Yates (1992) includes a stemmer and a stoplist algorithm:

`ftp://ftp.vt.edu/pub/reuse/IR.code/ir-code/`

The book *Information Retrieval* by van Rijsbergen (1979) includes discussion of similarity measures and other retrieval issues:

`www.dcs.gla.ac.uk/Keith/`

Alignment and translation memory demos are at the RALI site:

`www-rali.iro.umontreal.ca`

Multilingual text processing tools from Multext including a bilingual aligner are at:

`www.lpl.univ-aix.fr/projects/multext/`

Computational Linguistics

For general NLP links including information about paper repositories see:

`www.cs.columbia.edu/~radev/u/db/acl/`

This site has links to special interest group pages including phonology, parsing and generation. The Association for Computational Linguistics has its own site with links to on-line versions of conference proceedings:

`www.aclweb.org`

Many articles on CL are available from the Computation and Language E-Print Archive:

`xxx.lanl.gov/archive/cs/intro.html`

The Linguistics Computing Resources page at the Summer Institute of Linguistics (SIL) and the Natural Language Software Registry have links to CL tools, including PC-KIMMO:

`www.sil.org/linguistics/computing.html`
`www.dfki.de/lt/registry/sections.html`

The HPSG web site contains useful links and articles on the theory:

`hpsg.stanford.edu`

Machine Translation

General and Transfer

The introduction to MT by Arnold et al. (1994) is available at:

`clwww.essex.ac.uk/~doug/book/book.html`

The regional components of the International Association for Machine Translation (IAMT) each have their own Web site:

Asia-Pacific

`www.jeida.or.jp/aamt/`

European

`www.lim.nl/eamt/`

American

`www.isi.edu/natural-language/organizations/AMTA.html`

The British Computer Society (BCS) has a Specialist group on MT with links to various resources:

`www.bcs.org.uk/siggroup/nalatran/nalatran.htm`

Federico Zanettin also maintains a list of useful links including commercial products:

`www.sslmit.unibo.it/zanettin/cattools.htm`

Using MT for Web pages is typified by AltaVista and its Babelfish service:

`babelfish.altavista.com`

The experimental KIT-FAST transfer system, running under SWI-Prolog is at:

`wave.cs.tu-berlin.de/~ww/mtsystem.html`

Interlingua MT

Articles on LCS translation can be downloaded from:

`www.umiacs.umd.edu/labs/CLIP/mt.html`

The KANT Web page includes several papers on the system:

`www.lti.cs.cmu.edu/Research/Kant/`

Similarly the Mikrokosmos site includes much information on the project:

`crl.nmsu.edu/Research/Projects/mikro/index.html`

The Ontology Resource Page lists conferences, research groups and specific ontologies:

`www.csi.uottawa.ca/dept/Ontology/`

The Natural Language Group at USC/ISI include a description of their KBMT system:

`www.isi.edu/natural-language/`

Other Approaches

An Introduction to MRS can be downloaded from:

```
hpsg.stanford.edu/hpsg/pubs.html
```

A Type Rewriting system can be obtained from:

```
www.ims.uni-stuttgart.de/~emele/TFS.html
```

Disambiguation

Chris Brew and Mark Moens, Brigitte Krenn and Christer Samuelsson, and Joakim Nivre have introductory guides to statistical techniques in NLP; respectively:

```
www.ltg.ed.ac.uk/~chrisbr/dilbook/dilbook.html
www.ling.gu.se/~nivre/kurser/wwwstat/compendium.ps
www.ling.gu.se/~nivre/kurser/wwwstat/index.html
```

Christopher Manning's page has links to corpora, analysers and other resources:

```
www.sultry.arts.usyd.edu.au/links/statnlp.html
```

An HMM tagger from Xerox is available from:

```
ftp://parcftp.xerox.com/pub/tagger/
```

Eric Brill's tagger can be downloaded from his home page:

```
www.cs.jhu.edu/~brill/home.html
```

Roget's Thesaurus can be downloaded via ftp from a number of sites. WordNet can be downloaded through:

```
www.cogsci.princeton.edu/~wn/
```

Information on its European counterpart project, EuroWordNet, is at:

```
www.let.uva.nl/~ewn/
```

SENSEVAL is a forum for the evaluation of sense disambiguation programs:

```
www.itri.brighton.ac.uk/events/senseval/
```

Evaluation

The TEMAA and EAGLES pages are at:

```
www.cst.ku.dk/projects/temaa/temaa.html
www.issco.unige.ch/projects/ewg96/ewg96.html
www.cst.ku.dk/projects/eagles2.html
```

The TSNLP project developed guidelines for creating test suites:

```
clwww.essex.ac.uk/group/projects/tsnlp/
```

References

Adorni, G. and M. Zock (1996). *Trends in Natural Language Generation*. Lecture Notes in Artificial Intelligence. Berlin: Springer.

Aho, A. V., R. Sethi, and J. D. Ullman (1986). *Compilers - Principles, Techniques, and Tools*. Reading, MA: Addison-Wesley.

Aït-Kaci, H., B. Boyer, P. Lincoln, and R. Nasr (1989). Efficient implementation of lattice operations. *ACM Transactions on Programming Languages and Systems 11*(1).

Aït-Kaci, H. and R. Nasr (1986). Login: A logical programming language with built-in inheritance. *Journal of Logic Programming 3*, 187–215.

Alam, Y. (1983). A two-level morphological analysis of Japanese. *Texas Linguistic Forum 22*, 229–52.

Allegranza, V., P. Bennett, J. Durand, F. van Eynde, L. Humphreys, P. Schmidt, and E. Steiner (1991). Linguistics for machine translation: The Eurotra linguistic specifications. See Copeland et al. (1991), pp. 15–125.

Allen, J. (1995). *Natural Language Understanding* (2nd ed.). Redwood City, CA: Benjamin/Cummings.

ALPAC (1966). *Languages and Machines: Computers in Translation and Linguistics*. Number 1416 in National Research Council Publications. Washington, DC: National Research Council. Report of the Automatic Language Processing Advisory Committee, Division of Behavioral Sciences, National Academy of Sciences.

Alshawi, H. (Ed.) (1992). *The Core Language Engine*. Cambridge, MA: MIT Press.

Alshawi, H. (1996). Head automata and bilingual tiling: Translation with minimal representations. In *Proceedings of the 34th Annual Meeting of the Association for Computational Linguistics - ACL-96*, Santa Cruz, CA, pp. 167–76.

Alshawi, H., S. Bangalore, and S. Douglas (1998). Automatic acquisition of hierarchical transduction models for machine translation. In *Proceedings of the 17th International Conference on Computational Linguistics and 36th Annual Meeting of the Association for Computational Linguistics - COLING/ACL-98*, Montreal, pp. 41–47. Association for Computational Linguistics.

Alshawi, H., A. L. Buchsbaum, and F. Xia (1997). A comparison of head transducers and transfer for a limited domain translation application. In *Proceedings of the 35th Annual Meeting of the Association for Computational Linguistics - ACL-97*, Madrid, pp. 360–65. Association for Computational Linguistics.

Alshawi, H., D. Carter, B. Gambäck, and M. Rayner (1992). Swedish-English QLF translation. See Alshawi (1992), Chapter 14, pp. 277–309.

Alshawi, H. and S. G. Pulman (1992). Ellipsis, comparatives and generation. See Alshawi (1992), Chapter 13, pp. 251–75.

Antworth, E. L. (1990). PC-KIMMO: A two-level processor for morphological analysis. Technical report, Summer Institute of Linguistics, Dallas, Texas. www.sil.org/pckimmo/pc-kimmo.html.

Arnold, D. (1996). Parameterizing Lexical Conceptual Structure for Interlingua Machine Translation. A Review of "Machine Translation: A View from the Lexicon". *Machine Translation 11*(4), 217–41.

Arnold, D., L. Balkan, R. L. Humphreys, S. Meijer, and L. Sadler (1994). *Machine Translation: An Introductory Guide*. Oxford: NCC and Oxford Blackwell. clwww.essex.ac.uk/~doug/book/book.html.

Arnold, D., D. Moffat, L. Sadler, and A. Way (1993). Automatic test suite generation. *Machine Translation 8*, 29–38. Special Issue on Evaluation.

Baker, C. L. (1995). *English Syntax* (2nd ed.). Cambridge, MA: MIT.

Baker, J. (1982). Trainable grammars for speech recognition. In *Speech Communication Papers for the 97th Meeting of the Acoustical Society of America*, pp. 547–50.

Baker, M. (Ed.) (1998). *Routledge Encyclopedia of Translation Studies*. London: Routledge.

Balari, S. and L. Dini (Eds.) (1998). *Romance in Head-driven Phrase Structure Grammar (HPSG)*. Stanford: CSLI.

Bar-Hillel, Y. (1960). The present status of automatic translation of languages. In F. L. Alt (Ed.), *Advances in Computers*, Volume 1, pp. 91–163. New York: Academic Press.

Barnett, J., I. Mani, E. Rich, C. Aone, K. Knight, and J. C. Martinez (1991). Capturing language-specific semantic distinctions in interlingua-based MT. In *Proceedings MT Summit III*, Washington DC, pp. 25–32.

Barwise, J. and J. Perry (1983). *Situations and Attitudes*. Cambridge, MA: A Bradford Book, The MIT Press.

Basili, R., M. T. Pazienza, and P. Velardi (1992). Combining NLP and statistical techniques for lexical acquisition. In *Intelligent Probabilistic Approaches to Natural Language - Papers from the 1992 Fall Symposium*, pp. 1–9. AAAI.

Bateman, J. A. (1995). On the relationship between ontology construction and natural language: A socio-semiotic view. *International Journal of Human-Computer Studies 43*(5,6), 929–44.

Beale, S., S. Nirenburg, and K. Mahesh (1995). Semantic analysis in the Mikrokosmos machine translation project. In *Proceedings of the 2nd Symposium on Natural Language Processing*, Bangkok, Thailand, pp. 297–307. crl.nmsu.edu/Research/Projects/mikro/htmls/misc-htmls/mikro-pub.html.

Beale, S., S. Nirenburg, and K. Mahesh (1996). Hunter-gatherer: Three search techniques integrated for natural language semantics. In *Proceedings of the Thirteenth National Conference on Artificial Intelligence (AAAI96)*, Portland, Oregon. American Association for Artificial Intelligence.

Bear, J. (1985). Interpreting two-level phonological rules directly. Technical report, SRI International, Menlo Park, CA.

Beaven, J. L. (1992a). *Lexicalist Unification Based Machine Translation*. Ph. D. thesis, Department of Artificial Intelligence, University of Edinburgh, Edinburgh, UK.

Beaven, J. L. (1992b). Shake-and-Bake machine translation. In *Proceedings of the 14th COLING*, Nantes, France, pp. 602–09.

Becker, T., W. Finkler, A. Kilger, and P. Poller (1998). An efficient kernel for multilingual generation in speech-to-speech dialogue translation. In *Proceedings of the 17th International Conference on Computational Linguistics and the 36th Annual Conference of the ACL - COLING/ACL 98*, Volume I, Montreal, Canada, pp. 110–16.

Bellman, R. (1957). *Dynamic Programming*. Princeton: Princeton University Press.

Bennett, P. (1993). The interaction of syntax and morphology in machine translation. See van Eynde (1993), Chapter 3, pp. 72–104.

Bennett, W. S. and J. Slocum (1988). The LRC machine translation system. See Slocum (1988), pp. 111–40.

Berger, A. L., S. A. Della Pietra, and V. J. Della Pietra (1996). A maximum entropy approach to natural language processing. *Computational Linguistics 22*(1), 39–71.

Bod, R. (1999). *Beyond Grammar - An Experience-Based Theory of Language*. CSLI/Cambridge University Press.

Borsley, R. D. (1996). *Modern Phrase Structure Grammar*. Oxford: Blackwell.

Bouma, G. (1992). Feature structures and monotonicity. *Computational Linguistics 18*(2), 183–203.

Bratko, I. (1990). *Prolog Programming for Artificial Intelligence*. Wokingham: Addison-Wesley.

Bresnan, J. (Ed.) (1982). *The Mental Representation of Grammatical Relations.* MIT Press Series on Cognitive Theory and Mental Representations. Cambridge, MA: The MIT Press.

Brew, C. (1992). Letting the cat out of the bag: Generation for Shake-and-Bake MT. In *Proceedings of the 14th COLING*, Nantes, France, pp. 610–16.

Brill, E. (1995). Transformation-based error-driven learning and natural language processing: A case study in part-of-speech tagging. *Computational Linguistics 21*(4), 543–65.

Bringhurst, R. (1997). *The Elements of Typographic Style.* Point Roberts, WA: Hartley & Marks.

Briscoe, E. and J. Carroll (1993). Generalised Probabilistic LR Parsing of Natural Language (Corpora) with Unification-Based Grammars. *Computational Linguistics 19*(1), 25–60.

Briscoe, E., A. Copestake, and V. de Paiva (Eds.) (1993). *Inheritance, Defaults and the Lexicon.* Cambridge, UK: Cambridge University Press.

Brown, P., J. Cocke, S. Della Pietra, V. Della Pietra, R. Mercer, and P. Roossin (1988). A statistical approach to language translation. In *Proceedings of the 12th International Conference on Computational Linguistics - COLING-88*, Budapest, Hungary, pp. 71–75.

Brown, P., J. Cocke, S. Della Pietra, V. J. Della Pietra, F. Jelinek, J. D. Lafferty, R. L. Mercer, and P. S. Roossin (1990). A statistical approach to machine translation. *Computational Linguistics 16*(2), 79–85.

Brown, P. F., S. A. Della Pietra, V. J. Della Pietra, J. D. Lafferty, and R. L. Mercer (1992). Analysis, statistical transfer, and synthesis in machine translation. In *Proceedings of the Fourth International Conference on Theoretical and Methodological Issues in Machine Translation – TMI-92*, Montreal, Canada, pp. 83–100.

Brown, P. F., S. A. Della Pietra, V. J. Della Pietra, and R. L. Mercer (1993). The mathematics of statistical machine translation. *Computational Linguistics 19*(2), 263–312.

Brown, P. F., J. C. Lai, and R. L. Mercer (1991). Aligning sentences in parallel corpora. In *Proceedings of the 29th Annual Meeting of the Association for Computational Linguistics - ACL-91*, University of California, Berkeley, pp. 169–76.

Burton-Roberts, N. (1997). *Analysing sentences: an introduction to English syntax* (2nd ed.). New York: Addison Wesley.

Butt, J. and C. Benjamin (1994). *A New Reference Grammar of Modern Spanish.* London: Edward Arnold.

Caraballo, S. A. and E. Charniak (1998). New figures of merit for best-first probabilistic chart parsing. *Compuational Linguistics 24*(2), 275–298.

Carbonell, J. G., T. Mitamura, and E. H. Nyberg, 3rd (1992). The KANT perspective: A critique of pure transfer (and pure interlingua, pure statistics, ...). In *Proceedings of the Fourth International Conference on Theoretical and Methodological Issues in Machine Translation – TMI-92*, Montreal, Canada, pp. 225–35.

Carpenter, B. (1992). *The Logic of Typed Feature Structures.* Tracts in Theoretical Computer Science. Cambridge, UK: Cambridge University Press.

Castaño, M. A., F. Casacuberta, and E. Vidal (1997). Machine translation using neural networks and finite-state models. In *Proceedings of the Seventh International Conference on Theoretical and Methodological Issues in Machine Translation - TMI-97*, Santa Fe, NM, pp. 160–67.

Chandioux, J. (1976). MÉTÉO: un systéme opérationnel pour la traduction automatique des bulletins météorologiques destinés au grand public. META *21*, 127–33.

Chapman, R. L. (Ed.) (1988). *Roget's International Thesaurus* (4th ed.). London: Collins.

Charniak, E. (1993). *Statistical Language Learning.* Cambridge, MA: A Bradford Book/The MIT Press.

Chierchia, G. and S. McConnell-Ginet (1990). *Meaning and Grammar.* Cambride, MA: MIT.

Chinchor, N., L. Hirschman, and D. D. Lewis (1993). Evaluating message understanding systems: An analysis of the third message understanding conference (MUC-3). *Computational Linguistics 19*(3), 409–49.

Chomsky, N. (1986). *Barriers.* Cambridge, MA: MIT Press.

Church, A. (1941). The calculi of lambda-conversion. In *Annals of Mathematical Studies*, Volume 6. Princeton, New Jersey: Princeton University Press. Reprinted by Klaus Reprints, New York, 1965.

Church, K. (1988). A stochastic parts program and noun phrase parser for unrestricted text. In *Proceedings of the 2nd Conference on Applied Natural Language Processing*, pp. 136–43.

Church, K. W. (1993). Char_align: A program for aligning parallel texts at character level. In *Proceedings of the 31st Annual Meeting of the Association for Computational Linguistics - ACL-93*, Columbus, Ohio, pp. 1–8.

Clews, J. (1988). *Language Automation Worldwide: The Development of Character Set Standards*. Number 5962 in British Library R & D reports. Harrogate, UK: SESAME Computer Projects. ISBN 1-870095-01-4.

Clews, J. (1992). Dealing with multiple languages in the computer industry. In *Translating and the Computer 13: A Marriage of Convenience*, pp. 47–60. The Association for Information Management.

Cohen, D. I. A. (1991). *Introduction to Computer Theory*. New York: Wiley.

Collins, B. and P. Cunningham (1997). Adaptation-guided retrieval: Approaching EBMT with caution. In *Proceedings of the Seventh International Conference on Theoretical and Methodological Issues in Machine Translation - TMI-97*, Santa Fe, New Mexico, pp. 119–126.

Comrie, B. (1981). *Language Universals and Linguistics Typology*. Oxford, UK: Basil Blackwell.

Coñi, J. M., J. C. González, and A. Moreno (1997). A lexical platform for engineering Spanish processing tools. *Natural Language Engineering 3*(3), 1–29. www.mat.upm.es:80/~aries/.

Copeland, C., J. Durand, S. Krauwer, and B. Maegaard (Eds.) (1991). *The Eurotra Linguistic Specification*. Studies in Machine Translation and Natural Language Processing. Luxembourg: Commission of the European Community.

Copestake, A., D. Flickinger, R. Malouf, S. Riehemann, and I. Sag (1995). Translation using minimal recursion semantics. In *Proceedings of the Sixth International Conference on Theoretical and Methodological Issues in Machine Translation - TMI-95*, Leuven, Belgium, pp. 15–32.

Copestake, A., D. Flickinger, and I. A. Sag (1998). Minimal recursion semantics: An introduction. hpsg.stanford.edu/hpsg/pubs.html.

Covington, M. A. (1994). *Natural language processing for Prolog programmers*. Englewood Cliffs, NJ: Prentice Hall.

Croft, W. (1990). *Typology and Universals*. Cambridge Textbooks in Linguistics. Cambridge, England: Cambridge University Press.

Cruse, D. A. (1986). *Lexical Semantics*. Cambridge: Cambridge University Press.

Crystal, D. (1987). *The Cambridge Encyclopedia of Language*. Cambridge, UK: Cambridge University Press.

Dagan, I. and K. Church (1997). Termight: Coordinating humans and machines in bilingual terminology acquisition. *Machine Translation 12*(1-2), 89–107.

Dagan, I., K. W. Church, and W. A. Gale (1993). Robust bilingual word alignment for machine aided translation. In *Proceedings of the Workshop on Very Large Corpora: Academic and Industrial Perspectives*, Columbus, Ohio, pp. 1–8.

Dagan, I. and A. Itai (1994). Word sense disambiguation using a second language monolingual corpus. *Computational Linguistics 20*(4), 563–96.

Dalrymple, M., S. M. Shieber, and F. C. N. Pereira (1991). Ellipsis and higher-order unification. *Linguistics and Philosophy 4*(4), 399–452.

Danlos, L. and P. Samvelian (1992). Translation of the predicative element of a sentence: category switching, aspect and diathesis. In *Proceedings of the Fourth International Conference on Theoretical and Methodological Issues in Machine Translation – TMI-92*, Montreal, Canada, pp. 21–34.

de Roeck, A. (1983). An underview of parsing. See King (1983), Chapter 1, pp. 3–17.

DeGroot, M. H. (1986). *Probability and Statistics* (2nd ed.). Reading, MA: Addison-Wesley.

Dermatas, E. and G. Kokkinakis (1995). Automatic stochastic tagging of natural language texts. *Computational Linguistics 21*(2), 137–63.

Devlin, K. (1991). *Logic and Information*. Cambridge, UK: Cambridge University Press.

DiMarco, C. and K. Mah (1994). A model of comparative stylistics for machine translation. *Machine Translation 9*(1), 21–59.

Dorna, M., A. Frank, J. van Genabith, and M. C. Emele (1998). Syntactic and semantic transfer with F-Structures. In *Proceedings of the 17th International Conference on Computational Linguistics and 36th Annual Meeting of the Association for Computational Linguistics - COLING/ACL-98*, Montreal, Canada, pp. 341–47.

Dorr, B. J. (1993). *Machine Translation : A View from the Lexicon*. Cambridge, MA: MIT.

Dorr, B. J. (1994). Machine translation divergences: A formal description and proposed solution. *Computational Linguistics 20*(4), 597–633.

Dorr, B. J. (1997). Large-scale dictionary construction for foreign language tutoring and interlingual machine translation. *Machine Translation 12*(4), 271–322.

Dorr, B. J., D. Lin, J. Lee, and S. Suh (1995). Efficient parsing for Korean and English: A parameterized message-passing approach. *Computational Linguistics 21*(2), 255–63.

Dorr, B. J. and M. B. Olsen (1996). Multilingual generation: The role of telicity in lexical choice and syntactic realization. *Machine Translation 11*(1-3), 37–74.

Dowty, D. R., R. Wall, and P. S. Peters (1981). *Introduction to Montague Semantics*. Dordrecht, The Netherlands: Reidel.

Durand, J., P. Bennett, V. Allegranza, F. van Eynde, L. Humphreys, P. Schmidt, and E. Steiner (1991). The Eurotra linguistic specifications: An overview. *Machine Translation 6*(2), 103–47.

EAGLES (1996). Expert advisory group on language engineering standards (EAGLES): Evaluation of natural language processing systems, final report. Technical Report EAG-EWG-PR.2, ISSCO, University of Geneva. www.issco.unige.ch/projects/ewg96/ewg96.html.

Earley, J. (1970). An efficient context-free parsing algorithm. *Communications of the ACM 14*, 453–60. Reprinted in *Readings in Natural Language Processing* (B. J. Grosz, K. Sparck Jones and B. L. Webber, eds.), pp. 25-33, Morgan Kaufmann, Los Altos, CA, 1986.

Elmasri, R. and S. B. Navathe (1994). *Fundamentals of Database Systems* (2nd ed.). Addison-Wesley.

Emele, M., U. Heid, S. Momma, and R. Zajac (1992). Interaction between linguistic constraints: Procedural vs. declarative approaches. *Machine Translation 7*(1-2), 61–98.

Emele, M. C. and M. Dorna (1998). Ambiguity preserving machine translation using packed representations. In *Proceedings of the 17th International Conference on Computational Linguistics and 36th Annual Meeting of the Association for Computational Linguistics - COLING/ACL-98*, Volume I, Montreal, pp. 365–71. Association for Computational Linguistics.

Esselink, B. (1998). *A Practical Guide to Software Localization*. Amsterdam: John Benjamins.

Estival, D., A. Ballim, G. Russell, and S. Warwick (1990). A syntax and semantics for feature-structure transfer. In *Proceedings of the Third International Conference on Theoretical and Methodological Issues in Machine Translation - TMI-90*, Austin, TX, pp. 131–44.

Evans, R. and G. Gazdar (1996). DATR: a language for lexical knowledge representation. *Computational Linguistics 22*(2), 167–216.

Evens, M. W. (Ed.) (1988). *Relational models of the lexicon: representing knowledge in semantic networks*. UK: Cambridge University Press.

Fisher, D. and E. Riloff (1992). Applying statistical methods to small corpora: Benefiting from a limited domain. In *Intelligent Probabilistic Approaches to Natural Language - Papers from the 1992 Fall Symposium*, pp. 47–53. AAAI.

Fontenelle, T., G. Adriaens, and G. de Braekeleer (1994). The lexical unit in the Metal MT system. *Machine Translation 9*(1), 1–20.

Frakes, W. B. and R. Baeza-Yates (Eds.) (1992). *Information Retrieval - Data Structures & Algorithms*. New Jersey: Prentice Hall PTR.

Frazier, L. and J. D. Fodor (1978). The sausage machine: A new two-stage parsing model. *Cognition 6*(4), 291–325.

Fung, P., M. Kan, and Y. Horita (1996). Extracting Japanese domain and technical terms is relatively easy. In *Proceedings of the Second International Conference on New Methods in Language Processing - NeMLap-2*, Ankara, Turkey, pp. 148–59.

Fung, P. and K. McKeown (1997). A technical word- and term-translation aid using noisy parallel corpora across language groups. *Machine Translation 12*(1-2), 53–87.

Furuse, O. and H. Iida (1994). Constituent boundary parsing for example-based machine translation. In *Proceedings of the 15th International Conference on Computational Linguistics - COLING-94*, Kyoto, pp. 105–11. International Committee on Computational Linguistics.

Gale, W. A. and K. W. Church (1993). A program for aligning sentences in bilingual corpora. *Computational Linguistics 19*(1), 75–102.

Gale, W. A., K. W. Church, and D. Yarowsky (1992). Using bilingual materials to develop word sense disambiguation methods. In *Proceedings of the Fourth International Conference on Theoretical and Methodological Issues in Machine Translation - TMI-92*, Montreal, pp. 101–12.

Gale, W. A., K. W. Church, and D. Yarowsky (1993). A method for disambiguating word senses in a large corpus. *Computers and the Humanities 26*, 415–39.

Gambäck, B., H. Alshawi, D. Carter, and M. Rayner (1991). Measuring compositionality in transfer-based machine translation systems. In *Natural Language Processing Systems Evaluation Workshop*, Griffiss Air Force Base, NY 13441-5700. Rome Laboratory, Air Force Systems Command.

Garey, M. R. and D. S. Johnson (1979). *Computers and Intractability: A Guide to the Theory of NP-Completeness*. New York: W. H. Freeman.

Garnham, A. (1985). *Psycholinguistics - Central Topics*. Methuen & Co.

Garside, R., G. Sampson, and G. Leech (1987). *The computational analysis of English: a corpus-based approach*. Harlow: Longman.

Gaussier, É. (1998). Flow network models for word alignment and terminology extraction from bilingual corpora. In *Proceedings of the 17th International Conference on Computational Linguistics and 36th Annual Meeting of the Association for Computational Linguistics - COLING/ACL-98*, Montreal, pp. 444–50. Association for Computational Linguistics.

Gaussier, É., J.-M. Langé, and F. Meunier (1992). Towards bilingual terminology. In *19th International Conference of the Association of Literary and Linguistic Computing. Proceedings of the Joint ALLC/ACH Conference*, Oxford, UK, pp. 121–4.

Gazdar, G., E. Klein, G. Pullum, and I. Sag (1985). *Generalised Phrase Structure Grammar*. Oxford, England: Blackwell.

Gazdar, G. and C. Mellish (1989). *Natural Language Processing in PROLOG: An Introduction to Computational Linguistics*. Wokingham, England: Addison-Wesley.

Goodman, K. and S. Nirenburg (Eds.) (1991). *The KBMT Project: A Case Study in Knowledge-Based Machine Translation*. San Mateo, CA: Morgan Kaufman.

Grefenstette, G. (1998). *Cross-language Information Retrieval*. Kluwer Academic.

Grimley-Evans, E., G. A. Kiraz, and S. G. Pulman (1996). Compiling a partition-based two-level formalism. In *Proceedings of the 16th International Conference on Computational Linguistics - COLING-96*, Copenhagen, Denmark, pp. 454–59. International Committee on Computational Linguistics.

Grosz, B. J., K. S. Jones, and B. L. Webber (Eds.) (1986). *Readings in Natural Language Processing*. Los Altos, CA: Morgan Kaufmann.

Grover, C. (1996). Parasitic gaps and coordination in HPSG. See Grover and Vallduví (1996), pp. 33–69. ftp://ftp.cogsci.ed.ac.uk/pub/grover/WP-12/grover.ps.

Grover, C. and E. Vallduví (Eds.) (1996). *Edinburgh Working Papers in Cognitive Science, Vol. 12: Studies in HPSG*. Scotland: Centre for Cognitive Science, University of Edinburgh.

Harada, T. (1986). NEC's machine translation system 'PIVOT'. *Japan Computer Quarterly 64*, 24–31.

Harrison, S. P. and T. M. Ellison (1992). Restriction and termination in parsing with feature-theoretic grammars. *Computational Linguistics 18*(4), 519–30.

Helmreich, S. and D. Farwell (1998). Translation differences and pragmatics-based MT. *Machine Translation 13*(1), 17–39.

Hindle, D. and M. Rooth (1991). Structural ambiguity and lexical relations. In *Proceedings of the 29th Annual Meeting of the Association for Computational Linguistics - ACL-91*, Berkeley,CA, pp. 229–36. Association for Computational Linguistics.

Hjelmslev, L. (1935). La Catégorie des Cas. Étude de Grammaire Générale. *Acta Jut-landica VII*(1).

Hjelmslev, L. (1978). *La categoría de los casos - Estudios de gramática general*. Number 279 in Biblioteca románica hispánica. Madrid, Spain: Editorial Gredos. Translated by F. Piñero Torre.

Hobbs, J. R. and J. Bear (1990). Two principles of parse preference. In *Proceedings of the 13th International Conference on Computational Linguistics - COLING-90*, Volume 3, Helsinki, pp. 162–167. International Committee on Computational Linguistics.

Horacek, H. and M. Zock (Eds.) (1993). *New Concepts in Natural Language Generation*. London: Pinter.

Hovy, E. and L. Gerber (1997). MT at the paragraph level: Improving English synthesis in SYS-TRAN. In *Proceedings of the Seventh International Conference on Theoretical and Method-ological Issues in Machine Translation - TMI-97*, Santa Fe, NM, pp. 47–54.

Hovy, E. H. (1988). *Generating Natural Language under Pragmatic Constraints*. Hillsdale, NJ: Lawrence Erlbaum Associates.

Huddleston, R. (1984). *Introduction to the Grammar of English*. Cambridge: Cambridge University Press.

Hudson, R. (1984). *Word Grammar*. Oxford, UK: Blackwell.

Huijsen, W.-O. (1998). *Completeness of Compositional Translation*. Ph. D. thesis, Utrecht Institute of Linguistics OTS, University of Utrecht, The Netherlands. www-uilots.let.uu.nl/~Willem-Olaf.Huijsen/.

Hutchins, J. (1997). From first conception to first demonstration: the nascent years of machine translation, 1947-1954. a chronology. *Machine Translation 12*(3), 195–252.

Hutchins, W. J. (1986). *Machine Translation - Past, Present and Future*. Chichester, England: Ellis Horwood.

Hutchins, W. J. and H. L. Somers (1992). *An Introduction to Machine Translation*. London: Academic Press.

Isabelle, P., M. Dymetman, and E. Macklovitch (1988). CRITTER: a translation system for agricultural market reports. In *Proceedings of the 12th International Conference on Computational Linguistics - COLING-88*, Budapest, pp. 261–66. International Committee on Computational Linguistics.

Jackendoff, R. (1983). *Semantics and Cognition*. Cambridge, MA: The MIT Press.

Jackendoff, R. (1992). Parts and boundaries. See Levin and Pinker (1992), Chapter 2, pp. 9–45.

Jackendoff, R. (1997). *The Architecture of the Language Faculty*. Cambridge, MA: MIT Press.

Jackendoff, R. S. (1990). *Semantic Structures*. Number 18 in Current Studies in Linguistics. Cambridge, MA: MIT Press.

Johnson, C. D. (1972). *Formal Aspects of Phonological Description*. Mouton.

Johnson, D. E. and H. Watanabe (1991). Relational-Grammar-Based generation in the JETS Japanese-English machine translation system. *Machine Translation 6*(1), 1–20.

Johnson, M. (1998). PCFG models of linguistic tree representations. *Computational Linguistics 24*(4), 613–32.

Jones, D. and J. Tsujii (1990). High quality machine-driven text translation. In *Proceedings of the Third International Conference on Theoretical and Methodological Issues in Machine Translation - TMI-90*, Austin, TX, pp. 43–46. Linguistic Research Center, University of Texas.

Jordan, P. W., B. J. Dorr, and J. W. Benoit (1993). A first-pass approach for evaluating machine translation systems. *Machine Translation 8*(1), 49–58. Special Issue on Evaluation.

Justeson, J. S. and S. M. Katz (1995a). Principled disambiguation: Discriminating adjective senses with modified nouns. *Computational Linguistics 21*(1), 1–27.

Justeson, J. S. and S. M. Katz (1995b). Technical terminology: Some linguistic properties and an algorithm for identification in text. *Natural Language Engineering 1*, 9–27.

Kameyama, M., R. Ochitani, and S. Peters (1991). Resolving translation mismatches with information flow. In *Proceedings 29th Annual Conference of the ACL*, Berkeley, CA, pp. 193–200.

Kamp, H. and U. Reyle (1993). *From Discourse to Logic – Introduction to Modeltheoretic Semantics of Natural Language, Formal Logic and Discourse Representation Theory*, Volume 42 of *Studies in Linguistics and Philosophy*. Dordrecht, The Netherlands: Kluwer Academic.

Kaplan, R. M. and J. Bresnan (1982). Lexical-functional grammar: A formal system for grammatical representation. See Bresnan (1982), Chapter 4, pp. 173–281.

Kaplan, R. M. and M. Kay (1994). Regular models of phonological rule systems. *Computational Linguistics 20*(3), 331–78. Special Issue on Computational Phonology.

Kaplan, R. M., K. Netter, J. Wedekind, and A. Zaenen (1989). Translation by structural correspondences. In *Proceedings of the Fourth Conference of the European Chapter of the ACL*, Manchester, UK, pp. 272–81.

Kaplan, R. M. and J. Wedekind (1993). Restriction and correspondence-based translation. In *Proceedings of the Sixth Conference of the European Chapter of the ACL*, The Netherlands, pp. 193–202. OTS, Utrecht University.

Karttunen, L. (1996). Contructing lexical transducers. In *Proceedings of the 15th International Conference on Computational Linguistics - Coling 94*, Volume I, Kyoto, Japan, pp. 406–11. www.rxrc.xerox.com/research/mltt/home.html.

Kasher, A. (Ed.) (1998). *Pragmatics - Critical Concepts*. London: Routledge. Vols I-VI.

Kathol, A. (1999). Agreement and the syntax-morphology interface in HPSG. See Levine and Green (1999). www.dfki.de/lt/HPSG/Bib/K.html.

Kay, M. (1980). The proper place of men and machines in translation. Technical Report CSL-80-11, Xerox PARC, Palo Alto, CA.

Kay, M. (1996). Chart generation. In *Proceedings of the 34th Annual Meeting of the Association for Computational Linguistics – ACL-96*, Santa Cruz, CA, pp. 200–04.

Kay, M., M. Gawron, and P. Norvig (1994). *Verbmobil: A Translation System for Face-to-Face Dialog*. Number 33 in Lecture Notes. Stanford, CA: CSLI.

Kay, M. and M. Röscheisen (1993). Text-translation alignment. *Computational Linguistics 19*(1), 121–142. Special Issue on Using Large Corpora: I.

Keck, B. (1991). Translation memory - a translation system based on statistical methods. Technical Report ESPRIT TWB 2315, WP 1.8, Fraunhofer Gesellschaft IAO, Stuttgart, Germany.

Keenan, E. L. (1985). Relative clauses. See Shopen (1985c), Chapter 3, pp. 141–70.

Kempson, R. M. (1977). *Semantic Theory*. Cambridge textbooks in linguistics. Cambridge: Cambridge University Press.

Khan, R. (1983). A two-level morphological analysis of Rumanian. *Texas Linguistic Forum 22*, 253–70.

Kilgarriff, A. (1998). Gold standard datasets for evaluating word sense disambiguation programs. *Computer Speech and Language 12*(4), pp. 453–72.

Kimball, J. P. (1973). Seven principles of surface structure parsing in natural language. *Cognition 2*, 15–47.

King, M. (Ed.) (1983). *Parsing Natural Language*. London: Academic Press.

King, M. (1991). Evaluation of MT systems – Panel discussion. In *Proceedings of MT Summit III*, Washington, DC, pp. 141–46.

King, M. (1996). Evaluating natural language processing systems. *Communications of the ACM 39*(1), 73–79.

King, M. and K. Falkedal (1990). Using test suites in evaluation of machine translation systems. In *Proceedings of the 13th COLING*, Helsinki, Finland, pp. 211–16.

Kiraz, G. A. (in press). *Computational Nonlinear Morphology*. Cambridge University Press.

Knuth, D. E. (1973). *The Art of Computer Programming*, Volume 3 - Sorting and Searching. Reading, MA: Addison-Wesley.

Knuth, D. E. (1986). *The METAFONTbook*. Reading, MA: Addison-Wesley.

Koskenniemi, K. (1983). Two-level morphology: A general computational model for word-form recognition and production. Publication No. 11, Department of General Linguistics, University of Helsinki.

Kugler, M., K. Ahmad, G. Heyer, M. Rogers, and G. Thurmair (1992). Translator's workbench - multilingual documentation and communication, final report. Technical Report ESPRIT

TWB 2315, Commission of the European Communities, Official Publications Office, L-2985 Luxembourg.

Kukich, K. (1983). Design and implementation of a knowledge-based report generator. In *Proceedings of the 21st Annual Meeting of the Association for Computational Linguistics*, Cambridge, MA, pp. 145–50. Massachusetts Institute of Technology.

Kupiec, J. (1993). An algorithm for finding noun phrase correspondences in bilingual corpora. In *Proceedings of the 31st Annual Meeting of the Association for Computational Linguistics - ACL-93*, Columbus, Ohio, pp. 17–22. Association for Computational Linguistics.

Kwon, H.-C. and L. Karttunen (1996). Incremental construction of a lexical transducer for Korean. In *Proceedings of the 15th International Conference on Computational Linguistics - Coling 94*, Volume II, Kyoto, Japan, pp. 1262–66.

Lakoff, G. (1987). *Women, fire and dangerous things. What categories reveal about the mind.* Chicago/London: University of Chicago Press.

Lakoff, G. and M. Johnson (1980). *Metaphors We Live By.* Chicago: University of Chicago Press.

Langacker, R. W. (1991). *Concept, Image and Symbol - The Cognitive Basis of Grammar.* Berlin: Mouton de Gruyter.

Lappin, S. (Ed.) (1996). *The Handbook of Contemporary Semantic Theory.* Oxford: Blackwell.

Lappin, S. and H. Shih (1996). A generalized reconstruction algorithm for ellipsis. In *Proceedings of the 16th International Conference on Computational Linguistics - COLING-96*, Copenhagen, Denmark, pp. 687–92. International Committee on Computational Linguistics.

Lascarides, A., T. Briscoe, N. Asher, and A. Copestake (1996). Order independent and persistent typed default unification. *Linguistics and Philosophy 19*(1), 1–90.

Lascarides, A. and A. Copestake (1999). Default representation in contraint-based frameworks. *Computational Linguistics 25*(1), 55–105.

Lehmann, W. P. (1997). Review of Whitelock and Kilby (1995). *Machine Translation 12*(3), 261–69.

Lehrberger, J. and L. Bourbeau (1988). *Machine Translation - Linguistic characteristics of MT systems and general methodology of evaluation.* Studies in French and General Linguistics. Amsterdam: John Benjamins.

Levin, B. and S. Pinker (Eds.) (1992). *Lexical & Conceptual Semantics.* Cognition Special Issues. Cambridge, MA: Blackwell.

Levine, R. and G. Green (Eds.) (1999). *Studies in Contemporary Phrase Structure Grammar.* Cambridge University Press.

Lindop, J. and J. Tsujii (1991). Complex transfer in MT: A survey of examples. Technical Report CCL/UMIST Report 91/5, Center for Computational Linguistics, UMIST, Manchester.

Lonsdale, D., T. Mitamura, and E. Nyberg (1994-1995). Acquisition of large lexicons for practical knowledge-based MT. *Machine Translation 9*(3-4), 251–83.

Lun, S. (1983). A two-level analysis of French. *Texas Linguistic Forum 22*, 271–78.

Lunde, K. (1999). *CJKV Information Processing.* Sebastopol, CA: O'Reilly & Associates, Inc.

Lyons, J. (1968). *Introduction to theoretical linguistics.* Cambridge: Cambridge University Press.

Macaulay, L. A. (1996). *Requirements Engineering.* Applied Computing. London: Springer.

Macklovitch, E. (1989). An off-the-shelf workstation for translators. In *Proceedings of the 30th American Translators Conference*, Washington DC.

Macklovitch, E. and M.-L. Hannan (1998). Line 'em up: Advances in alignment technology and their impact on translation support tools. *Machine Translation 13*(1), 41–57.

Magnúsdóttir, G. (1993). Review of *An Introduction to Machine Translation* by Hutchins, W. J. and Somers, H. L. *Computational Linguistics 19*(2), 383–384.

Maier, E. and E. Hovy (1993). Organising discourse structure relations using metafunctions. See Horacek and Zock (1993), pp. 69–86.

Mallinson, G. and B. J. Blake (1981). *Language Typology, Cross Linguistic Studies in Syntax.* North-Holland Linguistic Series 46. Amsterdam, The Netherlands: North Holland.

Mann, W. and S. Thompson (1988). Rhetorical Structure Theory: Toward a functional theory of text organization. *Text 3*, 243–81.

Manning, C. D. and H. Schütze (1999). *Foundations of Statistical Natural Language Processing* (Cambridge, MA ed.). MIT Press.

Marcus, M. P., B. Santorini, and M. A. Marcinkiewicz (1993). Building a large annotated corpus of English: The Penn Treebank. *Computational Linguistics 19*(2), 313–30.

Matthews, P. H. (1974). *Morphology*. Cambridge: Cambrige University Press.

Maxwell, D., K. Schubert, and T. Witkan (Eds.) (1988). *New Directions in Machine Translation*. Number 4 in Distributed Language Translation. Dordrecht, The Netherlands: Foris.

McCord, M. C. (1989). Design of LMT: A Prolog-based machine translation system. *Computational Linguistics 15*(1), 33–52.

McTait, K. and A. Trujillo (1999). A language neutral, sparse-data algorithm for extracting translation patterns. In *Proceedings of the Eighth International Conference on Theoretical and Methodological Issues in Machine Translation - TMI-99*, Chester, UK.

Melby, A. K. (1987). On human-machine interaction in translation. See Nirenburg (1987), pp. 145–54.

Melby, A. K. (1995). *The possibility of language: a discussion of the nature of language, with implications for human and machine translation*. Amsterdam: John Benjamins.

Mellish, C. (1988). Implementing systemic classification by unification. *Computational Linguistics 14*(1), 40–51.

Mel'čuk, I. and A. Zholkovsky (1988). The explanatory combinatorial dictionary. See Evens (1988), Chapter 2, pp. 41–74.

Mel'čuk, I. A. (1979). *Dependency Syntax: Theory and Practice*. New York: SUNY.

Mey, J. L. (1993). *Pragmatics - An Introduction*. Oxford: Blackwell.

Mikheev, A. (1997). Automatic rule induction for unknown-word guessing. *Computational Linguistics 23*(3), 405–23.

Minnis, S. (1993). Constructive machine tranlation evaluation. *Machine Translation 8*, 67–75.

Minsky, M. L. (1975). A framework for representing knowledge. In P. H. Winston (Ed.), *The Psychology of Computer Vision*, pp. 211–77. New York: McGraw-Hill.

Mitamura, T. and E. H. Nyberg, 3rd (1995). Controlled English for knowledge-based MT: Experience with the KANT system. In *Proceedings of the Sixth International Conference on Theoretical and Methodological Issues in Machine Translation - TMI-95*, Leuven, Belgium, pp. 158–172.

Mitchell, G. H. (Ed.) (1972). *Operational Research: techniques and examples*. London: The English Universities Press.

Mitkov, R. and N. Nicolov (Eds.) (1996). *Recent Advances in Natural Language Processing*, Volume 136 of *Current Issues in Linguistic Theory*. Amsterdam: John Benjamins.

Mohri, M. and F. C. N. Pereira (1998). Dynamic compilation of weighted context-free grammars. In *Proceedings of the 17th International Conference on Computational Linguistics and 36th Annual Meeting of the Association for Computational Linguistics - COLING/ACL-98*, Montreal, Canada, pp. 891–97.

Mohri, M. and R. Sproat (1996). An efficient compiler for weighted rewrite rules. In *Proceedings of the 34th Annual Meeting of the Association for Computational Linguistics - ACL-96*, Santa Cruz, CA. Association for Computational Linguistics.

Montague, R. (1974). *Formal Philosophy. Selected Papers of Richard Montague*. New Haven/London: Yale University Press. Edited by R. H. Thomason.

Morita, M. (1985). Japanese text input system. *IEEE Computer 18*(5), 29–35.

Nagao, M. (1984). A framework of a mechanical translation between Japanese and English by analogy principle. In A. Elighorn and R. Banerji (Eds.), *Artificial Intelligence and Human Intelligence*, pp. 173–80. Amsterdam: North-Holland.

Nagao, M. (Ed.) (1989). *Machine Translation Summit*, Ohmsha, Tokyo.

Nagao, M., J. Tsujii, and J. Nakamura (1988). The Japanese government project for machine translation. See Slocum (1988), pp. 141–86.

Nirenburg, S. (Ed.) (1987). *Machine Translation - Theoretical and Methodological Issues*. Studies in Natural Language Processing. Cambridge, UK: Cambridge University Press.

Nirenburg, S., J. Carbonell, M. Tomita, and K. Goodman (1992). *Machine Translation: A Knowledge Based Approach*. San Mateo, CA: Morgan Kaufman.

Nirenburg, S., C. Domashnev, and D. J. Grannes (1993). Two approaches to matching in example-based machine translation. In *Proceedings of the Fifth International Conference on Theoretical and Methodological Issues in Machine Translation - TMI-93*, Kyoto, pp. 47–57.

Oakes, M. P. (1998). *Statistics for Corpus Linguistics*. Edinburgh Textbooks in Empirical Linguistics. Scotland: Edinburgh University Press.

Onyshkevich, B. and S. Nirenburg (1995). A lexicon for knowledge-based MT. *Machine Translation 10*(1-2), 5–57. crl.nmsu.edu/Research/Projects/mikro/index.html.

Ortony, A., J. Slack, and O. Stock (Eds.) (1992). *Communication from an Artificial Intelligence Perspective: Theoretical and Applied Issues*. Heidelberg: Springer.

Parry, J. (1992). Computer character sets: their evolution and impact. In *Translating and the Computer 13: A Marriage of Convenience*, pp. 61–67. The Association for Information Management.

Parsons, T. (1990). *Events in the Semantics of English: A Study in Subatomic Semantics*. Number 19 in Current Studies in Linguistics. Cambridge, MA: MIT Press.

Pereira, F. C. N. and S. M. Shieber (1987). *Prolog and Natural-Language Analysis*. Number 10 in CSLI Lecture Notes. Stanford, CA: Center for the Study of Language and Information.

Pereira, F. C. N. and D. H. D. Warren (1980). Definite clause grammars for language analysis - a survey of the formalism and a comparison with augmented transition networks. *Artificial Intelligence 13*, 231–78. Reprinted in Grosz et al. (1986).

Phillips, J. D. (1993). Generation of text from logical formulae. *Machine Translation 8*(4), 209–35.

Pinkal, M. (1995). *Logic and Lexicon: the semantics of the indefinite*. Dordrecht/London: Kluwer. Translated from the German *Logik und Lexikon* by Geoffrey Simmons.

Pollard, C. and I. Sag (1987). *Information Based Syntax and Semantics: Vol. 1*. Lecture Notes. Stanford, CA: CSLI.

Pollard, C. and I. A. Sag (1994). *Head Driven Phrase Structure Grammar*. IL: Chicago University Press. hpsg.stanford.edu/.

Popowich, F., D. Turcato, O. Laurens, P. McFetridge, J. D. Nicholson, P. McGivern, M. Corzo-Pena, L. Pidruchney, and S. MacDonald (1997). A lexicalist approach to the translation of colloquial text. In *Proceedings of the Seventh International Conference on Theoretical and Methodological Issues in Machine Translation - TMI-97*, Santa Fe, NM, pp. 76–86.

Poznański, V., J. L. Beaven, and P. Whitelock (1995). An efficient generation algorithm for lexicalist MT. In *Proceedings of the 33rd Annual Meeting of the Association for Computational Linguistics*, Boston, MA.

Poznanski, V., P. Whitelock, J. IJdens, and S. Corley (1998). Practical glossing by prioritised tiling. In *Proceedings of the 17th International Conference on Computational Linguistics and 36th Annual Meeting of the Association for Computational Linguistics - COLING/ACL-98*, Montreal, pp. 1060–66. Association for Computational Linguistics.

Pulman, S. G. (1996). Unification encodings of grammatical notations. *Computational Linguistics 22*(3), 295–327.

Quirk, R., S. Greenbaum, G. Leech, and J. Svartik (1985). *A Comprehensive Grammar of the English Language*. London: Longman.

Rabiner, L. R. (1989). A tutorial on hidden Markov models and selected applications in speech recognition. *Proceedings of the IEEE 77*(2), 257–285.

Ramsay, A. (1988). *Formal Methods in Artificial Intelligence*, Volume 6 of *Cambridge Tracts in Theoretical Computer Science*. Cambridge, UK: Cambridge University Press.

Raskin, V. and S. Nirenburg (1998). An applied ontological semantic microtheory of adjective meaning for natural language processing. *Machine Translation 13*(2-3), 135–227.

Rayner, M., H. Alshawi, I. Bretan, D. Carter, V. Digalakis, B. Gambäck, J. Kaja, J. Karlgren, B. Lyberg, P. Price, S. Pulman, and C. Samuelsson (1993). A speech to speech translation system built from standard components. In *Proceedings of the 1993 ARPA workshop on Human Language Technology*, Princeton, NJ.

Rayward-Smith, V. J. (1983). *A First Course in Formal Language Theory*. Computer Science Texts. Oxford, UK: Blackwell Scientific Publications.

Rayward-Smith, V. J. (1986). *A First Course in Computability*. Computer Science Texts. Oxford, UK: Blackwell Scientific Publications.

Reiter, E. and R. Dale (1997). Building applied natural language generation systems. *Journal of Natural Language Engineering 3*(1), 57–87.

Reiter, E. and R. Dale (2000). *Building Natural Language Generation Systems*. Cambridge University Press.

Reyle, U. (1993). Dealing with ambiguities by underspecification: Construction, representation and deduction. *Journal of Semantics 10*(2), 123–179.

Ritchie, G. D., G. J. Russell, A. W. Black, and S. G. Pulman (1992). *Computational Morphology: Practical Mechanisms for the English Lexicon*. Cambridge, MA: The MIT Press.

Roche, E. and Y. Schabes (1995). Deterministic part-of-speech tagging with finite-state transducers. *Computational Linguistics 21*(2), 227–53.

Rosetta (pseud.), M. T. (Ed.) (1994). *Compositional Translation*. Dordrecht: Kluwer Academic.

Ross, S. M. (1994). *A First Course in Probability* (4th ed.). New York: Macmillan College Publishing.

Rupp, C. J., M. A. Rosner, and R. L. Johnson (Eds.) (1994). *Constraints, Language and Computation*. London: Academic Press.

Russell, G., A. Ballim, D. Estival, and S. Warwick (1991). A language for the statement of binary relations over feature structures. In *Proceedings of the Fifth Conference of the European Chapter of the ACL*, Bonn, Germany.

Russell, S. and P. Norvig (1998). *Artificial Intelligence – A Modern Approach* (2nd ed.). Prentice Hall.

Sadler, L. and H. Thompson (1991). Structural non-correspondence in translation. In *Proceedings of the Fifth Conference of the European Chapter of the ACL*, Bonn, Germany, pp. 293–98.

Sag, I. A. (1997). English relative clause constructions. *Journal of Linguistics 33*(2), 431–84. hpsg.stanford.edu/hpsg/papers.html.

Sag, I. A. and T. Wasow (1999). *Syntactic Theory: A Formal Introduction*. Stanford, CA: CSLI. hpsg.stanford.edu/hpsg/sw-tb.html.

Sager, J. C. (1994). *Language Engineering and Translation: Consequences of Automation*. Amsterdam: John Benjamins.

Samuelsson, C. (1994). Notes on LR parser design. In *Proceedings of the 15th International Conference on Computational Linguistics - COLING 94*, Volume I, Kyoto, Japan, pp. 386–90.

Samuelsson, C. (1996). Example-based optimization of surface-generation tables. See Mitkov and Nicolov (1996).

Sanfilippo, A., E. Briscoe, A. Copestake, M. Marti, M. Taule, and A. Alonge (1992). Translation equivalence and lexicalization in the ACQUILEX LKB. In *Proceedings of the Fourth International Conference on Theoretical and Methodological Issues in Machine Translation – TMI-92*, Montreal, Canada, pp. 1–11.

Sato, S. (1995). MBT2: a method for combining fragments of examples in example-based translation. *Artificial Intelligence 75*(1), 31–49.

Sato, S. and M. Nagao (1990). Towards memory based translation. In *Proceedings of COLING '90*, Helsinki, Finland.

Schubert, K. (1988). The architecture of DLT - interlingual or double direct? See Maxwell et al. (1988), pp. 131–44.

Shieber, S., G. van Noord, F. C. N. Pereira, and R. C. Moore (1990). Semantic-head-driven generation. *Computational Linguistics 16*(1), 30–42.

Shieber, S. M. (1985). Using restriction to extend parsing algorithms for complex-feature-based formalisms. In *Proceedings of the 23rd Annual Conference of the ACL*, Chicago, IL, pp. 145–52.

Shieber, S. M. (1986). *An Introduction to Unification-based Approaches to Grammar*, Volume 4 of *CSLI Lecture Notes*. Stanford, CA: CSLI.

Shieber, S. M. (1988). A uniform architecture for parsing and generation. In *Proceedings of COLING '88*, Budapest, Hungary.

Shieber, S. M. (1993). The problem of logical-form equivalence. *Computational Linguistics 19*(1), 179–90.

Shopen, T. (Ed.) (1985a). *Language Typology and Syntactic Description Vol. III: Grammatical Categories and the Lexicon*. Cambridge, UK: Cambridge University Press.

Shopen, T. (Ed.) (1985b). *Language Typology and Syntactic Description. Volume I: Clause Structure*. Cambridge, UK: Cambridge University Press.

Shopen, T. (Ed.) (1985c). *Language Typology and Syntactic Description. Volume II: Complex Constructions*. Cambridge, UK: Cambridge University Press.

Simard, M., G. F. Foster, and P. Isabelle (1992). Using cognates to align sentences in bilingual corpora. In *Proceedings of the Fourth International Conference on Theoretical and Methodological Issues in Machine Translation - TMI-92*, Montreal,Canada, pp. 67–81.

Simard, M. and P. Plamondon (1998). Bilingual sentence alignment: Balancing robustness and accuracy. *Machine Translation 13*(1), 59–80.

Slocum, J. (Ed.) (1988). *Machine Translation Systems*. Studies in Natural Language Processing. Cambridge, UK: Cambridge University Press.

Smadja, F. (1993). Retrieving collocations from text: Xtract. *Computational Linguistics 19*(1), 143–77.

Smadja, F., K. R. McKeown, and V. Hatzivassiloglou (1996). Translating collocations for bilingual lexicons: A statistical approach. *Computational Linguistics 22*(1), 1–38.

Somers, H. (1987). *Valency and Case in Computational Linguistics*. Edinburgh, Scotland: Edinburgh University Press.

Somers, H. L. and A. C. Ward (1996). Some more experiments in bilingual text alignment. In K. Oflazer and H. Somers (Eds.), *Proceedings of the Second International Conference on New Methods in Language Processing*, Ankara, Turkey, pp. 66–78. Bilkent University.

Sparck Jones, K. and J. R. Galliers (1995). *Evaluating Natural Language Processing Systems: An Analysis and Review*. Berlin: Springer.

Spencer, A. (1991). *Morphological Theory*. Oxford: Basil Blackwell.

Sproat, R. (1992). *Morphology and Computation*. ACL-MIT Press Series in Natural Language Processing. Cambridge, MA: MIT.

Stolcke, A. (1995). An efficient probabilistic context-free parsing algorithm that computes prefix probabilities. *Computational Linguistics 21*(2), 165–201.

Sumita, E. and H. Iida (1991). Experiments and prospects of example-based machine translation. In *Proceedings of the 29th Annual Conference of the ACL*, Berkeley, CA.

Talmy, L. (1985). Lexicalization patterns: semantic structure in lexical forms. See Shopen (1985a), Chapter 2, pp. 57–149.

TEMAA (1997). A testbed study of evaluation methodologies: Authoring aids - TEMAA final report. Technical Report D16, Center for Sprogteknologi, Copenhagen. Project sponsored by the European Union.

Thompson, H. (1977). Strategy and tactics: A model for language production. In *Papers from the 13th Regional Meeting, Chicago Linguistics Society*, Chicago, IL, pp. 651–68.

Trujillo, A. (1992). Spatial lexicalization in the translation of prepositional phrases. In *Proceedings of the 30th Annual Conference of the ACL, Student Session*, Newark, Delaware, pp. 306–08.

Trujillo, A. (1995a). Bi-lexical rules for multi-lexeme translation in lexicalist MT. In *Proceedings of the Sixth International Conference on Theoretical and Methodological Issues in Machine Translation – TMI-95*, Leuven, Belgium, pp. 48–66.

Trujillo, A. (1995b). Towards a cross-linguistically valid classification of spatial prepositions. *Machine Translation 10*(1-2), 93–141.

Trujillo, A. (1997). Determining internal and external indices for chart generation. In *Proceedings of the Seventh International Conference on Theoretical and Methodological Issues in Machine Translation – TMI-97*, Santa Fe, New Mexico, pp. 143–50.

Trujillo, A. and S. Berry (1996). Connectivity in bag generation. In *Proceedings of the Sixteenth International Conference in Computational Linguistics – COLING '96*, Copenhagen, Denmark, pp. 101–106.

Tsujii, J. and K. Fujita (1991). Lexical transfer based on bilingual signs: Towards interaction during transfer. In *Proceedings Fifth European Conference of the ACL*, Berlin, Germany.

Uchida, H. (1989). ATLAS II: a machine translation system using conceptual structure as an interlingua. See Nagao (1989), pp. 93–100.

Ungerer, F. and H.-J. Schmid (1996). *An introduction to cognitive linguistics*. Harlow: Longman.

Unicode (1996). *The Unicode Standard : Version 2.0*. Reading, MA: Addison-Wesley.

van Deemter, K. and S. Peters (Eds.) (1996). *Semantic Ambiguity and Underspecification*. Stanford: CSLI.

van der Eijk, P. (1993). Automating the acquisition of bilingual terminology. In *Proceedings of the Sixth European Conference of the ACL*, Utrecht, The Netherlands, pp. 113–19.

van Eijck, J. and R. C. Moore (1992). Semantic rules for English. See Alshawi (1992), Chapter 5, pp. 83–115.

van Eynde, F. (Ed.) (1993). *Linguistic Issues in Machine Translation*. London: Pinter.

van Noord, G. (1994). Head corner parsing. See Rupp et al. (1994), Chapter 12, pp. 315–38.

van Noord, G. (1997). An efficient implementation of the head-corner parser. *Computational Linguistics 23*(3), 425–56.

van Rijsbergen, C. J. (1979). *Information Retrieval* (2nd ed.). London: Butterworths.

Vasconcellos, M. (1987). Post-editing on-screen: machine translation from Spanish into English. In C. Picken (Ed.), *Translating and the Computer 8: A Profession on the Move*, pp. 133–146. London, England: Aslib.

Viegas, E., K. Mahesh, and S. Nirenburg (1999). Semantics in action. In P. Saint-Dizier (Ed.), *Predicative Forms in Natural Language and in Lexical Knowledge Bases*. Kluwer Academic Press.

Vinay, J.-P. and J. Darbelnet (1995). *Comparative stylistics of French and English: a methodology for translation*. Amsterdam: Benjamins.

Voss, C. and B. Dorr (1995). Toward a lexicalized grammar for interlinguas. *Machine Translation 10*(1-2), 143–84.

Wahlster, W., E. André, S. Bandyopadhyay, W. Graf, and T. Rist (1992). WIP: The coordinated generation of multimodal presentations from a common representation. See Ortony et al. (1992), pp. 121–44.

Wang, Y.-Y. and A. Waibel (1998). Modelling with structures in statistical machine translation. In *Proceedings of the 17th International Conference on Computational Linguistics and 36th Annual Meeting of the Association for Computational Linguistics - COLING/ACL-98*, Montreal, pp. 1357–63. Association for Computational Linguistics.

Watanabe, H. (1994). A method for distinguishing exceptional and general examples in example-based transfer systems. In *Proceedings of the 15th International Conference on Computational Linguistics - COLING-94*, Kyoto, pp. 39–44. International Committee on Computational Linguistics.

Watanabe, H. (1995). A model of a bi-directional transfer mechanism using rule combinations. *Machine Translation 10*(4), 269–91.

Watanabe, H. and K. Takeda (1998). A pattern-based machine translation system extended by example-based processing. In *Proceedings of the 17th International Conference on Computational Linguistics and 36th Annual Meeting of the Association for Computational Linguistics - COLING/ACL-98*, Montreal, pp. 1369–73. Association for Computational Linguistics.

Weischedel, R., M. Meteer, R. Schwartz, L. Ramshaw, and J. Palmucci (1993). Coping with ambiguity and unknown words through probabilistic models. *Computational Linguistics 19*(2), 359–82.

Whitelock, P. (1992). Shake-and-Bake translation. In *Proceedings of the 14th COLING*, Nantes, France, pp. 784–91.

Whitelock, P. (1994). Shake-and-Bake translation. See Rupp et al. (1994), pp. 339–59.

Whitelock, P. and K. Kilby (1995). *Linguistic and Computational Techniques in Machine Translation System Design*. London: UCL Press.

Whitley, M. S. (1986). *Spanish/English contrasts : a course in Spanish linguistics*. Washington, DC: Georgetown University Press.

Wilcock, G. and Y. Matsumoto (1998). Head-driven generation with HPSG. In *Proceedings of the 17th International Conference on Computational Linguistics and 36th Annual Meeting of the Association for Computational Linguistics - COLING/ACL-98*, Montreal, pp. 1393–1397. Association for Computational Linguistics.

Wilks, Y. (1975a). An intelligent analyzer and understander of English. *Communications of the ACM 18*(5), 264–74. Reprinted in (Grosz et al. 1986).

Wilks, Y. (1975b). A preferential, pattern-seeking semantics for natural language inference. *Artificial Intelligence 6*, 53–74.

Wood, M. M. (1993). *Categorial Grammars*. London: Routledge.

Wood, M. M. and B. J. Chandler (1988). Machine translation for monolinguals. In *Proceedings of the 12th International Conference on Computational Linguistics - COLING-88*, Budapest, pp. 760–63.

Wu, D. (1994). Aligning a parallel English-Chinese corpus statistically with lexical criteria. In *Proceedings of the 32nd Annual Meeting of the Association for Computational Linguistics - ACL-94*, Las Cruces, NM, pp. 80–87.

Wu, D. (1996). A polynomial-time algorithm for statistical machine translation. In *Proceedings of the 34th Annual Meeting of the Association for Computational Linguistics – ACL-96*, Santa Cruz, CA.

Wu, D. (1997). Stochastic inversion transduction grammars and bilingual parsing of parallel corpora. *Computational Linguistics 23*(3), 377–403.

Wu, D. and X. Xia (1994). Large-scale automatic extraction of an English-Chinese translation lexicon. *Machine Translation 9*(3-4), 285–313.

Yarowsky, D. (1992). Word sense disambiguation using statistical models of Roget's categories trained on large corpora. In *Proceedings of the 14th International Conference on Computational Linguistics - COLING-92*, Nantes, France, pp. 454–60. International Committee on Computational Linguistics.

Zajac, R. (1989). A transfer model using a typed feature structure rewriting system with inheritance. In *Proceedings of the 27th Annual Conference of the ACL*, Vancouver, Canada, pp. 1–6.

Zajac, R. (1990). A relational approach to translation. In *Proceedings of the Third International Conference on Theoretical and Methodological Issues in Machine Translation - TMI-90*, Austin, TX, pp. 235–54. Linguistic Research Center, University of Texas.

Index

291